LIBRARY
OKALOOSA-WALTON JUNIOR COLLEGE

D0891440

THE EDWARDIAN NOVELISTS

The
Edwardian Novelists

John Batchelor

Fellow of New College, Oxford

Duckworth

PR
881
B33
1982
C. 1

Second impression 1983
First published in 1982 by
Gerald Duckworth & Co. Ltd
The Old Piano Factory
43 Gloucester Crescent, London NW1

© 1982 by John Batchelor

All rights reserved, No part of this
publication may be reproduced, stored in a
retrieval system, or transmitted, in any
form or by any means, electronic, mechanical,
photocopying, recording or otherwise, without
the prior permission of the publisher.

ISBN 0 7156 1109 7 (cased)

British Library Cataloguing in Publication Data

Batchelor, John
  The Edwardian novelists.
  1. English Fiction – History and Criticism
  I. Title
  823'.912   PR826

  ISBN 0-7156-1109-7

Photoset by
Specialised Offset Services Limited, Liverpool
and printed in Great Britain by
Unwin Brothers Limited, Old Woking, Surrey.

LIBRARY
OKALOOSA-WALTON JUNIOR COLLEGE

Contents

Preface   vii

Chapter One   EDWARDIAN LITERATURE   1
  1. 'Edwardian'   1
  2. Edwardian anxieties   5
  3. A patriotic myth: rural England   8
  4. A patriotic writer: Kipling's England   12
  5. Dandyism   17
  6. The imperial adventure   20
  7. The role of the hero   23

Chapter Two   CONRAD   27
  1. Early works: the image of the hero   27
  2. *The Nigger of the Narcissus* and 'Youth'   31
  3. *Heart of Darkness*: action and lying   36
  4. *Lord Jim*: creative love   45
  5. *Nostromo*   57
  6. *The Secret Agent*   66
  7. *Under Western Eyes*   74
  8. *Chance* and *Victory*   81
  9. The writer as hero   88

Chapter Three   FORD MADOX FORD   92
  1. Ford's myth of himself   92
  2. The collaboration with Conrad   97
  3. The man of letters   101
  4. *The Fifth Queen*   105
  5. Gallantry and *The Good Soldier*   109
  6. Tietjens and others: honest Edwardians   113

Chapter Four   H.G. WELLS   119
  1. Wells the prophet and *Tono-Bungay*   119

81596

2. *Love and Mr. Lewisham*   126
3. *Kipps*   131
4. *The History of Mr. Polly*   137
5. Wells the polymath: the drive towards freedom   142

Chapter Five   ARNOLD BENNETT   150
1. 'The whole contention'   150
2. *Clayhanger*   152
3. *A Man from the North* and *Anna of the Five Towns*   161
4. 'The Death of Simon Fuge'   167
5. The form of *The Old Wives' Tale*   170
6. 'The meaning of the word success'   178

Chapter Six   GALSWORTHY   183
1. John Galsworthy and Giles Legard   183
2. *The Man of Property*   188
3. *The Country House*   195
4. *Fraternity*   198
5. 'Danäe', *The Patrician* and the ascetic ideal   202

Chapter Seven   E.M. FORSTER   208
1. *Maurice* and Edwardian Forster   208
2. *Where Angels Fear to Tread*   213
3. *The Longest Journey*   217
4. *A Room with a View*   221
5. *Howards End*   225
6. The defeat of comedy   230

Afterword   233
Bibliography   235
Index   249

Illustrations between pages 118 and 119

Preface

This book was initiated by the question: why does Conrad look so isolated a figure? At an early stage of my reading I began to feel that his apparent isolation is an illusion created by the way in which we read and write about him. There are dozens of monographs on Conrad; there are few studies which relate him to his literary context. The reasons for this are perhaps self-evident: he is a difficult writer, there is a great deal of secondary material. Yet to read Conrad in isolation is obviously to distort him.

As I read Conrad's contemporaries the purpose and shape of the book changed; while Conrad remained my principal exhibit, so to speak, the Edwardian period as a whole began to seem to me the true subject of my interest. In the following chapters, therefore, I discuss six major novelists of the period: Conrad and Ford Madox Ford, Wells and Bennett, Galsworthy and Forster. I have chosen to confine the discussion to the novel because to do justice to the poets and (especially) to the dramatists (in a period which includes such important figures as Shaw and Granville-Barker) would have made the book unwieldy. I exclude Hardy and Henry James from my consideration on the grounds that the shapes of their careers as novelists were established (and in Hardy's case completed) by 1901. I exclude Lawrence and Joyce because they did not have major work *published* in the decade although *The White Peacock*, early drafts of *Sons and Lovers*, *Dubliners* and the unfinished *Stephen Hero* were all written within these years.

For Wells, Bennett, Galsworthy and Forster the Edwardian decade was a period of high achievement (though obviously Forster's major novel, *A Passage to India*, was to add a wholly new dimension to his career in 1924). For Ford Madox Ford the decade was a period of painful growth, and he can be seen as Edwardian in the special sense that having struggled with several kinds of failure and some unrecognised success (in his *Fifth Queen* trilogy), he then wrote major retrospective works, *The Good Soldier* and the Tietjens novels, in which he makes exemplary use of the lessons learnt in those years. Much of the dramatic interest of Ashburnham and Tietjens lies in the fact that they are Edwardian heroes adrift in a post-Edwardian world.

Many people have helped with this book. The late T.R. Henn supervised my Cambridge Ph.D. thesis, some of which has found its way into my first chapter. I am much indebted to the published work (and in several cases to the personal help) of David Lodge, Samuel Hynes, Bernard Bergonzi, John Bayley and P.N. Furbank. I regret that Ian Watt's *Conrad in the Nineteenth Century* was published too late for me to make use of it. I am particularly grateful to Richard Ellmann, both for his writing on the Edwardian period and for the generosity with which he made time to read the whole of my text at different stages of its existence. The Warden and Fellows of New College granted a period of sabbatical leave which enabled me to finish the writing, and my colleague, Anne Barton, nobly took more than her share of our joint duties when my work was at a critical stage. Colin Haycraft has shown inexhaustible patience and tact as publisher and editor.

For permission to quote copyright material I am grateful to the following: Madame Eldin, the estate of Arnold Bennett and Keele University Library for quotations from Bennett; The Provost and Fellows of King's College, Cambridge and Edward Arnold Ltd for quotations from E.M. Forster; Professor G.P. Wells and the estate of H.G. Wells for quotations from Wells; The Bodley Head for quotations from Ford Madox Ford; William Heinemann Ltd for quotations from John Galsworthy; The Society of Authors and the estate of George Bernard Shaw for quotations from Shaw.

I am grateful to Mr Frank Wells and the estate of H.G. Wells for photographs of Bennett and Wells as young men; to the B.B.C. Hulton Picture Library for photographs of Conrad, Bennett, and Wells; to Cornell University Library for the photograph of Ford Madox Ford in uniform; and to King's College, Cambridge, for the photograph of E.M. Forster.

New College, Oxford   J.B.
1981

To the memory of Thomas Rice Henn, 1901-1974

Chapter One: Edwardian Literature

The phrase 'Edwardian Literature' is not often heard.[1]

An 'age' is a system of agreed meanings in time.[2]

1. 'Edwardian'

To re-read Richard Ellmann's essay, 'The Two Faces of Edward', is to be reminded of the lasting truth of many of its observations and also to note that things have changed since 1959 when it was first published. While it is no longer true that the phrase 'Edwardian literature' is not often heard, it is true, as P.N. Furbank wrote in 1974,[3] that 'Edwardian' is not an established term quite like 'Romantic' or 'Augustan'. The term is still used with circumspection, although there are two distinguished collections of essays by Samuel Hynes, *The Edwardian Turn of Mind* (1968) and *Some Edwardian Occasions* (1972), and the existence of an Edwardian age to which one can confidently refer is assumed in the content, though not in the title, of Bernard Bergonzi's *The Turn of a Century* (1973).

For Cyril Connolly, writing in the 1930s, the Edwardian period had been characterised by 'the struggle between literature and journalism'.[4] He believes that the only Edwardian reputations which had actually been enhanced in the 1930s were those of Forster and Somerset Maugham, while 'Galsworthy, Bennett, Lawrence, Firbank are dead and also out of fashion' (p. 5) and the stocks of Shaw, Wells and Kipling have remained stationary. Frank Swinnerton wrote in 1935 that 'Edwardian' was used in the 1920s as a term of abuse: 'The object was to suggest that Shaw, Wells, Conrad and Bennett were out of date'.[5]

Certainly the 1920s found it necessary to be rude about the Edwardians. Apart from Virginia Woolf's famous attack on Wells, Bennett and

---

[1] Richard Ellmann, 'The Two Faces of Edward' (1959), in *Golden Codgers* (1973), p.113.

[2] J.P. Stern, *On Realism* (1973), p.158.

[3] P.N. Furbank, 'Chesterton the Edwardian' *G.K. Chesterton: A Centenary Celebration* (1974), p.16.

[4] Cyril Connolly, *Enemies of Promise* (1938), p.23.

[5] Frank Swinnerton, *The Georgian Literary Scene, 1910-1935* (1935), p.2.

Galsworthy in *Mr Bennett and Mrs Brown* (1924) there are Roy Campbell's aside about the 'prophets of Domestic Comfort, Shaw, Wells and Bennett' who have sold the 'experience of the human race' for 'a few patent bath-taps',[6] and Rebecca West's affectionate attack in *The Strange Necessity*: 'All our youth they hung about the houses of our minds like Uncles, the Big Four: H.G. Wells, George Bernard Shaw, John Galsworthy, and Arnold Bennett. They had the generosity, the charm, the loquacity of visiting uncles.'[7]

The Edwardian period is muzzy at the edges. Does it begin in 1895 with the destruction of Wilde and the emergence of Wholesomeness as a literary desideratum? Or does it begin with the death of Queen Victoria? Equally, where does it end? Virginia Woolf had it that human nature changed in 1910, but not everyone would agree with her. 1914 was certainly the end of everything that the Edwardians had taken for granted, but had the sense of literary ending come earlier than that? One could propose at least three frames for the period: the reign of King Edward is not the least important, since writers were conscious of, and affected by, the fact that what Wells spoke of as the 'great paperweight' of Victoria's presence had been removed and that they were working in the virgin years of a new century. Alternatively, the Boer War and the Great War could provide an intelligible frame. The myth of Empire was dented beyond repair by the first, the credibility of the English upper class – with much else – was drastically eroded by the second.

Equally, the Wilde *débâcle* and the first issue of *Blast* could be taken as the parameters. The fall of Wilde signalled the retreat of aestheticism and Edwardian literature can be seen to be casting about for its models and imperatives. If the favoured models are established earlier successes – Wells, Galsworthy and Forster follow Dickens and Meredith, Shaw adapts opera and melodrama, Granville-Barker closely follows Chekhovian musical form – and the imperatives loosely humanist, the period remains notable for its lack of a dominant artistic direction. *Blast*, in 1914, gave a clear new lead.

Exactly what would have happened to literature without the intervention of the Great War is an unanswerable question, but there can be little doubt that Wyndham Lewis and Pound would have had a decisive effect on the direction that it took.

The simple problem presented by the question of dates is compounded by the competing mythologies that the word 'Edwardian' has attracted to itself. Its associations include bloomers, bicycles, Fabians, suburbs, the Liberal Landslide, the People's Budget; garden parties, *Peter Pan*, the upper ten thousand, Lord Russell's imprisonment for bigamy, the King's affairs with

---

[6] Roy Campbell, 'Contemporary poetry', in Edgell Rickword (ed.), *Scrutinies* (1928), p.169.
[7] Rebecca West, *The Strange Necessity: Essays and Reviews* (1928), p.199.

Lady Warwick and Mrs Alice Keppel;[8] or realism, mysticism, symbolism, psychical research, high-minded homosexuality, *Principia Ethica* and 'The Free Man's Worship'.

Frank Kermode has claimed that since 1890 to 1900 is very clearly an ending, the next decade may properly be regarded as a beginning: 'You sometimes hear people say, with a certain pride in their clerical resistance to the myth, that the nineteenth century really ended not in 1900 but in 1914. But there are different ways of measuring an epoch. 1914 has obvious qualifications, but if you wanted to defend the neater, more mythical date, you could do very well. In 1900 Nietzsche died; Freud published *The Interpretation of Dreams*; 1900 was the date of Husserl's *Logic*, and of Russell's *Critical Exposition of the Philosophy of Leibnitz*.'[9]

Richard Ellmann in the article referred to above speaks of the self-reliant 'doughtiness' of the Edwardians (p. 114). Of their moral outlook he remarks that they were 'thoroughly secular' and that having rejected Christianity they 'felt free to use it, for while they did not need religion they did need religious metaphors' (p.116). Their attitude to 'Life' is sacramental: 'The capitalised word for the Edwardians is not "God" but "Life"' (p.120). The plots of Edwardian novels and plays (he refers particularly to Conrad and Forster) are characterised by sudden transformations, 'secular miracles', alterations of the personality by which the individual attains selfhood (pp.121 and 130). And in the absence of clear external moral imperatives the writers subordinated themselves to the primacy of their art: 'The Edwardian writer is an artist not because he proclaims he is, as Wilde did, but because his works proclaim it' (p.129).[10]

The Edwardians inhabited what may be called a contracting moral universe, in which the received moral imperatives had lost their urgency. The Victorian dismantling of Christianity had taken place slowly: its ascendancy in national and institutional life had sustained a series of blows in the latter part of the century. The impact of evolutionary thinking after the publication of Darwin's *Origin of Species* in 1859 remains the biggest single factor in what has been called 'The Disappearance of God'.[11]

George Eliot is quoted as saying that God was inconceivable, Immortality unbelievable, and Duty 'peremptory and absolute'.[12] Though it would

---

[8] For a representative 'high life' treatment of the Edwardian period see R.J. Minney, *The Edwardian Age* (1964).

[9] Frank Kermode, *The Sense of an Ending* (1967), p.97.

[10] See my discussion of 'Dandyism' below, pp.17-20.

[11] See J. Hillis Miller, *The Disappearance of God* (1963). For the impact of Darwin's work on literature and literary criticism see also Leo J. Henkin, *Darwinism in the English Novel, 1860-1910* (1963) and Tom Gibbons, *Rooms in the Darwin Hotel: Studies in English Literary Criticism and Ideas, 1890-1920* (1973).

[12] Quoted from F.H.W. Myers by David Daiches, *Some Late Victorian Attitudes* (1967), p.10.

probably be true to say that God no longer functioned as an effective sanction in the lives of most thinking people in the last quarter of the nineteenth century, there is no doubt that after-images which derived their energy from Christian habits of mind survived. George Eliot's sense of duty is one of these, Pater's equally cogent sense of beauty is another.[13] The dethroning of God created strain and distress: it was necessary to put something in his place. These substitutions may be seen as of progressively diminishing grandeur. Duty in the exalted abstract gives way to practical duty to the nation or the empire, duty to the beloved and the family and finally duty to oneself, 'heroic endurance for its own sake'.[14]

In the arts, Pater's passionate conviction that there is an aesthetic 'ecstasy' which can glorify the flux of time and confer 'success in life'[15] gives way to Arthur Symons's claim for the function of the symbol: the expression of the 'ultimate essence', the 'soul of whatever exists and can be realised by the consciousness'. In Symons the substitution of aesthetic principles for Christianity is quite explicit. In its 'revolt against exteriority' symbolism becomes 'a kind of religion, with all the duties and responsibilities of a sacred ritual'.[16]

The Edwardians were conscious of the need to fill the moral vacuum surrounding them. G.E. Moore approached his moral philosophy with the question 'What is Good?' (*Principia Ethica* (1903), Ch. 2 and *passim*). The answer, in his book, is the notion of 'human relationships' which for Bloomsbury was taken to mean close friends, passionate acquaintances and E.M. Forster's 'Love the Beloved Republic'.[17]

For a student of the Edwardian period Moore's answer is less interesting than his question. The fact that the nature of 'good' needed to be considered in terms so radical and pragmatic is at once revealing and representative. Moore's book is a clear instance of a leading Edwardian anxiety, the anxiety over what was good, what was right, where duty lay, what the direction of man should be. Conrad gives his own retrospective account of this anxiety in his 'Author's Note' to *An Outcast of the Islands* (1896): 'The discovery of new values in life is a very chaotic experience; there is a tremendous amount of jostling and confusion and a momentary feeling of darkness' (p.vii).

Some Edwardian novelists write from a specifically Christian viewpoint: notably Chesterton, especially in *The Man Who Was Thursday* (1908) and

---

[13] See Graham Hough's discussion of aestheticism as an expression of a dethroned religious impulse in *The Last Romantics* (1948).

[14] Daiches, p.11.

[15] Walter Pater, *The Renaissance* (1873), p.236.

[16] Arthur Symons, *The Symbolist Movement in Literature* (1899), p.10. Here the process described by Ellmann in which Christianity, having died, is revived in the form of metaphor, can be seen taking place.

[17] For the influence of Moore's book on the Bloomsbury Group, see J.K. Johnstone, *The Bloomsbury Group* (1954).

Manalive (1912). Although Christian, Chesterton's perspective was not yet Catholic: he was not received into the Catholic Church until 1922. An interesting minor Catholic novelist of the period is R.H. Benson, whose *Lord of the World* (1907) is a mixture of an invasion novel and a Wellsian utopian prophecy in which a Messiah of the future meets a (German) anti-Christ in an apocalyptic encounter. The most worthwhile of Benson's other books are perhaps *None Other Gods* (1911), the story of a young aristocrat who becomes a vagrant Christian martyr and in some ways anticipates Evelyn Waugh's Sebastian Flyte, and *The Sentimentalists* (1906), a notably temperate novel about his former friend Frederick Rolfe, Baron Corvo (whose attitude to Benson at this date was one of snarling vindictiveness). In Benson's novel Corvo as 'Christopher Dell' is freed from his lacerating and destructive egotism by a form of Christian psychotherapy.[18]

A symptom of the continuing popular taste for Christianity in literature is the enormous commercial success of Robert Hitchens's Catholic novel *The Garden of Allah* (1904).[19] With these obvious exceptions it would seem to be broadly true to say that the Edwardian imagination was secular.

2. Edwardian anxieties

One difference between the Victorian and the Edwardian mind is indicated by the ease with which at Cambridge the young G.E. Moore captured the audience which had formerly attended to the neo-Hegelian 'idealist', J. McT.E. McTaggart. 'It would be too much to say that Moore dethroned McTaggart, who was essentially undethronable, but he did carry the younger men by storm, and caused Lytton Strachey to exclaim, "The age of reason has come!" ... Moore's steady questioning as to what *is* good? What *is* true? had ... torn some large holes in the McTaggartian heaven'.[20]

The freedom celebrated by Forster here and by Russell in, for example, 'The Free Man's Worship'[21] carries an accompanying intensification of

---

[18] R.H. Benson was a Catholic priest, a convert, the son of an Archbishop of Canterbury, and the brother of two other writers. The Benson brothers occupy a representative minor place in literary scene. E.F. Benson's *The Babe, B.A.* (1897) is a readable comic novel about undergraduate life and his *As we Were* (1930) is a modish memoir of the 1890s and the Edwardian period. A.C. Benson, Master of Magdalene College, Cambridge, and author of the stiflingly complacent don's reminiscences *From a College Window* (1906) also wrote the words for Elgar's 'Land of Hope and Glory'.

[19] See the discussion of this novel in Claud Cockburn, *Best-Sellers: The Books that Everyone Read, 1900-1939* (1972).

[20] E.M. Forster, *Goldsworthy Lowes Dickinson* (1934), p.92.

[21] First published in *The Independent Review*, I, 3 (December 1903), pp.415-24. This was one of a series of articles by atheist philosophers on religious experience in a Godless world. Goldsworthy Lowes Dickinson, who was on the *Independent*'s editorial board, contributed several such articles between 1903 and 1907. Compare also William James's *The Varieties of Religious Experience: A Study in Human Nature* (1902).

anxiety, which characteristically manifested itself as an acute awareness of what Ian Watt has called the 'epistemological crisis' through which the period was passing: 'A crisis most familiar to literary history under the twin rubrics of the disappearance of God and the disappearance of the omniscient author.'[22]

The epistemological crisis is a product of the contracting moral horizons of the period, a steady erosion of the old certainties leaving Edwardian man confronted with the self and nothing beyond the self, unable to trust in anything other than his immediate sense impressions and his own actions. Bertrand Russell's autobiography registers this transition. As the nineteenth century closed he had a confident sense of intellectual territory securely grasped and mapped out: 'The time was one of intellectual intoxication. My sensations resembled those one has after climbing a mountain in a mist, when, on reaching the summit, the mist suddenly clears, and the country becomes visible for forty miles in every direction.'[23]

With the year 1900 came an abrupt change in his outlook: 'Oddly enough, the end of the century marked the end of this sense of triumph, and from that moment onwards I began to be assailed simultaneously by intellectual and emotional problems which plunged me into the darkest despair that I have ever known.'[24]

The popular tradition which sees Edwardian life in terms of Victoria Sackville-West's *The Edwardians* (1930) is at least partly right. The decade was indeed a period of luxury and expanding wealth flavoured with a marked increase of private licentiousness. This growth was accompanied by a terror of the increasingly dispossessed working-class. Literature reflects this in the ubiquitous image of the 'abyss' to describe the life of the urban poor. In *The Time Machine* (1895) H.G. Wells identifies with the aristocratic Eloi, descendants of the Victorian aristocracy, while the terrifying Morlocks who live on the Eloi's flesh are descendants of the industrial proletariat who now live in caverns deep in the earth. There is no doubt that *The Time Machine* reflects and expresses current middle-class anxiety about the urban poor. As Bernard Bergonzi remarks, 'From his schooldays in Bromley he had disliked and feared the working class in a way wholly appropriate to the son of a small tradesman.'[25]

It seems likely that the metaphor of the 'abyss' originated with another Wells fantasy, 'In the Abyss' (*The Plattner Story: and Others*, 1897), in which a deep-sea diver encounters biped intelligent reptiles on the ocean bed; these creatures have a developed urban civilisation and the diver is adopted by

---

[22] Ian Watt, 'Impressionism and symbolism in "Heart of Darkness"', in Norman Sherry (ed.), *Joseph Conrad: A Commemoration* (1974), p.40.

[23] Bertrand Russell, *Autobiography* (1970), p.145.

[24] Ibid., p.145.

[25] Bernard Bergonzi, *The Early H.G. Wells* (1961), p.56.

them as a visiting deity and worshipped. In the Edwardian period the currency of the word to describe the plight of the urban poor received impetus from C.F.G. Masterman's anonymous pamphlet about slum life, *From the Abyss* (1902), and his 'secular sermon', 'The Social Abyss' (W.H. Hunt (ed.), *Preachers from the Pew* (n.d.), pp.75-84). Jack London's *The People of the Abyss* (1903) uses the image to express with pungency a view of London which becomes central to *Howards End*, Wells's *Tono-Bungay*, Galsworthy's *Fraternity* and C.F.G. Masterman's *The Condition of England*: 'The London Abyss is a vast shambles. Year by year ... rural England pours in a flood of vigorous strong life, that not only does not renew itself, but perishes by the third generation' (p.38).

City life is causing the population to decline and is damaging the human stock of the nation: it is 'an unnatural life for a human' and produces degenerate children, 'a weak-kneed, narrow chested, listless breed' (pp.43-5). Forster's Leonard Bast lives on the edge of the 'abyss' in *Howards End* (1910): 'He was not in the abyss, but he could see it, and at times people whom he knew had dropped in, and counted no more' (p.43). As he develops his portrait of Leonard Bast as an exemplary victim of urban poverty, Forster could almost be quoting Jack London: 'One guessed him as the third generation, grandson to the shepherd or ploughboy whom civilisation had sucked into the town.' Margaret Schlegel notes 'the spine that might have been straight, and the chest that might have broadened' (p.113).[26]

The metaphor of the 'abyss' is used often by Arthur Morrison in his sensational novel of slum violence, *A Child of the Jago* (1896) and his more romantic, but still violent low-life adventure story *The Hole in the Wall* (1902).[27]

The fear that the race was degenerating had been expressed in such sensational works as Max Nordau's *Degeneration* (published in English in 1895) and *The Malady of the Century* (1896) and is probably one of the reasons for the Edwardians' obsession with their *health*. Tennis, sea-bathing, hot water after meals and 'mind-cures' are among the panaceas of the period. 'Sandow's Exercises', named after Eugene Sandow, an Englishman who made a career for himself in America in the 1890s as a 'body-builder', were the fashion among Edwardian suburban men. William James is entertaining on these trends in *The Varieties of Religious Experience* where he notes the 'Gospel of Relaxation', the 'Don't Worry Movement', and those who say

[26] For further examples of the 'abyss' and of the descent into working-class life seen as anthropological exploration, see Peter Keating (ed.), *Into Unknown England 1866-1913* (1976).

[27] Somerset Maugham's *Liza of Lambeth* (1897) and Robert Tressell's *The Ragged Trousered Philanthropists* (1914) are similarly based on the degenerative effects of urban poverty, although in these images the specific image of the 'abyss' does not occur in the same way. It is an odd coincidence, incidentally, that the heroine of *Liza of Lambeth* (a story of prostitution and urban violence) and the heroes of *The Hole in the Wall* (a story of smuggling and murder) and of Conrad's and Ford's *Romance* (a story of piracy and adventure) all have the surname 'Kemp'.

'Youth, Health, Vigour' as they dress themselves every morning (p.95). Arnold Bennett, himself a hypochondriac, was exploiting the market for 'health' with his books *Mental Efficiency* (1911; originally published as *The Reasonable Life*, 1907) and *How to Live on Twenty-Four Hours a Day* (1908).

Another dominant anxiety of the period is fear of invasion. 'England and Germany are bound to fight' is one of the themes of *Howards End*, and H.G. Wells's *The War in the Air* (1902) concerns a future war with Germany. The invasion novel is a distinct sub-genre of the period.[28] Germany is usually the aggressor, as in William Le Queux, *The Great War in England in 1897* (1894) and *The Invasion of 1910* (1906). The latter, with an introductory letter by Lord Roberts, is little more than a piece of rearmament propaganda in fictional form. Saki in *When William Came: A Story of London under the Hohenzollerns* (1914) gives a satirical account of England's unpreparedness for war and the social humiliation (curiously mild) of living in London under the Germans. By far the best of this group of novels is Erskine Childers' *The Riddle of the Sands* (1903) in which the Englishman's superior seamanship in small craft enables him to outwit the Germans in the North Sea.

The aggressor was not always Germany: in an extraordinary romance by M.P. Shiel, *The Yellow Danger* (1898), the enemy are the Chinese, and the English victory involves drowning the whole population of China in a monstrous whirlpool. In G.K. Chesterton's *The Flying Inn* (1914) the aggressor is Turkey, and the story concerns a patriotic hero who resists the Turkish occupation of England by travelling the country with a giant cheese and a liquor supply (the 'Flying Inn' of the title) in defiance of Moslem prohibition of alcohol.

The invasion novel was sufficiently clearly established as a form for P.G. Wodehouse to write an effective parody of it in *The Swoop! Or How Clarence Saved England* (1909). The Germans, the Russians, the Chinese and a number of smaller and less likely nations invade England simultaneously and fight each other. The bombardment of London has excellent results: 'The Albert Hall, struck by a merciful shell, had come down with a run, and was now a heap of picturesque ruins ... The burning of the Royal Academy proved a great comfort to all' (p.42).

3. A patriotic myth: rural England

The urban poor were felt as a threat from below, 'odours from the abyss' in Margaret Schlegel's phrase (*Howards End*, p.115). The ambitions of other nations, mainly Germany but also Russia and China, were felt as threats

---

[28] For an extensive list of invasion novels and a brief discussion of the genre, see Bernard Bergonzi, *The Early H.G. Wells*, pp.12-14.

from outside. But how did the literature of the period perceive the England that was being threatened? The positive aspects of English life were seen in terms of two leading, and related, myths: the country house and the land.

Much of the serious literature of the period re-examines and scrutinises these myths. The growth of the cities, and in particular the spread of middle-class suburbs, were facts to which the myth had to accommodate itself. An important insight in Masterman's *The Condition of England*, and one that he shares with Wells and Forster, is the recognition of suburban man as an irreversible feature of modern England. Forster on the whole deplores the suburbs (though he finds virtue in 'half-suburban' Summer Street in *A Room with a View*), Wells in *Tono-Bungay* (1909) sees them as a form of morbid, diseased growth; endless reproductions in miniature of the country house and its aspirations, necessary extensions of Bladesover, the country house which dominates the first part of the novel: 'It is this idea of escaping parts from the seventeenth-century system of Bladesover, of proliferating and overgrowing elements from the Estates, that to this day seems to me the best explanation, not simply of London, but of all England' (p.80).

Masterman's view of the suburbs is presumably coloured by Wells's (he was a friend of Wells and read the proofs of *Tono-Bungay* while writing *The Condition of England*) but is awkwardly uncertain, balanced uncomfortably between acceptance and rejection. Suburban man has 'drifted away from the realities of life' and is 'divorced from the ancient sanities of manual or skilful labour, of exercise in the open air, absorbed for the bulk of his day in crowded offices adding sums or writing letters' (p.94). It closely resembles Jack London's and Forster's lament for the countryman sucked into the town.[29] But Masterman goes on to say that suburban life is at least better than the life of the inner cities. In the suburbs the grip of the city is 'loosened' so that 'something of the large sanities of rural existence could be mingled with the quickness and agility of the town' and the suburbs at their best contain 'clean and virile life' and the 'healthiest and most hopeful promise for the future of modern England' (p.95).

What Masterman is really saying is that the suburbs were a reasonable compromise between urban and rural life. It is precisely the 'compromised' aspect of suburban life that Forster passionately rejects. Forster, with Kenneth Grahame, Saki, Edward Thomas, W.H. Hudson and Kipling, subscribes to the myth of England as a golden rural world, a place where right feeling is still to be found. Given Forster's satirical and acutely observing intelligence the hold that this myth had on him could only be damaging. It is responsible for the soggier parts of *Howards End* with its romancing about 'yeomen' and the countryside that would vote liberal 'if left to itself' in Hertfordshire, and is seen at its worst in *Maurice* where Maurice

[29] See above, p.7.

and his lover retreat from English suburban life and take refuge in 'the greenwood' to work as woodcutters in a pastoral idyll.[30]

Pastoral and suburban make a fixed, if false, antithesis in the Edwardian mind. Defeated modern man is descended from a heroic past: Masterman's suburb dwellers, Forster's corrupted yeomen, Edward Thomas's agricultural labourer who finds the 'unrelated multitude' of the contemporary urban world an 'endless riddle' (*The South Country*, 1909, p.65).

Nostalgia is the most striking feature of Thomas's prose works about rural England. In his *The Heart of England* (1906) London's hills are lost to the eye except at night, when 'we can see them as though the streets did not exist' (p.8). Forster's Leonard Bast has a similar experience in his night walk through the suburban hills in *Howards End*. And *Howards End*'s resentment of the petrol engine is anticipated in Thomas's book: a tramp tries to find a stretch of road where he can 'make a bit of fire' without being disturbed by the stink and dust of the motor-car, which is resented throughout Thomas's book for its disturbance of rural peace (p.8).[31]

To love the landscape is the act of a patriot. This became particularly clear from the retrospect of the Great War, when the landscape as a threatened ideal was thrown sharply into focus as a pole of the poetic sensibility.[32]

Some of the most vivid expressions of this nostalgia are to be found in the fantasies of the period. Fantasy, 'Fauns and Dryads and slips of the memory ... Pans and puns, all that is medieval this side of the grave',[33] is an irresponsible form, retrogressive, infantile, seeking appropriate arenas in which to escape from the pressures of the day. It is a significant feature of the period if only because so much of it was published: many of Forster's, Saki's and Kipling's short stories, most of the works of such minor writers as Algernon Blackwood, M.P. Shiel and Richard Marsh. Pan is a figure of major importance in these fantasies. In Forster's 'The Story of a Panic' and 'The Curate's Friend' he is an image of sexual freedom,[34] and in James Stephens's *The Crock of Gold* (1912), he is again a sexually liberating, and here mischievous and satirical, force. These pieces draw on the full tradition of Pan, both in what can fairly be called his phallic character (the aspect exploited in Arthur Machen's sensational tale of the macabre, *The Great God Pan* (1894) and in Forrest Reid's homosexual idyll, *The Garden God* (1905)) and in his more decorous literary role as the great custodian of the natural world.

---

[30] See my discussion of *Maurice* below, pp.208-13.

[31] This was a much discussed topic in enlightened circles. There are several articles deploring the motor-car's encroachment on rural peace in G.M. Trevelyan's *Independent Review* (1903-7), some of them by Forster's friend Goldsworthy Lowes Dickinson. Kipling, on the other hand, loved motoring and writes lyrically about its pleasure in the opening pages of 'They'.

[32] See Paul Fussell, *The Great War and Modern Memory* (1975).

[33] E.M. Forster, *Aspects of the Novel* (1927) p.115.

[34] E.M. Forster, *The Celestial Omnibus: And Other Stories* (1911), pp.1-42, 129-42.

In the extraordinary seventh chapter of *The Wind in the Willows* (1908) Pan, the 'Friend and Helper', appears in person as though to guarantee for ever the nostalgic values of the river-valley in which Rat and Mole live out their lives of innocuous undergraduate friendship (p.155).

The Wind in the Willows is a completely successful fantasy, a work in which the inner compulsions of the author become locked, at some level well below the surface, with his material: the result is a self-contained and self-sustaining world.

The Toad plot came first, and the river, the wild wood and the Rat and Mole friendship were added later: the stages of this process mark the retreat of Grahame's imagination into a backward-looking arcadia.[35] Toad still has one foot in the adult world, the word of the 'Olympians', the unsympathetic uncles and aunts from Grahame's short story published in *The Golden Age* (1900).

He is the only one of the animals to live in a house rather than a hole (although Badger's hole incorporates a Roman ruin and Mole's has suburban furnishings) and to have adventures involving the human world: the stolen motor-car, the comic-grotesque magistrate, the gaoler's daughter, the barge-woman, the engine-driver. Yet these human figures are heavily distorted, and deprived of the threatening reality that they would have in a 'real' adult world. Toad dresses up as a washer-woman and takes violent revenge on the barge-woman, but only a perversely Freudian critic would read these as fantasies of transvestism and sadism: they are rather expressions of an *infantile* wish to dress up and exercise power. The only opening for something more specifically sexual is in the relationship with the gaoler's daughter, but here Toad is pushed firmly back into his identity as an 'animal', and a 'poor animal' at that, while the rest of adult humanity – policeman, magistrates, engine-driver – treat him as a small but responsible *man*. The gaoler's daughter is a mother to Toad, never a mistress.

The closer Toad gets to the 'real' world the more heavily distorted it becomes. His imprisonment, the most harsh of his contacts with the human world, is elaborately distanced and Gothicised in a sustained pastiche of Wardour Street historical romance: 'Across the hollow-sounding drawbridge, below the spiky portcullis, under the frowning archway of the grim old castle ... up time-worn winding stairs, past men-at-arms in casquet and corselet of steel, darting threatening looks through their vizards' (pp.141-2) and so on.

The Wind in the Willows is a concentric work. On its circumference is the modern world, the trains, motor-cars and penal systems of the Toad-plot. Within that margin is the more comprehensible but still dangerous Wild Wood, in which Philistine violence has become extinct (the badgers occupy

[35] See Peter Green, *Kenneth Grahame* (1959).

the buried Roman city) but can still have sporadic rebirths (as stoats and weasels). At the centre is the sunlit river valley of the opening chapters in which Rat and Mole preserve intact their own mythical version of rural England. But the author knows that it exists only in a child's gentled fantasy world. Outside that the train whistles, the motor-car roars, the prisons gape for the violent.

4. A patriotic writer: Kipling's England

Kipling's image of England is at once unique and representative. His Indian and soldier tales of the 1880s and 1890s culminate in *Stalky and Co.* (1899) and *Kim* (1901): on the whole they are aggressive and forward-looking, they celebrate action, they subscribe, although with much subtle qualification (as recent criticism has recognised) to the myth of empire. In his Edwardian stories about Sussex, *Puck of Pook's Hill* (1906), *Rewards and Fairies* (1910), and 'They' (1904), he explores the resources of English myth and the relationships between landscape and personality.

Stalky and Co. is, of course, the unsurpassed account in English of the education that produces successful Imperial administrators. Study Number 5 opposes all comers and resists by stealth the formal values of the school, yet the Headmaster, the 'Prooshian' Bates (whose insight is un-English and would be well suited to England's great imperial competitor) recognises the subversiveness and individualism of Stalky, Beetle and McTurk as exactly the qualities that the empire needs. The early stories in *Stalky* present an innocent, savage world in which the boys take personal revenge on another house by pushing a dead cat under their floor-boards ('An Unsavoury Interlude') and punish a pair of bullies by subjecting them to their own primitive tortures ('The Moral Reformers').

In the last three stories of *Stalky and Co.* the adult world for which the boys are being prepared breaks into this innocence. In 'The Flag of Their Country', a tactless politican 'who has come to address the United Services College on "Patriotism"' (p.212), tramples on the boys' feelings. He unfurls the Union Jack in front of the assembled school: 'They had certainly seen the thing before ... But the College never displayed it; it was no part of the scheme of their lives; the Head had never alluded to it; their fathers had not declared it unto them. It was a matter shut up, sacred and apart' (p.213).

Patriotism is like sexual maturity, something they must grow towards and not be forced into prematurely. Any charge of jingoism brought against Kipling must be examined in the light of this story where, in this passage in particular, cheap patriotism is presented as a form of indecent assault.

Kim illustrates the division between the aggressive 1890s Kipling and the nostalgic Edwardian Kipling with an almost mythic neatness. Kim himself,

the young white imperialist who is supremely successful in The Game, shares
the narrative with the Lama who seeks his spiritual and physical home, his
River and the mountains where the 'years fall from him' as he breathes the
'diamond air'.

Kim is the aggressive pragmatist, the Lama the nostalgic idealist. In the
early chapters Kim is all eye and ear, an innocent led into experience by The
Game and The Road. His knowledge of his identity is limited to the amulet
round his neck and his personal myth of a Red Bull on a Green Field. While
the Lama's quest for his river is his central preoccupation, Kim's 'quest' for
the Red Bull barely holds his attention 'for twenty minutes at a time' (p.61).
His chance encounter with the Mavericks, his father's Regiment (whose flag
is the Red Bull of Kim's quest), his re-entry into the world of the Sahibs and
his schooling at St Xavier's at Lucknow creates a problem of identity like
that of the Indian Prince, Shere Ali, who is sent to Eton and Oxford and as a
result rebels against the British when he returns to India in A.E.W. Mason's
The Broken Road (1908).

The novel weaves continuously, without strain, between the perspectives of
Kim and the Lama, while the reader is obliged intermittently to be aware of
a third pattern: the conflict between Britain and her enemies in India. If
asked to name a famous Edwardian novel about keeping the Russians out of
Afghanistan one would be non-plussed: yet that *is Kim's* plot. It is part of
Kipling's unfailing artistry that the work of The Game against the imperial
competitors is never obscured but at the same time never allowed to
dominate the novel's interest. Angus Wilson believes that there is no 'evil' in
Kim: my own view is that evil is invisible to Kim and the Lama but present in
the novel. The Russian who strikes the Lama is a bullying thug, the priest
whom Kim outwits is a systematic parasite representative of vicious, endemic
petty corruption in Indian life. The child of thirteen astride Zam-Zammah
who has 'known all evil since he could speak' (p.4) might well grow into an
evil parasite himself were it not for his encounters with the Lama and the
English. This leads to the simplest and most effective of the book's
paradoxes. Kim's value to the British is his talent for duplicity, his capacity
to tell lies, to be a Sahib disguised as many kinds of Indian, an agent posing
as (as well as actually *being*) the Lama's loyal *chela*, a master of all dialects
and manners. But what enslaves his loyalty to both the Lama and the
English is that they tell the *truth*.

In Kipling's Edwardian English stories the land itself is the custodian of
truth. In *Puck of Pook's Hill* and *Rewards and Fairies*, the history of England is
presented to two children, Dan and Una, by Puck, Shakespeare's figure who
has become a subversive nature spirit like the Pans and Fauns employed by
Forster, Saki and other contemporaries. A field in Sussex belonging to the
childrens' father becomes a microcosm for the whole of England. Puck
describes his own survival as a minor deity who has always kept close to the

earth (compare the Faun in Forster's 'The Curate's Friend', left behind in Wiltshire when the Romans went home). The other deities have not done so well: the God Weland, in 'Weland's Sword', has become a blacksmith shoeing horses for ungrateful farmers: 'Farmers and Weald clay ... are both uncommon cold and sour' (p.21). Hugh, a novice monk, frees Weland from his immortality by giving him thanks and good wishes: in gratitutde Weland forges Hugh a magic sword and he becomes a warrior, the friend and companion of Sir Richard Dalyngridge, one of the Norman invaders. Between them these two friends bring good management to the land.

Friendship, good management and the power of the land are themes running through the Puck stories. As in *Stalky and Co.* good management is better than high principles: the story of Parnesius, the young centurion who works in an effective but unorthodox way on Hadrian's wall by cooperating closely with the Picts, is a reminder of Kipling's admiration and affection for the young subalterns and administrators who deal with the day-to-day practicalities of India as against the politicians and generals who 'govern' her.

In terms of dramatic dating most of the stories in *Rewards and Fairies* post-date the stories in *Puck of Pook's Hill*. 'The Knife and the Naked Chalk' is an exception. 'Weland's Sword' from the previous volume and 'The Knife and the Naked Chalk' are in a sense complementary versions of the same story, the one magical and the other prehistoric. Weland's magical sword gives power to Sir Hugh and helps bind together Saxon and Norman; stone-age man's need for iron knives leads mankind to collaborate against the wolf, the common enemy. Obviously the notion of uniting against a common enemy to defend England was relevant to the nervous and xenophobic atmosphere of 1910.

Kipling's 'They' (*Traffics and Discoveries*, 1904, pp.303-5) links the general nostalgia for rural and historical England in the Puck stories with the theme of the country house as the representative of English upper-class values which is a feature of the period, and the interest in the supernatural and extra-sensory perception which characterises some of the earlier stories (notably 'The Brushwood Boy', *The Day's Work*, 1898). It is also a personal story, an indirect expression of Kipling's grief for the death of his six-year-old daughter Josephine in America in the winter of 1898-9.

'The Other Side of the County', East Sussex, where Kipling lived at Bateman's, Burwash, is the world of the living: the contrast between this world and the 'House Beautiful', the Elizabethan house containing a blind woman and the spirits of dead children, is what the story is really about. Angus Wilson praises the story's evocation of landscape,[36] but perhaps

---

[36] Angus Wilson, *The Strange Ride of Rudyard Kipling* (1977), p.268.

stresses insufficiently this contrast between the Elizabethan house and the 'other side of the county'.

The story opens with a sense that the House Beautiful is difficult of access except to those chosen and invited. The narrator is not willing his journey there but is carried by the unfolding of the landscape and the effortless pleasure of riding in his motor-car: 'One view called me to another; one hill top to its fellow' (p.303).

The symmetry between the blind lady and the puzzled narrator is exact but unobtrusive: the beauty of her setting is closed to her as though she were in a purgatorial state to expiate some unknown sin, but in compensation she is allowed the companionship of the spirit children (although she is unmarried and childless). As the narrator's motor-car breaks into this both paradisal and purgatorial world the language reacts appropriately: 'It was *sacrilege* [my italics] to wake that dreaming house-front with the clatter of machinery' (p.307). And when he sets out to return to his home the lady has to send her butler (himself a bereaved parent) to guide him back to the world: 'We are *so out of the world* [my italics], I don't wonder you were lost!' (p.310).

At the end of the story the mystified narrator encounters his dead daughter and at last understands why he has been brought here: the dead child takes his hand, turns it and kisses it in the palm, 'A fragment of the mute code devised long ago' (p.332). With this comes enlightenment and also the knowledge that it is 'wrong' for him to commune with the dead. The lady intuitively knows this: 'For you it would be wrong'. And she pities him: 'You who must never come here again!' (pp.334, 335). Angus Wilson regrets this ending: 'He fudges the excellent story a little because none of the answers satisfies him and he hopes to get away with leaving a mystery.'[37]

Perhaps, though, the lines of the story are clearer than this comment suggests. The House Beautiful in 'They' is designed to free the narrator from his personal obsessions in the way that Friars Pardon cures the American millionaire, George Chapin, of his vaguely defined physical and psychological illnesses in 'An Habitation Enforced' (*Actions and Reactions*, 1909, pp.3-50).

Like the American Chapins, the narrator of 'They' is socially *placed*, and admonished as well as mystified by the House Beautiful. Bits of discreet snobbishness in the narration work *against* the narrator throughout: 'A butler appeared noiselessly at the miracle of old oak that must be called the front door' (p.310). Socially, the narrator behaves like a provincial tourist: 'If I am not packed off for a trespasser ... Shakespeare and Queen Elizabeth at least must come out of that half-open garden door and ask me to tea' (p.305).

[37] Wilson, p.266.

He is disapproved of by 'the fat woman who sells sweetmeats' in the village (Mrs Madehurst, whose grandchild later dies and joins the spirit children in the House Beautiful); he asks questions about the house and the blind woman and is made to feel that he is an upstart: 'The fat woman ... gave me to understand that people with motor cars had small right to live – much less "go about talking like carriage folk"' (p.312).

Like 'young Mr Meyer', the Jewish businessman who doesn't know how to shoot properly in 'The Treasure and the Law' (*Puck of Pook's Hill*) the narrator has valuable but crude energies which need to be civilised by the House Beautiful. But if he became a constant visitor to the house his bereavement would narrow his perceptions and become obsessive like that of Helen for her illegitimate son killed in the Great War, in the much later story 'The Gardener' (*Debits and Credits*, 1926). He must leave the House Beautiful and return to the cycle of life suggested by the movement of the car over the landscape and the turning of the year: his last visit is made in the early autumn when the 'elder and the wild rose had fruited'.

The idea of a stranger being *socially* educated by a landscape is taken up and treated centrally in 'An Habitation Enforced'. The American George Chapin has come to Sussex for a complete rest following an illness. His wife Sophie is descended from the Lashmars whose land Sir Walter Conant now owns; as a result Sophie and her husband find themselves accepted into the community of the village despite their wealth and their ignorance of English manners, whereas a Brazilian millionaire who has also moved into the neighbourhood – Sangres the 'nigger' – never will be. Kipling delights in this, in the sense of social distinctions being established by a combination of accidents of history and acts of will.

The story could easily be insufferably snobbish, but fortunately it is handled with sufficient tact and indirection to make its points gracefully. And as with 'They' and 'The Gardener' the fact that the story is *personal* gives it an added dimension, this time a happy one: it is clearly a tribute to Carrie, Kipling's American wife, who had courageously and successfully settled in England for life. Kingsley Amis writes that in his Sussex stories and especially in the poem 'Sussex' Kipling is 'too emphatic', it is 'the work of a man pushing down his roots by will-power'; and of this story in particular 'the tone and content of the story are Anglophile, something which a real Englishman cannot be.'[38]

This seems fair. As well as a tribute to his wife the story can be read as a placebo for personal unease. Among the gentry Kipling himself is an outsider, born in India of parents who were distinctly middle- rather than upper-class. His purchase of Bateman's, a gloomy, grand, damp house is a typical Victorian gesture: the self-made man making himself into a squire. If

[38] Kingsley Amis, *Rudyard Kipling and His World* (1975), pp.97, 98.

one accepts this view of Kipling as successful parvenu then his view of the English social order becomes, interestingly, not unlike Wells's (although Wells obviously had further to rise): the envious, resentful, admiring, simplified perception that an intelligent outsider might be expected to have of the life of the English ascendancy.

5. Dandyism

In the 1890s writers responded to the anxieties of the day by detaching themselves, by insisting on their isolation. They developed the myth of the heroically isolated and doomed artist, Yeats's 'Tragic Generation', or they adopted what Holbrook Jackson describes as the role of the 'Dandy', 'whose media are himself and his own personal appearance [and who] looks upon his personality as a movement in the pageant of life.'[39] If one thinks of Wilde, Beardsley, Richard Le Gallienne, Beerbohm, Henry Harland and Corvo, one can see that these two roles, the solitary and the dandy, were closely related. All these writers created for themselves public identities which were loosely upper-class and – this is the important point – detached from the economic and social laws governing modern urban society. Harland and Corvo invented fake aristocratic titles for themselves, Le Gallienne adopted the 'Le' when he moved to London from Liverpool. Wilde's belief in his own detachment from the laws, in both the general and the restricted sense, which governed the rest of mankind can be seen to have contributed substantially to his downfall. After 1900 when, as Yeats put it, 'Everybody got down off his stilts' (introduction to the *Oxford Book of Modern Verse*, 1936) the cult of the *invented* literary personality and the notion of the artist's self-tormenting isolation tended to fade.

Yet there were interesting and important exceptions to this. Arthur Machen and Corvo, for example, perpetuated the 1890s styles in their works and their lives. Arthur Machen was a writer of considerable talent who rightly believed that his career had been eclipsed by the Wilde scandal, and poured his frustrations with the literary life into an important novel, *The Hill of Dreams* (completed by 1897 but not published until 1907).

In the hero of *The Hill of Dreams*, 'Lucian Taylor', Machen creates a figure like Joyce's Stephen Dedalus, an isolated provincial writer seeking an appropriate image. Joyce's Stephen finds his image of the self in the winged figure, the 'fabulous artificer' ascending above Sandymount Strand in the central epiphany of *A Portrait of the Artist as a Young Man* (1916). Lucian finds no such consoling image: instead he becomes lost in a labyrinthine inner

[39] Holbrook Jackson, *Romance and Reality* (1911), pp.198-9. See also Ellen Moers, *The Dandy* (1960).

world with its own imaginary civilisation – the Roman city of Avallaunius, which is revealed to him beneath the Welsh hills of his home – and its own religion, the practice of Witchcraft.

The Hill of Dreams could be taken to exemplify the epistemological crisis: none of the supposed facts in the novel are reliable, Lucian's hallucinations and the outer reality are indistinguishable until they are put into perspective by the novel's close. Lucian has suffered loss of memory in London and dies of drug-addiction in a slum-house belonging to a prostitute (the witch-mistress of his imagination) who has robbed him. For most of the novel's length the reader is trapped in the inner drama of Lucian's consciousness and finds himself in a treacherous continuum of experience of which the elements are inseparable.

If Machen's Lucian Taylor is an extreme portrait of the self as solitary hero, Corvo's Arthur Rose in *Hadrian VII* (1904) is a striking continuation of the 1890s hero-as-dandy. Corvo's personal life was one of a dandyism by which he formalised his aggressions and secured for himself a social ascendancy based on nothing. The imaginary Italian title, 'Baron Corvo', the non-existent ordination implied by the 'Fr.' to which he contracted his first name, Frederick, the polite Venetian address from which he sent his appeals for money and his pornographic letters (the Bucintoro Rowing Club: Corvo was, indeed, a member and often slept there in a boat when he was penniless and homeless) all contribute to that precarious magnificence wrung from circumstances of awesome humiliation which characterises Corvo's career.

Hadrian VII is a compelling novel up to and including the moment at which George Arthur Rose is elected Pope:

> 'It was on him, on him, that all eyes were, why did he not kneel?
>
> 'Again the voice of the Cardinal-Archdeacon intoned, "Reverend Lord, the Sacred College has elected thee to be the Successor of St Peter. Wilt thou accept pontificality?"
>
> 'There was no mistake. The awful tremendous question was addressed to him.
>
> 'A murmur from the bishop prompted him, "The response is *Volo* – or *Nolo*".
>
> 'The surging in his temples, the booming in his ears, miraculously ceased. He took one long slow breath: crossed right hand over left upon his breast: became like a piece of pageant; and responded "I will"'
> (pp.84-5).

'Became like a piece of pageant': the phrase anticipates Holbrook Jackson's definition of a Dandy as one who 'looks upon his personality as a movement in the pageant of life' (see above, p.17). It also points to the novel's central weakness. The difficulty with the novel from this moment onwards is that the plot runs out of invention and the Pope is more 'a piece of pageant' than a human being. Beyond covering the walls of the Vatican with brown paper, impressing the Cardinals by his capacity to digest cream and displaying a childish arbitrariness over details of ritual, Pope Hadrian *does* very little. The novel is like two insignificant islands linked by a disproportionately ornate bridge. The islands are Rose's penury and his shadowy involvement as Pope in European politics – the plot, in short – and the bridge is the obsessive elaboration of his own image as Pope which is the novel's real subject.

Dandyism in its more frivolous sense is continuously present in the minor and popular literature of 1890-1914, as though the differences between Victorian and Edwardian felt in the upper literary atmosphere were scarcely registered in these lower depths. The undergraduate hero of Benson's *The Babe, B.A.: Being the Uneventful History of a Young Gentleman at the University of Cambridge* (1897) is the ancestor of Saki's graceful and infuriating young men Clovis Sangrail in *The Chronicles of Clovis* and Bassington in *The Unbearable Bassington* (both 1912). P.G. Wodehouse's Psmith, the upper-class anarchist who is expelled from Eton, is of the same mould.

Indeed, in Wodehouse's work the dandy, already an 1890s survival into the Edwardian world, was perpetuated for much of the twentieth century. His schoolboy stories of the Edwardian period are taken by Orwell, rightly I think, as works of a precocious maturity in which Wodehouse remained stuck for the rest of his long life (George Orwell, 'In Defence of P.G. Wodehouse', *The Collected Essays*, vol. 3 (Secker and Warburg, 1968), pp.341-55).

Psmith's characteristics are faintly reminiscent of Stalky's in *Stalky and Co.*, physical courage, disregard of the rules, tribal solidarity and cunning. But unlike Kipling's schoolboys, who are capable of complex emotions (Stalky's sense of personal affront in 'The Flag of Their Country', for example), Wodehouse's figures are capable only of aggression. The dominant motif of the dialogue is the insult, of which there are many good examples. One of the boys says of his adolescent moustache: 'Heaps of people tell me I ought to have it waxed'. 'What it really needs is a top-dressing with guano', replies Psmith (*Mike: A Public-School Story*, 1909, p.241). Psmith becomes the central figure of the first Wodehouse novel to have an adult setting, *Psmith in the City* (1910). After the Great War Psmith splits into two: his effortless social superiority becomes an attribute of Bertie Wooster, his guile and know-how become characteristics of the indispensable Jeeves.

In the Edwardian romances of high life by Elinor Glyn and Henry Harland dandyism becomes associated with sexual passivity. Three of Harland's Edwardian novels, *The Cardinal's Snuffbox* (1900), *The Lady Paramount* (1902) and *My Friend Prospero* (1904) have identical plots: strong rich girl meets weak rich boy, complications involving mistaken identities are cleared away, they close with each other. Each novel is characterised by enormous wealth, Italian settings, cardinals, and elegant dialogue filled with literary quotations. They are all readable in a tinselly way, and the last novel, *The Royal End*, completed by Harland's widow and published posthumously, has had stronger claims made for it.[40] This novel has a Jamesian heroine, Ruth Adgate, whose personality is filled out with rather more detail than is to be found in the preceding novels and who marries only the *second* richest man in the cast of characters.

While Harland's novels were commercial entertainments Elinor Glyn's *Three Weeks* (1907) was the work of a writer who took herself seriously and saw the writing of her sexually explicit novel as an act of personal liberation.[41] Paul Verdayne, her gentleman hero, is 'polished and lazy and strong', a 'clear, insular, arrogant Englishman', a 'Sleeping Beauty' who needs to be sexually awoken by the dominant foreign lady, the 'Imperatskoye', whom he meets in a hotel (p.64). *Three Weeks* is an uneven, naive, touching work which should not be consigned immediately to the dustbin. Its snobbishness is breath-taking (Paul 'left Oxford with a record for all that should turn a beautiful Englishman into a beautiful athlete' (p.6)) but its sexual energy is effective where it manages to avoid being absurd.

6. The imperial adventure

The figure of the dandy is balanced by the imperial adventurer who enjoys an equally unbroken continuity in popular literature from the nineteenth to the twentieth centuries. The assumptions underlying Rider Haggard's romances are present and unchanged in such works as A.E.W Mason's *The Broken Road* (1908) and John Buchan's *Prester John* (1910).[42] *Prester John* is a readable and in some ways subtle work. The central protagonists are Davie Crawfurd, the nineteen-year-old Scottish narrator, and his opponent John Laputa, the black Napoleon of Southern Africa who is planning a nationalist rising against the whites. Laputa is a figure of masculine force presented with what seems unmistakable, though presumably unconscious, homoerotic excitement by the adolescent narrator.

Davie Crawfurd sees Laputa stripped naked for the mysterious ceremony in which he puts on the ruby necklet which had belonged to the legendary black King Chaka and originally, it seems, to the Queen of Sheba. Stirred by this sight he acknowledges Laputa as a natural hero: 'I knew that, to the

[40] See Karl Beckson, *Henry Harland: His Life and Work* (1978).

[41] Galsworthy's *Joceylyn* is a comparable case; see the discussion of Galsworthy, below pp.183-8.

[42] See the discussion of these novels in Brian V. Street, *The Savage in Literature: Representations of 'Primitive' Society in English Fiction, 1858-1920* (1975).

confusion of all talk about equality, God has ordained some men to be kings and others to serve' (*Prester John*, p.187).

The use of an adolescent narrator is strategically successful. Davie Crawfurd does not have the settled racial attitudes of a mature white imperialist (though he *is*, of course, loyal to the empire) and he can be temporarily demoralised by Laputa's physical presence: 'I longed for a leader who should master me and make my soul his own' (p.192) he exclaims, and in the course of his lyrical response to Laputa's physical splendour notes that 'he put a hand on my saddle, and I remember noting how slim and fine it was, more like a high-bred woman's than a man's' (p.150).

When he recovers from this intoxication he quotes (again, presumably unconsciously) the title of Conrad's famous story of a white imperialist's moral collapse: 'Last night I had looked into the heart of darkness, and the sight had terrified me' (p.200).

The most conspicuous literary debt is to Rider Haggard: the notion of a tradition of heroism handed down to the modern African from an extinct civilisation, the fabulous hidden treasure (the Chaka's necklet) and the mysterious cavern in which Davie is almost trapped are obvious borrowings from *She* and *King Solomon's Mines*. It is possible that the villainous Portuguese trader, Henriques, known to Davie as the Portugoose, owes something to Conrad's Cornelius. But the novel is interesting precisely for the way in which it refuses to be like Conrad. In young Davie it has a potentially Conradian narrator, flexible, pragmatic, emotionally stirred by the force animating the opposing side. But the fundamental imperial assumption of the novel is so secure that Davie's sympathy for Laputa cannot disturb it. The political frame and the emotional energies of the novel exist apart from each other, so to speak, as though unaware of each other's existence.

One of the confusing features of the period, then, is the way in which popular literature continues to reproduce the received dramatic stereotypes as though nothing had changed. With certain obvious exceptions (Wells and Shaw, Chesterton and Belloc) it is broadly true that among the major Edwardian writers there is a tendency for the artist to subordinate his personality to his art. Joyce's perception of the artist-as-hero formulated (though not published) within the decade, is relevant here. The artist is 'like the God of the creation', a remote figure 'paring his fingernails' whose relationship with his work is one of detachment: he is 'within or behind or beyond or above his handiwork'.[43]

With this sense of a need to subordinate the self to the craft went a willingness to collaborate, to work together. In *The Private Papers of Henry Ryecroft* (1903) Gissing describes with stoic detachment the harm that his

[43] James Joyce, *A Portrait of the Artist as a Young Man* (1916), p.160.

self-imposed isolation as a writer had done to his art (pp.21-2). The Edwardians, by contrast, even those who were temperamentally solitaries like Conrad and Ford, were willing to get together. They pooled ideas, they argued about technique, they joined the Fabian movement, they collaborated on periodicals: Forster, though not on the editorial board, worked closely with Lowes Dickinson on *The Independent Review*, Wells and Shaw were associated with *The New Age* (edited by Alfred Orage and Holbrook Jackson), and Conrad can be regarded as a joint founder, with Ford Madox Ford, of *The English Review*.

Simple proximity, too, helped to break down the isolation of these writers' lives: Kipling, Wells, Henry James, Conrad and Ford all lived for a time within easy reach of each other in Kent and Sussex, and attracted a steady flow of literary visitors. And the emergence of the literary agent as an intermediary between author and publisher gave a new kind of cohesiveness and professionalism to the literary life. There is a needed book waiting to be written about J.B. Pinker, the tough Scot who was literary agent to Bennett, Wells, Ford, Conrad, Galsworthy and Henry James. It was easy for a writer to make a living (though Conrad did not find it so): indeed the printed word, as a medium, was enjoying its last few years of undisputed primacy, and it was possible for best-selling writers like Wells and Bennett to enjoy the kind of life-styles that were to be associated with film stars in the 'twenties and 'thirties.

Working in a period of anxiety and acute moral uncertainty, socially integrated but morally bereft, the major Edwardians can be seen to be living a paradox. Their gregariousness is a form of defence from the epistemological crisis. Reliably sensitive to the pressures of his time, C.F.G. Masterman expressed the situation in these terms: 'Belief in religion, as a conception of life dependent upon supernatural sanctions or as a revelation of a purpose and meaning beyond the actual business of the day, is slowly but steadily fading from the modern city race. Tolerance, kindliness, sympathy, civilisation continually improve. Affirmation of any responsibility, beyond that to self and to humanity, continually declines' (*The Condition of England*, 1909, p.266).

At a personal level tolerance, kindliness and sympathy work very well: the Bloomsbury cult of personal relations, the loyalty that all Conrad's friends showed him in his financial difficulties, the surprising kindness that Wells showed to Gissing are local examples of these virtues in action. But beyond the personal context the period displays a gap, a lack of connection, between moral conviction and effective action. Some commentaries have suggested that this disfunction, or paralysis, is the over-riding factor which permitted England to drift into the Great War.[44]

---

[44] See especially George Dangerfield, *The Strange Death of Liberal England* (1935).

Individual energy directed to the public arena seems to have been largely fruitless. The enormous labours of Beatrice and Sidney Webb, the powerhouse of the Fabian movement, had little impact on national policy. In prominent altruistic writers like Galsworthy and Granville-Barker there was a vivid awareness of social evils without much in the way of proposals for their correction. Granville-Barker's *Waste* points to the suicidal hypocrisy of a system which can destroy a gifted, innovative politician because of his sexual behaviour. Galsworthy's *Strife* is specific about the evils of industrial conflict and mismanagement but has no clear recommendations to make. The case of Galsworthy's *Justice* is slightly different: it seems likely that Galsworthy's 'Minute on Separate Confinement' personally forwarded to the Home Secretary by his friend Masterman combined with the publicity attracted by the play did contribute to the reduction of the mandatory term of solitary confinement to a uniform three months for all prisoners.[45]

Wells, of course, had very specific proposals for reordering the nation, but was too impatient to study carefully (as the Webbs did) the political realities he was dealing with. Central to his doctrine in the Edwardian period was the notion that scientific intelligence – himself and those who thought like him – should form an oligarchy to govern the state.[46] Also Wells was too impatient to be politically effective; when people failed to take up his ideas immediately he lost his temper and sulked. Hence the image of the sighted man who is hounded to his death by the blind in 'The Country of the Blind' (1911) and the new master-race of giants who are persecuted by frightened normal-sized humanity in *The Food of the Gods* (1904).

7. The role of the hero

Effective moral action in the public arena is the role of a hero, and one of the persistent, shared intuitions of the major Edwardians is that the modern world is inhospitable to heroism. Conrad and Ford write with an acute consciousness of the problem of a hero in a world which has no role for him to play. Conrad's Heyst and Ford's Tietjens are the most fully articulated embodiments of this theme, but it is present throughout their work. The whole of *Nostromo* can be seen as an ironic study of traditional male heroic qualities neutered by the conditions of the modern world; and to compound the irony Conrad has set his study of the male will to power and its final ineffectiveness, the self-destructiveness of the pressures within Gould,

[45] Catherine Dupré, *John Galsworthy: A Biography* (1976), p.151.

[46] See the conception of the 'Samurai', the oligarchy in Wells's *A Modern Utopia* (1905) and the discussion of this idea in the first number of *The New Age* 1, no.1 (2 May 1907), pp.9-11.

Nostromo and Decoud, in a South American setting where the word *macho* was coined, a culture which sets supreme value on male force.[47]

In his Victorian novel *Cashel Byron's Profession* (1886, revised 1901) Shaw displays a robust faith in effective male force, aggression, *virtu*. Cashel, the gentleman turned boxer, is personally irresistible, a glamorous violent animal among the inhibited urban males of London: 'His light alert step, and certain gamesome assurance of manner, marked him off from a genteelly promenading middle-aged gentleman, a trudging workman, and a vigorously striding youth' (pp.152-3).

At the turn of the century and in the Edwardian period, by contrast, Shaw's plays reflect the irrelevance and inefficacy of male force in the modern world. In many of his plays power is vested in the female: Vivie Warren defeating Sir George Crofts in *Mrs Warren's Profession*, Lady Cicely Waynflete outfacing both Captain Brasshound's romantic vindictiveness and Sir Howard Hallam's impersonal murderousness in *Captain Brassbound's Conversion*, Anne Whitefield subordinating Jack Tanner to the 'eternal purpose' – the perpetuation of the species – in *Man and Superman*, Eliza demonstrating to Henry Higgins that she can do without him in *Pygmalion*.

If the man does win he does so by guile rather than force. Undershaft, in *Major Barbara* (performed 1905, published 1907), is an armaments manufacturer whose career is a triumph of the will, of the doctrine 'thou shalt starve ere I starve' (p.172). He defeats the play's strong women, his wife Britomart who is an embodiment of aristocratic obstinacy, and his daughter Barbara, the Salvation Army 'Major' of the title whose faith he destroys by demonstrating that the Salvation Army depends on money produced by amoral industrialists like himself. By the end of the play he has won over the whole of his initially outraged family (and his adopted son, the 'foundling' Adolphus Cusins) to his view that 'money and gunpowder' are the 'two things necessary for salvation' (p.116), and that the seven deadly sins are 'food, clothing, firing, rent, taxes, respectability and children' (p.172).

Heartbreak House (written 1916-17) gives a retrospect of the theme of heroism in Shaw's Edwardian plays. Undershaft, the Mephistopheles of *Major Barbara*, has become senile Captain Shotover, the octogenarian armaments inventor who is kept going by gin. Captain Brassbound's successor is Hector Hushabye, international adventurer, liar and braggart (both portraits owe something to Cunninghame Graham's reputation). The dominant women of the previous plays are succeeded by Ellie Dunn, the mesmerist who is able to hypnotise and control 'Boss' Mangan, a violent capitalist, and Captain Shotover himself.

These figures, with their different kinds of strength, are powerless in the

---

[47] I am indebted to John Patterson, of Linacre College, Oxford, for this point.

context of the war. England is a ship navigated by an upper class which has fatally abdicated from its responsibilities:

Captain Shotover: 'The captain is in his bunk, drinking bottled ditch-water; and the crew is gambling in the forecastle. She will strike and sink and split. Do you think the laws of God will be suspended in favour of England because you were born in it?' (p.177) The image is perhaps a conscious recall of Captain Brassbound's exclamation of despair when he has been deprived of his purpose in life – avenging his mother's death – by Lady Cicely's intervention: 'I was steering a course and had work in hand. Give a man health and a course to steer; and he'll never stop to trouble about whether he's happy or not' (*Captain Brassbound's Conversion* (performed 1900, published 1901, p.411)).

An endangered ship as an image of humanity's loss of moral direction is a constant feature of Conrad's writing – in *The Nigger of the Narcissus,* 'Typhoon', 'Falk', *Lord Jim, Chance* – and is also used with considerable power by Masterman and Bertrand Russell. In Masterman's *The Condition of England* the image is associated with the topical fears of invasion, class war, and the degeneracy of the race:

'With the vertical division between nation and nation armed to the teeth, and the horizontal division between rich and poor which has become a cosmopolitan fissure, the future of progress is still doubtful and precarious. Humanity – at best – appears but as a shipwrecked crew which has taken refuge on a narrow ledge of rock, beaten by wind and wave; which cannot tell how many, if any at all, will survive when the long night gives place to morning. The wise man will still go softly all his days; working always for greater economic equality on the one hand, for understanding between estranged peoples on the other; apprehending always how slight an effort of stupidity or violence could strike a death-blow to twentieth-century civilisation, and elevate the forces of destruction triumphant over the ruins of a world' (p.303).

In his extraordinarily emotional essay, 'The Free Man's Worship', Russell uses a version of the same image to express man's solitariness in a godless universe:

'We see, surrounding the narrow raft illumined by the flickering light of human comradeship, the dark ocean on whose rolling waves we toss for a brief hour; from the great night without, a chill blast breaks in upon our refuge; all the loneliness of humanity amid hostile forces is concentrated upon the individual soul, which must struggle alone, with what of courage it can command' (pp.421-2).

Edwardian England, then, is a relatively stable and yet uneasy culture in which 'odours from the abyss' reminded the upper classes of a level of poverty and 'degeneracy' which they preferred not to acknowledge, and in which the threat of a European war was increasingly felt: a culture in which the great Victorian imperatives, Christianity, Monarchy, Empire had largely been replaced by secular consolations which for some writers were still current – rural England, adventure in action, the sense of social ascendancy which expressed itself in dandyism – but for others were themselves devalued and under attack.

Chapter Two: Conrad

1. Early works: the image of the hero

In *The People of the Abyss*, Jack London writes about a young fireman in the East End of London who lived only for drink and had given up any hope of marrying: 'His head was shapely, and so graceful ... that I was not surprised by his body that night when he stripped for bed. I have seen many men strip, in gymnasium and training quarters, men of good blood and upbringing, but I have never seen one who stripped to better advantage than this young sot of two-and-twenty, this young god doomed to rack and ruin in four or five short years, and to pass hence without posterity to receive the splendid heritage it was his to bequeath' (pp.37-8). London had been tramp, convict, seaman. His response to male beauty is vivid perhaps as a result of homosexual experience in prison. Throughout his life he made a cult of the 'perfect male body'.[1]

A man of action whose life has given him a streak of acquired, and probably unconscious, homosexuality: the description would fit Conrad as well as it fits Jack London, if a recent study of homosexuality in literature is to be believed: '*Victory* is a deliberate compromise between Conrad's desire to write openly about homosexuality and his need to suppress the theme and to surround the sexual core of the novel with reticence and evasion.'[2] This study suggests that *Victory* is like an equation with one of its terms suppressed. Heyst sees Jones as another self, a 'secret sharer' or *Doppelgänger*; Jones' overt homosexuality speaks to the repressed homosexuality in Heyst which is the hidden cause of his ineffectiveness as a man and his lack of sexual initiative with Lena.[3]

At the same time Orwell was certainly right in suggesting that Conrad's view of man is simple and old-fashioned: 'He had the outlook of a European aristocrat, and he believed in the existence of the "English gentleman" at a time when this type had been extinct for about two generations.'[4] But Orwell

---

[1] Andrew Sinclair, *Jack: A Biography of Jack London* (1978), p.104.
[2] Jeffrey Meyers, *Homosexuality and Literature: 1890-1930* (1977), p.77.
[3] Ibid., p.87.
[4] George Orwell, Review of *The Nigger of the Narcissus* and other works, *Collected Essays*, vol. 3, p.389.

was wrong in attributing this belief in English gentlemen to Conrad's Polishness; his collaborator Ford believed in gentlemen even more loyally, perhaps desperately, than Conrad did.[5]

In Conrad the young hero is there to be admired but also to be educated. The hero is himself both an ideal image of man, a *kouros*, and an immature seeker, the hero of a *Bildungsroman* or novel of initiation and development.[6] In Conrad these young heroes – Willems, young Marlow in *Youth*, Jim in *Lord Jim*, Powell in *Chance* – must relate themselves to mature men in the course of the difficult process of establishing their own manhood. It has been suggested that this pattern in Conrad's work reflects his own relationships with two older men, his father and his uncle.[7]

Bound up with the question 'What is a man?' is the question 'What is the significance of his life?' Conrad's imagination is that of an atheist using Christian concepts, as is perhaps inevitable for someone brought up in early childhood as a Catholic. The great works of his central period, *Heart of Darkness*, *Lord Jim*, *Nostromo* and *Under Western Eyes*, ask these questions *together*. 'What is man? What is the significance of his life?' circle the male figures of these narratives. The answers are oracular, and consist of the questions rephrased: 'Need man's life have a meaning? Need man have an identity?'

So much has been written on Conrad, he is now so much an academic heavy industry, that with him more than with most major figures it is important to recover the freshness of the amateur reader: to stand back from the works and ask oneself 'Why do I read Conrad? What do I find in him?'

My own answer to that would be that I find in him the *loneliness* of human beings caught and communicated with a vividness unsurpassed in any other writer.

In Conrad's first two novels, *Almayer's Folly* (1895) and *An Outcast of the Islands* (1896), a central pattern in his later work is adumbrated: male figures are forced to test themselves and confront their own limitations in drastically simplified settings. The limitation of these two early novels, as has often been pointed out, is that they are 'exotic' in too literal a sense. They depend rather heavily on the appeal of their remote and little-known settings.

The pattern of male figures seeking an appropriate model of masculinity on which to base themselves is established in outline in Almayer's relationship with Lingard in *Almayer's Folly*, and is developed much more successfully in the Willems-Lingard relationship in *An Outcast of the Islands*. Willems's story can be seen as the seed-bed for the stories of Jim, Razumov and perhaps Roderick Anthony and Heyst in the later works. The nature of

[5] See Geoffrey Wagner, 'Ford Madox Ford: the honest Edwardian', *Essays in Criticism* 17 (1967), pp.75-88.

[6] See J.H. Buckley, *Season of Youth: The Bildungsroman from Dickens to Golding* (1974).

[7] See R.R. Hodges, *The Dual Heritage of Joseph Conrad* (1967).

Willems is firmly grasped on the first page of this novel, as a weak anti-hero who is altering his world for the worse by compromising with his conscience: 'When he stepped off the straight and narrow path of his peculiar honesty, it was with an inward assertion of unflinching resolve to fall back again into the monotonous but safe stride of virtue as soon as his little excursion into the wayside quagmires had produced the desired effect' (p.3).

He is a petty lordling enjoying the small-scale veneration of his wife's family, the half-caste Da Souzas whose 'admiration was the great luxury of his life. It rounded and completed his existence in a perpetual assurance of unquestionable superiority' (p.4).

Willems is ignorant, boastful, the worst kind of colonial shirker and braggart, the kind of man that Jim fatally allows himself to associate with in chapter 2 of *Lord Jim* (1900): 'They were attuned to the eternal peace of Eastern sky and sea. They loved short passages, good deck-chairs, large native crews, and the distinction of being white' (p.13). He also has Jim's young man's attractiveness, the quality that first commends Willems to Lingard's charity when he deserts his Dutch ship as a boy.

Lingard has rescued Willems and set him up in his present employment with Hudig. The novel opens with Willems in the act of disgracing himself by misappropriating funds; he is sacked by Hudig and thrown back on Lingard's mercy.

Lingard unwisely takes his disgraced protegé back under his protection. Lingard has a secret, a river, which 'with infinite trouble [he] had found out and surveyed – for his own benefit only' (p.200). It is his private source of wealth, and also (like Jim's Patusan and Morrison's starving villages in *Victory*) the focus of a philanthropic dream: 'Knowing nothing of Arcadia – he dreamed of Arcadian happiness for that little corner of the world which he loved to think all his own' (p.200).

As well as a genuine philanthropist Lingard can be seen as a romantic megalomaniac whose misplaced loyalty to Willems is an expression of vanity; he prefers not to believe that a protegé of his own is rotten to the core. Willems is lazy and dishonest but he also feels, with justice, that he has been manipulated by Lingard. His betrayal of Lingard's secret river to the Arab traders is treachery, certainly, but is also a necessary act of self-assertion on the part of the younger man, a bid for freedom from Lingard's oppressive benevolence.

The writing is at its best in two passages involving Willems, the first when he is sacked by Hudig and stumbles out of the office feeling short of breath and with his visual perceptions heightened; both well-observed physical reactions to the threatened situation in which he finds himself: 'A thin rope's end lay across his path and he saw it distinctly, yet stumbled heavily over it as if it had been a bar of iron. Then he found himself in the street at last, but could not find air enough to fill his lungs. He walked towards his home, gasping' (p.22). One is struck by the accuracy with which Conrad observes the physical aftermath of a humiliating experience: the distressed breathing, the sense of unreality.

The moment at which Willems is shot by Aissa, his mistress, when she learns that he is married, is so much better than anything else in the novel that it threatens the book's integrity (the dots here are all Conrad's): 'He saw a burst of red flame before his eyes, and was deafened by a report that seemed to him louder than a clap of thunder. Something stopped him short, and he stood aspiring in his nostrils the acrid smell of the blue smoke that drifted from before his eyes like an immense cloud ... Missed, by Heaven! ... Thought so! ... And he saw her very far off, throwing her arms up, while the revolver, very small, lay on the ground between them ... Missed! ... He would go and pick it up now. Never before did he understand, as in that second, the joy, the triumphant delight of sunshine and of life. His mouth was full of something salt and warm. He tried to cough; spat out ... Who shrieks: in the name of God, he dies! – he dies! – Who dies? – Must pick up – Night! – What? ... Night already ...' (p.360).

Too often, in these early works, the writing is incantatory and somnolent using an omniscient narrative voice which dwells too lovingly on the settings. The tropical vegetation surrounding the love-making of Dain Maroola and Nina in *Almayer's Folly* anticipates the Turkish delight quality of *The Blue Lagoon* (1908), H. de Vere Stacpoole's exotic best-seller: 'Above, away up in the broad day, flamed immense red blossoms sending down on their heads a shower of great dew-sparkling petals that descended rotating slowly in a continuous and perfumed stream; and over them, under them, in the sleeping water; all around them in a ring of luxuriant vegetation bathed in the warm air charged with strong and harsh perfumes, the intense work of tropical nature went on: plants shooting upward, entwined, interlaced in inextricable confusion, climbing madly and brutally over each other in terrible silence of a desperate struggle towards the life-giving sunshine above – as if struck with sudden horror at the seething mass of corruption below, at the death and decay from which they sprang' (*Almayer's Folly*, p.71).

The languor of this passage is partly a result of Conrad's refusal to be economical with language, and partly of the way his phrases tend to fall into triplets: 'over them, under them, in the sleeping water'; 'plants shooting upward, entwined, interlaced'.

In *An Outcast*, even where he is writing about the virile virtues of the seagoing life, Conrad's ear betrays his narrative voice into the same kind of rhythmical chanting: 'The sea, perhaps because of its saltness, roughens the outside but keeps sweet the kernel of its servants' soul. The old sea; the sea of many years ago, whose servants were devoted slaves and went from youth to age or to a sudden grave without needing to open the book of life, because they could look at eternity reflected on the element that gave the life and dealt the death. Like a beautiful and unscrupulous woman, the sea of the past was glorious in its smiles, irresistible in its anger, capricious, enticing, illogical, irresponsible; a thing to love, a thing to fear. It cast a spell, it gave joy, it lulled gently into boundless faith; then with quick and causeless anger it killed. But its cruelty was redeemed by the charm of its inscrutable mystery, by the immensity of its promise, by the supreme witchery of its possible favour. Strong men with childlike hearts were faithful to it, were content to live by its grace – to die by its will' (p.12).

In chapter 1 the reader has been introduced to Willems who, as the lost boy whom Lingard rescued, was 'hopelessly at variance with the spirit of the sea' and had 'an instinctive contempt for the honest simplicity of that work' (p.17). The lyrical opening of chapter 2 quoted above introduces Lingard, who has all the good sea-going qualities but also a fatal conviction of his own superiority. The passage is again weakened by triplets ('it cast a spell, it gave joy, it lulled gently'; 'by ... its inscrutable mystery, by the immensity of its promise, by the supreme witchery') and a gratuitous chanting tone ('the old sea; the sea of many years ago'), but what it says about the sea in fact closely resembles the *content* of the much stronger writing about the sea in *The Nigger of the Narcissus*.

2. The Nigger of the Narcissus *and 'Youth'*

A man tries his strength against the sea. This primitive formula, which has attracted the poetic imagination from Homer to Hemingway, is the strong base on which *The Nigger*, 'Youth', 'Typhoon', 'Falk' and much of *Lord Jim* and *Chance* are constructed, and stands in the background of the more complicated contest taking place in *Heart of Darkness*. In *The Nigger* (1897) 'Old' Singleton, the oldest seaman on board, 'through half a century had measured his strength against the favours and the rages of the sea' (p.98). The respective strengths of Singleton and Captain Allistoun are challenged by the sea and the unsettled state of the crew. The sea is as 'mischievous and discomposing as a madman with an axe' (p.57). Singleton sees it as his life-long partner and comments on Allistoun's combativeness: 'The old man's in a temper with the weather, but it's no good bein' angry with the winds of heaven' (p.53). But Singleton's strength is over-taxed by the gale. As the oldest of the 'children' in the forecastle he becomes abruptly conscious that he himself will die:

'Old! It seemed to him he was broken at last. And like a man bound treacherously while he sleeps, he woke up fettered by the long chain of disregarded years ... He looked upon the immortal sea ... and he saw an immensity tormented and blind, moaning and furious, that claimed all the days of his tenacious life, and, when life was over, would claim the worn-out body of its slave' (p.99).

For the crew the trial of strength is a struggle with their own weaknesses. James Wait, the cowardly and mortally sick 'Nigger' seaman appeals to 'the latent egoism of tenderness to suffering' (p.138), and unfits the crew for their work: 'through him we were becoming highly humanised, tender, complex, excessively decadent' (p.139). Donkin appeals to egoism of another kind, envy of the officers and a desire to upset the ship's working order: 'inspired by Donkin's hopeful doctrines they dreamed enthusiastically of the time when every lonely ship would travel over a serene sea, manned by a wealthy and well-fed crew of satisfied skippers' (p.103).

From experience and habit as well as from conviction Conrad was autocratic. Despite his marriage and his circle of English literary friends he remained curiously isolated from English life and, especially, from the political liberalism by which most English writers of the day (even Kipling) were touched.[8] As Graham Hough has said of him: 'There is only one kind of society that Conrad had ever known intimately, had fully participated in as an adult human being – the society of a ship at sea.'[9] Graham Hough goes on to point out that the heirarchy of a ship at sea, with its fixed chain of command and its urgent priorities, is radically simpler than any social order, however rigid, to be found on land; and he makes a general statement about Conrad's narrative method which seems to illuminate Conrad's work as a whole: 'The complexities of his narrative method are, as it were, layers of protecting covering to an essentially simple heroic vision' (p.220).

The story reflects the current belief that the urban working class was morally and physically degenerating. The men of Singleton's generation, 'who could understand his silence' were 'those men who knew how to exist beyond the pale of life and within sight of eternity. They had been strong, as those are strong who know neither doubts nor hopes' (p.25). That generation of primitive heroes has been replaced by the present crew of the *Narcissus*, 'highly humanised', 'excessively decadent'. Stevie in *The Secret Agent* is identified by Ossipon as a degenerate partly because he has thin prominent ears: Donkin in this story has the same physical feature: 'His big ears stood out, transparent and veined, resembling the thin wings of a bat' (p.110).

The Nigger closes by asking a question: 'Haven't we, together and upon the immortal sea, wrung out a meaning from our lives?' (p.173). The experience of the sea defies and finally expels degeneracy – Donkin is given a bad discharge – and enforces the traditional moral sanction of the primitive fable, man against the sea. After lifting this simple contrast into a full light Conrad

[8] See above, Chapter One.
[9] Graham Hough, 'Chance and Joseph Conrad', *Image and Experience* (1960), p.215.

ends his story by inverting its antithetical shape and simultaneously enlarging its meaning.

Having survived the threats to their strength of Wait and Donkin, the sailors become 'castaways' in the life of the town which is now presented in the imagery of the sea: 'The roar of the town resembled the roar of topping breakers, merciless and strong, with a loud voice and cruel purpose' (p.172).

The writing of *The Nigger* represents a major technical advance on the earlier works. One mark of this advance is that what was formerly simile – in *An Outcast* the sea is '*like* a beautiful and unscrupulous woman', the sailor can see 'eternity *reflected* on the element' [the water] – becomes metaphor in *The Nigger*. In *The Nigger* the sea *is* eternity, *is* God: 'On men reprieved by its disdainful mercy, the immortal sea confers in its justice the full privilege of desired unrest. Through the perfect wisdom of its grace they are not permitted to meditate at ease upon the complicated and acrid savour of existence. They must without pause justify their life to the eternal pity that commands toil to be hard and unceasing' (p.90).

The greater assurance of the writing in *The Nigger* is a product, also, of greater sophistication over the question of narrative presence. The story is in free indirect speech, like *Almayer's Folly* and *An Outcast*, but in *The Nigger* the narrative voice is closely associated with figures in the story. In the first of the five chapters it is in the forecastle with the sailors, in chapter 2 when the Narcissus has put to sea on its homeward voyage from Bombay it moves round the sailors as they contemplate the sick figure of James Wait who lives with death, his 'hateful accomplice' (p.41), his 'awful and veiled familiar' (p.43), and whose life consists of a succession of 'interminable last moments' (p.37). It contemplates the trouble that James Wait and Donkin are beginning to cause: Jimmy's friend 'Belfast' steals from the galley the officers' fruit pie, 'to tempt the fastidious appetite of Jimmy' (p.38) while Donkin, who 'stood on the bad eminence of a general dislike' (p.40), has one of his teeth knocked out by Mr Baker for his insolence (p.41). He and James Wait are drawn to each other: 'Jimmy seemed to like the fellow!' (p.41). And the narrative voice can pull right back from the dramatic content of the story to set the ship in a global context:

'The ship, a fragment detached from the earth, went on lonely and swift like a small planet. Round her the abysses of sky and sea met in an unattainable frontier' (p.24). In chapter 3 the narrator joins 'Belfast', Archie Knowles, and Wamibo, the unintelligible Russian Finn, as they try to release James from the cabin in which he is in danger of being drowned. In chapter 5 the narrator looks on as Donkin sadistically terrifies and then robs Jimmy in the last moments of his life. The omniscient narrator joins the God-like sea in its judgment of Donkin's action: 'The immortal sea stretched away, immense and hazy, like the image of life, with a glittering surface and lightless depths. Donkin gave it a defiant glance and slunk off noiselessly as if judged and cast out by the august silence of its might' (p.155).

The Nigger can be seen as a story organised round four major figures: Wait and Donkin, the destructive elements, and Singleton and Allistoun, the sustaining figures who hold the ship through the memorable and lovingly written gale in chapter 3.

In this pivotal chapter the four central figures interact and reveal each other. Allistoun 'seemed with his eyes to hold the ship up in a superhuman concentration of effort' (p.65), while Singleton at the wheel steers for thirty hours, 'forgotten by all, and with an attentive face. In front of his erect figure only the two arms moved crosswise with a swift and sudden readiness, to check or urge again the rapid stir of circling spokes. He steered with care' (p.84). When the *Narcissus* is blown on her beam ends Donkin, who has hitherto established a kind of power for himself among the sailors, is revealed as cowardly and useless, screaming 'curses' and 'filthy words' at the skipper for his refusal to cut the masts and abruptly silenced by the hostile reaction he provokes: 'One of his rescuers struck him a back-handed blow over the mouth' (p.60).

Jimmy, sick in his cabin, has to be rescued from drowning and displays a hysterical cowardice which succeeds in demoralising the men where Donkin has failed: 'He screamed piercingly, without drawing breath, like a tortured woman; he banged with hands and feet. The agony of his fear wrung our hearts so terribly that we longed to abandon him, to get out of that place deep as a well and swaying like a tree, to get out of his hearing, back on the poop where we could wait passively for death in incomparable repose' (p.67).

Between the strength of Allistoun and Singleton and the cowardice of Donkin and Jimmy Wait a fifth figure, the young Charley, is thrown into prominence in a moment of extraordinary tenderness: 'Between two bearded shellbacks Charley, fastened with somebody's long muffler to a deck ring-bolt, wept quietly, with rare tears wrung out by bewilderment, cold, hunger, and general misery. One of his neighbours punched him in the ribs asking roughly: "What's the matter with your cheek? In fine weather there's no holding you, youngster." Turning about with prudence he worked himself out of his coat and threw it over the boy. The other man closed up, muttering: "'Twill make a bloomin' man of you, sonny." They flung their arms over and pressed against him. Charley drew his feet up and his eyelids dropped' (pp.61-2).

This has an obvious and direct relevance to the theme of initiation into male maturity. As the chapter closes the maturing process in Charley has begun. The sea has forced him to relinquish his cheeky, privileged persona for one humbler and more timid: 'Charley, subdued by the sudden disclosure of the insignificance of his youth, darted fearful glances' (p.74).

Despite its many strengths, its magnificent storm passage, its strong five-part structure, its carefully studied interplay between the major figures and the confidently 'known' quality of the masculine world that it presents, *The Nigger* is finally less perfect a form than 'Youth' (1902). The floating narrator in *The Nigger* has access to all the minds but is anchored in none until he surprisingly speaks in the first-person at the end of the story. In 'Youth' Conrad establishes the narrative device which contributes incalculably to the success of two of his major performances, *Heart of Darkness* and *Lord Jim*.

'Youth' begins, as *Heart of Darkness* begins, with a group of four mature men listening to a fifth man, Marlow, telling a story. Marlow is still in the merchant navy, the others were sailors as young men and have now gone into safe land jobs: law, industry, accountancy. Both stories begin with a frame, an anonymous outer narrator who establishes the relaxed, affectionate male solidarity of the after-dinner audience and introduces Marlow. The outer narrator of 'Youth' doesn't know Marlow well; this is perhaps the first occasion on which they have met. We are to imagine *Heart of Darkness* as being narrated at a later date, since here the outer narrator (clearly the same person) is well acquainted with Marlow although not, it seems, a close friend. In *Lord Jim* the after-dinner situation is taken for granted – it is sketched in perfunctorily at the end of chapter 4, as though the reader is expected to supply it from his memory of the earlier stories. The outer narrator here has the important function of establishing an omniscient and detached view of Jim in the first four chapters, before Marlow's special pleading takes over in chapter 5.

The identity of Marlow has been much discussed in criticisms of Conrad. He may well be based on Cunninghame Graham, whose own prose has the unrevised, colloquial quality that Conrad revises in Marlow. Or he may be conceived loosely as any man of action who recalls his experiences, like Captain Fred Burnaby, author of *A Ride to Khiva*, which went through many editions in the Victorian period and is read by young Marlow in 'Youth' and greatly preferred to Carlyle's *Sartor Resartus* (p.7).

Whatever the source for Marlow, he was a timely gift to Conrad's art: a pragmatist and man of action, unsubtle but reflective, affectionate as well as self-seeking. A contrast to, without being an antithesis of, the intensely sensitive, ambitious, over-scrupulous and self-pitying, not to say neurotic, personality of his creator.

The primitive myth, in which a man tries his strength against the sea, is at its simplest in 'Youth'. The middle-aged Marlow recalls his younger self, at the age of twenty, making his first voyage to the East. The whole enterprise is beset with comic misadventure. The ship, the *Judea*, is an old wreck which tries to put to sea three times with its cargo of coal for Bangkok and eventually has to be dry-docked, recaulked and completely refurbished. The voyage then begins; ominously, the rats choose this moment to leave the ship. The sailors laugh at the rats' stupidity; they stayed with the ship while it was a leaking ruin, they are leaving it now that it is reconditioned and safe. But the rats are proved right: the danger now is not the ship but the cargo. The cargo of coal has been re-loaded too often in bad weather during the work on the *Judea*, it has been broken up and become damp and produces gas which ignites on the voyage. After long delays caused by the obstinacy of the old skipper, Captain Beard, whose first command this is, the crew abandon the burning ship and the young Marlow sails into an Eastern port at the tiller of *his* 'first command': a lifeboat manned by two exhausted sailors and sailing under an improvised rig consisting of an oar, a tarpaulin and a boat-hook.

The weeping Charley in *The Nigger* is told at the height of the storm that the experience will 'make a bloomin' man of you, sonny' (see above, p.34). His successor, the twenty-year-old Marlow, sails his life-boat to an unknown Eastern port: 'I did not know how good a man I was till then' (p.36).

The firm narrative frame provided by the Marlow device is strengthened by the carefully established contrast between the middle-aged man, an ironist with few illusions left, and the idealistic younger self. From one point of view 'Youth' can be seen as ironic: the foolish ardour of the young Marlow is balanced against the foolish obstinacy of old Captain Beard, over-protective towards his wife, endangering his crew by refusing to allow them to leave the burning *Judea* until the ship is fully ablaze.

Once the reader is engaged with the excitement of the story's central contest, though, the irony seems unimportant. In 'Youth' the sea is like chaos at the beginning of creation, 'white like a sheet of foam, like a caldron of boiling milk' (p.11: cf. the same image in *Nigger*, p.78). The energy of the sea forces Marlow to measure his own young strength against it while the ship becomes a gallant old female whom the young sailor defends:

> 'The *Judea*, hove to, wallowed on the Atlantic like an old candle-box. It blew day after day: it blew with spite, without interval, without mercy, without rest. The world was nothing but an immensity of great foaming waves rushing at us, under a sky low enough to touch with the hand and dirty like a smoked ceiling.
>
> '... There was no rest for her and no rest for us. She tossed, she pitched, she stood on her head, she sat on her tail, she rolled, she groaned ...' (p.10)

This and similar passages ensure for 'Youth' a place among the Conrad stories that will always be re-read.

3. Heart of Darkness: *action and lying*

'Youth' was an exposed work, carrying its significance on its surface. The middle-aged man recaptures the moment of maturing and self-discovery in his own younger self. In later works the interest in this moment of self-discovery – in Lord Jim and Razumov – will be extended and bound up with the unanswerable epistemological questions which themselves give a generative force to Conrad's art. In 'Youth' the process of initiation is finite, the personality is fully knowable. The young man who 'did not know how good a man I was till then' has reached the East and won his long-drawn battle with the sea; at the same time he has undergone a quasi-sexual consummation with the East. An 'aromatic' puff of wind reaches him from the land, 'impalpable and enslaving, like a charm, like a whispered promise of mysterious delight' ('Youth', p.37).

'Youth' leaves one quite clear as to what the story has been 'about'. *Heart of Darkness* permits no such confidence. The reader himself is forced into the epistemological wilderness in this wrestle with the text; the normal premises, the normal contractual relationship between writer and reader have been discarded. The reader is not permitted to know which of the two figures, Marlow and Kurtz, is the 'subject' of the story, nor to know how reliable Marlow is as narrator. He is a simple Englishman of action with enough sensibility and experience to communicate his story at the level of primitive narrative but with at the same time a limitation of outlook and sophistication which enables the novelist constantly to hint that the story's significance lies beyond and behind the narrative surface. In the three major Marlow narratives, *Heart of Darkness, Lord Jim* and *Chance*, all the most sophisticated uses to which the device of the limited narrator can be put are explored. In this Conrad is working within a well-established English tradition, if one thinks of Ellen Dean and Lockwood in *Wuthering Heights*, Esther Summerson in *Bleak House*, the soldiers who narrate Kipling's barrack-room stories, the children who provide the frames for the stories in Kipling's *Puck of Pook's Hill* and *Rewards and Fairies*.

The outer narrator of *Heart of Darkness*, the dinner-guest who introduces Marlow to the reader (as he does in *Youth*) alerts the reader not to take the surface of the text on trust: 'We were fated ... to hear about one of Marlow's *inconclusive* experiences' (my italics) (*Heart of Darkness* (published in Blackwood's Magazine, 1899, and in book form in 1902), p.51).

Heart of Darkness can be read as a modernist fiction, perhaps the first consistently self-referential fiction in English.[10] Its surface can be taken as a system of signs and secrets, mysteries leading to other mysteries none of which are explained. The journey of exploration itself is a literary metaphor, an analogy illustrating the way the mind moves through a text responding to its images and signs.

In reading *Heart of Darkness* one encounters opposing principles which may

---

[10] See the rather different but very interesting discussion of the novel's self-referential features in Jeremy Hawthorn, *Joseph Conrad: Language and Fictional Self-Consciousness* (1979).

be termed 'action' and 'the lie'. Action is irreducible. In the world of the epistemological crisis a man's words, intentions, concepts of himself are all vulnerable while his actions are irrefutable as well as irreversible. This thought lies behind the celebrated letter of 1902 to William Blackwood when Conrad was slowly producing *Nostromo*. Blackwood had unwisely let slip that Conrad's work was a bad risk financially:

> 'I am *modern*, and I would rather recall Wagner the musician and Rodin the sculptor who both had to starve a little in their day – and Whistler the painter who made Ruskin the critic foam at the mouth with scorn and indignation ... My work shall not be an utter failure because it has the solid basis of a definite intention – first: and next because it is not an endless analysis of affected sentiments but in its essence it is action ... nothing but action – action observed, felt and interpreted with an absolute truth to my sensations (which are the basis of art in literature) – action of human beings that will bleed to a prick, and are moving in a visible world.'[11]

Marlow finds relief, or therapy, in action against the stagnation and malice that he finds among the Belgian traders. He must restore his sunk steam-boat. (The manager of the trading station has probably scuttled it to impede Marlow's career, since he jealously imagines that Marlow, like Kurtz, has been selected for rapid promotion by the Head Office back in Brussels, the whited sepulchre.)

The steam-boat 'had given me a chance to come out a bit – to find out what I could do. No, I don't like work. I had rather laze about and think of all the fine things that can be done. I don't like work – no man does – but I like what is in the work – the chance to find yourself. Your own reality – for yourself, not for others – what no other man can ever know. They can only see the mere show, and never can tell what it really means' (p.85).

The quest for Kurtz brings in the other opposing principle, 'the lie'. 'I would not have gone so far as to fight for Kurtz, but I went for him near enough to a lie. You know I hate, detest, and can't bear a lie, not because I am straighter than the rest of us, but simply because it appals me. There is a taint of death, a flavour of mortality in lies – which is exactly what I hate and detest in the world – what I want to forget. It makes me miserable and sick, like biting something rotten would do' (p.82).

Marlow's progress through the story is a movement towards knowledge of Kurtz and of the nature of the heart of darkness, a movement which is blocked at almost every turn by lies, shams, impostures. The colonialists

---

[11] To William Blackwood, 31 May 1902, *Joseph Conrad: Letters to William Blackwood and David S. Meldrum* (1958), pp.155-6.

have imposed on the continent a fraudulent linguistic frame, a verbal umbrella like Orwell's Newspeak under the protection of which they can exercise any degree of tyranny. Chained together in work-gangs, the Africans are 'called criminals' (p.64); when shelled by the French man-of-war ('it appears that French had one of their wars going on thereabouts', p.61), they are 'enemies'; when they are dying in the 'grove of death' they are former 'workers' (p.66: the text adds: 'They were not enemies, they were not criminals, they were nothing earthly now'). When Marlow finally reaches Kurtz's inner station to find Kurtz's house surrounded by severed heads on posts, Kurtz's naive young Russian disciple explains that these are the heads of 'rebels'. Marlow's mind revolts: 'Rebels! What would be the next definition I was to hear? There had been enemies, criminals, workers – and these were rebels' (p.132).

The celebrated imagery of 'hollow men' in the story is directly related to this pattern of fraudulent language. The word 'Kurtz' is itself a lie: 'Means short in German – don't it? Well, the name was as true as everything else in his life – and death. He looked at least seven feet long' (p.134). The ambitious brick-maker with a forked beard – who sees himself as competing with Marlow for the favour of the company and rapid promotion – is a 'papier-mâché Mephistopheles'; 'if I tried I could poke my forefinger through him, and would find nothing inside but a little loose dirt' (p.81). Marlow decides to play up to the illusion in the mind of this 'young fool' and feels himself become a fiction, a 'pretence' (p.82).

Kurtz is 'hollow at the core' (p.131), and the hollowness within him and the other hollow men is identified with the 'wilderness', which is itself an increasingly potent word in the story: it is the vacuum left behind a word when the word is part of a lie, the vacancy inside Kurtz which 'invades' Kurtz and 'speaks' to him.

The mass of commentary on *Heart of Darkness* reveals two major emphases. One tradition sees it as a major piece of anti-imperialist fiction.[12] Another sees it as a story about private sensibility which reflects especially the new interest of the 1890s in psychology and reflects also the Darwinian intellectual background of the period.[13]

A recent critic in this tradition, C.B. Cox, confidently reads *Heart of Darkness* as a 'journey into the wilderness of sex'.[14] An earlier notable sexual and psychological approach to this story is in the important 'psychoanalytic biography' by Bernard Meyer.[15]

---

[12] See Raymond Williams, *The English Novel from Dickens to Lawrence* (1974), Irving Howe, *Politics and the Novel* (1957), Eloise Knapp Hay, *The Political Novels of Joseph Conrad* (1963), Jeffrey Meyers, *Fiction and the Colonial Experience* (1973).

[13] See Tom Gibbons, *Rooms in the Darwin Hotel*, and above, p.3.

[14] C.B. Cox, *Joseph Conrad: The Modern Imagination* (1974), p.46.

[15] Bernard Meyer, *Joseph Conrad: A Psychoanalytic Biography* (1967).

Heart of Darkness plainly does reflect late Victorian anxieties over matters of major topical interest: the status and function of the Empire in a period when its mid-Victorian Christian justification was on the ebb, and the subversive and unassimilable pressures of the demands for sexual freedom and a humanist morality. In some ways Conrad is more representative of the 1890s and the Edwardian period than any native-born writer could be; a sensitive outsider responsibly and minutely observing the major concerns of the age. Eloise Hay quotes Flaubert's doctrine, 'The artist should have neither religion, country, nor even any social conviction', and comments that Conrad 'had neutralised himself in all three of these points by the time his writing life began'.[16] The surface of his life shows the case for this view: he had left Poland, he had married into the English lower middle-class, he was no longer a practising Catholic. But part of the pressure of evolutionary and psychological thinking in the 1890s is towards the position that one cannot, and should not, sever one's roots. These intellectual currents thus have a conservative as well as a radical effect by forcing the individual to acknowledge his place in the natural order and come to terms with his own biological history.

Therefore I am sympathetic to Bernard Meyer's suggestion that 'powerful and poignant overtones of a deep and abiding devotion to [his] early Catholic faith'[17] are found in Conrad's work and that bound up with these is an emotional commitment to his father and Catholic Poland[18] and a tendency to celebrate his own sufferings as a writer as though they were reflections of Christ's passion and Poland's suffering.[19]

It is certain that Conrad responds to images of power in a non-rational way, or, to express it from the opposite point of view, in a religious way. He obviously believes deeply in order, in a chain of command, in the love and 'human solidarity' of the crew of a merchant ship at sea. The Preface to *The Nigger of the Narcissus* describes the novelist's duty to 'speak to' the reader's 'feeling of fellowship with all creation' and 'to the subtle but invincible conviction of solidarity that knits together the loneliness of innumerable hearts' (p.viii). This binds together man's place in the evolutionary continuum and his role as an individual member of the ship's company.

From a broad view of Conrad's work one may judge that he sees subversion (Donkin and Wait, the anarchists in *The Secret Agent*) as a major threat to the 'feeling of fellowship', the 'conviction of solidarity'. But *coercive* authority – the Russian regime in *Under Western Eyes*, the British penal

[16] E.K. Hay, *The Political Novels of Joseph Conrad* (1963), p.1.

[17] Meyer, p.351.

[18] Ibid., pp.281-6.

[19] Ibid., p.355. Bernard Meyer's biography had a mixed reception from Conrad scholars, but in his distinguished study of the creative personality, *The Dynamics of Creation* (1972), the psychiatrist Anthony Storr remarks that Meyer's book is indispensable to an understanding of Conrad (pp.2 and 109).

system in *Chance* – is equally fatal to human solidarity. The right ordering of human societies depends upon a form of authority which is simultaneously absolute and dependent on consent.

An ideally run merchant ship may approximate to such a society, but in its perfect form this social ordering would presumably be found in Christianity ideally expressed.

In a letter to Edward Garnett, 23 February 1914, Conrad (in the context of a discussion of Tolstoy) expresses a dislike of Christianity: 'The base from which he [Tolstoy] starts – Christianity – is distasteful to me. Great, improving, softening, compassionate it may be but it has lent itself with amazing facility to cruel distortions and is the only religion which, with its impossible standards, has brought an infinity of anguish to innumerable Souls – on this earth.'

He follows this vigorous passage with a joke which suggests that he has overstated his anger and knows that it is irrational: 'Why I should fly out like this on Xtianity which has given to mankind the beautiful Xmas pudding I don't know, unless that, like some good dogs, I get snappish as I grow old.'[20]

In *Heart of Darkness* it is possible to see Conrad writing as a non-Christian who still innately is sharing specifically Christian responses to the paradox of authority and then seeking to clarify them in secular terms. Kurtz makes himself into a god and establishes his own liturgy:

'His – let us say – nerves went wrong, and caused him to preside at certain midnight dances ending with unspeakable rites, which – as far as I reluctantly gathered from what I heard at various times – were offered up to him – do you understand? – to Mr Kurtz himself' (pp.117-18).

Marlow himself is forced to acknowledge Kurtz as a deity:

'I had, even like the niggers, to invoke him – himself – his own exalted and incredible degradation. There was nothing either above or below him, and I knew it. He had kicked himself loose of the earth. Confound the man! He had kicked the very earth in pieces' (p.144).

I am not suggesting, as some have, that Conrad is in a sense condoning and covertly approving Kurtz's self-deification.[21] Kurtz's epiphany is presented in language of recoil: 'unspeakable rites', 'incredible degradation'. The wilderness possesses Kurtz in what could be a diabolical parody of an account of God invading the life of a saint: 'The wilderness ... had taken him, loved him, embraced him, got into his veins, consumed his flesh and sealed his soul to its own by the inconceivable ceremonies of some devilish initiation' (p.115). If one substituted 'God' for 'the wilderness' and removed the word 'devilish' the passage could almost have been lifted from, say, the

---

[20] Edward Garnett (ed.) *Letters from Conrad, 1895-1924* (1928), p.265.

[21] See K.K. Ruthven, 'The Savage God: Conrad and Lawrence', *Critical Quarterly* 10, 1 and 2 (Spring and Summer 1968), pp.39-54.

agonies of St Margaret Mary preceding her vision of the Sacred Heart. But of course the word 'devilish' cannot be removed. Conrad is determined – at all costs, as it were – that the act of veneration shall be perceived as a monstrous evil. He is like a former alcoholic writing about the perils of drink.

It seems to me, then, that in this story Conrad is writing with the temperament of a theist and the convictions of an atheist, and that this traps him in a contradiction which runs like a bottomless fissure through *Heart of Darkness* and helps to account for the difficulty and evasiveness of the surface of the text. The visible expressions of the religious impulse are there to be hated and rejected. At the same time the story begins and ends with the questions forced by Conrad's title: what lies at the heart of man's intellectual darkness? What is the significance of the totality of his being? These are ultimate questions about the nature of life: religious questions, in short. That Conrad should ask such questions is consistent with the view that he is a man of *repressed* religious impulses. This is distinct from the suggestion made by the 'savage god' adherents[22] that he is a man of *secret* religious impulses. The latter suggests a respectable citizen who is a secret drinker, but the right analogy for Conrad is a former alcoholic who has become a strict teetotaller.

One would guess that the writing of this story came as an exhilarating release, the unblocking and unlocking of a hidden region of the creative self. The title and theme address themselves to the problem of whether it is possible to arrive at and communicate a total world-view. The question then has sub-sections: is the world-view attainable from the advanced evolutionary vantage point of Western man? Or from that of primitive man engaged in the struggle for survival? Or, possibly, from that of man in the act of worship? It is as though the former alcoholic were to test himself by asking himself, cautiously, whether he wants a drink, and the answer comes in the form of a passionate and cathartic rejection.

Marlow's maleness, his generous virility, fills the vacuum left by the hollowness and negation surrounding him in *Heart of Darkness*. The deadness and hollowness of the traders is contrasted with the vitality of the Africans: 'They shouted, sang; their bodies streamed with perspiration; they had faces like grotesque masks – these chaps; but they had bone, muscle, a wild vitality, an intense energy of movement, that was as natural and true as the surf along their coast' (p.61).

The fascinating whiteness that Conrad as a child had seen at the centre of Africa 'in 1868, when nine years old or thereabouts' (*A Personal Record* (1912) p.13) has given way to a 'darkness' which is alive while Brussels is a white sepulchre. Black is energy, white is death; the equation is not mechanical or rigid, but it is sufficiently clearly marked to give its own additional richness to the text. The doors of the trading company offices leading into the

---

[22] See Ruthven, op. cit.

darkness are opened by a white-haired secretary.

The elegant white-suited, clean-collared clerk, 'amazing', sits in the middle trading-station on the Congo keeping his ledgers accurately while a groaning man dies at his feet. The ivory itself, the goal of this cruel and incompetent imperialism, takes its place in the black-white symbolism which is rounded off by the grouping of peripheral female figures in the story: in Brussels, the whited sepulchre, two women, one old and fat, one younger and thin, knit black wool 'guarding the door of Darkness' (p.57). The black girl, 'savage and superb, wild-eyed and magnificent' (pp.135-6) sums up the vitality of the savages in her sexual passion and loyalty to Kurtz. She gives way in turn to her rival the 'Intended', the white girl in a black setting, dressed in mourning but characterised by her 'forehead, smooth and white' which 'remained illuminated by the unextinguishable light of belief and love' (p.158). This pattern of imagery has been much discussed and is familiar. The point arising out of it which is of interest to me is that Conrad is a *macho* novelist in this story as in much of his other work. The women are unimportant. They are part of the frame; but the story does not pretend to be interested in heterosexual relationships as such: 'They – the women I mean – are out of it – should be out of it. We must help them to stay in that beautiful world of their own, lest ours gets worse' (p.115).

As Marlow here implies, the important relationships are between men.

Kurtz's blacks 'adored' him (p.128), the naive young Russian is possessed by him: 'The man filled his life, occupied his thoughts, swayed his emotions' (p.128). But Marlow comes closer to him than these idolators: 'I knew him as well as it is possible for one man to know another' (p.158).

Kurtz at least has purposiveness. He has come to the colony a romantic idealist, 'humanising, improving, instructing' (p.91), preparing his grandiloquent and philanthropic report for the International Society for the Suppression of Savage Customs: 'By the exercise of our will we can exert a power for good practically unbounded' (p.118). The surprise post-scriptum, 'Exterminate all the brutes!' indicates purposiveness of another kind. The Kurtz that Marlow meets has become hollowed out by wickedness, but he is still more of a 'man' than the 'pilgrims' with their 'staves' and the flabby manager with his petted over-fed black 'boy' from the coast who is allowed to cheek the agents without reproof.

The manager is devoid of normal human drives, the pilgrim's 'staves' are like impotent reified phalluses, emblems of the purposelessness of their lives: 'strolling aimlessly about ... with their absurd long staves in their hands' (p.76). The French gun-boat shelling the bush is attended by another symbol of sexual impotence: 'Her ensign drooped[23] limp like a rag; the muzzles of the long six-inch guns stuck out all over the low hull; the greasy, slimy swell swung

[23] 'dropped', 1946, 'drooped' Ms. and modern editions.

her up lazily and let her down' (pp.61-2). The six-inch guns have shrunk through the successive drafts of the story; in the Ms. they are 'ten-inch' and in *Blackwoods Magazine* 'eight-inch'. One of Conrad's editors has suggested, rather convincingly, that the sexual symbolism here is overt and refers to a specific European male's anxiety about the superior sexual potency of black men.[24]

Marlow is romancing when he describes Kurtz's cry, 'The horror. The horror!' as a moral victory. Marlow is a generous, virile temperament who will create moral positives where they don't exist. He prefers outright wickedness to 'hollowness'. Violence and greed are 'strong, lusty, red-eyed devils, that swayed and drove men – men, I tell you'. Among the Belgian traders he encounters 'a flabby, pretending, weak-eyed devil of a rapacious and pitiless folly' (p.65). In the sharpest contrast with this shabbiness and pretention is the nobility of the starving cannibal crew of the steamer. Marlow wonders why they do not fall on the white men and eat them: 'They were big powerful men, with not much capacity to weigh the consequences, with courage, with strength ... And I saw that something restraining, one of those human secrets that baffle probability, had come into play there' (p.104). The key to the human secret is in Marlow himself. Marlow is innately modest and is unable to see himself. It doesn't need much ingenuity for the reader to see that Marlow himself is, in reality, all that the naive Russian imagines Kurtz to be: a philanthropic, hard-working, morally upright being – in short, that rare phenomenon in the *serious* (as against popular) literature of that period, the good imperialist. It is Marlow's leadership that restrains the cannibals, Marlow's superiority that inspires envy and rage in the manager of the central station and the Mephistophelean brick-maker, Marlow's bearing and obvious honesty that inspire confidence in the 'Intended'.

The lie marks a change, perhaps the beginnings of 'corruption' but equally to be regarded as a gain in flexibility. Marlow is a pre-lapsarian Lord Jim, a 'limited' narrator in the sense in which a good man seeking to describe a wholly evil universe is limited – he can't believe the full iniquity of what he sees.

Marlow speculates that self-knowledge 'came to [Kurtz] at last' (p.131), with his dying cry, 'The horror! The horror!' It seems equally likely, though, that this is the last and most provoking of the story's evasions. The reader's understanding of this final cry is heavily coloured by Marlow's commentary: 'It was an affirmation, a moral victory paid for by innumerable defeats, by

---

[24] Robert Kimbrough, private communication: editor of the Norton Critical Edition of *Heart of Darkness* (1971). This point is perhaps weakened by the fact that the measurements refer, of course, to the *width*, not the length, of the barrels, and Conrad may well have made these changes simply because six-inch guns were the appropriate armoury for a small gun-boat. (I am indebted to John Bayley for this *caveat*.)

abominable terrors, by abominable satisfactions. But it was a victory! That is why I have remained loyal to Kurtz to the last' (p.151).

Why? How can Marlow know that this is 'a victory'? Marlow is too generous a man to be able to tell the story of Kurtz with full understanding. His own virility balances the hollowness of Kurtz, the lack of sexual drive in the manager, the externalised phallic symbols of the pilgrims' staves and the heads on stakes.

He has already warned the reader that his experience of meeting Kurtz will prove incommunicable: 'I've been telling you what we said – repeating the phrases we pronounced – but what's the good?' (p.144). Here we have unconscious proof, so to speak, of that failure. 'Affirmation', 'moral victory', 'abominable terror', 'abominable satisfaction', these are all evasions, words and phrases indicating nothing except the fact that there is a mystery still concealed. The action/lying antithesis is brought into focus with Kurtz's cry. The words 'The horror! The horror!' tell the reader nothing, their function is not to communicate but to provoke and stimulate further questions, to drive the reader and Marlow yet further on their collaborative quest for the story's 'whole meaning' or 'kernel' (p.48).

'The horror' is the last of Kurtz's lies; a form of words that compels respect, has an air of oracular communication, and reveals nothing. The 'whole meaning' for Marlow is to be found in Marlow's own actions: his life has been decisively changed by the loyalty that Kurtz has generated in him. He finds the Intended and tells her his own deliberate lie, performs the action that has the flavour of death for him, thereby revealing the extent to which Kurtz's imprinting has affected him.

4. Lord Jim: *creative love*

A.J. Guerard memorably describes *Lord Jim* (1900) as 'the first novel in a new form: a form bent on involving and implicating the reader in a psycho-moral drama which has no easy solution, and bent on engaging his sensibilities more strenuously and more uncomfortably than ever before.'[25]

This seems right: at the same time one may note that the narrative method of *Lord Jim* is obviously a development of that of *Heart of Darkness* and also that narrative indirection can often serve (intentionally or otherwise) to mask structural weakness.

The story of Jim's struggle with Gentleman Brown, the murder of Dain Waris by Brown and the killing of Jim himself by his former friend Doramin do not mesh well with the wonderful subtlety of the first part of the novel. Conrad acknowledged to Garnett (12 November 1900) that 'the division of

[25] A.J. Guerard, *Conrad the Novelist* (1958), p.126.

the book into two parts' was its 'plague spot'.[26] This final part of the novel has a curiously simple moral polarity, a brightly coloured 'flatness', and it introduces in Gentleman Brown a straightforward villain who would be more at home in one of the later novels, *Victory* or *The Rover*, than among the complex characterisations of Conrad's central period. The discussion of Jim's moral predicament involves exploring the possibility that the human condition is always a matter of moral relativity, and with the wicked figure of Brown Conrad seems to be throwing his hard-won insight overboard. It is as though the end of *Lord Jim* were drawn from a part of Conrad's mind different from, and shallower than, the consciousness that has created the bulk of the novel.

I think Conrad succeeds, just, in 'smuggling' the flatness of this ending past the reader's demand for consistency by adopting a new narrative technique for it. The first four chapters of the novel are spoken by an omniscient narrator, chapters 5 to 35 are Marlow's after-dinner narration, and the remainder is pieced together by Marlow from the testimonies of Jewel, Tamb' Itam and Gentleman Brown and sent in a letter to one of his after-dinner audience, the 'privileged man' who has been especially attentive to the story.

The 'privileged man' receives four documents from Marlow in all: a covering letter, Marlow's narrative, the fragment of paper on which Jim on hearing of Dain Waris' death has written 'an awful thing has happened – I must now at once ...', and the last letter that Jim received from his father, the 'good old parson', who 'fancied his sailor-son', a few days before he joined the *Patna* (pp.340-1).

The altered frame, then, invites one to expect that this final section of the novel will have significant differences from the main narrative. It is written, not spoken; it is not drawn from personal experience but from the stories of Jewel and Tamb' Itam whom Marlow has encountered taking refuge in Stein's house after Jim's death, and from the malignant death-bed narrative of Gentleman Brown, who spitefully recounts his victory over Jim to Marlow as he chokes to death with asthma; and it is addressed to the 'privileged man' who is a man of action and adventure and of simple outlook. Marlow comments on the privileged man's prejudices: 'you said ... that "giving your life to them" (*them* meaning all of mankind with skins brown, yellow or black in colour) "was like selling your soul to a brute"' (p.334). It is not improper to see this story of Jim, Jewel, Dain Waris, Doramin and Brown, this story of simple good and evil and idealised love and friendship, as designed for the understanding of the 'privileged' man who has the conventional white imperialist attitudes of the day.[27]

---

[26] Garnett, *Letters from Conrad*, p.172.
[27] As reflected in A.E.W. Mason and John Buchan; see above, pp. 20-3.

Much has been written on *Lord Jim* as an analysis of the morality of action. With its narrative complexity and its exhaustive evaluation of Jim from all points of view it becomes a troubled mirror in which the reader may study his own moral being. As Guerard expresses it, we are asked 'to evaluate a romantic pride, a romantic conscience, an exalted egoism as solutions to the essential problem of "how to be" [Stein's phrase, *Lord Jim*, p.213]. We must locate on a moral spectrum "a sort of sublimated, idealised selfishness" [*Lord Jim*, p.177]. What we as readers are likely to think of such attitudes, or of Jim as a person, will depend partly on the persons we are, and not merely on the novel's success or failure. But *Lord Jim*'s impressionistic structure prevents us from bringing to bear too easily our preconceptions.'[28]

While not dissenting from this I would add that most critics have tended to under-emphasise Jim's youthfulness and his romanticism, both of which place him in the tradition of the *Bildungsroman*; the novel of initiation and development.[29]

Despite the loss of depth once the narrative has reached Patusan, the contrast in narrative tone between the two parts of the novel is an aesthetic necessity if the reader is to get the sense of Jim moving from a childlike to an adult condition.

Whereas the first part of the book could be said not to have a plot in the conventional sense, the Patusan part is if anything over-plotted. Jim is caught up in the web of relationships with Dain Waris, Doramin, Jewel, Cornelius, Brown. Initially he establishes himself at Patusan by freeing the community from the grip of the Arab trader, Sherif Ali, and successfully challenging the authority of the villainous old Rajah Allang. The plot is so organised that Jim's nobility destroys him. Gentleman Brown, the disgraced Englishman whose history has a superficial resemblance to Jim's, forces Jim to make the fatal mistake of sparing his life. In the course of their retreat down-river Brown and his piratical companions make a wantonly vindictive attack in which Dain Waris is killed. Jim himself is shot dead by Dain Waris's father, Doramin, who tragically misunderstands Jim's motives and believes him to be a racial traitor who has joined the white marauders at the expense of his adopted Malays.

In chapter 6 of the novel Marlow remarks that the official enquiry is not asking the right questions: 'Its object was not the fundamental why, but the superficial how, of this affair' (p.56). This gives the reader a signal of Marlow's own motivation for the interest in Jim and the telling of the story: a desire to know 'the fundamental why'. Marlow wants to know why this figure who is 'one of us', a representative near-heroic English gentleman, broad-shouldered, 'an inch, perhaps two, under six feet' (p.3), with all the

---

[28] Guerard, pp.144-5.
[29] Above p.28.

apparent marks of dignity and courage, has gone soft. The question once asked relates to other questions: why does Brierly, a more mature figure in the same mould, kill himself? Having 'eaten dirt' at the trial and received public humiliation as though he were voluntarily undergoing punishment, why does Jim abandon each of the subsequent jobs that Marlow finds for him as soon as the *Patna* story is known? By what standard he is measuring himself?

The further the narrative develops, the more the answers to these questions recede. The technique of *Lord Jim* defies the normal expectation in reading a novel that one's knowledge of the characters should be deepened as the narrative proceeds. In this novel the first four chapters, spoken by the outer narrator, achieve a concise objective picture which presents Jim's moral outline with some clarity: more clarity, at least, that is arrived at by Marlow in the hundreds of pages to come. Taken on their own these chapters reveal Jim as dreamy, idealistic, easily paralysed by fear, pleasure-loving, tending towards laziness; close to Willems of *An Outcast of the Islands* and surprisingly close, too, to the newspaper accounts of the real-life officers of the *Jedda*.

It is convenient here to outline the factual background to *Lord Jim*. Conrad had probably met Augustus Podmore Williams, the Chief Officer of the *Jedda*; a young man whose career was ended by the celebrated *Jedda* scandal of 1880, and who thereafter became a ship's chandler's water-clerk, married a native girl and settled respectably in Singapore. The *Jedda* set out with 900 Moslem pilgrims from Singapore to Jedda in 1880. The ship encountered stormy weather and began to leak. The Moslem passengers began to fight with the crew for possession of the life-boats. The Captain had his wife on board and was so anxious for her safety that he became incapable of making decisions. Williams, the Chief Officer, effectively took command and lowered a life-boat for the Captain and his wife and some other officers, after which he was pushed overboard by the enraged pilgrims and fished out of the water into the life-boat. This boat reached Aden and the Captain reported that the *Jedda* had sunk. On the following day the *Jedda* was towed into Aden with the Moslem pilgrims aboard and it became obvious that the officers had deserted the ship and then lied to cover their cowardice.

Conrad's alterations of this source are all designed to give Jim at least the makings of a case within the terms of the *legal* code, quite apart from the morals of the situation. The *Patna* is old and rusting in contrast with the comparatively new *Jedda*. Whereas Williams took the lead in deserting the ship Jim is entirely passive, excluding only the jump itself; he is entirely out of sympathy with the German captain and the others and they for their part make no attempt to include him in their escape.[30]

In chapter 2 Jim takes a course of action by which he is adversely judged

---

[30] See Norman Sherry, *Conrad's Eastern World* (1966), pp.65-72.

by the unsparing omniscient narrator of these chapters: he chooses to take service on a native-owned ship, having been left behind in the East with an injury. His initial disgust for the soft white men who 'loved short passages, good deck-chairs, large native crews and the distinction of being white' gives way to 'fascination in the sight of those men, in their appearance of doing so well on such a small allowance of danger and toil. In time, beside the original disdain there grew up slowly another sentiment', *envy*, presumably; 'and suddenly, giving up the idea of going home, he took a berth as chief mate of the *Patna*' (p.13).

Once he is committed to the *Patna* the omniscient narrative becomes loaded with proleptic images of increasing severity. Jim will later leave the pilgrims supposedly to drown, and as they board the *Patna* the imagery already suggests that they are threatening to sink it: they 'over-flowed down the yawning hatchways, filled the inner recesses of the ship – like water filling a cistern, like water flowing into crevices and crannies, like water rising silently within the rim' (p.14). The ship crosses a sea where the sun is like God's unforgiving eye, and the night comes as a merciful veil: 'The ship, lonely under a wisp of smoke, held on her steadfast way black and smouldering in a luminous immensity, as if scorched by a flame flicked at her from a heaven without pity. The nights descended on her like a benediction' (p.16).

The universe has become part of a system of moral judgment in imagery which seems to recall *The Ancient Mariner*: heat, phantoms, life-in-death, a false calm: 'Under the sinister splendour of that sky the sea, blue and profound, remained still, without a stir, without a ripple, without a wrinkle – viscous, stagnant, dead. The *Patna*, with a slight hiss, passed over that plain luminous and smooth, unrolled a black ribbon of smoke across the sky, left behind her on the water a white ribbon of foam that vanished at once, like the phantom of a track drawn upon a lifeless sea by the phantom of a steamer' (pp.15-16). Marlow is an ancient mariner under a compulsion to tell his tale, Jim labours under a guilt the nature of which is ostensibly obvious – he has jumped – and ultimately obscure.

After the severity of the first four chapters, Marlow's narrative gives a welcome alternative perspective, and an ingratiatingly humane tone of voice. His function is to disconcert the reader, to force us to see the attractive humanity, the appealing young-mannishness of Jim as well as the bald fact of his disgrace. In strict chronology Jim's jump should be narrated in chapter 5, but it is held back until chapter 9 giving Marlow an opportunity to expose the reader to the charm of Jim's personality while judgment is still suspended. By the time the consummate close of chapter 9 is reached the reader, forced,to collaborate with Marlow, already loves Jim:

'"She was going down, down, head first under me."

'He raised his hand deliberately to his face, and made picking motions with his fingers as though he had been bothered with cobwebs, and afterwards he looked into the open palm for quite half a second before he blurted out –

'"I had jumped ..."'

'He checked himself, averted his gaze ...'

'"It seems," he added' (p.110).

Part of Jim's defence is that his actions were determined, he could not withstand the cries of the other white men calling from their life-boat, he did not have free will: 'I told you I jumped; but I tell you they were too much for any man. It was their doing as plainly as if they had reached up with a boat-hook and pulled me over' (p.123). Confronted by his distress Marlow feels 'helpless before a childish disaster' (p.110) and wherever the jump from the *Patna* is mentioned there will be a neighbouring reference to Jim's youthfulness: 'You had to listen to him as you would to a small boy in trouble. He didn't know. It had happened somehow' (p.111). The child on the training-ship in the first chapter and the man in disgrace are the same person. In the first chapter Jim as a boy is too late to take part in a dramatic rescue: he is passively determined by events, delayed by 'a push' which made him 'stagger' (p.7). As in 'Youth', *The Nigger* and *Typhoon* the sea is setting a test of manhood. Jim's passivity is caused by an unacknowledged fear of the gale; a fear which he denies, with bitter romanticism, as soon as the danger is past: 'It seemed to him he cared nothing for the gale. He could affront greater perils. He would do so – better than anybody' (p.8)

He isolates himself in heroic fantasy: 'He could detect no trace of emotion in himself, and that final effect of a staggering event was that, unnoticed and apart from the noisy crowd of boys he exulted with a fresh certitude in his avidity for adventure, and in a sense of many-sided courage' (p.9). Like Joyce's Stephen Dedalus he sees himself living apart from other adolescents, luxuriously dedicated to an exalted private destiny.

His immature perception misses the menace of the seascape and responds only to its beauty: 'the certitude of fostering love upon the placid tenderness of a mother's face' (p.17). *After* his jump he sees the harsh, punitive face of the sea. Marlow quotes him: 'For two or three minutes the end of the world had come through a deluge in a pitchy blackness. The sea hissed "like twenty thousand kettles". That's his simile, not mine' (p.112). It is surprising to find Jim expressing himself in imagery of any kind, and this image marks him growing up.

Stein's advice, 'to the destructive element submit' (which he later rephrases in the form of words quoted by Marlow and by most of the novel's readers, '*in* the destructive element *immerse*'), has been called one of the 'strange, high-sounding phrases whose implications are deliberately left unclear.'[31] But to my mind this phrase has a specific meaning which is relevant to the *Bildungsroman* character of the work.

Nothing is fixed or certain for Conrad in his central period, and Stein's phrase, in its first form, reminds the reader of that. Life is a *process*, not a fixed fact, and no formulation which treats it as a fixed fact can encompass it; it is a 'destructive element' (*Lord Jim*, p.214) in the sense that it will break down and wash away any formulation with which man tries to define himself. A man can only attain selfhood, can only undergo the necessary transition from young to mature, from bound to free,[32] by submitting himself, by making the necessary *willed* 'jump' (the escape from the palisade) as against the involuntary leap from the *Patna*, by engaging in action.

Conrad was developing a philosophy of the reality of action at the time of writing *Lord Jim*; witnesses the passage of *Heart of Darkness* and the letter to Blackwood of 1902 that I have referred to above:[33] his work is based on 'action observed, felt and interpreted with an absolute truth to my sensations', and for Marlow, in *Heart of Darkness*, action enables a man to know himself: 'Your own reality – for yourself, not for others.'

Within Conrad's epistemological wilderness the actions of the self and the appearances of the physical world are the only evidences. There may well be constants, parameters, which are more stable than the welter of subjective experience would suggest. But the narrating mind has only the subjective experience to go on. There is a further inherent paradox, of which Conrad was increasingly aware as he developed the use of Marlow as narrator, in that the narrating mind is itself a constant, a parameter, the subjective factor that continually modifies the observed instabilities of the experienced world. Where everything else has become elusive and contingent the printed word remains a fixed fact, a self-evident constant, a parameter of the simplest kind.

In *Heart of Darkness* Marlow was a 'Buddha' and the way he tells the story suggests that he has arrived at this Buddha-like state as a result of the experience described in the story, the maturing 'immersion' of the exploratory journey and the disturbing encounter with Kurtz. This Buddha becomes a priest, confessor and father-figure to Jim in *Lord Jim*. Marlow's own identity as a man is of critical importance: Jim's story is one of a tragicomic near-miss transformed into surprising romantic success by the maieutic influence of a lucky friendship. The cycle of aspiration to an unattainable self-image is broken by Marlow's love for him which enables him not so much to come to terms with himself – the image of the 'veiled familiar at his side' suggests that he can do this only at the moment of death – as to win achievement with the energy generated by neurotic conflict.

[31] Cox, *Joseph Conrad*, p.18.

[32] See the discussion of self-possession in H.M. Daleski, *Joseph Conrad: The Way of Dispossession* (1977).

[33] See p.38.

Since Marlow speaks in the first person the reader's sense of his identity has to be intuited from his style. When speaking of 'style' one is discussing two related matters: the restricted sense of the word refers to the organisation of sentences, the large sense to the temperament of the man presenting the tale as sensed in the manner of the telling.

The temperaments of the mature male figures surrounding Jim give the reader alternative modes of approaching this truth while simultaneously hinting that a clear formulation of such a truth may not in the end be possible. Brierly, Doramin, Chester, the German skipper, the French Lieutenant, Jim's father, Brown, Stein as well as Marlow himself are all more mature men than Jim whose styles form a pattern, inviting the reader to make analogies which may well be false. The first law of the epistemological wilderness is that the self is isolated and can know nothing beyond its own frontiers. But this novel is full of male characters who seem to assert the opposite: that the self is a comprehensible, socially determined entity, that Jim's difficulty is a matter of vanity, refusal to face facts, over-sensitivity to criticism.

Marlow likes rogues, 'bad company'; he reminds the after-dinner group to whom he tells his story that they are 'respectable thieves of commerce', and of Jim's association with the officers of the *Patna* he remarks tolerantly that 'there are times when a man must act as though life were equally sweet in any company' (p.41). Marlow also likes Jim's company, and Jim likes Marlow's. Jim is deified in Patusan, 'Tuan' Jim, and this moral sanction enables him to impose an order which in turn reinforces the deification. In a more sophisticated way Jim 'worships' Marlow: Marlow is the point of reference in his mind which validates his own being, the man whose good opinion he must retain even after they have separated for the last time. And in still broader terms Marlow venerates Jim as emblematic man, reminding him of his youth's belief in the ideal of human solidarity now much flawed and battered by 'bad company': 'He came from the right place; he was one of us. He stood there for all the parentage of his kind' (p.43).

With the exception of Jim's father and Gentleman Brown the white males in the novel have much in common with each other. They are men of action, adventurers in a world heavily weighted in their favour by the late-Victorian expansion of Europe's commercial and political power. Divided though Conrad may seem about the morality of imperialism, in one sense this whole book is an expression of it: without the conditions created by imperialism the setting for *Lord Jim* and the code of virtue by which Jim measures himself – the unspoken code which is never formulated – would vanish, and the underlying assumption of *Lord Jim* is to that extent identical with the code of Kipling's subalterns and schoolboys who are being trained to survive and conduct themselves well as imperial administrators. He looks like one of Kipling's 'clean-run' subalterns and he has gone wrong initially by deserting his *country*, not his ship: by taking exployment with a 'native-owned' in preference to a British line.

Yet it would plainly be wrong to suggest that the high Victorian ideal of empire is in some sense, even unconsciously, the final moral referent of *Lord Jim*. It may well be the hidden ultimate referent of the intensely self-regarding Brierly; it is possible that after witnessing Jim's humiliation Brierly sees Jim's failure to live up to the imperial ideal reflected in himself, and finds the experience intolerable. But if this is true of Brierly it is no more applicable to Jim's own inner struggle than are the French Lieutenant's rigid code of honour or the tame domestic English Christianity of Jim's father. In any case, since life is process and a 'destructive element', no code can be final. In this case the visible expression of the authority of empire is as ugly as Gentleman Brown's quasi-imperial rapacity: the court of which Brierly is a member is a cold and ungenerous mechanism, with a chief magistrate who looks like a dying invalid. The chill of the courtroom and the pallor of this magistrate are contrasted with the joyous indifference of life outside, the brilliant sunshine, the smells and clamour of an eastern port.

If there is an ultimate moral referent for Jim we need not look for it in the values and order laid down for the British Empire. Yet it is obvious – indeed, it is a truism without which the novel could not exist – that Jim perceives himself as a moral being.

One way to express Jim's experience is to see it in religious terms as a private revelation, binding but incommunicable. Marlow's anxiety in his presence goes to support this: 'He was not speaking to me, he was only speaking before me, in a dispute with an invisible personality, an antagonistic and inseparable partner of his existence – another possessor of his soul ... He appealed to all sides at once – to the side turned perpetually to the light of day, and to that side of us which, like the other hemisphere of the moon, exists stealthily in perpetual darkness, with only a fearful ashy light falling at times on the edge' (p.93).

Marlow senses that Jim has access to a moral and psychological truth, something that both enables him to see a 'moral order' beside which all man-made codes look like interim and clumsy mechanisms, and also brings into play the whole of his (and Marlow's) being, the daylight self and the 'other hemisphere'. One might object that Conrad's language is rhapsodically inexplicit at this point, but it seems to me that the diction is exactly right for Marlow's temperament as it responds to Jim: the 'style' in both senses is appropriate. The discomfort and mixed feelings, the embarrassed use of 'Inconceivable' are consistent with what one intuits of Marlow. His pain here is the pain of a rational man exposed to a friend who has had a religious experience.

The right order of things exists only in Jim's head, locked up with his private revelation. His good work in Patusan is an approximation to that order, and certainly owes much to the way both empires and ships should be governed in the real world – Doramin and Dain Waris as first and second mates, Jim as the heroic young skipper – but it transcends both these models. Jim is Christ-like, forgiving Brown, refraining from the use of power, unapproachable. Marlow tells his story as hagiographers recorded the lives of the saints, because its central figure was distinguished by remarkable action and has access to an inner truth. The book itself, the product of the pragmatic narrator's attempt to organise the records of a man now dead, is like a gospel or even a church, a meeting place between sacred and secular, between men caught in the web of circumstance and the isolated self which has received an intense, transfiguring illumination.

If Jim is finally unknowable, can the view of the novel as a *Bildungsroman* hold? Certain aspects of him, his movement from unsuccessful to successful arenas of action and his growth from boy to man are confidently grasped by Marlow's consciousness. As he discusses him with Stein he calls Jim 'the youngest human being now in existence' (p.214) and speaks of the 'insolence' of his youth: 'Youth *is* insolent; it is its right – its necessity; it has got to assert itself, and all assertion in this world of doubts is a defiance, an insolence' (p.236). As he takes leave of Jim in chapter 23 Marlow becomes aware that Jim has been becoming adult through his reversals, that his youthfulness is receding. They are intimate 'as though his risk set off against my years had made us more equal in age and in feeling ... He exerted himself to soothe me as though he had been the more mature of the two' (p.241).

On the *Patna* and in the subsequent jobs that Marlow has made shift to find for him – with Denver in the rice mill, in Bangkok with Yucker, as water-clerk in various far-Eastern ports – Jim is the victim, the bound man whose actions are determined.

In Patusan he is at last a free man asserting his own will. The difference is immediately registered. The boy who lacked the will to join the cutter from the training-ship or to stick to his duty on the *Patna* becomes the man who discovers the instinctive will to rescue himself from the murderous old Rajah Allang by leaping over a palisade. He then runs like a machine until he finds himself buried in mud in a creek, and with his eyeballs 'bursting' and chest straining he demonstrates a primitive will to survive, 'culminating in one mighty supreme effort in the darkness to crack the earth asunder, to throw it off his limbs – and he felt himself creeping feebly up the bank' (p.254). He re-enacts in his own person the evolutionary struggle and is reborn from the slime a mature and self-determining man.

To explore further the use of freedom in the novel is to come up against a paradox. Freedom brings responsibility which in turn brings a new kind of bondage: 'The land, the people, the friendship, the love, were like the jealous guardians of his body. Every day added a link to the fetters of that strange freedom' (p.262).

Marlow remains the loving, human, limited narrator whose urgent interest in Jim's personality keeps up the novel's narrative drive to its conclusion. The oracular aspect of Marlow in *Heart of Darkness* – the Buddha-like detached observer who sees man dwarfed by the evolutionary process, so that the young Romans who were 'men enough to face the darkness' and about to undergo their 'initiation' into 'such mysteries' (p.50) are identified with his own younger self seizing the 'chance to find yourself' (p.85) – is taken by Stein, the oracular, semi-oriental Bavarian trader who has outlived man's normal drives and now devotes himself to his collection of Coleoptera. He has been a celebrated adventurer, and at the height of his adventures he found a perfect specimen of a rare butterfly: '"On that day I had nothing to desire; I had greatly annoyed my principal enemy; I was young, strong; I had friendship; I had the love" (he said 'lof') "of woman, a child I had, to make my heart very full – and even what I had once dreamed in my sleep had come into my hand, too!"' (p.211).

The normal attributes of human success have proved short-lived. Stein strikes a match: '"Friend, wife, child", he said, slowly, gazing at the small flame – "phoo!" The match was blown out' (p.211).

In Stein's stoical view of the world it is right to detach oneself from human beings and collect butterflies. The butterfly is a perfectly adapted product of evolution: '"Look at the accuracy, the harmony. And so fragile! And so strong! And so exact! This is Nature – the balance of colossal forces. Every star is so – and every blade of grass stands *so* – and the mighty Kosmos in perfect equilibrium produces – this. This wonder; this masterpiece of Nature – the great artist"' (p.208). Stein's chapter, the twentieth chapter of the novel, is the pivot of the structure, the axis on which are hung the two parts of the hinged diptych in which the two aspects of Jim, his youth and maturity, are presented. The image of the butterfly could be taken as making a point about the structure of the novel, with the identity of Jim held at its centre. The analogy can only be tentative, though, Stein's butterfly leading as it does to his carefully qualified account of man himself. Whereas the butterfly is perfectly adapted, man is 'amazing', an aberration in the creator's plan, 'making a great noise about himself, talking about the stars, disturbing the blades of grass' (p.208). His celebrated image of the 'destructive element' catches up the themes of survival and rebirth in the story of Jim: '"A man that is born falls into a dream like a man who falls into the sea. If he tries to climb out into the air as inexperienced people endeavour to do, he drowns – *nicht wahr?* ... No! I tell you! The way is to the destructive element submit yourself, and with the exertions of your hands and feet in the water make the deep, deep sea keep you up"' (p.214).

In this complicated metaphor the surface of the sea replaces the meeting-point of the 'colossal forces' as the point of balance, and man at this point of balance (replacing the butterfly) is held in his place by his own small action –

his will – working with the destructive element to sustain himself by treading water.

Equally the destructive element is an image of the narrative itself, simultaneously dissolving and renewing the identity of Jim, the central figure. Marlow's problem is the problem of seeing Jim clearly. Stein helps to define the parameters of the problem. Man has a soaring and diving spirit, 'he wants to be a saint, and he wants to be a devil' (p.213) and he is 'romantic, romantic' which is both good and bad (p.216). Marlow's problem is not exactly clarified by Stein's thinking, but the terms of the problem are extended. Listening to Stein, Marlow reflects that 'at that moment it was difficult to believe in Jim's existence', meaning his social existence – parson's son, sailor, disgraced exile – but that 'his imperishable reality came to me with ... an irresistible force!' as though 'we had approached nearer to absolute Truth, which, like Beauty itself, floats elusive, obscure, half-submerged' (p.216). Jim's 'reality' has been the subject of Marlow's quest from the beginning: 'He was not – if I may say so – clear to me' (p.177). This paragraph about Truth and Beauty is the most elusively phrased, and the least characteristic, of Marlow's inquiries into Jim's nature. Marlow is not helped, the phrases remain emblems of intangible standards borrowed from Stein's reminder that man is Romantic: absolute Truth, Beauty itself are watchwords of literary romanticism.

Marlow will fall back on his feelings. The rehabilitation of Jim has become Marlow's life-work because his affection runs so deep that it is as though his own survival, as well as Jim's, were at stake: 'He had reached the secret sensibility of my egoism' (p.152). The fact that Marlow constantly retells this tale, like the Ancient Mariner with only one theme, is itself evidence of the central importance of Jim in his own life. Jim is his foster-son and his creation, since without Marlow's help Jim would immediately have dropped into the 'abyss'[34] after the *Patna* case: 'As soon as he left my room ... he would take his place in the ranks, and begin the journey towards the bottomless pit' (p.179).

Because Marlow is the narrator, inherently modest and self-deprecating, Jim's love for *him* is revealed patchily and indirectly. Jim's last words to him despite their shyness and hesitancy clearly reveal an emotional commitment to Marlow: ' "I must stick to their [the people of Patusan's] belief in me to feel safe and to – to..." he cast about for a word, seemed to look for it on the sea ... "to keep in touch with" ... His voice sank suddenly to a murmur ... "with those whom, perhaps, I shall never see any more. With – with – you, for instance" ' (p.334). Quoting Stein's 'he is romantic, romantic', Marlow modestly brushes aside this revelation of feeling, leaving the reader to make of it what he will.

[34] See the currency of the 'abyss' as an Edwardian metaphor, above, pp.6-7.

As disaster finally overtakes him Jim sits down to write to Marlow: 'It was then, I believe, he tried to write – to somebody – and gave it up. Loneliness was closing in on him' (p.409: Marlow considers briefly the possibility that Jim is writing to Stein, p.340; another instance of Marlow's modesty). Marlow and Jim have set up for themselves overlapping mythologies in which each is the central figure in the world-view of the other. If Jim is Marlow's foster-son, Marlow is for Jim the experienced judge of right action, a guarantor of the possibility of goodness in a fallen world, the man to whom he turns in his extremity. He seems to see his relationship with Marlow as mystical; the good conduct of his own life will permit him to 'keep in touch with' a man whom he will never see again (p.334). But loneliness closes in; the novel leaves Jim at the moment of his death isolated, out of Marlow's reach. It finally communicates the bleakest and most central of Conrad's insights, the ultimate loneliness of human beings.

Freedom and bondage, pragmatism and romanticism, isolation and solidarity, order and worship; ostensibly *Lord Jim's* diptych form holds in balance the contrasting elements of these linked antitheses. In the experience of reading, though, the last emphasis always falls on romanticism, isolation, self-worship and freedom *in* bondage. The balance of idealism and action is not a real balance; it is the idealism in which we are interested, and the subjective presentation of idealism and the problems which it has created that yields Conrad's most vivid and strenuous writing.

5. Nostromo

The loving celebrations of the individual male in 'Youth', *Heart of Darkness* and *Lord Jim* give way, in the next three novels, to enquiries into societies. The questions about the ultimate nature and significance of man's life are never dropped, but the interest in the individual is overlaid by other considerations. The story of Charles Gould in *Nostromo* (1904) is a reconsideration of the story of Jim. Gould is the young imperial hero who becomes corrupted by 'material interests'. His patron, the American millionaire Holroyd, is a debased successor of Lingard and Stein, the middle-aged patrons of energetic young men. Holroyd loves Gould because he nakedly relishes the exercise of power: 'He was not running a great enterprise there; no mere railway board or industrial corporation. He was running a man!' (p.81).

The interest in the individual spans these political novels, and returns with the celebrations of Conrad's romantic heroes in the post-Edwardian novels; Roderick Anthony in *Chance*, Heyst in *Victory*, Real in *The Rover*.

The return to the study of the individual is marked by the return of Marlow as narrative voice; he is dropped after *Lord Jim* and restored twelve years later with *Chance*. To my mind the movement of the narrative voice, the blend of omniscience and subjective engagement, in *Lord Jim*, is a technical success that was never to be surpassed in Conrad. Nevertheless the willingness to throw Marlow overboard and adopt a much more complicated and impressionist narrative method in *Nostromo* arguably indicates a writer who is more confident, more 'free', than the writer of *Lord Jim*. The remoteness and unreality of the setting of *Nostromo* would support this: in *Lord Jim* Conrad keeps quite close to his source while in *Nostromo* the setting is one that he barely knew.[35]

Decoud's letter to his sister and Captain Mitchell's obtuse and pompous 'explanation' of the republic to a hapless hypothetical visitor make two important secondary 'islands' of narration in the text, but for most of its length the novel is presented by a third person narrator who is allowed as much 'omniscience' as is enjoyed by the flexible narrating voice in *The Nigger of the Narcissus*.

The degree of access that this narrating voice has to the inner experiences of the characters varies. Decoud is exhaustively known from within, Old Giorgio Viola and his wife the Padrona Teresa are half ironically but very sympathetically explored, Dr Monygham is steadily approached by the narrative so that his personality, which is at first baffling, becomes less opaque as the novel develops. Charles Gould is fully known as a schoolboy, and as a young man grieving for his father's death and courting his Emily in the ruined palazzo of the decayed aunt at Lucca, but as a mature man he is accessible only partially and in patches. Nostromo himself is seen almost entirely externally, a folk-hero discernible in terms of his actions; his inner temperament becomes accessible only in his post-lapsarian state once he has surrendered to the seduction of the silver.

The setting, the mythical Costaguana, is a sequestered paradise. To some extent it is a fantasy world, a 'Vanished Arcadia'[36] a secret place in which laws of probability can be simplified though never suspended. The opening paragraph stresses the difference between it and the 'real' world of economic forces: 'Sulaco had found an inviolable sanctuary from the temptations of a trading world in the solemn hush of the deep Golfo Placido as if within an enormous semi-circular and unroofed temple, open to the ocean, with its walls of lofty mountains hung with the mourning draperies of cloud' (p.3.).

It is an invented world, possibly consecrated to ancient mysteries (an 'unroofed temple'), certainly backward-looking, and probably regretting

[35] See 'A note on the background to *Nostromo*' in C.T. Watts (ed.), *Conrad's Letters to Cunninghame Graham* (1969), pp.37-42, and Norman Sherry, *Conrad's Western World* (1971), pp.147-8.

[36] To quote the title of Cunninghame Graham's book about Venezuela which is one of Conrad's sources; another is G.F. Masterman's *Seven Eventful Years in Paraguay* which gives the source for Dr Monygham and many names for other characters, Barrios, Corbelàn, Decoud, Gould and Fidanza (some of which are also found in Cunninghame Graham's *Portrait of a Dictator*). See *Conrad's Letters to Cunninghame Graham*, p.38.

('mourning') a heroic past. The paragraph is also ironic: inviolable Sulaco is soon to be violated. Commercial imperialism, British and American, is soon to break into this sanctuary.

Nostromo defies its reader to form a broad view of its events simply by turning the pages and following the narration from paragraph to paragraph. The reader has to build up the sequence of events retrospectively from the testimonies of Mitchell, Decoud, and the omniscient narrator, and by imposing a chronology on the dramatised scene. If *Lord Jim* forced the reader to collaborate in the exercises of writing Jim's biography, *Nostromo* forces the reader to collaborate in the writing of a history.

The novel exemplifies more drastically than any of its precursors the epistemological crisis that Conrad inhabits. There are no fixed rules by which to observe the world, no knowledge is to be gained easily. The challenge it presents gives its own high intellectual delight, otherwise we would not read it, and the narrative indirection is never there for its own sake. It has the effect of stripping away the reader's preconceptions about narratives and about societies: assumptions about order, trade, honour, personality, and the action of time, are unsettled. With the figures of Charles Gould and Decoud at its centre the narrative peels away layers of fixed or obsolete assumptions until the particular individuality of these figures is fully exposed.

The form of the novel is notoriously 'imperfect'. Its imperfection is well suited to its subject. The narrator's vain struggle to impose order on his material reflects Charles Gould's struggle to impose order on Costaguana. Conrad is surely aware that a novel presented in so complicated a way cannot achieve the wholeness towards which Henry James in, for example, *The Ambassadors* (1903) and *The Golden Bowl* (1904) is working.

The cracked marble vase in the ruined palazzo of the impoverished aunt at Lucca seems to me a carefully placed image, with more than a suggestion of James's golden bowl about it, for the well-turned, but fractured, form of the novel. (I am not, of course, suggesting direct influence. The novels were being written at the same time.) The hall of the palazzo 'was furnished with exactly one gilt armchair, with a broken back, and an octagon columnar stand bearing a heavy marble vase ornamented with sculptured masks and garlands of flowers, and cracked from top to bottom' (p.61).

If one takes the characters of Gould and Nostromo, leaving Decoud on one side for the moment, one can see the novel as taking further the innovations of *Lord Jim*. These are two strong characters whose inner natures are inaccessible. The narratives not only have to encompass the mystery presented by both of them but also to establish whether their secrets are identical, related, complementary or separate.

The three parts of the novel, 'The Silver of the Mine', 'The Isabels', 'The Lighthouse' are articulated with extreme artfulness. The apparently arbitrary opening, in which Nostromo is defending Old Giorgio and his wife from the Monterist rebellion and fulfilling his role as their adopted son, their 'Gian' Battista', is balanced by the tragi-comic close in which Giorgio shoots him dead. The Nostromo story is thus a frame surrounding the youth, maturity and personal tragedy of Charles Gould and the complex interplay of forces, native and imperial, orderly and anarchic, economic and social, which encompass him.

If one looks at the inner situation first, it is immediately plain that the contradictions inherent in imperialism are again firing Conrad's imagination. As in *Lord Jim* the fact of imperialism is the given situation without which the novel could not exist. Costaguana has been invaded throughout its history. Only the Indian mine workers who call Don Pépé 'father' because he wears shoes have any substantial claim to be considered indigenous. The 'first families' of Spanish settlers who live on the plain on the patriarchal estates, the three generations of Goulds, the influx of Italian railroad workers who are the select *clientele* of the Casa Viola, and the two modern economic imperialists, Holroyd and Sir John, are all equally foreign to the place.

Conrad was alive to the nomadic nature of all human communities; at the beginning of *Heart of Darkness* he reminds us that the Thames at the time of the Roman invasion was as the Congo is now. But he could hardly have used an English setting as he uses this *emigré* community where will can rapidly be translated into action, where governments change from week to week and the sense of continuity taken for granted in Europe is unknown. Such a situation gives freedom to those strong enough to take the appropriate initiatives; Gould can transform himself from the powerless son of a ruined man to 'King of Sulaco' in the space of a few years.

I agree with Graham Hough's view that Costaguana is less 'real' than some of Conrad's other settings, especially the ships but also the Congo and even Patusan.[37] Imperialism is both good and bad; the silver and the railway are both beneficial and destructive. The sequestered, beautiful, mourning province evoked in the first paragraph is to be plundered and dragged into the modern world of the late nineteenth century in order to enrich other nations. The heroic values asserted by Giorgio the Garibaldino (ironically undercut though his heroism is by the fact that he was Garibaldi's *cook*), Don José, Dr Monygham and minor figures such as Father Corbelàn and Hernandez (a South American Robin Hood), the heroic values of which Nostromo seems for most of the novel to be the most developed representative, must give way to 'material interest'. The old order is doomed: 'The great owners of estates on the plain, grave, courteous, simple men, caballeros of pure descent, with small hands and feet, conservative, hospitable, and kind' (p.34). Their small hands and feet are perhaps a mark of overbreeding, and their place is to be usurped by illiterate peasant bastards, Montero and his brother the 'General', who

37 Hough, p.216.

break into the power vacuum created by the dangerous chaos of Costaguanan politics (p.39).

Holroyd, the American financier, is an equally mongrel figure – 'his parentage was German and Scotch and English, with remote strains of Danish and French blood' (p.76) – exercising by his investment in the mine a form of coercive authority which is just as unacceptable, though less crude in its expression, as the murderousness of the Montero brothers.

Conrad resented having to pay Income Tax. There is an anecdote, pleasing and characteristic but probably apocryphal, to the effect that when he was offered a knighthood in 1924 by Ramsay MacDonald he thought that the official envelope contained an Income Tax demand and left it for a time unopened on his desk. He refused the knighthood. This refusal has proved a ticklish matter for Conrad scholars. He may well have declined it, as Baines thinks, because he felt (as had his friend Galsworthy, who also refused a knighthood) that it was an inappropriate honour for an artist.[38] The Polish scholar Zdzislaw Najder suggests another reason: 'His refusal in 1924 to accept a knighthood is most easily explained by the fact that the Korzeniowskis [his father's family] had been noblemen for generations.'[39] Frederick Karl, Conrad's most recent biographer, sees the refusal as consistent with Conrad's Tory anarchist outlook: 'The argument that he refused the honour because the offer came from a socialist government is nonsense. Conrad heaped ridicule on all government: the institution itself was suspect.'[40]

Bearing in mind this future event in Conrad's life and his general dislike of the intervention of governments, it is interesting to consider this paragraph about Charles Gould's father when the San Tomé Silver Mine concession is forced on him:

> 'Man is a desperately conservative creature, and the extravagant novelty of this outrage upon his purse distressed his sensibilities. Everybody around him was being robbed by the grotesque and murderous bands that played their game of governments and revolutions after the death of Guzman Bento. His experience had taught him that, however short the plunder might fall of their legitimate expectations, no gang in possession of the Presidential Palace would be so incompetent as to suffer itself to be baffled by want of a pretext' (p.56).

Charles Gould's father is perhaps based on the obsessive, depressive

[38] Jocelyn Baines, *Joseph Conrad: A Critical Biography* (1960), p.435.

[39] Zdzislaw Najder (ed.), *Conrad's Polish Background: Letters to and from Polish Friends* (1964), p.28.

[40] Frederick Karl, *Joseph Conrad: The Three Lives* (1979), p.908.

personality of Conrad's own father. Charles Gould inherits his father's economic individualism, but brings to the problem of the mine an aggressive Victorian energy which transforms failure into success. In the context of the gangster-governments of Costaguana his high Victorian laissez-faire individualism becomes an attractively radical Toryism ('splendidly disobedient' as Emily Gould phrases it): 'Only let the material interests once get a firm footing, and they are bound to impose the conditions on which alone they can continue to exist. That's how your money-making is justified here in the face of lawlessness and disorder. It is justified because the security which it demands must be shared with an oppressed people' (p.84). Because he has moved right away from the European context, Conrad can set up a model of imperialism more sophisticated than any he has used before.

Nostromo reflects more finely than any of Conrad's other works – more even than *The Secret Agent* which is a much more specifically 'Edwardian' novel – the absence of direction in the contemporary world as Conrad perceived it. Conrad and Kipling can be seen as having this in common. For them British imperialism of the late nineteenth century is a matter of stoical action which is autotelic, performed for its own sake or for the sake of the 'craft' involved, unsanctioned by any overriding moral imperative. The 'art for art's sake' of the aesthetic movement is echoed by 'action for action's sake' in these writers.[41] This view sees *Nostromo* as a development of the outlook expressed in a letter from Conrad to Cunninghame Graham in 1898: 'L'homme est un animal méchant. Sa méchanceté doit être organisée. Le crime est une condition nécessaire de l'existence organisée. La société est essentiellement criminelle – ou elle n'existerait pas. C'est l'égoisme qui sauve tout – absolument tout – tout ce que nous abhorrons, tout ce que nous aimons' (*Letters to Cunninghame Graham*, p.117). Given the essential wickedness and disorder of human communities, man's egoism should be allowed full play and the community will right itself: 'material interest' will create a government by consent, just as the common will to survive a gale makes for social cohesiveness on board ship.

The twin notions that self-interest is the only rational basis of social order and that stoic action is self-validating come together in the figure of Charles Gould. After the death of his father, killed by his obsessive anxiety over the San Tomé silver mine, Charles Gould's mind turns to the therapy of action: 'Action is consolatory. It is the enemy of thought and the friend of flattering illusions. Only in the conduct of our action can we find the sense of mastery over the Fates' (*Nostromo*, p.66).

The story of Charles Gould dramatises a conflict between two high Victorian ideals which were becoming anachronisms in the Edwardian

[41] See David Daiches, *Some Late Victorian Attitudes* (1967), Lecture 1.

period: married love and economic individualism. The dramatic date of the novel is itself in the past (the 1880s), the theft of the silver is based on a story which Conrad heard in the 1870s when he was 'very young' (p.xv).

It is interesting that Conrad writes in this preface that after finding the story of the Italian sailor who steals a lighter of silver he felt that 'perhaps, perhaps, there still was in the world something to write about' (p.xvii). He had had wider and more adventurous experience than any other English novelist and it is amazing to find him even temporarily lost for a subject. But one can well believe that after the ferment of *Heart of Darkness* and *Lord Jim* Conrad felt temporarily 'dried up'. With *Nostromo* he takes an arena at once more remote and more 'public' than before, the narrator no longer masked but nakedly confronting the reader; and for concepts he moves back into the Victorian past.

As well as being a representative Victorian individualist Charles Gould has the stoic reticence of the Victorian public schoolboy. This reticence, which passes for a virtue, is a deep-seated symptom of moral anxiety. From the 1890s onward the received Victorian sanctities were under attack. In order to maintain good order the state required that its schools should produce men who would 'get on with the job' without asking questions.[42] Kipling both celebrates this and recognises its inherent absurdity. Forster in *A Passage to India*, when writing about the collective madness of the British community making its 'tribal' reaction to the supposed attack on Adela Quested in the Marabar Caves – the central mystery of that beautifully constructed novel – takes this critique much further.

In his own life Conrad was the opposite of stoic. His letters are packed with lamentation and outcry, he was one of the most noisily self-pitying of agonised writers. At the same time his fascination with men of action makes it natural and inevitable that he should celebrate the established style of the ruling English upper-middle class. And although born in Costaguana and speaking with the accent of the country Charles Gould exerts this fascination by his sheer physical presence; his height, red-haired taciturnity, and air on horse-back of having just ridden out of a green meadow on the other side of the world.

For two-thirds of the novel Gould's economic doctrine can be seen to work: witness the 'steadying effect of the San Tomé mine upon the life of that remote province' (p.95). It is a consistent implication of Conrad's political novels that interim stability is the best that humanity can hope for at the level of political action. Although Gould's ambitions turn sour Costaguana does not revert to the primitive brutality that existed under Guzman Bento, the earlier dictator whose methods provoked Don José's unpublished history, 'Fifty Years of Misrule'. At the same time Gould's *personal* history is one of

---

[42] See Daiches, op. cit.

failure. He sees himself as 'competent because he has no illusions' (p.85), but he suffers one overwhelming illusion. He imagines himself to be a free man, but from the beginning he is 'owned' by Holroyd, who is 'running a man' (above p.57). Further, Gould makes Lord Jim's mistake of supposing that in his case the laws of human society will be suspended, and that he can remain uncontaminated by his associates: he has to accommodate himself 'to existing circumstances of corruption so naively brazen as to disarm the hatred of a man courageous enough ... He made use of it with a cold, fearless scorn, manifested rather than concealed by the forms of stony courtesy which did away with much of the ignominy of the situation' (pp.142-3). For the best British reasons – stoicism again – he underestimates the 'irresistible potency' of corruption to 'ruin everything it touched', and 'he refused to discuss the ethical view with his wife' (p.143).

Dona Emilia is often seen as a custodian of positive values in this book, and this seems to me right, although there is also the opposite view that she errs by isolating herself, that her perfection is sterile. Her doll-like appearance, the cloistered feeling of the Casa Gould and the artificiality of her tea-parties might support this view, but it seems to me that she is forced into her isolation by Charles's failure to confide in her and failure to love her. At the beginning the mine is their joint enterprise, she travels with him recruiting labour, she praises his economic individualism, her courage and commitment to action seem as complete as his until he wantonly detaches himself from her. Even after she and Charles have drifted apart she continues to perform effective human actions in her care for the mineworkers and for the victims of the Monterist rebellion. But her full capacity for good action is blocked by her husband's coldness. Conrad's traditional view of marriage is relevant here: 'A woman's true tenderness, like the true virility of a man, is expressed in action of a conquering kind' (p.67). One may compare also Don José's failure to recognise the great worth of his daughter Antonia's love for him: 'He accepted it in the benighted way of men, who, though made in God's image, are like stone idols without sense before the smoke of certain burnt offerings' (p.140). The tragedy of corrupted idealism becomes the tragedy of chilled personal relations. By taking too far his public school self-reliance and 'stony courtesy', Gould has sinned against the one clear moral positive of the book.

If Nostromo and Gould are men of action by instinct, Decoud is a man of action by default. There is no male inner drive in Decoud: the Costaguanero of the Boulevards becomes editor of the *Porvenir* and revolutionary leader of Costaguana without any conviction, and lover of Antonia Avellanos as an exercise of the intellect, a testing of his own skill in the art of counterfeit. Once he is alone on the Isabels with the cargo of silver which he and Nostromo have shipped out of Sulaco, Decoud's intelligence fails him and he loses hope and kills himself.

His despair is one of the most memorable of Conrad's achievements. It can be taken as a dramatised presentation of the epistemological crisis which enabled Conrad to write a novel of such complexity. The omniscient narrator introduces Decoud's suicide as though it were a case in a psychological text-book: 'The truth was that he died from solitude, the enemy known but to few on this earth, and whom only the simplest of us are fit to withstand' (p.496). His sense of his own identity has been sustained by social contact and by action both of which are now denied him: 'In our activity alone do we find the sustaining illusion of an indpendent existence as against the whole scheme of things of which we form a helpless part' (p.497).

Convinced that the counter-revolution has failed, that Nostromo and Antonia and the Goulds are defeated by the Monterists, he sets out in the dinghy. The *silence* becomes a physical image: 'The solitude appeared like a great void, and the silence of the gulf like a tense, thin cord to which he hung suspended by both hands' (p.498). After nights of wakefulness a 'merciless' dawn finds him disintegrating: 'The silence appeared again before him, stretched taut like a dark, thin string' (p.500). The only possible release from this tension is to shoot himself, which Decoud does, asking, with a final irony, the question that Nostromo has asked about him: 'I wonder how that Capataz died?' (p.501).

Just as the 'tense, thin cord of silence' seems to replace Decoud's sense of his own identity, so the silver seems to replace – almost to suck and hollow out – Nostromo's identity. It is reasonable to ask, if Gould and Decoud are the psychologically explored figures in the novel, why it is called *Nostromo*? The function of the silver seems to be crucially bound up with this question.

The Nostromo story provides the frame of the novel, and the framing device gets into the picture and becomes central to the reader's understanding of what Costaguana loses as it surrenders to modern imperial forces. A heroic view of man has given way to an urban view of man. A celebrated passage in which Nostromo himself is presented, after the theft of the silver, as an awakening Adam reborn into a fallen world, marks the point at which Nostromo makes the transition from the heroic to the urban state: 'Nostromo woke up from a fourteen hours' sleep, and arose full length from his lair in the long grass. He stood knee deep among the whispering undulations of the green blades with the lost air of a man just born into the world. Handsome, robust, and supple, he threw back his head, flung his arms open, and stretched himself with a slow twist of the waist and a leisurely growling yawn of white teeth, as natural and free from evil in the moment of waking as a magnificent and unconscious wild beast. Then, in the suddenly steadied glance fixed upon nothing from under a thoughtful frown, appeared the man' (pp.411-12).

Once Nostromo has lost his primitive strength the silver, like an alien life-form making a better evolutionary success of things than any of the human beings in the novel, takes over; indeed the novel can be seen as finally creating an environment in which the silver will survive and be perpetuated.

The silver is obviously a pervasive image. It provides old Giorgio with his silver-framed spectacles so that he can read his bible. He values religion but despises priests, and retains a severe, austere ideal of liberty synonymous, one comes to feel, in his mind with God. His singlemindedness goes with metaphorical and literal shortsightedness; when he takes up his last residence on the Great Isabel manning the lighthouse above Nostromo's hoard of silver, his myopia – his inflexible attitude towards his daughters' love affairs – leads him to mistake Nostromo's identity and shoot him. Nostromo has been part of the old man's conception of ideal manhood, and his son and his saint, his Gian' Battista who would have been the same age as his son who died in infancy.

Nostromo and Decoud take the places of the ghosts of the two gringos whose legend introduces the novel; they fill out the myth and make it history. Decoud has shot himself and sunk to the bottom of the Golfo Placido, as the omniscient narrator knows, with bars of silver in his pockets to help him down: 'Weighted by the bars of San Tomé silver, disappeared without a trace, swallowed up in the immense indifference of things. His sleepless, crouching figure was gone from the side of the San Tomé silver; and for a time the spirits of good and evil that hover near every concealed treasure of the earth might have thought that this one had been forgotten by all mankind. Then, after a few days, another form appeared [Nostromo, returned to conceal the treasure] ... And the spiritis of good and evil that hover about a forbidden treasure understood well that the silver of San Tomé was provided now with a faithful and lifelong slave' (p.501).

The silver confirms its mastery by making a guy of Nostromo – he is seen with the 'vigour and symmetry of his powerful limbs lost in the vulgarity of a brown tweed suit' (p.527) – and grotesquely blocking his other impulses: his sex drive is cut across by the silver. He secretly loves Giselle but agrees to marry Linda as a 'cover' for his visits to his hoard of silver on the island. The effect is of disconcertingly flat and mechanical plotting. It is as though the silver's last and unexpected triumph is to damage the novelist's art, though what the novel's ending loses in probability it gains in symmetry. Gould is separated from his wife by the mine, which she sees as a tyrant 'more pitiless and autocratic than the worst Government' (p.521), and he and Nostromo are revealed as hollowed out and destroyed by this inanimate master that they have mistaken for a servant.

6. The Secret Agent

If Conrad can be seen as in a sense bored with his characters at the end of *Nostromo*, *The Secret Agent* (1907) is characterised by an icy distaste for human beings which gives the novel its extreme ironic detachment and also a shapeliness unique among Conrad's works. The techniques of *Heart of Darkness, Lord Jim* and *Nostromo* are collaborative; the reader is forced to stand side by side with the novelist and engage with him in the struggle to perceive and record the persons or the world in front of his eye. The struggle is sustained by a quasi-sexual energy; the reader experiences the need to know, to embrace and possess, the characters and the situation.

The ironic technique of *The Secret Agent* holds the reader at a distance from the material. The desire to know is replaced by disgusted knowingness; the human spectacle is relentlessly, repellently visible. Love has been replaced by hatred as the fuel of the narrative drive.

The connection between the central event of Conrad's novel and its source is clear. Conrad refers in his note to the attack on the Greenwich Observatory in 1894 and Ford Madox Ford's comments on it. One Martial Bourdin had approached the observatory with a bomb which had detonated prematurely; it blew off one of his hands and opened his stomach so that the intestines hung out. He lived for an hour or so after the explosion. In his adaptation Conrad is careful to show that the bomb is not at fault. Stevie has tripped and fallen on top of the bomb which has disintegrated him and excavated a large hole.

The sources for *The Secret Agent* are indicated in Conrad's note and have been discussed in detail.[43] As with *Lord Jim* Conrad is working from a sensational news item which hit the headlines of the day. What strikes one is that where in *Lord Jim* he refines and complicates the clear outlines of the *Jedda* scandal, in *The Secret Agent* he takes the story of the anarchist and simplifies it. The London of *The Secret Agent* is as unreal and isolated as any of his exotic settings, and becomes like a ship carrying a closely knit and envenomed group of characters through the fog.

There are no heroes in *The Secret Agent*. The novel denies the existence of moral positives in man. Dedicated to Wells, 'the chronicler of Mr Lewisham's love, the biographer of Kipps and the historian of the ages to come', and ironically designated 'this simple tale of the nineteenth century', *The Secret Agent* takes the Wellsian anti-hero and puts him in hell. The Wellsian lower-middle-class world is recognisably present in Verloc himself, born of 'industrious parents for a life of toil', who has diverted the characteristic ambition and energy of the lower-middle-class to a life of idleness: 'He had embraced indolence from an impulse as profound as inexplicable and as imperious as the impulse which directs a man's preference for one particular woman in a given thousand' (p.12). As an indolent failed salesman of pornographic goods, a seedy small shopkeeper turned double-agent to shore up his income, Verloc is Wells's Mr Polly with

[43] Norman Sherry, *Conrad's Western World*, pp.228-47.

a vicious streak, a Mr Polly who is denied the pastoral refuge of the Potwell Inn and has found another kind of refuge in the easy money offered by sinister and finally dangerous sources.[44] It is as though Conrad suggests that *Love and Mr Lewisham*, *Kipps* and *Mr Polly* are childishly euphoric works, identifying the moral squalor of the urban lower-middle-class world but then throwing away this valuable insight in favour of fantasy.

The novel is about heredity and environment, the effect on man of degeneracy in the human stock and the overdetermined urban world in which it lives. Ossipon's lecherous and brutal condition has been determined by heredity; he is blonde, 'typically' British, but has flattened 'negroid' features as though the lower-middle-class had been infected by the subject races of the empire. Fascinated by Lombroso's theories of biological degeneracy, he is himself shown to be a degenerate when his obsessive anxiety over Winnie Verloc's secret drives him mad in the closing pages of the novel.

The economic world celebrated by Dickens in *Dombey and Son*, *Bleak House* and *Little Dorrit* in which the individual is trapped in a determining web of forces, has here become a decayed world, devoid of energy.[45] Positive impulses are deformed or aborted: Ossipon's sexual drive, Karl Yundt's sense of justice, the Professor's Messianic conviction of his own righteousness, the stifling marital fidelity practised by the Verlocs, Heat's tenacity and discretion. The Professor's temperament is a parody of the early Victorian protestant ethic: he has inherited his self-possession from his father, 'An itinerant and rousing preacher of some obscure but rigid Christian sect – a man supremely confident in the privileges of his righteousness. In the son, individualist by temperament, once the science of colleges had replaced thoroughly the faith of conventicles, this moral attitude translated itself into a frenzied puritanism of ambition. He nursed it as something secularly holy' (pp.80-1).

Heat can be seen as a more devious and less courageous Mr Bucket, Sir Ethelred as a dimmer and more powerful Leicester Dedlock, and the Lady patroness of Michaelis as having Lady Dedlock's social ascendancy without her vulnerability. The Professor is a deadlier Smallweed, the 'nice and privileged child' who is Sir Ethelred's secretary is a successor of the tribe of Barnacles in *Little Dorrit*, and his name, 'Toodles', is borrowed from the family of Paul Dombey's wet-nurse in *Dombey and Son*. The anarchists are

[44] I am not, of course, suggesting that *The History of Mr Polly* is a source for *The Secret Agent*. *The History of Mr Polly* was not published until 1910.

[45] It is reasonable to see Conrad's view of nineteenth-century England as Dickensian: Dickens was one of the first English writers that Conrad read. He began reading him in Polish translations as a child: his 'first introduction to English imaginative literature' was *Nicholas Nickleby* (*A Personal Record*, 1912, p.71) and *Bleak House* was a 'work of the master' for which he had an 'intense and unreasoning affection' (p.124).

vicious equivalents of Dickens' low-life figures in *Little Dorrit*, and the theme of imprisonment, focused on Michaelis and Dorrit *père* respectively, echoes through both books.

Perhaps for Conrad at the time of writing *The Secret Agent* the whole of Victorian civilisation, both as observed and as reflected in literature, had come to seem a pool of degeneracy breeding malignant and abortive political movements to match its malignant and abortive people.

It is by no means only the low-life figures that are sneered at. As in the 'Condition of England' novels of the period by Galsworthy, Forster and Wells, the entire social fabric is exhibited for the reader's scorn. Verloc walks in the Row watching the fashionable displaying themselves: 'Carriages went bowling by, mostly two-horse broughams, with here and there a Victoria with the skin of some wild beast inside and a woman's face and hat emerging above the folded hood' (p.11).

This post-Darwinian stress on the kinship of woman and wild beast is followed by a systematically Wellsian sneer at the world that Verloc is employed to protect: 'All these people had to be protected. Protection is the first necessity of opulence and luxury. They had to be protected; and their horses, carriages, houses, servants had to be protected; and the source of their wealth had to be protected in the heart of the city and the heart of the country; the whole social order favourable to their hygienic idleness had to be protected against the shallow enviousness of unhygienic labour' (p.12).

One can understand why *The Secret Agent* caused dismay among Conrad's Edwardian readers. He seems to have discarded the subject matter native to him, the growth into full masculinity of young men, the ships, the sea, action as the test of manhood, and to have adopted instead a nightmare version of a field in which Wells was already established and arguably more successful, certainly better informed: the life of the urban dispossessed, the 'condition of England' seen in terms of the strains imposed on the individual by the social and economic pressure of urban life.

Both Wells and Conrad can be seen to be working with a convention of the urban novel established by Dickens, and in addition to the features of characterisation and milieu that I have noted in *The Secret Agent* there are significant aspects of technique that Conrad seems to have in common with Dickens.[46] Dickensian synecdoche and reification, the transformation of persons into things and the use of things, or bits of things, to stand for persons or groups of persons, are recurrent features of *The Secret Agent*.

[46] It seems likely that *The Princess Casamassima* (1886), Henry James's novel of terrorist conspiracy and mobility between the upper and lower classes of Victorian London, has also contributed to *The Secret Agent*. Elsa Nettels in her book on James and Conrad notes this possibility but goes on to argue that *The Princess Casamassima* can be fruitfully related to Conrad's *Under Western Eyes* (1911). I find this latter suggestion implausible. Elsa Nettels, *James and Conrad* (1977), pp.22, 208-14.

In the fake medieval tavern where Ossipon and the Professor are meeting in Chapter Four, the pianola has more life than any of the human beings.[47] It is the day of the fateful explosion which destroys Stevie. The Professor discusses the bomb that he carried at all times on his person, and looks round him to judge how many people in the tavern would be killed if he detonated his bomb. The fatalities would include a couple going up the stairs past the mechanical piano: as he remarks this, the piano springs to life as though refuting the Professor's confidence in the superior strength of death 'which knows no restraint and cannot be attacked' (p.68). The piano 'clanged through a mazurka with brazen impetuosity as though a vulgar and impudent ghost were showing off. The keys sank and rose mysteriously' (p.67).

Verloc's hat is more animate than Verloc, moving in the wind after his murder in mockery of his own immobility in life; a 'thick' police constable, 'part of inorganic nature, surging apparently out of a lamp-post' (p.14), gives no sign that he recognises Verloc, whom he knows to be a police informer. Lively images of disaster recall Dickens's apocalyptic effects. In a proleptic image of his violent disintegration Stevie, by way of political protest, lets off fireworks in the offices of a 'preserved milk firm', as a result of which 'silk hats and elderly businessmen could be seen rolling independently down the stairs' (p.9).

The difference from the world of Dickens or of any other mid-Victorian novelist is, of course, that however 'dark' Dickens's imagination became—in *Little Dorrit*, for example – his world rests on certain assumptions which remain intact: that order and honest work are good, that there is a consensus of 'Christian' values, loosely defined, to which a novelist can confidently refer. Behind Conrad's work there is no such consensus. A social order which has to be sustained by Heat, Vladimir and Verloc in order to preserve 'the gorgeous perambulator of a wealthy baby being wheeled in state across the Square' (p.23), is an artifice in which all classes are equally 'degenerate'. Dickens's imagination in its darkest moods would never have allowed itself to hate babies.

The sanctions preserving this society are largely inoperative and inappropriate. The only figure to be substantially affected by them is the innocent and harmless Michaelis, transformed into a swollen cripple by his imprisonment. The only dangerous figure, the Professor, has secured his immunity from punishment by the known strength of his will to destroy himself rather than be captured. There is no difference between policemen and criminals. Inspector Heat, the most prominent defender of the social order, is motivated by 'vanity of power' and 'vulgar love of domination' (p.122), and to his mind thieving is a job of work whose difference from other

[47] See Cox, ch.5.

forms of work 'consisted in the nature of its risk' (p.92). The social order is blindly coercive and devoid of inherent 'right'. Winnie Verloc, whose utterances are likely to be less ironic than those of the other characters, explains the function of the police to Stevie in these terms: 'They are there so that them as have nothing shouldn't take anything away from them who have' (p.173).

Does *The Secret Agent* contain any positives at all? If they are present, they are to be sought in the female characters, and where they appear they seem qualified out of existence. There is value of a kind in the notion of wifely loyalty as practised by Winnie, but she has drastically compromised with her feelings, and been dishonest to Verloc, by marrying him in preference to the butcher's boy in order to give Stevie a home. On a higher social level Michaelis's patroness seems to be an analogous figure. Cherishing Michaelis is almost as pointless an investment of human feelings as loving Stevie. Michaelis is as futile a human being as Stevie, childlike and pampered, writing an unpublishable book about his experiences. With her invincible stupidity and autocratic outlook the patroness is an interesting instance of the dangerous obtuseness of the governing class, a theme in which Conrad here surprisingly resembles Wells and Galsworthy.

The patroness adores Michaelis, and regards his neo-Marxist ideas as a defence of the upper-class against the middle-class: 'She disliked the new element of plutocracy in the social compound, and industrialism as a method of human development appeared to her singularly repulsive in its mechanical and unfeeling character. The humanitarian hopes of the mild Michaelis tended not towards utter destruction, but merely towards the complete economic ruin of the system. And she did not really see where was the moral harm of it. It would do away with all the multitude of the 'parvenus', whom she disliked and mistrusted, not because they had arrived anywhere (she denied that), but because of their profound unintelligence of the world ... With the annihilation of all capital they would vanish too: but universal ruin ... would leave the social values untouched. The disappearance of the last piece of money could not affect people of position' (p.111). In this wonderfully funny vignette of an 'absolutist mind' Conrad seems to me to have beaten Wells and Galsworthy on their own ground.

Traditionally, discussion of the novel has it that the novel's moral positives are to be found clustered round Stevie: that Winnie Verloc's love for her idiot brother and her mother's compassionate decision to go and live in the alms houses in order not to impose a strain on Verloc's charity are small expressions of selfless love in an otherwise morally bankrupt world. There are undoubtedly good *intentions* at work in both women, but what is the effect of these intentions? It seems to me that here Conrad's irony goes very deep indeed. All Winnie's actions tend with Sophoclean inevitability towards the destruction of Stevie.

By marrying Verloc in the first place Winnie puts Stevie under the protection of the man who will kill him. By encouraging Verloc to make friends with Stevie she unwittingly awakens her husband to the possibility that Stevie might serve as an accomplice; by implanting in Verloc the habit of taking Stevie for walks with him she suggests the elementary deception by which he decoys Stevie away from Michaelis's cottage on the day of the planned bombing.

The decision of Winnie's mother to move to the almshouses takes further this pattern of the futility of good action.[48] It is because Stevie pines after his mother's departure to the almshouses that he is sent to stay at Michaelis's cottage in the country (and thereby deprived of Winnie's protective vigilance). The destruction of Winnie herself can also be seen to stem from their mother's removal. Winnie writes Stevie's address inside his coat in order that he can make the journey to the almshouses without getting lost. It is this address label on the fragmented remnant of Stevie's coat-collar, and this only, that links Stevie with Verloc's shop, brings the knowledge of Stevie's death back to Winnie, and thence leads Winnie to the murder of Verloc and her subsequent suicide.

The one action in the book which is 'good' not only in intention but also in *effect* is Stevie's reproach to the cab-driver. Stevie's mother travels to the almshouses by cab, and Stevie reproaches the cab-driver for ill-treating his horse: as a result the man dismounts and leads his horse away on foot. Unquestionably Stevie has succeeded; unquestionably, then, he is the one *effectively* 'good' character in the book. Surely, though, the implication of this is immediately seen as ironic: goodness in such a person is a contradiction in terms, a society which harbours goodness only in the weak-minded has given clinching evidence of its irreversible depravity. Stevie's goodness is like an animal's, characterised by a complete absence of mind: his 'desire to make the horse happy and the cabman happy, had reached the point of a bizarre longing to take them to bed with him. And that, he knew, was impossible. For Stevie was not mad' (p.167). But he is near enough to it to make no difference within an unsympathetic urban world, and the cabby's compassion towards his horse is still observed with an icy objectivity which nullifies any appeal to the reader's feelings that it may threaten to have: 'The short, thick man limping busily, with the horse's head held aloft in his fist, the lank animal walking in stiff and forlorn dignity, the dark low box on wheels rolling behind comically with an air of waddling' (p.168).

The Secret Agent is a monument to the futility of all aspiration and almost all

---

[48] This was first noticed by a friend of Conrad's in a contemporary review: Edward Garnett, unsigned review, *The Nation*, 28 September 1907 (Norman Sherry (ed.), *Conrad: The Critical Heritage* (1973), pp.191-3).

action, the incident of the cabhorse being the exception which seems to prove the rule. It is underpinned by the paradox that existed for many in the period in the doctrine of evolution. There was hope for man as a perfectible species but with this hope went a sensational, and to many minds thrilling, doubt: might man be on the *decline*, in evolutionary terms? Wells's *The Time Machine* is organised round this idea.

The theories of Lombroso are invoked to show Stevie as 'degenerate'.[49] His bat-like ears resemble those of Donkin in *The Nigger* and Winnie's face takes on a startling resemblance to Stevie's at the moment at which she murders Verloc; she too shares the degenerate state of modern man: 'Into that plunging blow, delivered over the side of the couch, Mrs Verloc had put all the inheritance of her immemorial and obscure descent, the simple ferocity of the age of caverns, and the unbalanced nervous fury of the age of bar-rooms' (p.263). Here Conrad gets in both parts of the evolutionary paradox. Winnie can be taken both as reverting to the violence of the cave-dwellers, and as betraying the decline of the human species as exemplified by her drunken father's 'nervous fury of the age of bar-rooms'.

Stevie and Winnie exemplify racial degeneracy as popularised by Max Nordau's books and the popular journalism of the day. At the same time she is in a sense an existential hero, like Jim or Razumov, moving (for a moment only in this book) from bondage into freedom, self-determinism.

The city has become drastically simplified, like the community of one of Conrad's ships. The sea of course drowns Winnie and frees her from her terror of the hangman. The sea is also interestingly present at the moment at which Winnie gains her freedom. She leans on the side of the sofa where Verloc lies dead 'because of the undulatory and swinging movements of the parlour, which for some time behaved as though it were at sea in a tempest...She was a woman enjoying her complete irresponsibility and endless leisure, almost in the manner of a corpse' (p.263). The freedom is an illusion of course, and is over before it had begun; the proleptic use of the word 'corpse' makes that clear. Ossipon, who looks like a Norwegian sailor, will cruelly protract the illusion for her, but in fact her freedom is lost and replaced by a new kind of bondage, a bondage to terror, from the moment that she hears Verloc's blood dripping: 'Mrs Verloc by the door was quite a different person from the woman who had been leaning over the sofa' (p.266). And as she runs from the shop the imagery again anticipates her death by drowning, more insistently than before: 'This entrance into the open air had a foretaste of drowning; a slimy dampness enveloped her, entered her nostrils, clung to her hair' (p.269).

---

[49] On Lombroso's theories, see Leo Henkin, 'Evolution and the idea of degeneration', *Darwinism in the English Novel* (1963), pp.221-32.

7. Under Western Eyes

Willems, Kurtz, Jim and Gould grew out of each other, while the figures in *The Secret Agent* and *Under Western Eyes* (1911) are created in response to external literary stimuli, Wells (with Dickens and James's *The Princess Casamassima* in the background) and Dostoievsky respectively. The parallels between *Crime and Punishment* and *Under Western Eyes* are well-known: the physical and psychological illnesses of Razumov and Raskolnikov following their crimes, and the identical roles of Ziemianitch the sledge-driver and the house-painter in *Crime and Punishment*. Both these figures are suspected of the crime and deflect suspicion from the hero so that Razumov and Raskolnikov find themselves in closely similar final situations: the confession, when it comes, is in each case made of his free will. And each is cared for by a self-sacrificing woman, Tekla or Sonia.

The differences, of course, are more interesting than the similarities. Dostoievsky's novel is Christian in its outer assumptions and in its conclusion. Conrad's inhabits a wholly secular frame of reference and could indeed be seen as a *parody* of *Crime and Punishment* in the same way as the story of Verloc could be seen as giving the world of Kipps and Mr Lewisham a diabolical twist.

In 1908 Conrad wrote to Galsworthy giving an early version of the plot of *Under Western Eyes*. It was to have been in two movements. The first was very much as we have it: the student Razumov, natural son of Prince K-, gives up secretly to the police his fellow student, Haldin, who seeks refuge in his rooms after committing a political crime. Haldin is hanged. The second movement was much more dramatic and consciously novelistic than the final version. Razumov meets Mrs Haldin and her daughter, marries the daughter, has a child by her. Mrs Haldin and the daughter are killed in a complicated plot which turns on the child's resemblance to the dead Haldin. One can be grateful that this somewhat Wardour Street device is replaced by the carefully-paced psychological unfolding which constitutes the action of the published novel. Conrad's letter indicates clearly enough his *central* concern, which is fully and successfully released by the pattern he finally chose: 'The psychological developments leading to Razumov's betrayal of Haldin ... form the real subject of the story.'[50] It is interesting that the earlier version of the plot is the same as the central domestic pattern in *The Secret Agent*, in which Mrs Verloc is married to her brother's killer.

Razumov is the most deracinated of Conrad's heroes. He stands in the same tradition as Jim and Decoud, but his situation is drastically simplified. He has no family in any real sense – Prince K- is no more to him than an available figure in authority to whom he can turn at the crisis precipitated by

[50] G. Jean-Aubry, *Joseph Conrad: Life and Letters*, vol 2 (1927), p.65.

Haldin – no mature male figure on which to base his sense of his own identity. He is 'officially and in fact without a family ... as lonely in the world as a man swimming in the deep sea' (p.10). One is struck by the resemblance of this to Stein's image of a man born to float in the 'destructive element'. His points of reference are idealised abstracts, the 'autocracy' which is the 'religion' of Russia: 'In Russia, the land of spectral ideas and disembodied aspirations, many brave minds have turned away at last from the vain and endless conflict to the one great historical fact of the land. They turned to autocracy for the peace of their patriotic conscience as a weary unbeliever, touched by grace, turns to the faith of his fathers for the blessing of spiritual rest. Like other Russians before him, Razumov, in conflict with himself, felt the touch of grace on his forehead' (p.34). The tone is ironic but complex. As Tony Tanner says of this and other passages: 'Anybody who reads *Under Western Eyes* as an anti-Russian polemic has not learned to respond to the full range of Conrad's wide-ranging irony ... nor to the depths of his insight into the human personality.'[51]

The political essay 'Autocracy and War' (1905), often quoted in conjunction with *Under Western Eyes*, is, by contrast, a direct and very angry piece: here Russia is 'a country held by an evil spell, suffering from an awful visitation for which the responsibility cannot be traced either to her sins or her follies' (p.98). It is possible to see Razumov in Part First a victim to the kind of oppression described in 'Autocracy and War', peculiarly open to the worship of Russia because he has no human alternative, he has nothing else to love.

Haldin throws the bomb which kills de P-, takes refuge in Razumov's rooms (relying on Razumov's reputation for 'English' discretion and unobtrusiveness), persuades Razumov to deliver a message to Ziemianitch the sleigh-driver who is to get him out of the city. Razumov finds Ziemianitch hopelessly drunk, and, after an explosion of temper in which he beats Ziemianitch with a stable-fork, wanders the streets anxiously wondering how best to serve his own interests in the unwelcome situation that Haldin has thrust on him. The Russian landscape presents itself to him as an epiphany of Russia's 'sacred inertia', and he experiences a messianic need for a strong political leader to embody the country's failing political ideal of itself: 'What it needed was not the conflicting aspirations of a people, but a will strong and one: it wanted not the babble of many voices, but a man – strong and one!' (p.33).

The theocratic vision of Russia and the barely formulated quest for a leader are drastically tested by his encounters with General T- and Mikulin. The existential agony which drives Razumov to betray Haldin first to Prince

---

[51] Tony Tanner, 'Nightmare and complacency: Razumov and the Western Eye', *Critical Quarterly* (autumn 1962), p.199.

K- (Razumov's father) and then to General T- is finely observed: 'He felt the need of some other mind's sanction' (p.39). This recalls the quotation from Novalis which serves as the epigraph to *Lord Jim*: 'It is certain my conviction gains infinitely the moment another soul believes in it.' Jim and Decoud both share this need: 'Razumov longed desperately for a word of advice, for moral support. Who knows what true loneliness is – not the conventional word, but the naked terror? To the lonely themselves it wears a mask. The most miserable outcast hugs some memory or some illusion. Now and then a fatal conjunction of events may lift the veil for an instant. For an instant only. No human being could bear a steady view of moral solitude without going mad' (p.39).

Under the pressure of his loneliness Razumov for a moment entertains the prospect of committing himself to Haldin and the revolutionaries: 'He embraced for a whole minute the delirious purpose of rushing to his lodgings and flinging himself on his knees by the side of the bed with the dark figure stretched on it; to pour out a full confession in passionate words that would stir the whole being of that man to its innermost depths; that would end in embraces and tears; in an incredible fellowship of souls – such as the world had never seen' (pp.39-40).

But he chooses autocracy and, after a brief embarrassed interview with Prince K-, goes to encounter the human reality of Russian authority in the person of General T-. General T- lives in a setting of cultivated luxury – 'there was a coal fire in an English grate; Razumov had never before seen such a fire' – which ironically contains a *kouros*, an image of the freedom for which Haldin has fought and which Razumov has betrayed: 'Filling a corner, on a black pedestal, stood a quarter-life-size smooth-limbed bronze of an adolescent figure, running. The Prince observed in an undertone – "Spontini's. 'Flight of Youth'. Exquisite." "Admirable," assented Razumov faintly' (p.43).

There is a tiny, but deft, juxtaposition of the aesthetic and the moral responses to art signalled by the contrast between the Prince's 'exquisite' and Razumov's 'admirable'. Razumov has not yet stifled his conscience (and will never do so completely): the Prince behaves as though he has never possessed a conscience. Razumov's moral perceptions continue to function as he confronts General T- in his elegant stronghold and notes the 'air of jovial, careless cruelty' behind his 'bright white flash of an automatic smile' (p.44).

After the betrayal and hanging of Haldin, Razumov writes out a political credo which is often taken to be Conrad's:

'Still-faced and his lips set hard, Razumov began to write. When he wrote a large hand his neat writing lost its character altogether – became unsteady, almost childish. He wrote five lines one under the other.

History not Theory.
Patriotism not Internationalism.
Evolution not Revolution.
Direction not Destruction.
Unity not Disruption.' (p.66)

He impales the list against the wall as though rearing his standard on the side of autocracy, rationalising and dignifying the decision to betray Haldin. My own view is that the writing of this credo is no evidence of Conrad's beliefs. It is part of the dramatic presentation: a psychological fact about Razumov, not a political fact about Conrad. Razumov is seeking to codify experience, to control the facts which are veering about him in a dizzying way, to stabilise a universe which has been disturbed by Haldin's invasion of his smug, inner-directed, 'bourgeois' (as Tony Tanner calls it) life-style. His dreams release the anxieties which the symmetry of the credo is designed to keep at bay: 'He woke up shivering from a dream of walking through drifts of snow' (p.66).

The loneliness experienced in the dream is intensified on the following day when he finds his rooms searched by the police. It becomes worse in the course of his dialogues with Mikulin. One of the best scenes in the whole of Conrad is the dialogue in which Razumov tries to fend off Mikulin at the end of Part First. Mikulin is in fact entirely friendly and is discreetly testing Razumov to see whether he might be pressed into service as an agent against the expatriate revolutionaries, but Razumov, now almost engulfed in paranoid dislocation, responds with an aggressiveness which anyone less patient than Mikulin would resent; Razumov is shadow-boxing with his own psyche.

'A man – strong and one', the 'flight of youth', a 'fellowship of souls': Razumov in Part First of the novel is seeking a hero, a male figure to whom he can relate and submit himself. From the ironic vantage point enjoyed by the reader it is clear that Haldin himself is the hero whom Razumov fails to recognise.

The novel is so structured that Part First and Part Fourth are continuous. In Parts Second and Third the novel presents the external actions of Razumov and the Geneva revolutionaries, in Parts First and Fourth the novel has inner access to Razumov's mind, and Part Fourth shows the steps by which Razumov has come to work for Mikulin. He is driven to it by Haldin's 'moral spectre', which presses on Razumov until his inner conscious purpose – his drive towards the Prize Essay and the career as a professor or civil servant – is disrupted. He reached out his hand towards his pen, 'steady in his great purpose', in order to continue with the prize essay, and the ghost intervenes: 'He happened to glance towards the bed. He rushed at it, enraged, with a mental scream: "It's you, crazy fanatic, who stands in the way!" He flung the pillow on the floor violently, tore the blankets aside ... Nothing there. And, turning away, he caught for an instant in the air, like a vivid detail in a dissolving view of two heads, the eyes of General T- and of Privy Councillor Mikulin side by side fixed upon him, quite different in character, but with the same unflinching and weary and yet purposeful expression ... servants of the nation!' (p.302).

By betraying Haldin Razumov has destroyed his own inner life, whereas if he had said nothing Haldin would have escaped undiscovered (as General T- points out) and Razumov could have continued undisturbed with the bourgeois progress that he wants. As it is he at last goes to Mikulin eagerly, driven by the pressure to escape from isolation: Mikulin is 'the only person on earth' with whom Razumov is able to discuss Haldin, thereby exorcising for a moment the 'falsehood-breeding spectre' (p.304). The ghost of Haldin on his bed drives him to Mikulin: the resemblance to Haldin in Natalie, who has a 'virile handshake' and 'masculine bearing' pulls him to fall in love with her and then drives him to confess his treachery. He is impelled here, again, by the need to escape from loneliness: 'Do you know why I came to you? It is simply because there is no one anywhere in the whole great world I could go to. Do you understand what I say? No one to go to. Do you conceive the desolation of the thought – no one – to – go – to?' (pp.353-4).

Following this confession he goes back to his rooms in Geneva and sits down to write out the narrative delivered to the language teacher. At midnight he reproduces the pattern of the night on which he betrayed Haldin, he is 'the puppet of his past', runs out of the house and goes to the gathering of revolutionists and repeats his confession. Most of those assembled are embarrassed and saddened but Nikita (himself, as we later learn, a double agent also employed by Mikulin) takes him outside and deafens him. Razumov wanders in his stricken state and is run down by a tram. Tekla looks after him in his crippled condition as she had formerly looked after the neglected cat at the Chateau Borel.

It could be said that once Razumov has made his confession to the assembled revolutionaries he has acquired an existential freedom similar to that achieved by Jim or Decoud. But this freedom at the end of the novel is heavily qualified. He lives in seclusion in Russia and gives counsel to the revolutionaries whom he had betrayed – a state of things bewildering to the language teacher – but beyond this oracular and hermit-like role he is as incapable of effective action as Stevie in *The Secret Agent*.

The *Doppelgänger* motif is constant in Conrad. In a benign form it is markedly present in the short story, 'The Secret Sharer', in which a young captain finds a naked man swimming alone and secretly takes him on board his ship. The stranger, Leggatt, is escaping from another ship where he had been awaiting trial for killing one of the sailors who was threatening the ship's safety. The skipper hides Leggatt in his cabin, and the narrative voice of the story reflects throughout on the physical similarity of the two men; anyone looking into the cabin would see them as a double man. An extraordinary intimacy is established. By sailing dangerously close to a rocky shoreline the skipper enables Leggatt to swim to safety; at the same time this risky piece of navigation has given the young skipper full possession of himself and mastery of his ship.

Malign forms of the *Doppelgänger* occur in the similarity-with-differences of Lord Jim and Gentleman Brown, Heyst and Jones, Heat and Verloc. In *Under Western Eyes* Razumov has the figure of Haldin before him throughout the novel, and the novel's pattern forces him to compare and contrast Haldin's moral being with his own.

If the contrast between Haldin's heroism and Razumov's caution is the major pattern dramatised by the novel it is reasonable to ask what, if anything, the narrative device of the language teacher contributes to it. The language teacher has been much disliked by commentators: C.B. Cox in particular sees the device as boring and played-out, overworked and incredible. At times, certainly, the reader's credulity is strained; the language teacher can seem disconcertingly articulate and perceptive about Razumov's sufferings which, after all, he knows only from brief contact and from the document in Russian in Razumov's handwriting. There are awkward scenes of great passion where, like Nelly Dean in *Wuthering Heights*, he seems to be intruding for no reason. The reader is inclined to echo Razumov's irritated question (as he makes his momentous confession to Natalie): 'How did this old man come here?'

The slowness and the laboriousness of the narrative method are justified, though, to my mind, by the grandeur of the cumulative effect. Razumov is seen subjectively in Part First, externally and from a distance in Part Second, still externally but more closely in Part Third (which is where the device is at its weakest: the language teacher is just not sufficiently characterised to convince the reader that he is, or can be, emotionally involved with Natalie) and subjectively again in Part Fourth. The effect of the narrative then is to present Razumov slowly to the mind, under different lights and with different degrees of access, inviting us both to know his mind and to observe his actions rather as Marlow's narrative in Lord Jim invites us to collaborate with him in his contemplation of Jim: with the difference that Razumov can be fully understood whereas Jim could not. Marlow as limited narrator could not capture the refinements of Jim's moral consciousness; the language teacher as narrator can perceive Razumov accurately, since they are both Western and bourgeois in outlook, but misses the 'mystical' quality of Russia presented at its best by Natalie Haldin and her mother.

When he first encounters the Haldin women the language teacher finds that he is struggling with an alien experience. Natalie Haldin tries to explain to him the nature of the struggle of the Russian people:

'"You think it is a class conflict, or a conflict of interests, as social contests are with you in Europe. But it is not that at all. It is something quite different."

'"It is quite possible that I don't understand," I admitted. That propensity of lifting every problem from the plane of the understandable by means of some sort of mystic expression is very Russian' (p.104).

Blind to the moral force of the Haldins, he writes it off as 'simplicity, a terrible corroding simplicity in which mystic phrases clothe a naive and hopeless cynicism' (p.104). Political oppression does not breed simplicity of outlook; confident imperialism does that, witness the late Victorian public-schoolboy. The English, as Natalie Haldin bitterly remarks, have 'made their bargain with fate' (p.114) and won their security at the expense of becoming stupid.

In Part Fourth the narrative doubles back on itself because Razumov himself becomes narrator: he begins to write the book which the language teacher is partly translating and partly amplifying. We may feel that there is no need for the frame to get into the picture in this way, that the novel is becoming like a system of self-reflecting mirrors, that the complications are wanton. But the act of writing is itself an important item among the aggregate of Razumov's actions. In Part Third the gallery of grotesque revolutionaries in Geneva force him into an increasingly false identity: he is taken up by Madame de S- who finds him attractive, he is insulted by Nikita, he is venerated by Sophia Antonovna who tells him that a fellow student has written admiringly of Razumov's stoicism and cool courage after the throwing of the bomb. The last of these deceived figures, Julius Laspara (whose dwarfish physique recalls the Professor in *The Secret Agent*) presses him to *write*, to record his experiences for a revolutionary journal of which Laspara is editor. This triggers in Razumov the frightening conviction that his actions are still being determined from outside by the ghost of Haldin: 'It seemed as though he were being looked after in a specially remarkable way. "If I believed in an active Providence," Razumov said to himself ... "I would see here the working of an ironical finger"' (p.289). The writing itself is another flight from solitude, a written confession like the spoken declarations to Mikulin, to Natalie and to the assembled revolutionaries. The written confession is delivered to the language teacher not because, like Marlow, he is a close friend or significant influence but precisely because of his detachment and insignificance, his secure absence from the mainstream of political or human action.

The novel's odd title is finally vindicated by this equally odd shape. The 'western eyes' of the language teacher and the reader cannot be expected to penetrate the 'mystic' Russian pattern with which the novel ends. The reader's expectations of justice are disappointed. The narration is transferred in the last few pages from the language teacher to Sophia Antonovna: she tells the language teacher that Razumov has now become a hermit and prophet, that Nikita has been exposed as a double agent, that Madame de S- has left all her money to reactionary relations and nothing to her parasitical lover Peter Ivanovitch, who in turn has defied expectation by marrying a peasant girl and returning to Russia. Even he, parasitical and bullying as he is, finally lives up to an ideal which is hidden from the 'western eye'. Sophia Antonovna's final line, 'Peter Ivanovitch is an inspired man' (perhaps echoing Marlow's equivocal phrase, 'Mr Kurtz is a remarkable man,' in *Heart of Darkness*), is a piece of subtlety which loses the language teacher altogether. All he can do is quote it, and leave its significance to the reader's judgment.

8. Chance *and* Victory

Graham Hough is surely right in his diagnosis of the problem of *Chance*: 'The complexities of the narrative method are ... layers of protecting covering to an essentially simple heroic vision.'[52]

Chance was the first of Conrad's novels to sell. It did so in the teeth of probability: Conrad was fifty-six and in poor health, and the country was concerned with the imminent threat of a European War. But it sold. Jocelyn Baines suggests possible reasons for its commercial success: it contains the traditional Conradian formula, an isolated protagonist – in this case two protagonists, Flora de Barral and Roderick Anthony – finding release and self-confidence in a contest with the sea. And it adds an element new in Conrad: a study of female sexuality. And it had a picture of a girl on the cover.

In a sense it conforms to a pattern, since all Conrad's novels can be seen as relating to existing currents of fashion: *Lord Jim* makes a bid for the imperial market, *The Secret Agent* for the Wells and Bennett market; *Under Western Eyes* acknowledges the late Edwardian craze for all things Russian: music, ballet, décor. *Chance* relates to the demythologising of women which had been a feature of recent literature: Hardy, Shaw, George Moore, and on the popular level Somerset Maugham and Elinor Glyn.

Hitherto most of Conrad's women had had old-fashioned virtues: Freya, the silent niece in 'Falk', Tekla in *Under Western Eyes*, Jewel in *Lord Jim*, Emily Gould in *Nostromo*. But there had been a counter-movement in the portraits of dominant or destructive women: Amy Foster, the patroness of Michaelis in *The Secret Agent*, Madame de S- in *Under Western Eyes*. In *Chance* (1913) Conrad presents a stark contrast between the sea, where the virtues of loyalty and courage are still practised, and the land which is populated by stunted or

[52] Graham Hough, *Image and Experience*, p.220.

perverted figures among whom dominant women are prominent.

Flora de Barral herself is not blankly virtuous, since she has practised deception: she marries Roderick Anthony partly in order to give her father a refuge when he comes out of prison, and she feels justified in this deception because she is convinced that she is unlovable, that Roderick Anthony has married her only out of pity. This misunderstanding has been forced on her by the two powerful female figures in the novel, her governess and Mrs Fyne, Roderick Anthony's sister.

The governess is one of the most vivid and surprising of Conrad's creations. She is 'avid' for pleasure with 'ungovernable [sexual] passions' (p.103) and she has cherished her envious hatred of Flora, her charge, 'in tiny amounts, treasuring every pinch carefully till it grows at last into a monstrous and explosive hoard' (p.110). When her father is known to be ruined financially Flora is told by the governess that she is unlovable, 'viciously assured that she was in heart, mind, manner and appearance an utterly common and insipid creature' (p.119). In thrall to the governess's authority, Flora 'could not help believing what she had been told' (p.236), and from this moment her childhood self-confidence has been 'brutally murdered' (p.139).

Flora goes to Mrs Fyne for comfort but Mrs Fyne, who is a feminist and appears also (from her behaviour) to be discreetly lesbian, is a further obstruction to Flora's happiness. Mrs Fyne is doctrinally opposed to marriage (though married herself to the 'pedestrian' Fyne): Flora is influenced by her views and 'in echo of her own stupid talk' writes her an unwise letter saying that she 'did not love her brother' (Roderick Anthony) but 'had no scruples whatever in marrying him' (p.443). In the last few pages of the novel it becomes clear that Mrs Fyne has reported this letter, or a version of it, to her husband who in turn has reported it to Roderick Anthony. Roderick is forced by this to believe that he is taking advantage of Flora's semi-orphaned state (her father has been imprisoned for seven years) and that she does not love him, is merely grateful to him (p.329).

The land people in *Chance*, then, obstruct love. This obstructiveness begins with a character who is not presented in the novel directly, the poet Carleon Anthony, father of Roderick Anthony and Mrs Fyne. Carleon Anthony can be presumed to have damaged the sexual development of both his children. He is himself a lyrical poet of married love, but also a sexually incontinent domestic tyrant who has worn out two wives and is destroying a third. In an important article on the sources of *Chance* Mrs Duncan-Jones has shown that Carleon Anthony is based on Coventry Patmore, who himself had a son in the merchant service with whom he had quarrelled, Milnes Patmore, a young man of whom Conrad would certainly have known and whom he may well have met. (Mrs Duncan-Jones also suggests persuasively that there is a resemblance between the Flora/governess relationship in *Chance* and the Flora/Miss Jessel relationship in James's *The Turn of the Screw*.)[53]

The other father, de Barral, becomes incestuous and murderous after his seven years imprisonment, which Marlow as narrator refers to as 'a maiming, crippling process ... the individual coming back damaged in some subtle way' (p.352). This father-figure also seems to have literary precursors. Mrs Fyne recalls him after the death of his wife walking hand in hand with Flora (as a child) on Brighton beach, 'pictures from Dickens – pregnant with pathos' (p.162).

The 'picture' is from *Dombey and Son*, the story of the cold, unbending businessman who rejects his daughter (Florence: the association with Conrad's Flora is self-evident) after his wife's death and walks with her on Brighton beach in the novel's final scene of reconciliation. Conrad's version of the father-daughter relationship suggests that love, in its perverted, landlocked form, can be worse than rejection: de Barral's feeling for Flora when he comes out of prison is incestuous possessiveness.

The sea people present all too simple a contrast to the land group. Young Powell, Roderick Anthony's second mate, 'Old' Powell, the clerk who because of the accident of their having the same name passes young Powell off as his nephew and thereby gets him his post on the *Ferndale*, Franklin, Brown and the ordinary seamen all have the simple sea-going virtues, loyalty and courage. Roderick Anthony himself is the novel's weakest point. He is the sailor-hero in his pure form, the object of Graham Hough's 'essentially simple heroic vision', but the difficulty with the characterisation of Anthony is that when the 'layers of protecting covering' have been penetrated there is nothing there. He is null, passive, invisible, and his sexual *impasse* with Flora is frankly incredible. Also it is damaging artistically: having got his characters into their impossible predicament Conrad resorts to a cheaply melodramatic ending to get them out of it.

Flora and Anthony set to sea in the *Ferndale* and one might expect their landlocked inhibitions to be lifted. But Flora's father, fresh from prison, accompanies them and the obstruction remains: the marriage is unconsummated, Flora shares a cabin with her father, not with her husband. It takes de Barral's attempt to murder Anthony to break down the barriers between the lovers and enable them to talk to each other.

The narration of *Chance* suffers from an over-sophistication of which all its readers have complained. There are three frames: the story is told by young Powell to Marlow (the Marlow of *Youth*, *Heart of Darkness* and *Lord Jim*, but here become unaccountably misogynist and cranky), who tells it to an

---

[53] E.E. Duncan-Jones, 'Some sources of *Chance*', *Review of English Studies*, 20 (November 1969), pp.468-71.

anonymous narrator who organises it into the narrative on the page. Henry James in 'The New Novel' (1914) complained of the method getting in the way of the material, the narrators being like 'successive members of a cue from one to the other of which the sense and the interest of the subject have to be passed on together, in the manner of the buckets of water for the improvised extinction of a fire, before reaching our apprehension: all with whatever result, to this apprehension, of a quantity to be allowed for as spilt by the way' (p.206).

As the novel proceeds its title is seen to be ironic: the lives revealed by this gratuitously complicated technique are inexorably determined. The inhibitions of Flora and Anthony and the psychopathic behaviour of Flora's father – the groundwork of the action – are the products not of 'chance' but of conditioning. Indeed nothing is left to 'chance', the novelist can be seen riveting the coincidences into their positions in the structure at every turn: young Powell owes his job to the fact that he has the same name as old Powell; the presence of the dog prevents Flora from jumping off a cliff in her despair when she is staying with the Fynes; the ship which nearly collides with the *Ferndale* sparks off Powell's love for Flora, who helps him to prevent the collision; an accidental breakage enables Powell to see, through a newly glazed window, de Barral's attempt to poison Roderick Anthony; Roderick is drowned in another collision thus leaving Flora to Powell and fulfilling the promise of the first chapter's title, 'Young Powell and his Chance'.

The novel is buttoned down by references to 'chance' throughout: Marlow's familiarity with the Fynes is a chance acquaintance, as is the friendship between Flora's mother and Mrs Fyne before her marriage, the product of the loneliness of two women who happened to be neighbours. Roderick Anthony is 'that man whom chance had thrown in Flora's way' (p.351), and Flora's traumatic experience with the governess is again a matter of contingency: she is left alone with the governess for those fatal few minutes while the cold-blooded Fynes, who know that they ought to intervene (although they don't know exactly what's happening) look on diffidently at the de Barral house from the other side of the street.

The word 'novel' suggests something that is new, full of surprises, open.[54] To organise a narrative round accidents *ought* to allow the reader to have experiences in art which are as open and surprising as those in life. But for me *Chance* has the opposite effect: I can see all the writer's choices at work, I can see each contingency being elaborately dwelt on. It is possible that Conrad is aware of this gap between his title and his effect and that the irony of the title is conscious: if so, it makes a sophisticated point about the nature of realism, that verbal art is fixed and ordered and planned, that its selections

[54] See Malcolm Bradbury's refreshing reconsideration of the word in his *Possibilities: Essays on the State of the Novel*, 1973.

cannot ever hope to match the flux of actual experience.

At the same time the intellectual effort of *Chance* is less pleasing than that of any of the previous major novels precisely because of the consciousness with which the title draws attention to the novel's cleverness. The title, the chapter headings, the insistence on the word 'chance' are pointers to the reader by which the novel congratulates itself on its own skilfulness as it unfolds. The cleverness is actually rather easy to unwrap, the reader is allowed to feel that he has penetration and insight without much exerting himself. It is the only major Conrad novel that does not demand to be read twice.

In *Under Western Eyes* heroic force in Haldin confronts bourgeois caution in Razumov, and loses. From *Chance* and *Victory* (1915) heroic force has disappeared to be replaced by something else, an asceticism or self-abnegation combined with sexual inhibition in both Roderick Anthony and Heyst. The difference between these two figures is that while Roderick Anthony is colourless (and is the weakest feature of *Chance*) Heyst's asceticism in *Victory* is drawn so vividly and acutely as to make him one of Conrad's most vivid characterisations. This full portrait stands at the centre of (and has perhaps been achieved at the expense of) a novel the rest of which is weirdly flat and unreal. Heyst is Christ-like, of course, and he is a flesh-and-blood Christ in a morality in which the other actors are puppets. Heyst's life is a denial of force: '"I've never killed a man or loved a woman – not even in my thoughts, not even in my dreams ... To slay, to love – the greatest enterprises of life upon a man! And I have no experience of either"' (p.212). If the form of *Victory* were entirely like that of a puppet show one would feel less unease than one actually does in reading it.

Conrad has not unlearnt the lessons of *Chance*, as he perhaps should have done if he is moving away from social reality into myth. Jones, Ricardo and Pedro are Skeleton, Cat and Ape, but they also have uneasily fitting psychological features: Jones's misogyny is complicated, and his putative homosexuality (does he kill Ricardo out of sexual jealousy?) adds a further complication. Pedro's loyalty to Jones and Ricardo seems to arise from more than sheer terror; Ricardo's 'feral' heterosexuality is coloured and filled out by the details of his foot-fetishism.

The opening page of the novel invites us to accept that the real and the magical worlds co-exist: 'There is, as every schoolboy knows in this scientific age, a very close chemical relation between coal and diamonds' (between the pragmatic and the fantasy worlds) (p.3). The narrator of the first part of the novel is a sailor, 'one of us' (in the phrase repeated from *Lord Jim*), a friend of fat, loyal Davidson who sails within view of Samburan once a month and reports his sightings of Heyst. The pragmatic, man-of-action narrator is useful because he is able to present Heyst's Christ-like altruism with a convincing lack of comment. He perceives Heyst as 'enchanted' by the islands (p.25), a man of 'finished courtesy' (p.29), a 'consummate good-society manner' (p.13) and 'a taste for solitude' (p.28).

With amused detachment the narrator quotes Schomberg's malicious gossip: Heyst 'the Enemy' (p.25) has 'turned hermit from shame' (p.31). Although none 'of us' believe Schomberg's version – that Heyst has sponged off Morrison and then sent him home to die – the narrator is perfectly capable of being securely callous about Morrison's death: 'He went into Dorsetshire to see his people, caught a bad cold, and died with extraordinary precipitation in the bosom of his appalled family' (p.22).

This narrator, then, is totally unlike the Marlow of *Lord Jim* who loves Jim and feels for him in his isolation: this narrator is as detached from Heyst as 'naive Heyst' appears to be from the rest of the world (p.23). The narrator is a good-natured gossip, contemptuous of Schomberg but too lazy to keep away from his hotel, using the colloquial, half-interested diction of men of action to describe someone whom he respects as a gentleman, distrusts slightly as a foreigner ('a Swedish baron or something', p.24), and would forget if Schomberg's hatred would let him.

The fat and friendly Davidson is more involved with Heyst than the narrator. Davidson marvels at Heyst's rescue of Lena, and the narrator's well-armoured callousness again comes to the surface:

> '"Only think what it means," wheezed Davidson, imaginative under his invincible placidity. "Just only try to think! Brooding alone on Samburan has upset his brain. He never stopped to consider, or he couldn't have done it. No sane man ... How is a thing like that to go on? What's he going to do with her in the end? It's madness."
>
> '"You say that he's mad. Schomberg tells us that he must be starving on his island; so he may end yet by eating her," I suggested' (p.45)

This narrator is unembarrassed in the presence of fine moral action: Heyst's Christ-like sacrifice for Morrison, for instance. Heyst's dispassionate demeanour brings Morrison to pour out the details of his financial ruin like a leper showing his sores: he is being forced by his creditors to sell his brig, the *Capricorn*, his means of livelihood. He has a great deal of money owing to him from villagers 'up dark creeks and obscure bays' who will never pay (p.10). Morrison thinks prayer is for women and children, not for men of action: 'I don't hold with a man everlastingly bothering the Almighty with his silly troubles' (pp.14-15). Nevertheless, in his desperation he prays, and Heyst, the answer to his prayer, immediately works the decorous and slightly chilly miracle of lending him the money to recover his impounded boat (p.15). Heyst and Morrison both make the mistake of playing God. Morrison has allowed himself to get into debt by his generosity to his villagers; Heyst will destroy himself by rescuing Lena and thereby incurring Schomberg's hatred – and, indeed, by helping Jones, Ricardo and Pedro ashore when they arrive at Samburan, prostrated with thirst and exhaustion in their boat.

Guerard argues that a fatal flaw in *Victory* is to be found in the fact that Heyst undergoes an inexplicable change of character.[55] But it is only the *limited* narrators, Davidson and the outer narrator who is 'one of us', who see an abrupt change in Heyst. As the outer narrator puts it at the opening of Part Three, Heyst had been 'a waif and stray, austerely, from conviction as others [are] through drink' until the moment at which he takes the 'plunge' and rescues Lena on 'that disturbing night' (p.92). But this narrator does not understand Heyst, mythologises him, makes him into a folk hero of comic legend: 'He suddenly reappeared in the world, broad chest, bald forehead, long moustaches, polite manner and all – the complete Heyst' (p.31). But this is not the 'complete Heyst', it is only the absurdly formal, 'enchanted' figure of common gossip. One returns to the central truth in Conrad, that actions are to be trusted more than words. Heyst's rescue of Lena is consistent with his sudden generosity to Morrison: 'Had the Swede [Heyst] suddenly risen and hit him on the nose, he could not have been more taken aback' (p.15). In short, it seems to me that Davidson and the outer narrator are used with great subtlety to transmit a common and partial understanding of Heyst, an outline which is then filled and enriched by the omniscient narrator's reportage of his extended dialogues with Lena on the island.

The sexual situation takes further the *impasse* of *Chance*. Heyst is Adam 'naming the animals of the paradise which he was so soon to lose' in his solitude on Samburan (p.174). 'Lena', known before as Alma or Magdalen, is one of the animals thus named. Her name recalls Rima, the mystical girl in the South American forests in W.H. Hudson's *Green Mansions* (1904) – a novel Conrad admired – and her tragedy is similar to Flora's in *Chance*. To convey to Heyst the depth of her love for him she has to sacrifice her own life. To take the knife from the murderous Ricardo is her 'victory': when Jones accidentally shoots her (instead of shooting Ricardo) she dies believing that she has saved Heyst's life, 'convinced of the reality of her victory over death' (p.406).

But Heyst, I believe, never learns to love. 'Fire purifies everything' (p.410), including despair, and it may be that Heyst burns himself to death less out of remorse than out of a final recognition of his own incompleteness. What he feels for Lena is not love but, in his father's phrase, 'that form of contempt which is called pity' (p.174).

Seen in the context of Conrad's Edwardian heroes Heyst is a sceptic like Decoud, a passive figure driven by events until he takes a climactic 'plunge'

---

[55] Guerard, p.234.

like Lord Jim, and a man caught up in the toils of his father's destiny like Charles Gould. Indeed there is a good deal of Gould in Heyst: they both have the impulses of the good imperialist. It is this impulse, together with his desire to silence Morrison's embarrassing gratitude, that has allowed Heyst to be won over by Morrison's mad scheme of mining coal from the islands: 'We doubted whether he had any visions of wealth – for himself, at any rate. What he seemed mostly concerned for was the "stride forward", as he expressed it, in the general organisation of the universe, apparently. He was heard by more than a hundred persons in the islands talking of "a great stride forward for these regions"' (p.6).

Like Gould he is possessed by his father's legacy; in Heyst's case the legacy consists of scepticism, furniture, and a great many books. The books written by Heyst's father take over part of the narrative and speak directly to the reader about love and guilt. Heyst sits on his island, Lena at his side, imagining that his father is telling him, from one of his books, that 'of the stratagems of life the most cruel is the consolation of love', and that 'men of tormented conscience, or of a criminal imagination, are aware of much that minds of a peaceful, resigned cast do not even suspect' (p.219). It is important that this is the voice of a *dead* philospher. For Heyst, the conflicts of love and guilt belong to the past, and in one sense the 'victory' of the title has been all too thoroughly won. While Decoud, Jim, Gould and Anthony are engaged in inner struggles with aspects of themselves, Heyst fights on the side of good against conspicuously obvious evil. Conrad's vision of man has become settled and clear in this novel, and it is a settled negative. Both the people Heyst tries to help, Morrison and Lena, die from a chain of events which begins with his intervention. Heyst's own death is a victory for his father: he was wrong to be hooked like a 'silly fish' into the world of 'action' (p.174).

Heyst is an explicit denial of the traditional attributes of the hero: purposefulness, self-assertion and sexual enterprise. He is a very successful piece of characterisation but the fiction constructed round him is barely readable as a novel; the new wine has burst the old wine-skin, the received form refuses to cooperate with the insights of the modernist imagination. *Victory* is perhaps best seen as a theoretical exercise demonstrating the difficulties of building a dramatic structure round a protagonist who is devoid of will.

9. The writer as hero

Nostromo is the turning-point in Conrad's work. In the novels and stories up to and including *Nostromo* Conrad explores the possibility that heroism in the traditional sense is still a reality. Decoud's suicide, the failure of Gould's marriage and the figure of Nostromo in his brown suit shambling through the streets of Sulaco mark the closure of that possibility. In *The Secret Agent* and *Under Western Eyes* Conrad's vision of man moves in the other direction. The two novels communicate a deep conviction of the futility of human aspiration, in the first on a national and in the second on a global level. There is a contrary movement, though, that works against this. *The Secret Agent* is characterised by an icy distaste for all human beings, while in *Under Western Eyes*, beyond the range of vision of the 'western eye', there is a 'mystic' dimension in which the heroic virtues of love and loyalty may still exist.

In *Chance* love and loyalty triumph, technically, in the reconciliation of Flora de Barral and her Roderick Anthony. But this reconciliation is the weakest part of a flawed, over-worked novel: Roderick Anthony is never quite credible as a personality, the sexual *impasse* between Roderick and Flora defies probability and the plot is obliged to become wildly melodramatic to get them out of it. In *Victory* the central figure behaves like a hero for anti-heroic reasons: Heyst rescues Lena, as he rescues Morrison, out of Christ-like abnegation. The whole character is built on the notion of an ascetic blocking, or inversion, of the normative impulses. Asceticism on this scale is itself, of course, heroism of a kind: that is one of the points of *Victory*'s title.

Conrad's central intuition, that a man is knowable only by his actions, sustains the great central novels. It returns to energise parts of the later work – *The Shadow-Line* and the end of *The Rover* – but there is no doubt that on the whole after *Under Western Eyes* the novels decline in quality, that the later works including *Victory* are marred by moral flattening into simple black-and-white polarities, and that *Chance* is a misguided attempt to recover by a willed technical complexity the depth and density of the earlier Marlow-narrations, *Heart of Darkness* and *Lord Jim*.

It is clear that Conrad's studies of the hero as man-of-action are closely bound up with his perception of himself as novelist. In 1898 he wrote to Garnett: 'I want to howl and foam at the mouth ... In the morning I get up with the horror of that powerlessness I must face through a day of vain efforts ... I seem to have lost all *sense* of style and yet I am haunted, mercilessly haunted, by the *necessity* of style.'[56] The quest for 'style' drove him to his tragi-comic collaboration with Ford, the collaboration which produced three books which are the worst work of either of the two writers: *The Inheritors, Romance, The Nature of a Crime*.

Conrad arrived at his own technical mastery after he had hit on the device of using a man of action – Marlow – as a narrator, and after he had begun to

[56] Letter to Garnett, 29 March 1898, Jean-Aubry, *Conrad*, pp.231-2.

use the metaphor of the man of action as the way in which to express his own identity as a writer: 'My work shall not be an utter failure because it has the solid basis of a definite intention – first: and next because it is not an endless analysis of affected sentiments but in its essence it is action ... nothing but action.'[57]

In his famous account of the writing of *Nostromo* the metaphor recurs:

> 'For twenty months, neglecting the common joys of life that fall to the lot of the humblest on this earth, I had, like the prophet of old, "wrestled with the Lord" for my creation, for the headlands of the coast, for the darkness of the Placid Gulf, the light on the snows, the clouds on the sky, and for the breath of life that had to be blown into the shapes of men and women, of Latin and Saxon, of Jew and Gentile.'[58]

And the same metaphor appears again in the essay on Henry James:

> 'Action in its essence, the creative art of a writer of fiction may be compared to rescue work carried out in darkness against cross gusts of wind swaying the action of a great multitude. It is rescue work, this snatching of vanishing phases of turbulence, disguised in fair words, out of the native obscurity into a light where the struggling forms may be seen, seized upon, endowed with the only possible form of permanence in this world of relative values – the permanence of memory. And the multitude feels it obscurely too; since the demand of the individual to the artist is, in effect, the cry 'Take me out of myself!' meaning really, out of my perishable activity into the light of imperishable consciousness.'[59]

Writing is intimately bound up with a sense of virility. While writing *Lord Jim* he found that the act of writing restored a sense of lost manhood: 'I am still at *Jim* ... I am old and sick and in debt – but lately I've found I can still write – *it* comes! *it* comes! – and I am young and healthy and rich.'[60] The writer is hero, man of action, or he is nothing. It probably begins with his first letter to Cunninghame Graham. The letters to Galsworthy and Garnett and Pinker are self-pitying and literary: the first letter to Graham dramatises the self as adventurer, a self-image which was to become steadily more robust and confident as the friendship with Graham developed (5 August 1897):

[57] Joseph Conrad, *Letters to Blackwood and Meldrum*, pp.155-6.

[58] *A Personal Record*, p.98.

[59] Joseph Conrad, 'Henry James: An Appreciation', *Notes on Life and Letters* (1905), p.13.

[60] 26 March 1900, to Edward Garnett: Edward Garnett (ed.), *Letters from Conrad*, p.169.

'Most of my life has been spent between sky and water and now I live so alone that often I fancy myself clinging stupidly to a derelict planet abandoned by its precious crew. Your voice is not a voice in the wilderness – it seems to come through the clear emptiness of space. If – under the circumstances – I hail back lustily I know you won't count it to me for a crime.'[61] Conrad, the solitary commander of the shipwrecked earth, finds one other living creature in a universe which he had thought uninhabited. And reacts 'lustily': with a young man's athletic strength, with toughness, with the strenuous qualities of the hero as a man of action, though the 'action', for this hero, is thought, invention and the toil of writing.

[61] *Letters to Graham*, p.46.

Chapter Three: Ford Madox Ford

1. Ford's myth of himself

At the end of the Edwardian decade Ford wrote of himself: 'I am a troublesome solitary nature without the least desire for companionship of any kind.'[1]

This letter was written in the aftermath of Ford's troubles over *The English Review*, when he may well have been feeling the need to isolate himself and lick his wounds. But the evidence of his autobiographical writings is that he was in fact a man who longed for, and thrived on, society, who enjoyed being 'in the swim' and looked back enviously at the solidarity and human community enjoyed by the Pre-Raphaelites among whom he had spent his childhood.

In *Ancient Lights: And Certain New Reflections* (1911) (the title itself suggests a contrast between Burne-Jones's stained glass and a modern mirror) he recalls the mutual delight and sustaining energies of the Brotherhood: 'The characteristic ... of all these men was their warm-heartedness, their enmity for the formal, for the frigid, for the ungenerous' (p.16).

In his present loneliness he envies them this solidarity: 'It is one of the saddening things in Anglo-Saxon life that any sort of union for an aesthetic or for an intellectual purpose seems to be almost an impossibility. Anglo-Saxon writers as a rule sit in the British Isles each on his little hill surrounded each by his satellites, moodily jealous of the fame of each of his rivals, incapable of realising that the strength of several men together is very much stronger than the combined strengths of the same number of men acting apart' (p.23). This reflects his own sense that he had been personally betrayed by Conrad and Wells (and everybody else) over *The English Review*, of which Conrad and Wells had been virtually co-founders with him. And reflects also the current difficulties of his relationship with Conrad.

Ford envies his grandfather, Ford Madox Brown, the exciting and sometimes explosive friendships with Morris, Holman Hunt, Swinburne and the Rossettis, and the extraordinary cohesiveness of their group. It is to him a

[1] To R.A. Scott-James, 10 January 1910, in Richard M. Ludwig (ed.) *Letters of Ford Madox Ford* (1965), p.40.

'mystery' how 'in the 'seventies and 'eighties such an inordinate number of poets managed to live in the gloom of central London' (p.34). The Pre-Raphaelites created an art characterised at once by its 'clearness' and its relevance to the situation in which they lived: 'I suppose they sang of Launcelot and Guinevere to take their minds off their surroundings' (p.34).

He discusses both sides of this paradox without necessarily drawing attention to (or noticing?) its paradoxical nature. Holman Hunt's religious paintings were 'blasphemous' because his portrait of Christ as a young Jew, in 'the Light of the World', was 'offensively realistic' (p.214). Ford Madox Brown's young labourers in 'Work' are heroic realism, the discovery that humble human material lying under one's hand and visible every day can be transformed into art. But while admiring them for being modern and 'realists' he also and equally admires them for the quality of anachronism in their lives: 'They seemed to date from the Regency, and to have skipped altogether the baneful influence of early Victorianism and of the commerciality that the Prince Consort spread through England' (p.17).

When one reflects that Lawrence, Pound and Wyndham Lewis were all published in his *The English Review* it seems extraordinary that Ford should regard the modern age as one of stagnation contrasted with the Pre-Raphaelites' fruitful upheaval. But by this stage of *Ancient Lights* he has evolved a formula: the Pre-Raphaelites were so good that their influence has lasted and become a form of tyranny. Their legacy to the present is 'the dreary shibboleth that literature must be written by those who have read the *Cuchullain Saga* [sic] or something dull and pompous' (p.249). And they have imposed on Edwardian literature the notion that good art is minority art whereas 'great literature is and always has been popular' (p.249).

At the same time social and economic conditions have altered, so that the Victorian writer who could command social respect – the status of a 'gentleman' which meant so much to Ford and which echoes like a paranoid refrain through all his work – has given way to a situation in which 'a writer has in England no social position; an officer in the Guards is at the top of the tree' (p.243).

The conditions of the market, Ford also complains, work against writers. Whereas in the halcyon days of the Bodley Head in the 1890s a writer had some standing and could control the length and shape of his work he now had to accept browbeating from publishers and editors.

As a statement about the Edwardian literary situation this is plainly not true. On the contrary, it was possible for a penniless writer to carve out for himself an almost unprecedented degree of wealth, prestige and artistic independence: one has only to think of the careers of Kipling, Wells, Bennett and Shaw. As an autobiographical comment, though, it has its own depressing truth. The flattery and recognition that Ford had enjoyed as a precocious young writer in the 1890s have given way to a world in which he feels *declassé* and snubbed. Like Gissing in *New Grub Street* he externalises the pain and makes it universal: 'I suppose that never before was the financial struggle among the literary classes so bitter and so ignoble' (p.158).

When the serialisation of *Tono-Bungay* in *The English Review* was being advertised, Wells complained to Ford that it was wrongly described as autobiographical: Ford soothingly wrote back: '*I* have never written a book that has not by someone or other been called autobiography.'[2] The charge was usually just: all Ford's non-fictional works tend to be fictions presenting a flatteringly idealised self-portrait as their central dramatic figure.

Ford presents an interesting contrast with Shaw in this respect. Shy, inhibited Shaw created an aggressive, dominant figure known as G.B.S.: emotional, selfish and quarrelsome Ford created a series of fictional and non-fictional self-portraits whose leading characteristics are heroic altruism and gentlemanly self-possession. Wells rudely describes him as 'a long blond with a drawling manner': 'What he is really or if he is really, nobody knows now and he least of all; he has become a great system of assumed personalities and dramatised selves. His brain is an exceptionally good one and when first he came along, he had cast himself for the role of a very gifted scion of the Pre-Raphaelite stem, given over to artistic purpose and a little undecided between music, poetry, criticism, The Novel, Thoreau-istic horticulture and the simple appreciation of life.'[3]

Ancient Lights is not so much a history as an autobiographical novel giving a fictional retrospect of the Edwardian period. It bears comparison with *The Fifth Queen* trilogy: the Pre-Raphaelites, upholders of the true faith (as Katharine Howard is an upholder of Catholicism in the trilogy) are the old order looking back to a civilisation which is even older: in *Ancient Lights* the freedom of the Regency, in *The Fifth Queen* the generosity and benign tyranny of late medieval monasticism.

Cromwell, founder of the modern secular state in *The Fifth Queen*, has his equivalent in the representative modern, managerial Edwardian in *Ancient Lights*: perhaps Pinker, Ford's agent, whom Ford despised because he was Jewish and not a gentleman, and who takes on the status of a hate-figure in Ford's letters. To be sure the Pre-Raphaelite world to which he looks back nostalgically was also a 'hothouse' which Ford felt had been bad for him, but its training left him with the conviction that the writer's role had 'something of the priestly' (p.95), that the secular world was not enough.

As an autobiographical novel contrasting the Victorian and modern literary situations *Ancient Lights* is a complete success. Chapter 11 gives a symbolic tableau bringing this into focus. Ford Madox Brown, Ford's grandfather, has half finished a painting, filling the canvas as far as the 'crux'

---

[2] Letter to H.G. Wells, 20 November 1908, *Letters*, p.28.
[3] H.G. Wells, *Experiment in Autobiography*, vol.2 (1934), p.617.

of his own name, the 'x' of Madox, in his signature. Then the old man dies.

The chapter ends with a paragraph giving the contents of Madox Brown's room as he sits by the fire with William Rossetti, Ford as a child present as an onlooker. Dark leather panelling, green doors, an old man's clutter on a table are left suspended in the final paragraph and the next chapter opens with an account of the excitement of the 1890s: the new literature that exploded into being as the Pre-Raphaelites receded. Kipling 'burst upon the world with a shower of stars' (p.277); Wells, Anthony Hope, J.M. Barrie, Olive Schreiner and others were founding their reputations.

Historically, Ford's scenario is that the stir of the 1890s was a precocious growth destroyed by the Wilde debâcle. The Bodley Head folds, Dr Garnett stands on the steps of the British Museum announcing that the imprisonment of Wilde marks the end of English poetry, the aspirations of the aesthetic movement give way to an atmosphere of triumphant philistinism in which the purist who wishes to 'express his own thoughts in the language of his own time' (p.52) is condemned to write only for the future: 'I desire immensely to be influential, expensive and all the rest of it. But still I go on writing for posterity. It is, I presume, in the blood, in the training' (pp.191-2).

Ford's myth of himself included the notions that he was an obstinate, loyal Tory and the exemplary 'stylist' of his day. Both self-images were thrown into flattering relief by the collaboration with Conrad in the first years of the century. In his memoir of Conrad he sees Conrad and himself as literary guerillas out to coordinate a 'conspiracy against a sleeping world': 'the world certainly did not want us; not at that date; and to be reputed the finest English stylist was enough, nearly, to get you sent to gaol' (*Joseph Conrad*, 1924, p.38).

That phrase about the stylist is sadly typical of the mixture of crowing and whining that characterises Ford's later works. As a book about Conrad the memoir is very much flawed, and indeed Ford withdraws its claims to be objective truth and speaks of it as a work of fiction: a 'novel exactly on the lines that Conrad and the writer evolved' (p.125). But two features of Ford's Conrad stick out from his book as persuasively real.

There is the paradox of Conrad's political convictions: socially Conrad saw himself as 'an English country gentleman of the time of Lord Palmerston' (p.57) and his political attitudes were those of the 'politician of the impasse' (p.48): 'If Conrad were the eternal loyalist, nevertheless the unimaginative and cruel stupidity of Crown and Government officials were an essential part of his creed' (pp.47-8).

Secondly there is the paradoxical nature of the relationship between the two men. Ford needed friends and was closer to Conrad during the years of their collaboration than he had been to anyone in his young life. Yet he can say of Conrad that he never knew what Conrad's feelings were. No doubt this reflects his sense of personal betrayal after they had quarrelled, but it also embodies an ideal of English social behaviour often voiced by Ford: 'i. I do not enquire into my neighbour's psychology; ii. I do not know my neighbour's opinions; iii. I give him credit for having such opinions as my own; iv. I tolerate myself; v. I tolerate him. And so, in these fortunate islands we all live very comfortably together' (*The Spirit of the People*, 1907, p.28).

One can believe, then, that the stodgy and unemotional quality that he perceives in his relationship with Conrad, 'two English gentlemen ... in a club' (*Joseph Conrad*, p.121), is something that Ford valued and admired. But at the same time he obviously wishes that he and Conrad had been able to express their emotions to each other: 'It is that that makes life the queer, solitary thing that it is. You may live with another for years and years in a condition of the closest daily intimacy and never know what, at the bottom of the heart, goes on in your companion' (p.123).

Ford personally had an intense irritable vanity: the opposite of the self-possessed, blandly assured image that he liked to cultivate. He found it difficult to relate to people, as his memoir of Conrad shows, and difficult, one may note in passing, to deal with emotions in any of his novels before *The Good Soldier*. This partly accounts for the failure of *A Call, The English Girl* and *Mr Apollo*.

In the long term this difficulty yielded an artistic gain. It seems likely that Ford sought to make up for his creative weakness by passionate attention, in the Edwardian period, to matters of technique. When at last he became 'unblocked' and was able to communicate his human experience in *The Good Soldier* and the Tietjens novels the combination of fully felt human experience and technical virtuosity resulted in major novels.

As a man, then, Ford can be seen as a mass of conflicting attitudes: Wells's 'system of assumed personalities and dramatised selves', a Tory anarchist, a clubbish townsman who loved Bohemian London where you 'may do very much what you like short of eating peas with a knife' (*The Soul of London*, 1905, p.117), but had tried self-sufficiency on the land for thirteen years, caught up by the fashion for 'idealising ... country life' started, in his view, by William Morris (*Ancient Lights*, p.230). A man who longed all his life for a peaceful relationship with a woman and failed to find it; who ostensibly admired objective and cool relationships with other men, and yet – unlike Conrad – was of an intensely affectionate sentimental disposition. From the pressure of these irreconcilable drives in himself the devotion to literary technique offered a refuge and consolation.

Return to Yesterday: Reminiscences, 1894-1914 (1931) is the fullest of Ford's memoirs, and although his recollection of the Conrad collaboration has become embroidered ('there never was a quarrel' he says, blandly (p.190)) it and Ford's memoir of Conrad taken together are interesting on the kind of novel that he and Conrad were working for.

2. The collaboration with Conrad

Conrad and Ford collaborated between 1898 and 1903, and the collaboration produced *The Inheritors* (1901), *Romance* (1903) and *The Nature of a Crime* (1924), which was first published under a comic pseudonym in *The English Review* (edited by Ford) in 1909. The Conrad-Ford collaboration has been well documented by Frederick Karl, Arthur Mizener and R.J. Andreach.[4]

The personal relationship between the two suffered strains in 1909-10, when *The English Review* was in a financial mess through Ford's mismanagement and Ford was in marital difficulties as well. Conrad had a good deal of sympathy and liking for Elsie Martindale, Ford's wife. Ford tried, in vain, to persuade Elsie to divorce him so that he could marry his mistress, Violet Hunt (who later left him and became the model for Sylvia Tietjens; one of the best bitches in English literature). Ford made ill-advised attempts to enlist Conrad's support against Elsie. They engaged in a bad-tempered exchange of letters creating a breach from which the relationship never recovered.

Yet throughout his life (as Karl's biography stresses) Conrad seems to have needed men friends: Ford, then Arthur Marwood, then Richard Curle, and in their early years it seems likely that Ford was Conrad's conception of the writer as hero: well-connected, 'one of us', talented, generous (for Ford *was* generous, with his time, his money and his house, to the Conrads), and with the highest possible conception of his art.

In *Return to Yesterday* he takes further his account of the Conrad collaboration. They saw themselves as radical innovators who took as their starting point the view that the idea of the novel as a work of art did not exist in England: it had 'only existed since 1850, and in the France of Flaubert alone, at that' (p.208). Their – or rather Ford's – notion of the art of the novel included impressionism (characters and events presented in the way in which they are presented to the consciousness in life) and an almost classical sense of the unities: 'I think we both started out with at least this much of a New Form in our heads: we considered a novel to be the rendering of an Affair ... of one embroilment, one set of embarrassments, one human coil, one psychological progression. From this the novel got its Unity. No doubt it might have its caesura ..., markings of time when the treatment called for them. But the whole novel was to be an exhaustion of aspects, was to proceed to one culmination, to reveal once and for all, in the last sentence, or the penultimate, ... the psychological significance of the whole' (pp.209-10). He recognises that Henry James has already achieved this 'miracle' in his own work while he and Conrad were groping towards it, but insists on the

[4] See Bibliography.

differences between their work and James's. 'For, in the end, Conrad and I found salvation not in any machined Form, but in the sheer attempt to reproduce in words life as it presents itself to the intelligent observer' (p.210).

Part of the mutual attraction between Ford and Conrad must have been the difficult temperamental qualities which finally contributed to their breach: anxiety, fits of despair, arrogance and obsequiousness by turns. Also, the collaboration seems to have met a need in each man to deny responsibility for his own work. They both felt that a 'third person', a hypothetical author arising out of, but distinct from, their own linked identities, had taken over the writing of *Romance* (*Joseph Conrad*, p.45). Ford willingly renounced *The Inheritors*, which was almost all his (apart from the last twenty pages) and allowed it to be published over Conrad's name alone in Conrad's collected works.

In *Return to Yesterday* Ford says that he had learnt from the collaboration on *Romance* 'the great part of what I know of the technical side of writing' (p.192). But the elements of this technique, the 'progression d'effet', the 'impressionist' handling of characterisation and dialogue, the 'unity' given by a single 'embroilment' did not help him to produce real novels until he came to write *The Good Soldier* and the Tietjens novels. And even *The Good Soldier* is disliked by some for having too much virtuosity and too little substance, for being all angles and glare.

Ford's work in the Edwardian period is characterised by a high degree of anxiety, a need to make himself acceptable to a readership which was willing to read Wells and Henry James and to a lesser extent Conrad but somehow wouldn't read Ford. In *Mr Apollo* and *The Inheritors* he is blatantly seeking to appeal to the market for prophecy and scientific romance that Wells had opened up. In *The Benefactor* and *The English Girl* he is very obviously imitating James and creating would-be prestigious novels about the Henry James civilisation as he, Ford, saw it: 'A Leisured Society that is fairly unavailing, materialist, emasculated – and doomed' (*Return to Yesterday*, p.216). And in *Romance*, the collaboration with Conrad which was Ford's idea and largely his work, he was trying for the biggest market of all, the popular market for stories about men of action in exotic settings.

Romance has to be one of the dullest adventure stories in literature. Only Ford could have made a novel about pirates as mannered, static and tortuous as this book.

The collaborators' desire to get in all their technical effects holds up the action at every turn, and if *Romance* demonstrates anything beyond the unwisdom of literary collaboration it is Ford's unfitness for writing novels about men of action: he is a novelist of passivity, urban consciousness and modern sexual suffering.

John Kemp in *Romance* is a notably passive hero: 'It was, I suppose, what I demanded of Fate – to be gently wafted into the position of a hero of romance, without rough hands at my throat' (p.30). This passivity is part of a recognisable tradition which includes Scott's Waverley, Stevenson's Jim Hawkins, John Buchan's Davie Crawfurd, and in Kemp's case it is compounded by his figuratively erotic surrender to Don Carlos; Don Carlos is the (impossibly stagy) 'Byronic' consumptive who has adopted John Kemp as heir to his South American estate and husband designate of his cousin, Seraphina: 'I imagined him [Don Carlos] an aristocratic scapegoat, a corsair – it was the Byronic period then – sailing out to marry a sort of shimmering princess' (p.36). Carlos takes leave of Kemp, who has opted for the 'respectable' middle-class English commercial world instead of the world of romance (a decision which is in due course reversed by the novel's action):

> '"I shall come back for you – one day." He looked at me and smiled. It stirred unknown depths of emotion in me. I would have gone with him, then, had he asked me. "One day," he repeated, with an extraordinary cadence of tone.
>
> 'His hand was grasping mine; it thrilled me like a woman's; he stood shaking it very gently ... He leaned over and kissed me lightly on the cheek, then climbed away. I felt that the light of Romance was going out of my life' (p.51).

Moments like this, where the novel seems about to break away from its dramatic stereotypes, are regrettably few. There are also few moments of significant action, although these, when they come, can be effective: as for example the stabbing of the villain, O'Brien, in a Jamaican prison: 'O'Brien's lips were pressed tightly together, the handle of the knife was against his ear ... As he lowered [his right arm] the blood spurted from his shoulder as if from a burst stand-pipe, only black and warm' (p.451).

When he does engage in action himself Kemp is helplessly gentlemanly, anticipating Ford's noble altruists, Moffat in *The Benefactor*, the idealised fictional self-portraits in the autobiographies, Tietjens of the tetralogy, Dowell of *The Good Soldier*. He spares the lives of his enemies in circumstances which strain one's sense of probability to breaking-point; he controls his sexual feeling for Seraphina with a decorum which is unintentionally comic. Seraphina is in any case a barely sketched outline of a character, a bundle of conventional idealised female attributes: but when the time comes this cardboard figure has to take the initiative and virtually force Kemp into her embrace.

Also, despite the 'unity' which Ford claimed for it *Romance* is a disjointed work. It has jerky, awkward transitions, odd repetitions, abrupt changes of tone and inadequately prepared surprises. Castro, Don Carlos's ape-like follower, becomes an old man with bewildering speed and undergoes uncertainly grasped changes of motivation in the long scene in which, with

LIBRARY

OKALOOSA-WALTON JUNIOR COLLEGE

John Kemp and Seraphina, he is being starved out of a cave by the villainous Manuel and the *Lugarenos*.

Using John Kemp as first-person narrator adds to the novel's difficulties. As well as being unintentionally spineless Kemp is required by the method to be implausibly stupid: he is a limited narrator from whom key facts have to remain hidden long after they have become rather obvious to the reader. For example, part of Don Carlos's attraction to Kemp is that he, Carlos, is in love – in a distant and theoretical way – with Kemp's sister Veronica. This not very significant secret is known to the alert reader with the first few scenes of the novel. In short, a fundamental requirement of the device of the limited narrator has been violated. The reader is not kept guessing, and the narrator's ignorance becomes irritatingly pointless.

It is hard to see what was learned or gained by Ford from the writing of *Romance*. The success of the *Fifth Queen* trilogy depends on quite different methods. *The Fifth Queen* has the virtues of an outstandingly good wax-work display. Aptly chosen tableaux illustrating significant historical events are presented in exhaustively elaborate settings; like the Chamber of Horrors the novels are honourably painstaking reconstructions of the circumstances surrounding cruelty.

It is probable, though, that *Conrad* learnt quite a lot from the work on *Romance*. *Romance* lies in the background of all the work that Conrad was doing between 1898 and 1903, the years of *Heart of Darkness, Lord Jim* and *Nostromo*. Carlos and Castro helping Kemp to escape from the charge of having aided Kentish pirates against the excise men could well be a rehearsal for the escape of Decoud and Nostromo (and the unwilling Hirsch) across the Golfo Placido with the lighter loaded with silver in *Nostromo*. The 'Capataz' Manuel, the villainous leader of the *Lugarenos* (the pirates of Rio Medio, Don Carlos's hereditary home) is a fiendish equivalent of the other Capataz in *Nostromo*. And the topography of Rio Medio, the contrast between its decayed aristocratic population 'leading a cloistered existence in the ruins of old splendour' and the violent *Lugarenos*, the 'thievish rabble' who live down by the waterfront (*Romance*, p.153) could well be a version of Costaguana. O'Brien, the evil Irish lawyer who intrigues his way into the Carlos household and competes with Kemp for the love of Seraphina is similar, in his villainous moral blackness, to Conrad's 'flat' villains, Gentleman Brown, Mr Jones and Scevola in *The Rover*. And Don Carlos's feeling for England may be compared with Natalie Haldin's hopeless envy of English security in *Under Western Eyes*.

Don Carlos turns the title of *Romance* inside-out. He uses the word to describe England's safety, while Kemp uses it to describe South American danger and glamour. In his dying speech Carlos uses this contrast as part of his attempt to persuade Kemp to marry Seraphina:

'"English things last forever – English peace, English power, English fidelity. It is a country of much serenity, of order, of stable affection" ... He had on him the glamour of things English ... of England stable and undismayed, like a strong man who has kept his feet in the tottering of secular edifices shaken to their foundations by an earthquake ... It was as if for him that were something fine, something romantic, just as for me romance had always seemed to be embodied in his features, in his glance, and to live in the air he breathed' (pp.150-1).

'Romance', here, has lost its sense of 'adventure' and has become instead synonymous with 'nostalgia': the wish to perpetuate the mythical England celebrated by the rural fantasies and patriotic lyrics of the Edwardian decade.

3. The man of letters

The founding of *The English Review* is an event of major importance in Edwardian literature and gave evidence of the extraordinary ability of Ford as a literary editor. It also gave an outlet to his judgments as a critic of contemporary literature and the literary situation. In the editorials of *The English Review* (collected with some revisions in *The Critical Attitude* (1911)), Ford reveals himself as a pungent and far-sighted commentator.

Kipling 'once ... wrote the best short stories that are to be found in English literature, but now, alas! *il pontifie*' (p.4). Wells's scientific romances, especially *The Invisible Man* and 'The Man who could work Miracles', are his best work because when he wrote them he was 'at his ease and comparatively serene' (p.101). But the noisy Edwardian Wells, the Wells of the utopian writings and political novels is 'a poet fascinated by the aspects, borne away by the emotions of the moment' (p.102). This Wells has become in a sense a romantic, clinging to 'old illusions, old chivalries and old heroisms' (p.104), writing 'without the help of any aesthetic laws, trusting to his personality alone ... He trusts to his personality, he revels in it. And, as each new thing interests him, he makes a book of it' (p.103). He is 'so much an enthusiast of the moment' that his books 'have the appearance of being driven along before the winds of brain-storms' (p.104).

Ford's account of Wells seems woundingly accurate. He responds with more favour to Bennett whom he sees, with justice, as a scrupulous realist working from French models as carefully as Conrad or George Moore (or Ford himself). Although his subjects, drawn from the displaced or lower-middle class milieux, are similar to Wells's, he is 'more composed' because 'more than Mr Wells he represents that side of modern life which has left romanticism behind' (p.104).

In Ford's overview of the literary history of the period Conrad, James and George Moore are upheld as the writers who withstand the modern pressures. They are the only writers whom 'we may regard as being wholly concerned with their Art, as belonging to the School which represents the main-stream of the current of European Literature, and as having no external considerations for anything but their individual presentation of life' (p.88). In a passage which I will quote from its original state in *The English Review* because it is abridged in *The Critical Attitude* he upholds Henry James as the aesthetic monitor of the period:

> 'What we so very much need today is a picture of the life we live. It is only the imaginative writer who can supply this ... In England, the country of Accepted Ideas, the novelist who is intent merely to register – to *constater* – is almost unknown. Yet it is England probably that most needs him, for England, less than any of the nations, knows where it stands, or to what it tends. Flaubert said that had the French really read his "Education Sentimentale" France would have avoided the horrors of the *Debâcle*. Mr James might say as much for his own country and for the country he has so much benefited by making it his own' (*The English Review* I, December 1908, p.160).

The founding of *The English Review* was not a modest act. It was seen by Ford as a major patriotic undertaking designed to give English intellectual life an identity which would in turn sharpen its sense of its national life. Ford's concern with the cultural health of England is as active as Matthew Arnold's (or Leavis's or Richard Hoggart's). In the letters that he wrote when the *Review* was failing he remained loyal to his original vision: 'The only motive that Marwood [Arthur Marwood, the friend of Conrad and Ford who put up much of the money to found the periodical] and I had for spending our money was the desire to establish an organ in which the better sort of work might see the light.'[5] His declared motives were to promote good work and set out the reasons why it is good: 'The chief value of the arts to the State is that they are concerned with Truth ... The life we live today renders us dependent on the arts for our knowledge of life in a degree that probably never before obtained' (*The Critical Attitude*, pp.26-7).

Writing retrospectively, Ford sees *The English Review* as a form of national rearmament against the threat of world war: 'Only from the arts can any safety for the future of the State be found' (p.29). The *Review* sought to bring together and present the work of a 'sober, sincere, conscientious, and scientific body of artists, crystallising, as it were, modern life in its several aspects ... It

[5] To Wells, at the height of their quarrel, 2 April 1910: *Letters of Ford Madox Ford*, p.43.

was for this definite and unashamed purpose that the English Review was begun' (p.29).

His personal control of *The English Review* lasted only a year, December 1908 to December 1909, but the *Review* continued to publish contributions accepted under Ford's editorship – such as Lawrence's 'Odour of Chrysanthemums' – until 1911. Ford's editorials for 1908-9, taken together, are a major document for the temperament of the period. The first editorial of the series throws down the nature of the challenge that the periodical is to present by treating the publication of Henry James's collected works in the New York edition as *the* major historical event of the year, overshadowing the imperial competition between England and Germany: 'The appearance of this great body of imaginative effort must be regarded as an event at least as important in the history of a civilisation as the recording of the will of a sovereign people with regard to some policy of exclusion, or admission, or humanitarianism, or pugnacity.[6] He sums up James's virtues as veracity, intellectual provocativeness and detachment: he presents 'a picture of the life we live', he has an ability to 'awaken thought', and an objectivity which keeps the author's personality hidden: 'Whatever the private views may be, we have no means of knowing them' (p.160).

The next three editorials continue the theme of 'The Functions of the Arts in the Republic'. On contemporary drama he writes (rather absurdly) that naturalism is impossible in London because the theatres are too big for the acting to get across: hence Shaw's 'operatic' writing and Barrie's sentimentality. These writers aside, there is more intellectual content in the average Music Hall turn than in the West End production (Editorial, *English Review* II, January 1909, p.320). In April 1909 he opposes Asquith's moves to expand the navy: '*The English Review* stands for peace ... it is only in times of peace that the arts flourish' (Editorial, *English Review*, April 1909, p.137).

It is sad that this figure who seems so confident (if occasionally wrong-headed) a critic should have written such feeble novels (apart from *The Fifth Queen*) in the Edwardian decade. *The Benefactor: A Tale of a Small Circle* (1905) is perhaps the worst, mannered and inert and blatantly self-congratulatory. George Moffat, whose relationship with his father ('a famous painter') is a sweetened version of Ford's with his grandfather Ford Madox Brown, is the benefactor of the title. In one of his memoirs Ford quotes Madox Brown's 'rule of life' which he, Ford, tried to follow: 'Never refuse a lame dog over a stile. Never lend money; always give it ... Beggar yourself rather than refuse assistance to anyone whose genius you think shows promise of being greater than your own' (*Ancient Lights*, pp.197-8).

The 'small circle' of the sub-title is, transparently, the literary group to

---

[6] Editorial, 'The Function of the Arts in the Republic', *The English Review* 1 (December 1908), p.159.

which Ford felt himself to belong, and from which he thought himself unjustly excluded after his various quarrels. In the novel all the geniuses discovered by George Moffat become alienated and ungrateful the moment they taste success: 'Seeing always, clearly enough, the end and aims of others; never having had any very conscious aim of his own, he had always been content to step out of the way, and to supply the immense incentive of applause. It was as if, recognising very fully the futility of human strivings, he were content himself to strive not at all' (*The Benefactor*, pp.214-15). As a novel it is hopeless; as an essay about the way in which Ford saw himself it is rather interesting.

Mr Apollo (1908) has been described by John A. Meixner as a unique production among Ford's works: a novel about *religion* and a defence, though not an impassioned one, of Catholicism.[7] *Mr Apollo* seems to me so feeble that it can't be said to defend anything. It sets out a series of utopian discourses loosely strung together round a central figure. The Wells fantasies on which it is obviously based, *The Wonderful Visit* and *The Sea Lady*, have primitive narrative virtues which are never lost. The reader remains interested in the basic devices: an angel which falls to earth and is unrecognised and strenuously resisted as a deformed human being, or a mermaid whose vigorously amoral attitude to pleasure upsets the middle-class society of a seaside resort. Ford's novel offers no such pleasures; it begins well and then peters out. The god Phoebus Apollo is arrested for loitering and gives his name as Phybus Poldo. After one good joke in which the policeman who has arrested him drops dead in the court-room, nothing whatever happens. It is true that the book makes vague gestures in the direction of the moral regeneration of modern London, but the defence of Catholicism detected in it by Meixner is not visible to me.

If *Mr Apollo* is a feeble imitation of Wells, *An English Girl* (1907) is an equally feeble imitation of James. Eleanor, the English girl of the title, becomes engaged to an enormously rich American, Don Collar Kellog. They move between English and American life-styles until, for obscure motives which have to do with a refined sense of decorum, as far as one can make out, the girl decides that the engagement must be broken off. The only flicker of interest in the novel comes at the end where 'Count Carlo', an Italian aristocrat whose name and spirit seem rather close to those of Don Carlos in *Romance*, rebukes Eleanor for her treatment of her lover. In so far as the book expresses any feelings at all they are misogynist. Carlo expresses a passionate solidarity with Don Collar Kellog, whom Eleanor has betrayed: 'You have stabbed my brother. May God forgive you' (p.300). For Carlo, in the closing pages of the novel, women are a purely destructive intrusion into masculine friendships: a point of view that the novel's shape does nothing to disturb.

[7] John A. Meixner, *Ford Madox Ford's Novels: A Critical Study* (1962), p.122.

4. The Fifth Queen

Given the deadliness of *The Inheritors, The Benefactor, The English Girl, Mr Apollo* and *The Call*, to read *The Fifth Queen* trilogy comes as a real surprise. It is an achievement of a quite different order. Difficult but rewarding, this long novel suggests that Ford, like Bennett, would command a much higher reputation among twentieth-century novelists if he had been content to publish only his best work. The difference is that Ford's bad novels are the novels of a talent that is locked in conflict with itself and can only produce abortions, angular, crippled and botched. Bennett's bad novels are the frankly trashy products of a commercial mind which knows what it is about.

The Fifth Queen covers a short space of dramatic time which in one sense is full of action. The action consists of the arrival of Anne of Cleves to marry Henry VIII and the consequent divorce; the fall of Cromwell engineered by his own former spy, Throckmorton; the marriage to the king of the Catholic Katharine Howard; and her own trial and execution for treason following charges of immorality brought against her by her uncle, the Duke of Norfolk, and Archbishop Cranmer.

Although death is constantly present in the novel, Katharine's own execution, which might have proved an irresistible temptation (to a minor writer) for a sensational closing scene, is not presented. Katharine is given a dignified closing speech in which she punishes Henry by forcing him to destroy her against his will, and the novel closes with a brief formal announcement of her execution, and the date.

It is a taxing novel, it assumes a certain amount of historical knowledge and a willingness to read slowly and to visualise elaborately. The scenes are set up like tableaux and, as Graham Greene has pointed out, are as carefully *lit* as a production in a theatre.[8] The impatient reader looking for action and sensation finds his own image in Sir Thomas Culpepper. In historical reality Culpepper was an elegant courtier but in this novel he is a passionate drunken oaf: a constant reminder to the reader that sensuality and passion are not enough.

The reader who may wish to object that Ford's Katharine is unlike what is known of the historical Katharine Howard will find himself rebuked by another figure, Throckmorton, the spy who loves Katharine but is unable (like the historian) to believe in her chastity. Ford had done a great deal of work on the period, both for his book on Holbein for the Popular Library of Art (*Hans Holbein the Younger: A Critical Monograph*, 1905) and for a biography of Henry VIII which was never published. There is no doubt that he is presenting his version of Katharine as history as well as fiction, and that he is offering a quite deliberate challenge to the received view of her.

[8] Graham Greene, Introduction to the *Bodley Head Ford Madox Ford*, vol.1 (1971), p.10.

Although they seem to encompass a great deal of action the three novels are really devoted to a single process, the preparation of Katharine for her martyrdom. The novels are full of elaborately placed proleptic images of Katharine's death. When she is first brought to court by Culpepper and sees the King for the first time, 'she raised her head [which will be cut off] and shrieked at the sight of him' (p.50). At the end of the first volume the conspiracies of Secretary Cromwell and of Gardiner, Bishop of Winchester, against her have been foiled and the King proposes marriage to her: 'She stretched out both her hands, being still upon her knees. Her fair face worked convulsively, her lips moved and her hood, falling away from her brows, showed her hair that had golden glints. "For pity sake let me go," she moaned. "For pity"' (p.321). The novel has already contained a remarkably effective prolepsis of Katharine's death in the dark house in the alley to which she is hurried by Throckmorton (this follows the scene in which she plays Persephone in a Masque at the Bishop of Winchester's Palace and charms the King with her beauty and talent): 'In the passage it was blacker than the mouth of hell, and her eyes still seemed to have in them the dazzle of light and triumph she had just left' (p.142).

The whole of Tudor London is a hell and a prison, with Cromwell as its presiding fiend. This physical hell in the alley is, paradoxically, a place of enlightenment. Throckmorton has brought Katharine to this lawless refuge of thieves and vagabonds because it is the one place where he can be sure there are no spies, and he works on her feelings (knowing that she is destined to be the King's next fancy) to enroll her in his own conspiracy against Cromwell. This is in fact the turning-point of the action of the first volume and from this moment, although she does not know it, Katharine is assured of victory over Cromwell.

The final victory, though, goes to the forces of darkness: the fiends that do, in truth, inhabit the pit. The first volume, *The Fifth Queen*, ends with Katharine's hood falling from her hair as though she is preparing to put her head on the block. The second, *Privy Seal* (Cromwell's official title) ends with a more explicit anticipation of her death.

Anne of Cleves has renounced her rights, Cromwell is defeated and it is clear that his life is forfeit: the King repeats his request that Katharine shall become Queen and she now has no sufficient reason to refuse him, despite her agonised misgivings. As she consents, 'the light of the candles threw their locked shadows along the wall and up the ceilings. Her head fell back, her eyes closed, so that she seemed to be dead and her listless hands were open in her skirts' (p.413). The proleptic image of a woman being executed has now been completed.

The conclusions to the first two novels are complementary, then, as are the big central set-pieces in the two books. The black cellar in which Throckmorton discloses his schemes to Katharine is balanced by the painted hall at Richmond in which Katharine visits Anne of Cleves: a place of light, clarity and stillness in contrast with the darkness, secrecy and noise of the thieves' alley:

> 'The Queen sat in her painted gallery at Richmond, and all around her her maids sewed and span. The gallery was long; along the panels that faced the windows were angels painted in red and blue and gold and in the three centre squares St George, whose face was the face of the King's Highness, in one issued from a yellow city upon a green plain; in one with a cherry-coloured lance slew a green dragon from whose mouth issued orange-coloured flames, and in one carried away, that he might woo her in a rose-coloured tower on a hillside, a princess in a black gown with hair painted of real gold' (p.365).

A Pre-Raphaelite tableau in which the Queen with her reputation for stillness and endurance forms the central figure:

> 'Her maids sewed; the spinning-wheels ate away the braided flax from the spindles, and the sunlight poured down through the high windows. She was a very fair woman then, and many that had seen her there sit had marvelled of the King's disfavour for her; but she was accounted wondrous still, sitting thus by the hour with the little hounds in the folds of her dress' (p.365)

Katharine comes and kneels at her feet to ask her whether she is willing that her marriage to the King should be dissolved; and, a separate but far more important point (for Katharine, who is a Catholic), whether the marriage has been consummated:

> 'The silence and the bright light of the sun swathed these two women's figures, so that Katharine seemed to hear the flutter against the window-glass of a brown butterfly that, having sheltered in the hall all winter, now sought to take a part in the new brightness of the world. Katharine kept her knees, her eyes upon the floor; the Queen, motionless and soft, let her eyes rest upon Katharine's hood ... The butterfly sought another window' (p.367).

Ford breaks this skilfully evoked stillness with a carefully selected, strategically economical movement:

> 'The Queen spoke at last.
> '"You seek my queenship" ...

'Katharine raised her eyes; they saw the imprisoned butterfly, but she found no words.

'"You have more courage than I," the Queen said.

'Suddenly she made a single gesture with her hands, as if she swept something from her lap: some invisible dust – and that was all' (p.367).

In terms of artistry this beautiful scene is the summit of the whole trilogy. Its qualities are sustained beyond Anne's gesture: she reveals herself as a lazy, comfort-loving, dirty woman who is clearly not a fit mate for the King at this juncture of his reign. It is what she reveals herself to be, rather than what she says, that hardens (and justifies dramatically) Katharine's decision to replace her. The image of the doomed butterfly underlines the fact that this sunlit gallery is as much a prison as all the other interiors in this novel. The butterfly is related to both queens: like Anne it is undistinguished (a *brown* butterfly), like Katharine it lives its own intense life and exerts a frail pathos. It is linked to the animal imagery that occurs throughout the trilogy with the persistence of the Jacobean dramatists (I am thinking particularly of Webster): the King's approach with the 'swish pad of his heavy soft shoes' is 'as if a bear were coming over the pavement' (p.45). Elsewhere he is 'hoggish' (p.486) and a 'beast that is stabbed to the heart' when he understands that Katharine's death is inevitable (p.585).

Gardiner, Bishop of Winchester, has 'snake's eyes under [his] flat cap' (p.31). The Duke of Norfolk is the King's 'dog whose nature it is to maul cats' (p.421), Lascelles is a fox, and Archbishop Cranmer is associated with a series of animals, the most striking of which is the snail that lives in his fireplace in Pontefract Castle: 'The soot of the chimney back was damp, and sparkled with the trail of a snail that had lived there undisturbed for many years, and neither increasing, because it had no mate, nor dying, because it was well fed by the ferns that, behind the present hangings, grew in the joints of the stones' (p.421).

The Fifth Queen has had a mixed critical history. Ford himself created confusion by speaking slightingly of it. In his memoir of Conrad he says that he knew that he himself would be unable to write mature work before the age of forty, and that earlier than that he 'disdainfully' wrote historical novels: 'A historical novel even at the best is nothing more than a *tour de force*, a fake more or less genuine in inspiration and workmanship, but none the less a fake' (*Joseph Conrad*, p.176).

Serious critics of Ford have worked to defend him from the effects of his own 'disdain'. *The Fifth Queen*'s characterisation has attracted sharply contrasted opinions: Katharine has been found 'rendered with an impressive complexity and subtlety and endowed with a rounded independent life',[9] and

---

[9] Meixner, p.53.

she has been found to be the fatal weakness of the whole enterprise: 'In the end his romantic need to turn her into an impossibly ideal figure makes her unconvincing, just as his romantic need to idealise the figures of his literary anecdotes so often carried them – for all his cleverness in managing them – beyond human possibility.'[10]

Katharine is like Browning's Pompilia in *The Ring and the Book*: a person whose moral rectitude and ascendancy increase rather than diminish as one gets to know her better. It is precisely the point of Ford's *historical* thesis that he wishes to press this fresh interpretation of her, to explore the possibility that she was a person of exalted intelligence and virtue whom history has smeared.

Personally I do not find the Katharine of the third volume, *The Fifth Queen Crowned*, 'impossibly ideal', although it is certainly true that she arrives by her own methods and experiences at an extreme and surprising moral position. Her 'confession' of adultery is a mixture of suicide and revenge. Suicide because she is indeed an idealist, and her vanity will not take the compromise status that Henry offers her (to live on as his separated wife and secret mistress): revenge in that she knows that her behaviour will work on him to inflict more pain than anything else could do: 'Never will I unsay [the formal 'confession' of adultery] ... for it is right that such a King as thou should be punished, and I do believe this: that there can come no agony upon you such as shall come if you do believe me false to you' (p.585).

This, then, is the last of Ford's surprises in his reworking of Katharine Howard. It was of her own deliberate will that she was recorded by posterity as an adulterer: it was part of her deliberate punishment of the King. Her rectitude and Henry's weak sensuality are not unlike the respective qualities of Leonora, who as an Irish Catholic is bound like Katharine by the 'Old Faith', and Edward Ashburnham in *The Good Soldier*. If we can believe in the personalities – as we obviously can – in that successful novel of Ford's maturity, then we can believe in Ford's Katharine Howard.

5. *Gallantry and* The Good Soldier

In his discussion of *The Good Soldier* Arthur Mizener sees the novel as part of the Edwardian response to 'the new affluence and the breakup of Victorian values.'[11] He sees the writers of the period dividing into those concerned with private experience (James and Conrad) and those concerned with public affairs (Wells and Shaw) and suggests that their work foreshadows 'the need for a form of fiction that would represent in a single image the public and private senses of reality and the exacerbating conflict between the two. Ford

[10] Arthur Mizener, *The Saddest Story*, p.475.
[11] Ibid., p.254.

was the first good writer to bring that conflict into sharp focus and to find a form for it.'[12]

In *The Good Soldier* Dowell sets out in a memorable image his notion of the scale of the tragedy that he is narrating: 'Some one has said that the death of a mouse from cancer is the whole sack of Rome by the Goths, and I swear to you that the breaking up of our little four-square coterie was such another unthinkable event' (p.17). In Part III of *Privy Seal*, titled 'The Sunburst' (the novel's image for the King) Culpepper is at Smithfield waiting to see the burning of Friar Forest for heresy when he is dragged away to court by a messenger from Cromwell. In his disappointment at missing the fun he makes himself a promise: 'This night I will hold a mouse on a chain above a coal fire. So I will see a burning' (*The Fifth Queen*, p.393).

If *The Good Soldier* is the first form which embraces public and private senses of reality, *The Fifth Queen* can be seen as its seed-bed. *The Good Soldier* compares the sack of Rome by the Goths to the scale of a drama of drawn-out sexual torture. *The Fifth Queen* sees the fate of England determined by the caprice of an unknowable old tyrant. The burning of a mouse and a friar are of equal importance. If Katharine had her way, of course, and the Old Faith were restored, the traditional moral horizons would be re-established. The duel between Katharine and Cromwell for possession of Henry VIII is reflected in the struggle between Leonora and Florence over the body of Ashburnham, presented in a series of stifling interiors by Dowell, the limited narrator.

It has taken Ford a long time to reach his maturity. This is partly because, as everyone observed, he was so many personalities coexisting: the English gentleman, the German aristocrat, the ninety-ish patron of the fine arts, the Jamesian explorer of 'affairs', the Conradian celebrator of male heroism.

The parallels between Edward Ashburnham and Henry are close: like Henry, Edward is hoggish, 'as obstinate as a hog' in his wish to build a chapel for Leonora (*The Good Soldier*, p.128). And being devoid, like Henry, of moral convictions, he is easily swayed by those whose convictions are strong: 'He was even hurt that Leonora's confessor did not make a strenuous effort to convert him. There was a period when he was quite ready to become an emotional Catholic' (p.129). He has a monarchical view of himself: he wishes to be a judge, father, benefactor and lord to his tenants instead of running his decayed estate as a business yielding an income.

Henry was a 'sun-burst', a 'red flare' in the distance: Edward and Leonora are 'fireships': 'two noble natures, drifting down life, like fireships afloat on a lagoon and causing miseries, heart-aches, agony of the mind and death' (p.146).

The climactic scene of the novel involves a recall of the historical context of

[12] Ibid.

The Fifth Queen, the convulsion of Europe caused by the Protestant
Reformation. Edward, Leonora and the Dowells are looking at the Protest
signed by Martin Bucer and Luther at the castle of 'M-', and Florence chooses
that moment to taunt Leonora about her Catholicism. The scene is based on a
visit by Ford and Violet Hunt in 1910 to see the Protest in Marburg castle:
Ford, who at that time saw himself as a German Catholic, was being teased by
Violet Hunt over his religion.[13]

Dowell, the limited narrator of *The Good Soldier*, is one of the best examples
of that technique that the English novel has to offer. (The framing narrators
in Conrad can often seem clumsy by comparison: in *Under Western Eyes*, for
instance, where the old language teacher is improbably and irritatingly
ubiquitous, and in *Chance* where the use of an outer narrator reporting
Marlow-reporting-Powell is needlessly cumbersome.) He has no suspicion of
the sexual liaison between his wife, Florence, and Edward Ashburnham,
though Leonora, Edward's wife, already knows everything: Florence's vanity
has driven her to flaunt her possession of Edward in front of his wife, and she
now dares to go further as they admire Luther's document:

Florence says to Edward:

' "There it is – the Protest ... Don't you know that is why we were all called
Protestants? ... It's because of that piece of paper that you're honest, sober,
industrious, provident and clean-lived. If it weren't for that piece of paper
you'd be like the Irish or the Italians or the Poles, but particularly the
Irish ..." And she laid one finger upon Captain Ashburnham's wrist' (p.48).
This is a fine and rightly admired passage, perhaps the most completely
satisfying episode in Ford's fiction.

The novel is 'Edwardian' in the sense that Mizener claims for it – its
particular relationship between private and public experience – and also in
its family resemblance to other Edwardian novels. It is Jamesian, obviously,
in subject matter and technique. An innocent American millionaire, Dowell,
whose money is unable to bring him happiness, presents the story of an
English gentleman enslaved by his appetites and decorously narrates a
situation which is essentially one of what James called 'horrors', ugly and
violent sexual drives. The human realities are fully known to Leonora,
Florence and Edward, and totally withheld from Dowell; who, nevertheless,
like James's Maisie in *What Maisie Knew*, is able from his innocent
observations to convey to the reader exactly what is going on.

Dowell has obvious affinities with Conrad's language teacher in *Under
Western Eyes*, and the novel's vicious sexuality has elements in common with
Chance (the governess, Mrs Fyne, Flora's father). It is also Conradian in many
small touches: Florence is a sexual imperialist, Ashburnham is her heart of
darkness: 'It was Florence clearing up one of the dark places of the earth,

[13] Ibid., p.203.

leaving the world a little lighter than she had found it. She would tell him the story of Hamlet; explain the form of a symphony, humming the first and second subjects to him, and so on' (p.45).

The way Dowell 'apologises' for the technique of the story is like the many apologies that Conrad's Marlow makes in *Heart of Darkness*, *Lord Jim* and *Chance*: 'I have stuck to my idea of being in a country cottage with a silent listener, hearing between the gusts of the wind and amidst the noises of the distant sea, the story as it comes ... I console myself with thinking that this is a real story and that, after all, real stories are probably told best in the way a person telling a story would tell them. They will then seem most real' (p.161). And there is a glancing reference to Wells's social Darwinism and Shaw's doctrine of the Life-Force in the fact that Leonora is the final victor and beneficiary of the plot's hideous entanglement: 'Edward was the normal man, but there was too much of the sentimentalist about him; and society does not need too many sentimentalists. Nancy·[Rufford, last of Edward's girls, who goes mad] was a splendid creature, but she had about her a touch of madness. Society does not need individuals with touches of madness about them. So Edward and Nancy found themselves steamrolled out and Leonora survives, the perfectly normal type' (p.205).

If *The Fifth Queen* trilogy may be seen as a seed-bed for *The Good Soldier*, *The Half Moon* bears the same kind of relationship to the Tietjens tetralogy. *The Half Moon* was planned as the first of a historical trilogy to be called *The Three Ships*; the other two novels were not written. The trilogy was to have been a sea-going historical cycle about seventeenth-century explorers; a sequel and complement to the land-based drama of Tudor intrigue in *The Fifth Queen*.

Like many of Ford's less successful novels *The Half Moon* (1909) has excellent moments. The description of the walled city of Rye, near which Ford lived for many years, and its silting up harbour is very successful, and there is a fine comic account of James I: it makes much of his uncouth Scottishness, his homosexuality and his disconcerting flashes of practicality and grasp of affairs. There is an entirely convincing characterisation of a sexually obsessed woman whose vanity is injured: Anne Jeal, determined to encompass the death of Edward Colman, a wool-merchant of Rye, because she fancies that he has slighted her.

But Edward Colman himself is transparently one of Ford's flattering self-portraits, 'sunny' and 'careless', gallant and courageous (p.94). And Ford wrecks his novel by deciding to have Anne Jeal destroy Edward Colman by witchcraft. The witchcraft would have worked moderately well in a short story about the supernatural, but mixed in with the realism of Edward's voyage across the Atlantic with Hudson the navigator it is ludicrous. Yet the witchcraft is a powerful metaphor of the malice of women, something Ford believed in and dramatises with chilling authority in the Tietjens novels.

The Tietjens books are both Ford's farewell to the Edwardian and his recognition of the realities of the modern. The Great War produced images of evil in the real world big and dark enough to match up to the profound intuition of evil always present in Ford's imagination.

6. *Tietjens and others: honest Edwardians*

The formulae used to express Anne Jeal's nature in *The Half Moon* became the underlying truths of the Tietjens novels. The white witch, Anne Jeal's enemy, warns Edward Colman to be on his guard against Anne: '"Women do not love; women's love is not like men's love. If a woman would have a man to love her she wounds him in play with gibes and little pouts and mockeries; but if he avoid and go in preference to another, then she will not tire till he be dead." What a woman asks is not, "Whom shall it profit?" but rather, "How may I find ease?"' (p.80). This is a fair paraphrase of the possessive hatred with which Sylvia pursues Tietjens. Sylvia is a woman driven by her own nature and Tietjens (with the novel) both hates and admires her for it.

In *Some Do Not* (1924) he recognises that the girl he loves, Valentine Wannop, and his wife Sylvia are 'the only two human beings he had met for years whom he could respect: the one for sheer efficiency in killing: the other for having the constructive desire and knowing how to set about it. Kill or cure! The two functions of man.' (p.161) Although Tietjens is yet another hero in Ford's own image, the novel succeeds in dramatising with detachment the qualities in him that make Sylvia hate him. Tietjens is unresponsive, loyal to his own sense of himself as a 'gentleman', and has an infuriating dignity. Sylvia's impulse is to destroy the dignity, break through the unresponsiveness and get at the man.

She throws a plate of food at him, missing him except for 'one, crouched, very green leaf ... on his shoulder strap' (p.197). She has an entirely persuasive outburst against his forgiving attitude and assumption of moral superiority: '"If ... you had once in our lives said to me: 'You whore! You bitch! You killed my mother. May you rot in hell for it' ... you might have done something to bring us together"' (p.216). And indeed, in addition to his obstinate 'gentlemanliness' there is a malicious side to Tietjens. He takes a self-lacerating satisfaction in his war-to-the-death with her, having convinced himself that it is an honourable war, like that which he (and Ford) believes England must fight against the French once the Germans have been defeated. Ford loved the Germans, his father's people, and saw the *French* as England's natural enemy.

Similarly, the witchcraft practised by Anne Jeal in *The Half Moon* enables her to feel close to her victim, Edward Colman, in the act of destroying him.

She holds out his wax image to the fire and as it melts 'she quivered and shook; it seemed to her that she held life – a human child, a baby – in the hand that she stretched to the coal and the logs' (p.223).

As Colman sickens from the effects of Anne's witchcraft, so Tietjens is aware of the injuries being done him by Sylvia's slanders, and the 'hatred coming to him in waves from the convent in which Sylvia had immersed herself' on the other side of the Channel, while he is fighting in France: 'He imagined Sylvia, coiled up on a convent bed ... Hating ... Her certainly glorious hair all round her ... Hating ... Slowly and coldly ... Like the head of a snake when you examined it ... Eyes motionless: mouth closed tight' (*No More Parades*, pp.67-8).

Although Sylvia is a fine extended characterisation of a bored woman who relieves her boredom by practising psychological torture, the Tietjens tetralogy is principally a study of Tietjens himself: the difficult, outspoken colleague who is too intelligent for his own good, the man who believes that 'all that was good in English literature ended with the seventeenth century' (p.100), whose appearance is too noble for common humanity. He is 'heavy; fixed. Not insolent, but simply gazing over the heads of all things and created beings, into a world too distant for them to enter' (p.118).

He perceives his own loyalty to truth and rectitude as a form of immaturity: '"I am really, sir, the English public schoolboy. That's an eighteenth-century product. What with the love of truth that – God help me! – they rammed into me at Clifton and the belief Arnold forced upon Rugby that the vilest of sins – the vilest of all sins – is to peach to the headmaster! That's me, sir. Other men get over their schooling. I never have. I remain adolescent"' (p.248).

This account of himself to General Campion is a valuable example of Tietjens' attempts to understand himself and of the distance that Ford is able to establish between Tietjens and the reader. Tietjens is the complete Edwardian hero, a man who has survived with obsolete values and an outmoded ideal of manhood into a ruthless, demoralised world. With this portrait Ford displays sustained and delicate self-knowledge. Tietjens is Ford's farewell, so to speak, to Edwardian Hueffer: wealth and privilege are over, there will be 'no more parades' (the title of the second of the Tietjens novels). The one positive, and it is a very much qualified positive, is the possibility that after the war there will be a new, simpler, post-apocalyptic world in which 'a man could stand up on a little hill' (*A Man Could Stand Up* is the title of the third volume). He hopes to live modestly with Valentine Wannop in a simpler, poorer, less arrogant world. Edwardian Hueffer, the over-ambitious man-about-town whose hopes crumbled with the failure of *The English Review*, the collapse of his marriage and the break-down of his relationship with Violet Hunt, has grown into Ford the novelist.

The difference between the detachment of the Tietjens books and the

anxious instability of Ford's earlier work is marked by the contrast between
A Call (1910) and the Tietjens novels. *A Call* turns on the improbable device
of a telephone call which causes madness. Dudley Leicester has married
Pauline Lucas: he then resumes an earlier sexual relationship with a woman
called Etta Stackpole, now Lady Hudson (presumably a rather wire-drawn
joke is at work here: Lady Hudson has the names of two of Henry James's
benign women, Henrietta Stackpole (from *The Portrait of a Lady*) and Mrs
Hudson (from *Roderick Hudson*) yet she behaves like one of the Jamesian
villainesses, Madame Merle or Christina Light). Leicester receives a
telephone call from an unknown man who knows his name: this causes an
acute nervous shock which can only be cured when his friend and counsellor
Robert Grimshaw reveals that it was he who made the telephone call.

Like the witchcraft in *The Half Moon*, the telephone call is poor material for
a novel but a good metaphor of psychological manipulation. The whole novel
deals in paranoia, the idea of 'things being said' behind one's back.
Grimshaw is a self-appointed secular priest whose mission is to punish sin
and 'torment the damned' as he puts it to Etta Stackpole. Towards the end of
the novel he engages in a significant conversation with a real (Greek
Orthodox) priest, to whom Grimshaw, being himself half Greek, unbares his
moral outlook. The priest deplores the timidity of the English, their social
caution, their reluctance to keep diaries or to enter 'entanglements' for fear of
what may be 'used against them' (p.221).

A much more thorough-going document of paranoia is *The Simple Life*
(1911): one of the satirical novels about Edwardian literary life that Ford
published under the pseudonym of Daniel Chaucer (the other is *The New
Humpty Dumpty*, 1912).

Being published pseudonymously gives these books a peculiar status
among Ford's works, as though he half wanted to disown them and at the
same time wanted the satisfaction of seeing his victims squirm. *The Simple Life*
is an unstructured and angry work, reading a little like Wyndham Lewis in a
venomous mood (as in his libellous novel *The Roaring Queen*). It could be
taken as expressing Ford's *private* feelings about his differences from Conrad.
In his 'official' accounts of Conrad Ford always takes care to be deferential.
In *The Simple Life*, by contrast, there is a richly vindictive portrait of Conrad
as 'Simon Bransdon': 'Simon Bransdon, whose real name was Simeon
Brandetski, was a possibly Polish, possibly Lithuanian, possibly Little
Russian Jew' (p.69).

In place of Conrad's career as a sailor Bransdon is given a ludicrous
'equivalent' career on land. He has worked on railways first as a tea maker,
then as a navvy, finally as a 'superintendent of plate layers' (Chief Officer?).
He has been building a new railway in British East Africa (a railway into the
Heart of Darkness?). Ford's spiteful point seems to be that ships and
railways are both merely forms of transport and that the glamour

surrounding Conrad the sailor is unearned.

A literary agent, 'Parmont' (Garnett), who enjoyed a certain ascendancy in the 1890s but is now *passé* – Ford must have enjoyed getting that in – suggests the pen-name Bransdon to Brandetski, and commissions Bransdon/Brandetski to write a book about his experiences in Africa 'on the other side of the Continent that it was then the custom to call "Dark"' (p.73). It would not take much ingenuity – the substitution of a C for the B – to see 'Bransdon' as a near-anagram of 'Conrad'.

The intellectual tendency of the day is towards socialism, but Brandetski/Bransdon is a conservative and imperialist who hates the blacks he works with on the railway: 'He said that the only thing for them was the whip' (p.71) (Conrad's attitude to Donkin?). In his memoir, *Joseph Conrad*, Ford hints that Conrad was incapable of getting on with his work without Ford's encouragement, self-sacrifice, willingness to write from Conrad's dictation, altruistic gift of plots and ideas, financial help. In this satire he goes much further: Bransdon/Brandetski is 'by inclination ... one of the laziest men that ever breathed ... He wanted to be in a hammock for ever and ever, and he was convinced that he led a dog's life' (p.73).

His conservatism is an aspect of his laziness. In Bloomsbury he has encountered advanced ideas but 'is too lazy to embrace them'. He grows a beard because he is 'too lazy to shave' (p.75). He becomes too lazy to write his own work so engages a secretary to whom he can dictate and then marries her 'to save trouble' (p.76): an unflattering view of Conrad's marriage to Jessie, who hated Ford from the outset.

Ford's feelings about Conrad must always have been double-edged: when they first met Conrad was older, poorer, foreign and in need of help but he soon became infuriatingly prestigious, attracting to himself exactly the kind of recognition that Ford regarded as his own due. It would be entirely reasonable to think that Ford hated Conrad by 1911 when this book was published.[14] But even more important than revenge was Ford's need to console his wounded ego.

In *The Simple Life* Ford gives himself yet another flattering self-portrait as Luscombe, a wealthy squire: 'A blonde, rather heavy man of perhaps thirty-five or a little more, he was dressed in a shooting-jacket, had a heavy jaw, a thick moustache and sagacious, rather dog-like eyes. He was a little slow in his actions and he had a pleasant smile which uncovered white and level teeth' (p.5).

Ford cannot resist making Luscombe a gentlemanly hero, the ideal undergraduate who 'pulled rather a good oar', and has a 'taste for the Latin Humaner letters' and 'a real passion for gardening' (p.10). The idle

[14] Ford often tried to accomplish some kind of reconciliation with Conrad – by such gestures as making Conrad his literary executor during the Great War and by being kind to Borys Conrad – but the friendship never fully recovered (see Mizener and Karl).

Bransdon is manoeuvred by one Gubb (Mizener (p.558) suggests that this is J.B. Pinker, the literary agent for both Ford and Conrad) to become a joint leader of – and philosopher to – a socialist rural community of the kind recommended by William Morris, Edward Carpenter and the Fabians. The situation is paradoxical: Bransdon is anti-socialist in all his views, and Gubb has the rapacious instincts of a conservative businessman. Gubb systematically exploits Luscombe's generosity until Luscombe rebels and refuses to support the Simple Lifers any further. This, for what it is worth, is the plot.

Based on such a small structure the novel is far too long, though it has some good comic moments. Bransdon rousing himself to work, despite his poor mental health: 'In two years he'd written no less than three short stories' (p.239). Bransdon's filthy cottage, the brick floor undermined by rats, nutshells and spilt honey everywhere, the sagging ceiling resting on the top of the loom on which Bransdon weaves (for reasons of economy, not 'socialism') his own and his family's clothes: probably recalling the confusion in which the Conrad family lived in Ford's cottage, the Pent (p.51).

An excellent article describing Ford as 'The honest Edwardian' makes the point that Edwardianism is 'a most inconclusive concept' and that the ellipses and aposiopeses characterising Ford's work reflect this inconclusiveness.[15] This article suggests that while Conrad's heroes are 'indifferent, apart, instruments of contemplation' destroyed by women, Ford's heroes are 'cases' in which Conrad's Apollonian objectivity has become a 'high Toryism' which is 'closer to sexual pathology than anything else' (p.81). Part of the case, though not a very major part, is that Ford's imagination is somewhat androgynous: Sylvia Tietjens is 'really a man', Valentine Wannop is a 'surrogate boy' (p.83). Ford lends support to this himself, of course, in his accounts of John Kemp's erotic response to Don Carlos, of the loyalties between men elsewhere in his work and the account of himself as a perpetual public-schoolboy. A perpetual social and emotional adolescence may be taken to characterise Ford the man and the novelist. The role of eternal immature idealist is an effective one to adopt in a period of contracting moral horizons and existential uncertainty.

Ford remarks about his habit of aposiopesis that *The Inheritors* was 'received with a paeon of abuse for the number of dots it contained ...' [*sic*] (*Joseph Conrad*, p.149). He defends this habit as a feature of his realism: English speech and behaviour *do* contain a lot of aposiopesis. Of the collaboration on *The Inheritors* he writes: 'We both desired to get into situations, at any rate when anyone was speaking, the sort of indefiniteness that is characteristic of all human conversations' (p.135). And all English

---

[15] Geoffrey Wagner, 'Ford Madox Ford: the honest Edwardian', *Essays in Criticism* 17 (1967), p.85.

conversations are fragmentary, consisting of 'allusions and unfinished sentences' (p.135).

The incomplete sentence goes with an incompleteness of moral outlook, the absence of clear moral imperatives in Edwardian life. In writing about Conrad, Ford reflects this void in his own way. He describes Conrad as a loyalist and a Papist: but he does so in a circular manner, so that what he is really saying in effect is that it was Conrad's habit to be loyal to loyalty. He writes that: 'out of the loyalty that is demanded of gentlemen we were both papists', but he has no real knowledge of Conrad's religious views except that, when out driving, he would 'turn back rather than meet two priests' (*Joseph Conrad*, p.123). His Conrad is a papist who hated priests, a 'Loyalist' to 'every regime that ever existed but passionately a Loyalist to Great Britain' (p.47), but at the same time an authoritarian who hated authority: 'The unimaginative and cruel stupidity of Crown and Government officials was an essential part of his creed. He was a politician – but a politician of the impasse' (pp.47-8).

One returns to Ford's *Joseph Conrad* because it is in some ways Ford's best *self*-portrait: in the course of his interplay with the personality of a man whom he has loved and quarrelled with he illuminates the contours of his own difficult nature, with his loyalty to loyalty, obstinate adherence to the identity of a 'gentleman', alienation from the contemporary world in all its aspects. All that is left is the figure of the writer himself: the writer emerges as the hero for Ford even more strongly than for Conrad. To fail in one's duty to squeeze 'the last drop of blood out of your subject when you are writing in a book' is 'the real crime against the Holy Ghost' (p.128).

In the later memoirs this notion that novel-writing is a religious act, or an act to be described in religious metaphor, is strengthened: in *Return to Yesterday* he writes that he owed to Conrad 'that strong faith – that in our day and hour the writing of novels is the only pursuit worth while for a proper man' (p.185). *The English Review* had given him a brief period of ascendancy, a time when he was a literary arbiter and leader, when he was not only in the swim but *was* the swim. Another brief period of such public influence was to come with *The Transatlantic Review* in the 1920s. For the rest of his life he saw himself as lonely, alienated, ignored: 'I may really say that for a quarter of a century I have kept before me one unflinching aim – to register my own times in terms of my own time, and still more to urge those who are better poets and better prose writers than myself to have the same aim. I suppose I have been pretty well ignored; I find no signs of my being taken seriously. It is certain that any conviction would gain immensely as soon as another soul could be found to share it.'[16]

---

[16] A deliberate quotation from the epigraph to *Lord Jim*, perhaps a reproach to Conrad for deserting him and leaving him isolated. (Ford Madox Hueffer, *Collected Poems* (1914), p.13.)

1. Joseph Conrad, 1911

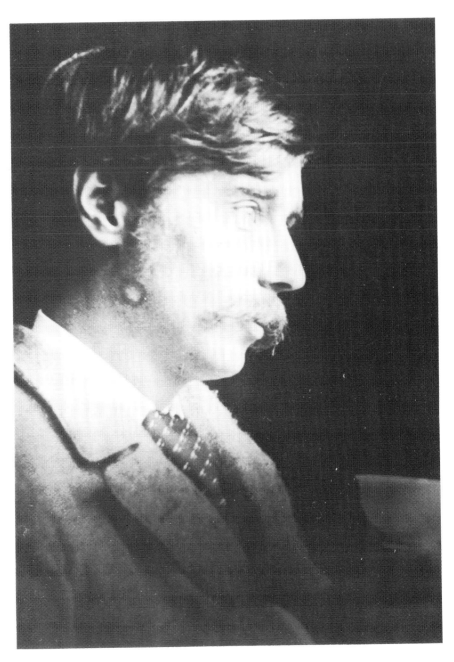

2. H.G. Wells, photographed by Jane Wells, *c.* 1900

3. H.G. Wells, *c.* 1912

4. Arnold Bennett, photographed by H.G. Wells at Sandgate, *c.* 1900

5. Arnold Bennett, *c*. 1929

6. Ford Madox Ford in uniform, *c.* 1915

7. John Galsworthy, 1911

8. E.M. Forster, *c.* 1913

Chapter Four: H.G. Wells

1. Wells the prophet and Tono-Bungay

The first decade of the twentieth century is inevitably identified with Wells. He had established himself in the last decade of the nineteenth century as a writer of scientific romances which have been convincingly characterised as decadent and *fin de siècle* in outlook.[1] The new century finds him moving out of fantasy into engagement with actual social conditions. If Wilde may be thought to have a symbolic relationship with the 1890s, Wells has a symbolic relationship with the Edwardian period. He was radically (at times, one may think, naively) excited by the *newness* of the new century. He greeted the emergence of a new kind of mind, the 'legislative' rather than the 'submissive', which 'thinks constantly, and by preference, of things to come, and of present things mainly in relation to the results that must arise from them' (*The Discovery of the Future* (1902), p.8).

It is as though history, as it turned the corner from the nineteenth to the twentieth century, released a new kind of man with a new kind of outlook. The representative, the exemplar, of this new kind of man is of course Wells himself. In *Anticipations* (1902) he does his first piece of extended 'legislation' for the future, a 'sincerely intended forecast of the way things will probably go in this century' (p.1). London of 2,000 AD will have 'suburb' (something Wells admires) extending to the 'south of Nottingham and east of Exeter' (p.46). The whole of England will be an extended garden city, like the England of Morris's *News from Nowhere*. And this future state is to be governed by 'New Republicans', an *elite* existing in and cutting across the 'social mass': 'picking themselves out more and more clearly from the shareholders, the parasitic speculator and the wretched multitudes of the Abyss' (p.278). Their connection with the ostensible forms of power will be indirect: 'The new Republicans will constitute an informed and open freemasonry. In all sorts of ways they will be influencing and controlling the apparatus of the ostensible governments' (p.278). A significant feature of *Anticipations* is the *religious* flavour of its prophecy. The New Republicans 'will be religious men

[1] See Bernard Bergonzi, *The Early H.G. Wells*.

... They will be disposed to find, and consequently they will find, an effect of purpose in the totality of things. Either one must believe the Universe to be one and systematic, and held together by some omnipresent quality, or one must believe it to be a casual aggregation, an incoherent accumulation with no unity whatsoever outside the unity of the personality regarding it. All science and most modern religious systems pre-suppose the former, and to believe the former is ... to believe in God' (p.281).

This religious conviction to be found in science and social organisation in the future is a response to a present need, the 'cry for faith that sounds in contemporary life so loudly, and often with so distressing a note of sincerity' (p.292).

The Edwardian sequels to *Anticipations* and *The Discovery of the Future* do not quite have the heady urgency of these early works. It is as though the intoxication of finding himself filling the role of his own New Republican, the herald of the future, abates somewhat as the century gets into its first decade. *Mankind in the Making* (1903) and *New Worlds for Old* (1908) are less assured, less exhilarated by their own daring, than *Anticipations*. *New Worlds for Old* treads carefully: 'On the whole ... things *get better*. There is a secular amelioration of life, and it is brought about by Good Will working through efforts of men' (p.6). Its 'legislation' is harshly prescriptive: 'Children must not be casually born' (p.134), 'Private property must be of terminable nature' (p.88). Eugenics is part of the programme for the future in his fantasy, *A Modern Utopia* (1905), and is set out in an even more bullying form in the pamphlet, *Socialism and the Family* (1906), part of which was a paper read to the Fabians, October 1906, called 'Socialism and the middle classes'. This has two points, both of them stimulated by Wells's personal situation in the Fabian movement. The first is an attack on the Fabians themselves, upper-middle class socialists who have no knowledge of what socialism means: 'They exact respect from inferiors; no touch of Socialist warmth or light qualifies their arrogant manners' (p.17).

The second point is that sexual freedom has arrived, and is to be enjoyed as one of the new conditions of the new century: 'The great terror of the eighties and early nineties that crushed all reasonable discussion of sexual relationships is, I believe, altogether over' (p.31).

This is part of Wells's personal defence from growing criticism of his private life in the Fabian society. The second part of the pamphlet takes further the point about sexual freedom, arguing that 'Free Love' is already a social reality, 'open to any solvent person', and that 'our restraints are purely restraints of opinion' (p.49): 'Our society today has in fact no complete system of sexual morals at all. It has the remains of a system' (p.50). He then returns to his bullying of parents in a new form. The Socialist state is to be the 'Over-Parent' and is to take away from the family the responsibility of looking after children, and to control breeding: 'Socialism denies altogether the right to beget children carelessly and promiscuously' (p.58). Further, and with more relevance to Well's personal situation, the socialist attitude towards marriage requires 'repudiation of private ownership of women and children' (p.59). The husbands and fathers who resented Wells's attentions to their women will have no rights in a Wellsian Socialist State.

Wells calls the Socialism of this pamphlet 'the form and substance of my ideal life, and all the religion I possess' (p.5). This echoes the man of the future in *Anticipations* who will 'know God only under the semblance of a pervading purpose, of which his own individual freedom of will is a part' (p.283).

The political writings and the novels run in parallel during the Edwardian period. In the political books the detailed attacks on exact targets – landlords, shareholders, husbands, fathers – are linked to large, loose and increasingly unstable claims for science as the new religion.

Wells's earlier novels of the Edwardian period – works like *Love and Mr Lewisham* (1900), *The Sea Lady: A Tissue of Moonshine* (1902), and *Kipps* (1905) – do not prepare the reader for the sweep, assurance and force of *Tono-Bungay*. As the first decade of his new century draws to a close Wells seems to rise to the challenge of his reputation as polymath and prophet, and to create a work which channels all the talents – preacher, satirist, realist, fantasist, demagogue – which he has distributed over widely differing works hitherto.

The creative strength and imaginative wealth of *Tono-Bungay* are partly products of its confusion. The ideas are unclear: the bullying Wells of *The Discovery* and *Socialism and the Family* merges with a generous, sprawling, exploratory, muddled temperament, caught in the cross-currents of the Edwardian liberal dilemma. The first confusion of *Tono-Bungay* is between what the narrator, George Ponderevo, thinks he is doing and what he is actually doing. The narrator thinks of himself as an observer presenting the nature of the age with his uncle Edward Ponderevo, the fraudulent tycoon who makes a fortune out of the quack medicine called 'Tono-Bungay', its representative hero.

The narrator knows himself to be confronting an intractable mass of material which is conditioned by his own personality: 'I suppose what I'm really trying to render is nothing more nor less than Life – as one man has found it. I want to tell – *myself*, and my impressions of the thing as a whole, to say things I have come to feel intensely of the laws, traditions, usages and ideas we call society, and how we poor individuals get driven and stranded among these windy, perplexing shoals and shallows' (p.13).

Tono-Bungay is *two* novels. In one Edward Ponderevo's dishonesty exemplifies the social and economic corruption of the modern world: in the other George Ponderevo, the narrator, is engaged in a religious quest, moving through society and exploring and testing a variety of moral imperatives. For a time he is held by the moral order represented by Bladesover, the country house where his mother works as housekeeper: this is an exact borrowing from Wells's childhood at Up Park, Sussex, where his own mother worked as housekeeper. George is prepared to concede some, at least, of Bladesover's claims to legitimacy: 'About that park there were some elements of a liberal education; there was a great space of greensward not given over to manure and food grubbing; there was mystery, there was matter for the imagination' (p.24). George is grateful to Bladesover for giving him a 'non-peasant' view of the world, and for enabling him to go to a local grammar school free both of social pretension and of working-class attitudes. But upper-class life is fatally weak. George as a child fights with Archie Garvell, a young visitor to Up Park: 'I hadn't fought ten seconds before I felt this softness in him, realised all that quality of modern upper-class England that never goes to the quick, that hedges about rules and those petty points of honour that are the ultimate comminution of honour, that claims credit for things demonstrably half done' (p.35).

The quack medicine 'Tono-Bungay' is itself a moral imperative, an object of veneration, a mystery of which George and Edward Ponderevo are the priests. When Edward takes George as a partner, George's job is to 'give Tono-Bungay substance and an outward and visible bottle' (p.120). This is an example of the religious language with which 'Tono-Bungay', the quack medicine, is often surrounded. Teddy Ponderevo acknowledges that what he is manufacturing is a form of religion: 'You put Faith in 'em ... Christian Science, really' (p.107). Ewart, the monument sculptor – an atheist who earns his living carving angels on gravestones – ironically describes Tono-Bungay as 'life'.[2]

Ewart is the bastard son of a famous artist, a lazy, hedonistic socialist, and therefore a useful figure for the novel: the sceptical outsider looking on at the bustling stupid activity of the Edwardian business world. As a detached sage he occupies the same kind of position in the novel as Chaffery, the fraudulent medium in *Love and Mr Lewisham* and Masterman, the consumptive socialist in *Kipps*. Ewart teases Teddy Ponderevo by identifying Tono-Bungay with 'Life': '"Think of the little clerks and jaded women and over-worked people. People overstrained with wanting to do, people overstrained with wanting to be ... The real trouble of life, Ponderevo, isn't that we exist – that's a vulgar error; the real trouble is that we *don't* really exist and we want to. That's what this – in the highest sense – muck [Tono-Bungay] stands for! The hunger to be – for once – really alive – to the fingertips!"' (p.125).

Ewart is linked again to the religious connotations of Tono-Bungay when he is invited by Teddy to design a chalice which is to be the object of a

---

[2] See the period's quasi-theological treatment of 'Life' with a capital L, above, p.3.

cynical public relations exercise, a gift to an East End Church from the makers of Tono-Bungay: 'Ewart had produced at once an admirable sketch for the sacred vessel surrounded by a sort of wreath of Millies [Milly is Ewart's girl] with open arms and wings, and had drawn fifty pounds on the strength of it' (p.204).

Ewart then fails to produce the chalice. Teddy is indignant, and his language comically betrays the distance between his own perception of the chalice and its intrinsic Christian significance:

> '"You see, George, they'll begin to want the blasted thing! ... That chalice, damn it! They're beginning to ask questions. It isn't Business, George."
>
> '"It's art," I protested, "and religion."' (pp.204-5)

These three terms, business, art and religion, acquire a resonance in the novel. 'Religion' embraces the other two, and in his quest for it George Ponderevo has for a time admired and venerated his uncle's success, even though he can never admire the product. The success of Tono-Bungay is symbolic of its age, 'the whole of this modern mercantile investing civilisation' which is 'such stuff as dreams are made of' (p.175). In the later stages of the novel George's attitude to Teddy changes. The ostentatious gift of the chalice is one of the ways in which Teddy is over-reaching himself: the building of Crest Hill, an enormous grandiose house left unfinished by the events of the novel, is another, his wish to diversify into banking is a third. A vindictive, spiteful side of Teddy's character, which one would not have suspected in the buzzing Wimblehurst shop-keeper of the early chapters, begins to be sketched in. He wants to go back to Wimblehurst to triumph in person over his former enemies: 'Give 'em ten minutes of my mind, George. Straight from the shoulder. Jes' exactly what I think of them' (p.207). And he is unfaithful to Aunt Susan; he takes a lady journalist as his mistress and tactlessly festoons her with diamonds (p.209).

These points are perhaps dramatic necessities. The novel must make Teddy deserve his punishments: bankruptcy, flight from the country in the airship built by George (*The Lord Roberts β*) and death of pneumonia in a French inn. But this forfeiting of sympathy for Teddy Ponderevo also marks growth and change of outlook in George. The building of flying machines replaces Teddy's career as the centre of George's interest. The language for this becomes elevated and quasi-religious, like the language earlier surrounding 'Tono-Bungay'. When the airship *Lord Roberts β* is completed it is an 'altogether triumphant vindication of my claims upon the air' (p.239). As George puts it to the Hon. Beatrice Normandy (an aristocrat, the steady erosion of whose social position is one of the novel's subplots) he is 'taking the Universe by the throat!' (p.240). As in Wells's prophetic books, then, the scientist is the modern priest, the Universe is the mystery that he celebrates.

The imagery and action suggest that the scientist's quest will finally lead nowhere. The journey to Mordet Island to collect 'quap', the radio-active matter which will restore the Ponderevo fortunes, is a physical quest with religious overtones like Marlow's quest in Conrad's *Heart of Darkness*. Indeed, the Roumanian-Jewish Captain of the *Maud-Mary* is based on Conrad's personality. In his autobiography Wells noted Conrad's 'incurable tendency to pronounce the last *e* in these and those' (*Experiment in Autobiography*, vol.2, p.616) and in his portrait of the Captain he embroiders on this characteristic: '"Eet is all middle-class, youra England. Everything you look at, middle-class ... Eet is all limited and computing and self-seeking. Dat is why your art is so limited, youra fiction, your philosophia, why you are all so inartistic. You want nothing but profit! What will pay! What would you?"' (p.253).

It could be Conrad on the philistinism of English readers and publishers.

Borrowings from Conrad's writings are suggested in other details: the psychological changes in George on Mordet Island may reflect the way Marlow finds himself becoming 'psychologically interesting' in *Heart of Darkness*. The ship's timbers being eroded by the radioactivity of the 'quap' on the return journey could echo the smouldering coal which destroys and sinks the *Judea* in Conrad's 'Youth'. The quap itself, this cancerous matter growing out of the earth, might be taken as a version of Kurtz's morally corroding ivory (much of which is 'fossil' in the sense that it has been buried by the natives for storage). And Conrad's configuration of a hostile landscape forcing an economic adventurer into self-awareness is repeated in Wells's novel: 'I found out many things about myself and humanity in those weeks of effort behind Mordet Island. I understand now the heart of the sweater, of the harsh employer, of the nigger-driver' (pp.260-1).

This pattern of quest and disillusionment is balanced, and to some extent contradicted, by the presence throughout the novel of traditional symbols which still exert a kind of authority. The clearest of these is not Bladesover but Lady Grove, the country house which has formerly belonged to an old Catholic family, the Durgans, and which Edward Ponderevo buys in the course of his meteoric social climb. Lady Grove carries more authority than Bladesover, which is early exposed as partly a sham: an exposure marked especially by the dreadful gentility of Mrs Mackridge, the retired lady's maid and intimate of George's mother who 'had a way of acknowledging your poor tinkle of utterance with a voluminous, scornful "Haw!" that made you want to burn her alive' (p.20). The social elevation of the Durgans of Lady Grove is more authentic: 'The spirit of the place was akin to Bladesover but touched with something older and remoter ... This family had sent its blood and treasure, time after time, upon the most romantic quest in history, to Palestine' (p.197).

The Crusades had failed and the Durgan family had died out 'century by century, and was now altogether dead' (p.196). When Aunt Susan is forced by Teddy's bankruptcy to leave Lady Grove she expresses it as an echo of the Fall of Man: '"Poor old Adam and Eve we are! 'Ficial Receivers with flaming swords to drive us out of our garden!"' (p.271).

The Vicar of Duffield, the village of which Lady Grove is the great house, is part of this older civilisation: 'These Oxford men are the Greeks of our plutocratic [Roman] empire' (p.197). Teddy Ponderevo's money can buy the building but it can't buy the tradition of Lady Grove: the portraits of the Durgans look down disdainfully from the walls (p.196). He is ill-suited to the role of country gentleman. There is a good comic scene in which Teddy declares, to the vicar's refined horror, his determination to 'buck up' the countryside:

> '"The English country is a going concern still; just as the Established Church – if you'll excuse me saying it, is a going concern. Just as Oxford is – or Cambridge. Or any of those old, fine, old things. Only it wants fresh capital, fresh idees [*sic*: Teddy's pronunciation], and fresh methods. Light railways, fr'instance – scientific use of drainage. Wire fencing – machinery – all that."
>
> 'The vicar's face for one moment betrayed dismay. Perhaps he was thinking of his country walks amidst the hawthorns and honeysuckle.
>
> '"There's great things," said my uncle, "to be done on Mod'un lines with Village Jams and Pickles – boiled in the country"' (p.201).

The comedy here works against both the vicar and Teddy. Wells's imagination, like Dickens's, perhaps like that of most of the great liberal comic writers in English, responds to images of power in contradictory ways. The hereditary authority of the church and the hall confronts the new authority of Ponderevo's money. One part of Wells unequivocally applauds success (Arnold Bennett's success, for instance, as Wells describes it in his autobiography), but the novel's handling of Ponderevo's success is equivocal. It is not *assured* success, since Ponderevo is bankrupted and also since his perception of himself is vulgar and overblown: the 'Overman idee, Nietzsche – all that stuff' and the 'Napoleonic legend' have contributed to the making of his self-image (*Tono-Bungay*, p.208).

Interestingly, also, Wells's response to the values of past and future is ambivalent, in this novel, though elsewhere his loyalty is firmly enlisted with the future. The antitheses of sacred past and secular present, illustrated by the contrast between Edwardian commercial London and Bladesover, Lady Grove and the vicar's 'Greek' Oxford sensitivity, lead to the fine closing image of the novel in which the Tower of London is contrasted with Tower Bridge: 'The dear little sunlit ancient Tower of London lying away in a gap among the warehouses ... overshadowed by the vulgarest, most typical exploit of modern England, the sham Gothic casings to the ironwork of Tower Bridge' (pp.303-4).

George's quest has been conducted honestly. One feels, as seldom in Wells, that the novelist is not forcing his conclusion. *Tono-Bungay* in its quest and failure has reflected accurately the Edwardian liberal dilemma. In his autobiography Wells was to say that his friendly, and not so friendly, rivalries with Conrad, Ford and Henry James brought him to declare himself against 'art': 'All this talk that I had with Conrad and Hueffer [Ford] and James about the just word, the perfect expression, about this or that being "written" or not written, bothered me, set me interrogating myself, threw me into a heart-searching defensive attitude ... In the end I revolted altogether ... "I am a journalist," I declared, "I refuse to play the 'artist'. If sometimes I am an artist it is a freak of the gods. I am journalist all the time and what I write *goes now* – and will presently die" '(*Autobiography*, vol.2, p.623).

The artistry of *Tono-Bungay* is much more than a 'freak of the gods'. It has been fully discussed by Kenneth Newell and David Lodge.[3] Like Bennett at his best, Wells in this book seems to invoke a standard of art itself to withstand the corrosiveness of life.[4] The philosophy of Ewart, the cynical hedonistic sculptor in *Tono-Bungay*, is a doctrine for survival in a world devoid of value. The Tower of London remains beautiful despite the monstrous bastard it has engendered in Tower Bridge.

Throughout the novel George, the narrator, claims that he does not know how to write fiction. This is not unlike the adroit 'plain man' disclaimers of Conrad's limited narrators, Marlow, the language teacher and 'Amy Foster's' Dr Kennedy. As a novel about Teddy Ponderevo as an exemplary figure of the Edwardian economic world, *Tono-Bungay* is an effective episodic satire. As a novel about George Ponderevo's quests and disillusionments it is a different kind of work, subtle, highly-wrought, and 'written' in as full as sense as Conrad, Ford and Henry James could wish.

2. Love and Mr. Lewisham

Wells's earlier Edwardian novels are studies of insubordination, of the drive towards freedom in the socially disadvantaged. Wells's father, a country boy trapped in the suburbs, was an insubordinate personality who lost job after job because he would not be 'told.'[5] Wells in his *Autobiography* cockily applauds his own self-will: 'I shall die, as I have lived, the responsible centre of my world. Occasionally I make inelegant gestures of self-effacement but they deceive

[3] Kenneth Newell, *Structure in Four Novels by H.G. Wells* (1968); David Lodge, 'Tono-Bungay and the Condition of England' *Language of Fiction* (1966), pp.214-42.
[4] See below, pp.170-1.
[5] Norman and Jeanne MacKenzie, *The Time Traveller* (1937), p.7.

nobody, and they do not suit me. I am a typical Cockney without either reverence or a sincere conviction of inferiority to any fellow creature' (vol.1, p.291).

Love and Mr Lewisham (1900) was a surprising sequel to the scientific romances. It was not liked by the critics[6] and was misunderstood by Wells's friends. Bennett wrote complaining that he had deserted his true talent, and Wells replied with characteristic aggressiveness: 'Why the Hell have you joined the conspiracy to restrict me to one particular type of story? I want to write novels and before God I *will* write novels. They are the proper stuff for my everyday work, a methodical careful distillation of one's thoughts and sentiments and experiences and impressions. But that other stuff which you would have me doing day by day is no more to be done day by day than repartees or lyric poetry. The Imagination moves in a mysterious way its wonders to perform. I can assure you that I am *not* doing anything long and weird and strong in the manner of *The Time Machine* and I never intend to.'[7]

The scientific romances are portentous, excitable, exhilarated by their own energies, consumed by their own nightmares: the omniscient view of history granted to the Time Traveller by his miraculous (in a secular sense) journey in *The Time Machine* is followed by the descent into a modern biologist's hell in *The Island of Dr Moreau*.

Following these powerful and extraordinary books the first impression made by *Love and Mr Lewisham* is one of modesty. In its serial publication it was subtitled 'The Story of a Very Young Couple'.[8] The novel is short, controlled, economical, remarkably sparing in metaphor and almost devoid of the 'editorial' interventions that take up so much space in later works like *Tono-Bungay*. Wells himself saw it as 'sedulously polished':[9] '*Love and Mr Lewisham* was written with greater care than any of the writer's earlier books. It was consciously a work of art; it was designed to be very clear, simple, graceful and human. It was not a very successful book, no critic discovered any sort of beauty or technical ability in it, and it was some years before the writer could return, in *Kipps* (1905) and *Tono-Bungay* (1909) to his attack on the novel proper.'

Its structure has been ably studied and shown to be tight and symmetrical.[10] It has a small cast, a narrow selection of settings, a short dramatic time-span, a strategic and economical pattern of symbols. Wells the over-reacher is here writing well within his range. Its story may be seen

---

[6] It was seen as having 'a disproportionate realism that almost amounted to vulgarity', *The Speaker*, June 16 1900 (quoted by the MacKenzies, p.152).

[7] Harris Wilson (ed.), *Arnold Bennett and H.G. Wells: A Record of a Personal and a Literary Friendship* (1960), p.45.

[8] *A Bibliography of H.G. Wells*, H.G. Wells Society (1968), p.6.

[9] H.G. Wells, *The Atlantic Edition of H.G. Wells*, vol.1 (1924), p.x.

[10] See Newell, op. cit.

as a young man's progress from error to truth, presented both analytically and organically.[11] Most of the novel's narrow energy is devoted to the presentation of Lewisham himself. This is done very well. The young Lewisham is closely known but the observation is consistently dispassionate. At the beginning of the novel he is an eighteen-year-old schoolmaster, 'called "Mr" to distinguish him from the bigger boys' (p.11). He is talented and ambitious. He is also sexually susceptible. The two subjects of the title are the substance of the story as far as it concerns Lewisham himself; although, as the beginning of the novel announces: 'The opening chapter does not concern itself with Love – and indeed that antagonist does not certainly appear until the third – and Mr Lewisham is seen at his studies' (p.11). The adolescent Lewisham 'thought little of Love but much on greatness' (p.11) but is easily attracted to Ethel Henderson, a visitor to the socially dead village of Whortley, Sussex, where Lewisham teaches at a shabby-genteel private school. Ethel Henderson is not his match intellectually and has shallow social pretensions: 'She proceeded to praise London, its public libraries, its shops, the multitude of people, the facilities for "doing what you like", the concerts one could go to, the theatres. (It seemed she moved in fairly good society.) "There's always something to see even if you only go out for a walk," she said, "and down here there's nothing to read but idle novels. And those not new"' (p.26).

Lewisham's own social inexperience betrays him into being naively impressed by her. Her background is in fact calamitously insecure. Her father, Chaffery, is a fraudulent medium whose career in the novel ends criminally; he steals £500 from a patron (by hypnotising him) and leaves his wife for a flashy mistress. Lewisham's adolescent self looks forward to an illusory career in which brilliant qualifications and 'pamphlets in the liberal interest' will lead to intellectual distinction and political influence: 'In those days much of Lewisham's mind was still an unknown land to him. He believed among other things that he was always the same consistent intelligent human being, whereas under certain stimuli he became no longer reasonable and disciplined but a purely imaginative and emotional person' (p.22).

Ostensibly the pattern of the novel is one of disaster, with Lewisham as an anti-hero. But in fact Lewisham's movement through the social world is from impotence to power: from being snubbed and bullied by the middle-aged mediocrity who is headmaster of Whortley Proprietary School, to his position at the end of the novel as the head of a household, the protector of Ethel and her mother and the father of Ethel's child.

Love and Mr Lewisham expresses every male adolescent's rage. The child insists that he shall be recognised as a man, the sexually potent, socially

---

[11] Ibid., pp.13 and 39.

impotent individual asserts himself by gathering a household round him. And the last chapter suggests that Lewisham may come to enjoy the form of freedom that Wells has won for himself: 'Ethel came into their room with a waste-paper basket she had bought for him, and found him sitting at the little toilet-table at which he was to "write"' (p.170).

The double title, love *and* Mr Lewisham, breeds doubleness, a reflexiveness in the novel's patterning which is a consistent feature of its structural virtue. The self-confident, self-esteeming man that Lewisham is seen to have become at the end of the novel is contrasted with the adolescent science student with a 'great' but opaque future: 'From his marriage until the final examination in June, Lewisham's life had an odd amphibious quality. At home were Ethel and the perpetual aching pursuit of employment, the pelting irritations of Madam Gadow's [their German landlady] persistent overcharges, and so forth, and amid such things he felt extraordinarily grown up; but intercalated with these experiences were those intervals at Kensington, scraps of his adolescence, as it were, lying amidst the new matter of his manhood, intervals during which he was simply an insubordinate and disappointing student' (p.135).

Unfortunately the narrative does not resist the temptation to close this paragraph with a commentary, to 'tell' as well as to 'show: 'At South Kensington he dwelt with theories and ideals as a student should; at the little rooms in Chelsea ... there was his particular private concrete situation, and ideals gave place to the real' (p.135).

At its best the novel is sparing with its commentary and achieves its effects by carefully wrought dramatic presentation and strategic use of imagery. Lewisham's courtship of Ethel in Whortley is marked by a spray of blackthorn that he picks for her, which scratches his hand and makes it bleed (p.33) and this is echoed in chapter 29 of the novel, 'Thorns and Rose Petals', where the Lewisham marriage is beset with difficulties. Lewisham is receiving letters from a fellow-student, a Miss Heydinger, which fill Ethel with jealousy. Ethel at the same time is being courted by a young 'decadent' poet, Edwin Peak Baines, whose work she has been typing. After a quarrel over Miss Heydinger Lewisham sends roses to Ethel to comfort her: she mistakenly thinks that the roses have come from Edwin Peak Baines and hides them in the bedroom. Lewisham discovers them and extracts from her her reasons for hiding them: 'Lewisham gave way to a transport of anger. He caught up a handful of roses and extended them ... His finger bled from a thorn, as once it had bled from a blackthorn spray' (p.153).

Spurred by jealousy he determines to leave Ethel and starts packing his case: 'He was inflicting grievous punishment and that gratified him' (p.155). His dramatic exit is blocked by the gas-light going out: the landlady switches off all the gas in the house when she goes to bed. The candle and matches are in the bedroom with Ethel so he is forced to go in to her. He finds her face down on the bed: 'And in her hand and close to her face was a rose' (p.157). The blackthorn has become the rose: both draw blood from Lewisham, both are accepted by Ethel as evidence of his love. The intractability of circumstance – the gas going out – has blocked Lewisham's exit just as it earlier obstructed his attempts to make a distinguished career for himself, and he now responds sexually to the pathos of Ethel's posture on the bed. The chapter ends with a delicately placed symbol suggesting the sexual arousal, climax and post-coital tenderness taking place between the Lewishams: 'The expiring candle streamed up into a tall flame, flickered, and was suddenly extinguished. The air was heavy with the scent of roses' (p.158).

Lewisham is the purest Wellsian hero, the closest to the young thruster of the early pages of the *Experiment in Autobiography*: 'The originative intellectual worker is not a normal human being and does not lead nor desire to lead a normal human life. He wants to lead a supernormal life' (p.16). The autobiographer in *The Experiment* never does come to terms with 'normal human life'. As the MacKenzies point out, the *Experiment in Autobiography* 'virtually terminates' in 1904. When not congratulating itself on the successes of Wells's youth it pleases itself with broad speculations about the future: 'The future now took the place of the past as his point of reference, but fulfilment in the present still eluded him'.[12] The novelist is more truthful than the autobiographer: Lewisham's desire for 'Greatness', Kipps's desire to be a 'Nawther', Teddy Ponderevo's 'Overman Idee' – all ambitions by which the young Wells himself was driven – are forced to give way to the demands of 'normal human life'.

None of the characters outside Lewisham can match his strength. Ethel is ignorant but her loyalty and responsiveness give her adequate claims to be Lewisham's partner. Miss Heydinger is physically unattractive and belongs to Lewisham's immaturity: she believes in his genius and hopes to rescue him for his 'greatness'. Perhaps she could – the novel leaves this open – but by the time she declares herself Lewisham is married to Ethel and is beyond her help. Mr Lagune, the rich elderly fellow-student who is gulled by Chaffery is a mature man who *ought* to be a figure of authority but instead is, so to speak, an anti-father whose weakness emphasises the power vacuum at the centre of the novel.

This power vacuum needs to be filled by some positive: science, religion, or simply a strong individual. In fact, of course, the space is usurped by Chaffery, the arch-imposter who offers both false religion and false science and is very much an individual, though not strong enough – as he knows – to use his intelligence in his own best interests. The ostensible pattern of the action is that Chaffery destroys Lewisham's moral principles with his own

---

[12] MacKenzies, p.182.

superficial but attractive perversion of social Darwinism: '"Honesty is essentially an anarchistic and disintegrating force in society ... Life is a struggle for existence, a fight for food. Money is just the lie that mitigates our fury"' (pp.113-14).

But Lewisham does not need Chaffery: he has already discovered moral relativity for himself. In chapter 13 of the novel he learns that Ethel is not the high-society girl that he has been led to believe but little more than a petty crook, assisting Chaffery in his cheating manifestations of spirits. She tells Lewisham to leave her in her disgrace but he refuses: '"No," he said, obstinately, and they stood face to face at the cardinal point of their lives ... "I don't care where you are, what your people are, nor very much whether you've kept quite clear of this medium humbug"' (p.67). The socially poised Ethel of the earlier scenes, who condescended to Lewisham, has herself become a social outcast needing his protection.

As the novel traces his growth Lewisham emerges as its one dominant and effective male: the vacuum is waiting for him to fill it, he is his own father-figure, he becomes his own myth. Carlyle and Huxley, the mistily perceived hero figures of his adolescence, are replaced by the solid figure of his domestic self as husband and father. When Chaffery absconds Lewisham literally replaces him by looking after his family. And on the last page of the novel he substitutes true, biological Darwinism for the false social Darwinism articulated by Chaffery earlier: '"The future is the Child. The Future. What are we – any of us – but servants or traitors to that? ... Natural Selection – it follows ... this way is happiness ... must be. There can be no other." He sighed. "To last a lifetime, that is."' (p.172).

3. Kipps

If *Love and Mr. Lewisham*, 'The Story of a Very Young Couple', is 'about' youthful sexuality, *Kipps*, (1905) 'The Story of a Simple Soul', is 'about' class attitudes. The pressures on Lewisham are 'real', economic survival, sexual need. The pressures on Kipps are artificial, the pressures felt by the outsider who is on the receiving end of the social coercion practised by the privileged for their own defence. Class antagonism is the novel's theme: the plot mechanism supporting it is a simple story of economic disaster.

Kipps as a young man is caught in the 'great stupid machine of retail trade' (p.37), freed from it by his unexpected inheritance, and then plunged back into poverty when 'Brudderkins' Walshingham, the brother of the genteel opportunist girl to whom Kipps has become 'engaged', absconds with his money. But Kipps has had the good fortune to invest in an apparently mad enterprise – the staging of a play called 'The Pestered Butterfly' (a comic reference to *The Wild Duck*) by his friend Chitterlow – and as a result of this is assured a small but steady income for life: 'Wealth rises like an exhalation all over our little planet, and condenses, or at least some of it does, in the pockets of Kipps' (p.255).[13]

It is not surprising that Henry James admired *Kipps*: 'The book has throughout such extraordinary life; everyone in it, without exception, and every piece and part of it, is so vivid and sharp and *raw*.'[14] James's 'raw' is, no doubt, double-edged. The subject of *Kipps* is Jamesian: two kinds of power, that of money and that of social initiation, are matched against each other. Kipps could be one of James's American millionairesses seeking recognition in the chill waters of European high society. The treatment is anything but Jamesian: it is broad, exposed and explicit. Originally it was much bigger, being part of a huge chronicle of Edwardian society called 'The Wealth of Mr. Waddy'.[15] Kipps was one of Wells's 'personalities thwarted and crippled by the defects of our contemporary civilisation' (Wells, *Atlantic Edition*, vol.7, p.ix).

As in *Love and Mr. Lewisham* there is an absence of authority, a power vacuum. The male figures are inadequate: the uncle who has brought Kipps up is ignorant, obstructive, fat, slow. His schoolmaster in Hastings, 'George Garden Woodrow', is a shabby impostor, a mix of Bonover and Chaffery from the earlier novel. Mr Shalford, the draper in Folkestone to whom Kipps is apprenticed, is supposed to teach Kipps 'the whole art and mystery of the trade'. But since he is under no legal obligation to carry this out he neglects it with the short-sighted ruthlessness of a 'sound, practical business man' (p.32). Coote, the house agent and Kipps's self-appointed social mentor is another impostor. He advises Kipps to send Helen Walshingham her engagement ring 'by post' and to call on her mother in a 'Frock coat' (p.131): he has no more knowledge of the social usages he professes to teach than has George Garden Woodrow of the academic curriculum.

The Walshinghams, more human and more fully drawn than these other figures, are the worst impostors of all: shabby-genteel people who batten on Kipps for his money. Helen Walshingham is an interestingly mixed character. She has some feeling for Kipps: 'indeed, he did not seem so bad to her' (p.129). But she suppresses this sympathy and pretends love for Kipps out of cold-blooded rapacity: 'Behind him was money and opportunity, freedom, and London, a great background of seductively indistinct hopes' (p.129).

---

[13] There is a clear resemblance to *Great Expectations*: Pip invests some of his mysterious legacy in Herbert Pocket, who is thus able to help Pip to a new career in Marine Insurance when Magwitch's wealth is forfeit.

[14] Letter, 19 November 1905. From Patrick Parrinder (ed.), *H.G. Wells: The Critical Heritage* (1972), p.126.

[15] H.G. Wells, *The Wealth of Mr. Waddy: A Novel* (ed. Harry T. Moore and Harris Wilson) (1969).

Her coldness and her ruthless snobbish bullying of Kipps ('I am going to give you a good talking to about this' when Kipps escapes from the appalling Anagram Tea (p.166)) is more repellent in its way than her brother's merely criminal speculation with Kipps's money.

The figures who are not impostors are those who at first sight seem least promising: Chitterlow, the drunken penniless playwright whose *Pestered Butterfly* makes so surprising a success, and Masterman, the venomous working-class intellectual dying of consumption who is based on Wells's close (and compassionate) relationship with Gissing in the last years of the latter's tragic life.

The full-length novel (with its familial similarity to *Great Expectations*) would have been Dickensian in scale and complication. It involved an introductory chapter on 'Mr Waddy's declining years and how he was adopted' by a woman who 'subsequently became Mrs. Chitterlow', and there were also 'the adventures of young Mr. Walshingham as a fugitive in France' (Wells, *Atlantic Edition*, vol.7, p.ix). Kipps is the illegitimate child of a working-class girl and her middle-class lover. Kipps's grandfather (the 'Mr. Waddy' who has the 'Wealth') prevented the two from marrying and Kipps's father died in Australia (shades of Magwitch). The grandfather on his deathbed remorsefully leaves his money to the unknown illegitimate child: hence Kipps's fortune.

The theme of *Kipps* is thus established on the first page. Class antagonism has wrecked the lives of Kipps's parents and is in his blood. His mother is sketched in the barest outline which leaves no room for pity: she is pleasure-loving and irresponsible. She deserts Kipps, leaving him with his aunt and uncle at the 'Little Shop at New Romney' (again like Dickens's Pip, brought up by his sister at the forge near Rochester): 'It is clear she handed him over to his aunt and uncle at New Romney with explicit directions and a certain endowment. One gathers she had something of that fine sense of social distinctions that subsequently played so large a part in Kipps's career' (p.11). His aunt and uncle have isolated themselves socially: 'They feared the "low" and they hated and despised the "stuck up", and so they "kept themselves *to* themselves", according to the English ideal' (p.13).

The assistants in Shalford's drapery shop in Folkestone have their own hellish microcosm of the social order. The male assistants have a convention by which the newest is snubbed and bullied by the others, and the girls have a more subtle system: those who are 'engaged' to one of the male assistants take precedence over those who are not. They have to be 'engaged' because 'walking-out' is a custom of servants: 'Such is the sweetness of human charity, that the shop young lady in England has just the same horror of doing anything that savours of the servant girl as the lady journalist, let us say, has of anything savouring of the shop-girl, or the really quite nice young lady has of anything savouring of any sort of girl who has gone down into the economic battlefield to earn herself a living' (p.40).

The only class which seems to the assistants immune from the social structure, the 'claw of the Beast', is that of writers. They discuss enviously and appreciatively the social ascent of Dickens, Thackeray and Johnson, and Kipps determines to pose as a 'Nawther': 'Here was a class that seemed to bridge the gulf ... Essentially low, but by fictitious circumstances capable of entering upon these levels of social superiority to which all true Englishmen aspire, these levels from which one may tip a butler, scorn a tailor, and even commune with those who lead "men" into battle' (p.52). Chitterlow, of course, achieves this and in the long run pulls Kipps up with him.

The scenes in which Kipps, having received his legacy, experiences the pressures of English class discrimination, have a high farcical success. Kipps getting his own back on the middle class by playing an Edwardian equivalent of a juke box at a fashionable hotel in Folkestone (p.191), Kipps in headlong flight from Mrs. Bindon Botting's Anagram Tea (p.197), Kipps when he overhears the same lady resolving to dismiss his childhood sweetheart, Ann, who now works as a housemaid, finally rebelling against the web of alien attitudes in which he has become enmeshed: 'Upon the troubled disorder of Kipps's table manners there had supervened a quietness, an unusual calm' (p.203). Following the dramatic success of these scenes Wells is unable, as so often, to resist the temptation to editorialise: 'We English—all the world, indeed, today – live in a strange atmosphere of neglected great issues, of insistent, triumphant, petty things; we are given up to the fine littlenesses of intercourse; table manners and small correctitudes are the substance of our lives' (p.216).

Lewisham cuts his hand on the blackthorn and the roses and sheds blood for love of Ethel. Kipps sheds blood for love of Helen Walshingham by cutting himself as he tries to open a window at his woodwork class, and this affords him a moment of much needed dramatic triumph: 'He glanced ... at the blood on his wrist, and it seemed to him that it was on the very point of dropping on the floor of that cultured class-room. So he very neatly licked it off, feeling at the same time for his handkerchief. "Oh, *don't!*" said Miss Walshingham' (p.48). This spontaneous action defeats the resources of gentility. A developed sense of class discrimination cannot cope with a boy with a cut wrist. In his inarticulate way Kipps discovers, as Polly was to discover in the later novel, that 'if the world doesn't suit you, you can change it'.[16]

His inarticulacy is Kipps's major difference from Lewisham. At Shalford's shop in Folkestone he dimly perceives that the 'machine' of retail trade is destroying him, but has no defence from this other than stock-like obtuseness

[16] See below, p.140.

or fantasy: 'He plumbed an abyss of boredom, or stood a mere carcass with his mind far away, fighting the enemies of the empire, or steering a dreamship perilously into unknown seas' (p.34). Kipps's under-nourished imagination resorts to the period's stock hero-figure, the imperial adventurer, and the 'abyss' (from Wells's own story 'In the Abyss') is, of course, another resonant Edwardian image.[17]

Sex is his only other resource: '[The] development of the sex interest was continuously very interesting to Kipps, and kept him going as much as anything through all these servile years' (p.41). After being plunged into wealth by his inheritance Kipps is rescued from the social trap set up by the Walshinghams by his sexual drive towards Ann, and the same force gives him a new self-assertiveness when his son is born. In this he is like Lewisham, but the difference between the two figures is still marked; Kipps's new self-possession has to be announced editorially by the novelist instead of being presented dramatically: 'Kipps was coming to manhood now. The once rabbit-like soul ... was at last facing the greater realities. He came suddenly upon the master thing in life – birth ... Ann ... had the look of one who emerges from some strenuous and invigorating act' (p.150).

It is perhaps because the central figure is so inarticulate that *Kipps* has *two* loquacious minor commentators, Chitterlow and Masterman, where *Love and Mr. Lewisham* had one (Chaffery). Like the Wells of the autobiography, Chitterlow has never acknowledged the superiority of any fellow creature: he is the 'fellow of Shakespeare and Ibsen and Maeterlinck' (p.62). In the long run he forces the world to accept him at his own value. Kipps, despite his unpromising childhood, has the same buoyancy. When he encounters genteel Helen at his woodwork class, 'it had not yet come to Kipps to acknowledge any man as his better in his heart of hearts. When one does that the game is played, and one grows old indeed' (p.47).

Masterman presents a sharp contrast to this. He is an impressive speaker: 'Society is one body, and it is either well or ill. That's the law ... This civilisation of ours is on the topple ... The great mass of men festers and breeds in darkness, darkness those others make by standing in the light' (pp.179-80). The Wells who wrote *The Discovery of the Future* might be expected to agree with these opinions, but there is no doubt that the novel finally witholds its sympathy from Masterman. His self-pity leads him to substitute snarling fury for action: '"Those Skunks shut up all the university scholarships at nineteen for fear of men like me"' (p.181).

Kipps is a much less carefully written book than *Love and Mr. Lewisham*. It allows itself a naive plot naively presented. Chitterlow is 'fortune' when he knocks Kipps over with his bicycle: 'Fortune came upon him, in disguise and

---

[17] See above, pp.6-7.

with a loud shout, the shout of a person endowed with an unusually rich, full voice, followed immediately by a violent blow in the back' (p.55). Chitterlow promptly leads Kipps to his legacy, pointing out to him the newspaper advertisement for one 'Arthur Kipps or Waddy' (p.69), which Chitterlow has cut out because he has used the name 'Kipps' for a character in one of his plays. Wells makes no attempt to mask the improbability of this contrivance but leaves it, in Henry James's word, 'raw'.

Much of the writing is also 'raw', unrevised and hastily assembled. After the novel's effective opening, giving the contrast between the respectable lower-middle-class Kippses and the frankly proletarian Pornicks who live next door, Wells explores the relationship between Kipps and young Sid Pornick. He then after an interval worryingly *re*-introduces Sid Pornick, as though for the first time, as 'the son of the irascible black-bearded haberdasher next door' (p.17). Obviously something has gone wrong: the sequence of this section presumably was re-arranged, and this piece of discontinuity missed in the process.

In its account of Kipps's education the novel again seems to go astray. One can accept that George Garden Woodrow's genteel private school, Cavendish Academy, would leave Kipps at the age of fourteen 'confused in his mind, and retreating in his manners' (p.28). But the school is specifically a *snobbish* school, an 'Academy for Young Gentlemen', many of whom 'had parents in "India" and other unverifiable places. Others were the sons of credulous widows' (p.15). Given the school's aspirations to gentility, and the anxiety that Kipps's mother, aunt and uncle all share about questions of social status, is it likely that Kipps would have unregenerate working-class speech, as he clearly does?

The trouble is that the figure of Kipps is being made to illustrate too many points. He illustrates the evils of shabby private education as against English 'Board Schools' or German State education: 'If Mr. Kipps had been so unfortunate as to have been born a German he might have been educated in an elaborate and costly special school ("over-educated – crammed-up" – old Kipps) to fit him for his end – such being their pedagogic way. He might – But why make unpatriotic reflections in a novel?' (p.28).

He also illustrates the evil effects of the English class system, and in order that he should be easily bullied by Helen, intimidated by the absurd Coote ('within the sphere of gentleman there are distinctions of rank indeed, but none of class' (p.151)), and gulled by Helen's rascally brother, Kipps has to be presented as a totally unpolished innocent product of the working-class. Yet precisely the objection to Cavendish Academy is that it offers a modicum of social polish and nothing else.

4. The History of Mr. Polly

The History of Mr. Polly (1910) is in all senses a more 'innocent' novel than its predecessors. Lewisham and Kipps become men: Mr. Polly moves retrogressively through the story until he becomes a child-like, plump figure – Mr. Toad without the mischievousness – sitting by the stream at the Potwell Inn, enclosed in a womb. The valley of the Potwell Inn lies 'as if everything lay securely within a great, warm, friendly globe of crystal sky. It was as safe and enclosed and fearless as a child that has still to be born' (p.159).

Polly exists between two worlds. The 'real' world which he perceives as the 'whole scheme of life' (p.10) and the 'inevitable' (p.122) is the product of unplanned contingencies: his damaged digestion, his appalling education, his boring years as a draper's apprentice. The other world is an interior one, inviolable, that his imagination never surrenders. After his schooling his conviction that there is 'interest and happiness in the world' has become a 'creature which has been beaten about the head and left for dead but still lives'. He never lets go of the belief that somewhere there are 'pure and easy and joyous states of body and mind' (p.14).

The childhood of Polly parallels the childhood of Kipps but is much less black. Polly is lazier and more intelligent than Kipps, and luckier in his companions. At the Port Burdock Drapery Bazaar 'Mr. Polly, who had been an only child, first tasted the joys of social intercourse'. 'There were girls! And friendship!' (p.16). Just as Kipps remembers his school holidays with Sid Pornick as 'stained glass windows' relieving the horrors of the Cavendish Academy, so Polly remembers his Sundays and holidays from the bazaar as 'diamonds among the pebbles' (p.19). These 'diamonds' are intimations of the second world, the arcadian English countryside with its peace and traditions.

The novel has been carefully structured to prevent the Potwell Inn from coming as a total surprise. Polly has had visions of paradise before. The novel itself appears to share Polly's innocence, and celebrates the English countryside with an unselfconsciousness which would be impossible in *Tono-Bungay* or most of Wells's other Edwardian works. Wells is enjoying himself: 'There is no countryside like the English countryside for those who have learned to love it; its firm yet gentle lines of hill and dale, its ordered confusion of features, its deer parks and downland, its castles and stately houses, its hamlets and old churches, its farms and ricks and great barns and ancient trees, its pools and ponds and shining threads of rivers, its flower-starred hedgerows, its orchards and woodland patches, its village greens and kindly inns' (p.20).

The prose ambles on, like a well-seasoned upper-class traveller, to compare the English landscape with characteristic European and American landscapes, and finds the English superior. Mr. Polly makes two boon companions, Platt and Parsons, and on one of their outings a girl at an inn gives them 'three yellow-green apples': 'If Platt and Parsons and Mr. Polly live to be a hundred, they will none of them forget that girl as she stood with a pink flush upon her, faintly smiling and yet earnest, parting the branches of the hedgerows and reaching down, apple in hand ...' (p.22).

Mr. Polly has the instincts of the *leisured* class and is well suited to the life of wealthy laziness enjoyed by, for instance, Henry Harland's or Elinor Glyn's characters. He is potentially 'Edwardian' in all the more conservative senses of the term. He 'dreamt always of picturesque and mellow things, and had an instinctive hatred of the strenuous life' (p.33). During a spell as a draper's assistant in Canterbury he imagines himself as a medieval mason: 'He would ... have sat upon a scaffolding and carved out penetrating and none-too-flattering portraits of church dignitaries upon the capitals' (p.34).

The subversiveness of his mind is entirely playful, it doesn't lead to anything that might resemble a set of ideas or a political posture. There are no philosophers in this book, no need is felt to fill the place occupied by Chaffery, Ewart or Masterman in the other Edwardian novels. Parsons reads, but like Polly he reads only for the sensuous delight of the experience, not for intellectual reasons. Polly's reading is guided by Parsons, and is his greatest pleasure. Parsons introduces him to Shakespeare, Chaucer, 'Bocashieu', 'Rabooloose'.

Polly is devoid of sexual drive. He marries his cousin Miriam out of laziness and lack of alternative, and takes fifteen years to learn to hate her enough to leave her. 'The strongest affection in his life had been for Parsons' (p.38), and he has a hopeless romantic encounter with a middle-class schoolgirl. His love for her is escapist, like the rest of his emotional and imaginative life: 'Mr. Polly fell in love, as though the world had given way beneath him and he had dropped through into another, into a world of luminous clouds and of a desolate, hopeless wilderness of desiring and of wild valleys of unreasonable ecstasy, a world whose infinite miseries were finer and in some inexplicable way sweeter than the purest gold of the daily life, whose joys ... were brighter than a dying martyr's vision of heaven' (pp.65-6).

Fat, romantic, undersexed: Polly has the mind of a spoilt child, and the violent pleasures also. The farcical scene in which his friend Parsons, a fellow assistant at the Port Burdock Drapery Bazaar, physically attacks the manager for disturbing his window display (p.25) is a mild preparation for the explosive excitement of the Great Fishbourne Fire. Here the novel displays the innocent delight in violence that Bernard Bergonzi has remarked as a feature of the period.[18]

[18] Bernard Bergonzi, *Heroes' Twilight: A Study of the Literature of the Great War* (1965), pp.22-3: Bergonzi refers particularly to the blood flowing in the streets of G.K. Chesterton's *The Napoleon of Notting Hill*.

The Fishbourne fire is a retrogressive fantasy masquerading as a blow for freedom. Tortured by debts and boredom Polly determines to kill himself: 'Why had he submitted to things, blundered into things? Why had he never insisted on the things he thought beautiful and the things he desired, never sought them, fought for them, taken any risk for them?' (p.110).

The attempted suicide and the attendant fire are rich farce, absolutely assured without any false effects. Polly prepares to cut his throat: 'He drew the blade lightly under one ear. "Lord! but it stung like nettles!"'' (p.111).

He has already set fire to the house. The catching alight of his trousers spurs him into self-defence, especially when he is afforded what is perhaps a foretaste of the hell in which Polly does not believe: 'A thin, tall, red flame came up through the hole in the stairs he had made and stood still, quite still, as it seemed, and looked at him. It was a strange-looking flame, a flattish, salmon colour, redly streaked. It was so queer and quiet-mannered that the sight of it held Mr Polly agape' (p.111).

Visual excitement and high comic virtuosity sustain this excellent chapter right through to its close. The spectacular possibilities of the fire are fully exploited, and the reader's attention moves delightedly between the rich visual effects and the wonderfully farcical dialogue between Polly and his neighbour Rumbold's deaf mother-in-law, whom he is trying to rescue from the flames. At the climax of the rescue operation the deaf old lady notices her son-in-law down below in the crowd: 'She fumbled in her garments mysteriously, and at last produced a wrinkled pocket-handkerchief and began to wave it' (pp.117-18).

Polly is reborn by this experience: '[He] descended into the world again out of the conflagration he had lit to be his funeral-pyre, moist, excited, and tremendously alive, amidst a tempest of applause' (p.119). The applause is the novelist's own, for the success of his own imagination, and is well-deserved.

It would be impossible for the rest of the novel to live up to the energy and delight of the Fishbourne fire. The valley of the Potwell Inn is rather placid, the plump, later 'fat' woman needs more characterisation, the fights with Uncle Jim are rather too figurative and farcical to seem very significant.

Published in the same year as *Howards End* and *Clayhanger*, *The History of Mr. Polly* clearly invites one to think of it with *Tono-Bungay* as another 'Condition of England' novel. The title seems to claim for itself some seriousness and some large public significance: it is both 'history' and 'Mr. Polly' that are presented. 'History' is represented in the novel by the 'gifted if unpleasant contemporary' (p.96), the economist with pince-nez who sits at leisure in the Climax Club and writes a book about small shopkeepers such as Mr. Polly whose lives are 'failures': 'Not the sharp and tragic failure of the labourer who gets out of work and starves, but a slow, chronic process of consecutive small losses which may end, if the individual is exceptionally fortunate, in an impoverished deathbed before actual bankruptcy or destitution supervenes' (pp.95-6).

Obviously in this book the Wellsian authorial presence dissociates itself from these views: yet they are very like the attitude to inefficiency set out in all seriousness in *A Modern Utopia* and the affectionate but unblinking adverse judgment of his own father in the *Experiment in Autobiography*. Polly's recall of *his* father trying to get a small sofa up a narrow winding staircase could be lifted unchanged from the account of Joe Wells in the autobiography: 'A weakly wilful being, struggling to get obdurate things round impossible corners – in that symbol Mr. Polly could recognise himself and all the troubles of humanity' (p.39). The function of the gentleman in pince-nez, who has no bearing on the action, is presumably to give the novel more significance than that of sheer entertainment: this in itself betrays uncertainty about what *kind* of novel this is and what kind of level of attention it is aimed at.

From *Love and Mr. Lewisham* onwards Wells has increasingly allowed himself authorial intervention, and in this novel the 'unpleasant gentleman' is matched and amplified by the narrator himself as commentator. The narrator gives a powerful but one may well think superfluous passage at the moment of Polly's decision, following the great Fishbourne fire, to walk out on Miriam: 'When a man has once broken through the paper walls of everyday circumstance, those unsubstantial walls that hold so many of us securely prisoned from the cradle to the grave, he has made a discovery. If the world does not please you, *you can change it*. Determine to alter it at any price, and you can change it altogether' (p.122).

This sounds important enough to be part of a serious novel about the triumph of the will. But will involves objectives – Ponderevo's 'Napoleonic Idee', Lewisham's 'Greatness' – and Polly has no objectives: 'He wanted – what *did* he want most in life? I think his distinctive craving is best expressed as fun – fun in companionship' (p.53).

Precisely the point of Polly, then, is his taste for ignoble ease. While the other lower-middle-class heroes – even Kipps – have recognisable mature male drives, Polly has none at all. Polly refuses to be heroic in any way. The joke is, of course, that he actually *gets* all the things he feebly desires: a cheap victory over Uncle Jim, who is really rather easily defeated, a picturesque and mellow setting at the Potwell Inn, and fun in the lifelong companionship of the plump (but now explicitly 'fat') woman.

The novel enlists itself firmly on the side of Polly's lazy anti-heroism and against the stock, discredited image of the hero suggested by the allegorical painting of the lady gesturing towards a distant objective which is part of Polly's early memories. The subject of the painting is 'Education' or perhaps 'the Empire teaching her sons':

'A glorious woman, with a wise and fearless face, stooping over her children, and pointing them to far horizons. The sky displayed the pearly warmth of a summer dawn, and all the painting was marvellously bright as if with the youth and hope of the delicately beautiful children in the foreground. She was telling them, one felt, of the great prospect of life that opened before them, of the splendours of sea and mountain they might travel and see, the joys of skill they might acquire, of effort and the pride of effort, and the devotions and nobilities it was theirs to achieve. Perhaps even she whispered of the warm triumphant mystery of love ... She was reminding them of their great heritage as English children, rulers of more than one-fifth of mankind, of the obligation to do and be the best that such a pride of empire entails' (pp.12-13).

The painting stands for the Victorian sanctities that intelligent Edwardians had on the whole recognised as discredited: patriotism, empire, the purity and nobility of womanhood. The painting's strenuous if dimly apprehended message is opposed to everything in Polly's experience: the bungled teaching by incompetents at board school and private school, like a surgical operation carried out by a 'butcher boy' and a 'left-handed clerk' (p.13); the dismal years of indigestion as a result of which 'every afternoon he discovered afresh that life as a whole, and every aspect of life that presented itself, was "beastly"' (p.9); his 'tattered and dissipated affectionateness' (p.38) which focuses on Parsons, the schoolgirl on the wall and finally (fatally) on his cousin Miriam; the richly dreadful funeral for his father with its cold boiled chickens, ham and brawn, for which his cousins have 'tied up the knocker with black crepe, and put a large bow over the corner of the steel engraving of Garibaldi' (p.43), and at which his appalling future mother-in-law offers 'from down the table with a large softness: "'Am, Elfred? I didn't give you very much 'am"' (p.49).
Paradoxically, though, there is something in the allegorical painting that answers Polly's vague, and vain, quest for beauty in his life. Beautiful landscape, blue sky, perfect woman and exemplary children correspond to a conception of beauty which survives in a mutilated form at the back of Polly's mind (and is signally absent from the outside world) in the magnificent opening paragraphs of the novel:

> '"Hole!" said Mr. Polly, and then for a change, and with greatly increased emphasis: "'Ole!"
> 'He paused, and then broke out with one of his private and peculiar idioms.
> '"Oh! Beastly Silly Wheeze of a hole!"
> 'He was sitting on a stile between two threadbare-looking fields, and suffering acutely from indigestion ... This afternoon, lured by the

delusive blueness of a sky that was blue because the March wind was in the east, he had come out in the hope of snatching something of the joyousness of spring' (p.9).

This establishes Polly as the microcosm of this disordered Edwardian world, with the indigestion as a strong and useful comic image of disorder to be sustained throughout the work (his digestion is healthy for the first time after the purgatorial – and purgative – experience of the Great Fishbourne Fire).

When he learns about Uncle Jim, the criminal who battens on the plump woman at the Potwell Inn, Polly's first instinct is to run away. The surprisingly solemn diction indicates the seriousness of this juncture for Polly: 'He knew – he knew now as much as a man can know of life. He knew he had to fight or perish' (p.139).

The symbols of the novel's opening, blue sky and green field, are invoked to enforce the decision imposed on Mr. Polly: 'The reality of the case arched over him like the vault of the sky, as plain as the sweet blue heaven above and the wide spread of hill and valley about him. Man comes into life to seek and find his sufficient beauty, to serve it, to win and increase it, to fight for it, to face anything and dare anything for it, counting death as nothing so long as the dying eyes still turn to it' (p.139).

The novel has subverted its own ironies: Polly here is being required in all seriousness to live up to the standard of strenuous idealism which, earlier, was mocked in the account of the allegorical painting. The anti-hero whose comic laziness and escapism have hitherto been applauded is now forced to see himself as 'a grumbling, inglorious, dirty, fattish little tramp, full of dreams and quivering excuses', with 'a paunch, and round shoulders, and red ears' (p.139). The test of manhood, then, is brought to bear on Polly. As patriotically as an imperial adventurer of popular literature he defends the pastoral England represented by the Potwell Inn from Uncle Jim's demoralised malignity, and the novel closes on an established and secure arcadia.

5. Wells the polymath: the drive towards freedom

In the Edwardian period Wells was everything. 'He was the most serious of the popular writers of his time, and the most popular of the serious.'[19] He was a prophet, socialist, 'realist', visionary, spokesman of the age and *enfant terrible*.

In his prefaces to the 'Atlantic' edition of his work published between 1924

[19] W.W. Wagar, *H.G. Wells and the World State* (1961), p.6.

and 1927, Wells gave his own retrospect of his Edwardian self. After 1914 he had convinced himself that he was a journalist rather than an artist,[20] and the general preface to the 'Atlantic' edition reflects this belief. The quarrel with James seems to be still going on in 1924, eight years after James's death. Wells notes that the appearance of a collected works of H.G. Wells might seem to invite comparison with the 'processional dignity' of the Henry James New York edition of 1907-9,[21] but his own writings, unlike James's, are 'essentially comments and enhancements of the interest of life itself' (p.xi) and 'it is far truer to call them Journalism than Art' (p.xi).

A pattern emerges from these prefaces. Wells tends to divide his Edwardian novels into those in which an individual disentangles himself or herself from a disadvantaged position (Lewisham, Kipps, Mr. Polly, Ann Veronica) and novels which address themselves to the whole state of life as he sees it (*The Sea Lady, The Food of the Gods, The War in the Air, Tono-Bungay, The New Machiavelli, Marriage*).

Wells links the disentangling characters, the first group, back to Hoopdriver, the counter-jumping draper for whom the bicycle represents freedom in *The Wheels of Chance*. Hoopdriver, Lewisham, Kipps, Polly and Ann Veronica are Wells's socially 'thwarted and crippled' personalities,[22] and their drive to freedom is a central impulse in Wells's imagination in the decade, the impetus for the novels which have emerged as indisputably major: *Love and Mr. Lewisham, Kipps* and *The History of Mr. Polly* and *Tono-Bungay*.

Love and Mr. Lewisham was 'consciously a work of art' (above, p.127). One modern critic dislikes this novel, seeing a 'yawning gap' between its 'slightness' and the claims Wells makes for it in this preface.[23] This seems to me quite wrong, and I have discussed above (pp.126-31) what I see as the virtues of *Love and Mr. Lewisham*; had it met with an encouraging reception Wells might have turned into a quite different novelist in the Edwardian period. Would one have wanted him to sacrifice his energy and multifariousness for formal perfection? I think not. Here I disagree with the drift of an essay by Bernard Bergonzi where he deplores the dissipation of Wells's talents, saying 'It is only art that endures'.[24]

Surely there was enough formal perfection in the period already in Conrad, James, George Moore, Ford? Wells's personality would have stagnated if he had kept to the model of *Lewisham*. *Tono-Bungay* may or may not have formal perfection – its champions (notably David Lodge and

---

[20] See the famous quarrel with Henry James, Leon Edel and Gordon N. Ray (eds.), *Henry James and H.G. Wells* (1958) and the autobiography.

[21] H.G. Wells, 'General Preface', *The Atlantic Edition of H.G. Wells*, vol.1 (1924), p.x.

[22] See above, p.132.

[23] Patrick Parrinder, *H.G. Wells* (1970), p.50.

[24] Bernard Bergonzi, 'Introduction', *H.G. Wells: A Collection of Critical Essays* (1976), p.6.

Kenneth Newell) insist that it has – but it is a most exhilarating book. Nothing approaching its sweep, scale and suggestiveness could have followed the *Lewisham* pattern.

Wells's son, Anthony West, wrote of Wells that his own social and political proposals actually 'grated on his aesthetic sense',[25] and that when he is attacking aesthetic values in *Boon* Wells's violence reflects a suspicion in himself that there was 'something profoundly wrong about his own inner course of development'. West concludes: 'He knew in his bones that the aesthetes were right, and that the writer's sole duty is to state the truth which he knows' (p.23).

What is the truth that he knows? He knows lower-middle-class life. No other writer of the period has quite his perspective on society; even Bennett's father became a 'professional' man (a solicitor) after an early struggle. Wells's father was a failed shop-keeper and his mother was a servant. Given that parentage and Wells's talent there was nowhere for him to go but up. All Wells's central figures are mobile: the Time Travellers and explorers of the scientific romances, the low-life figures of the realist novels and the scientists and philosophers of the discussion novels all have this mobility – up or out – in common.[26]

He knows the small-town life of the south-east. The sense of locality in works as diverse as *The War of the Worlds, The History of Mr. Polly* and the opening chapters of *The New Machiavelli* is achieved with vivid particularity. Wells cycled round Woking discovering particular points where the Martians might have landed and carefully noted the background for such scenes as Kipps in Canterbury Cathedral and Hoopdriver in Midhurst, Guildford and Chichester.

He knows from first-hand experience what it is to be a sexual anarchist challenging convention. He first expresses this in the pamphlet, *Socialism and the Family* (1906), where he teasingly remarks that since sexual constraint is a matter of opinion rather than law there is no reason why one should conform to it: 'Free Love is open to any solvent person today' (p.49). This pamphlet was written partly to annoy the Fabian Old Guard, especially the Webbs, and partly to vindicate Wells's own sexual behaviour. In retrospect he came to see the pamphlet as the first of a series of defences of sexual freedom which included several of the novels: *Ann Veronica, The New Machiavelli, Marriage, The Passionate Friends, The Wife of Sir Isaac Harmon.*

Wells was notoriously high-handed over sexual freedom: 'Our society today has in fact no complete system of sexual morals at all. It has the remains of a system' (*Socialism and the Family*, p.50). Yet despite his sturdy insistence that sexual behaviour was a matter of opinion, he was extremely

---

[25] Anthony West, 'H.G. Wells', *Wells: Critical Essays*, p.19.

[26] See Robert P. Weeks, 'Disentanglement as a theme in H.G. Wells's fiction', *Wells: Critical Essays*, pp.25-31.

irritated when he found opinion going *against* him. The sexual freedom of *Ann Veronica* (1909) was, in his view, 'attacked with hysterical animosity by people who did not like the heroine or disapproved of her thoughts and ways. There were futile attempts to boycott the book. The criticism of fiction in England and ... America has still to rise above the level at which the villain is hissed and the "nice" characters applauded' (Wells, *Atlantic Edition*, vol.13, p.ix). *Ann Veronica* is closely based on Wells's sexual liaison with a young Cambridge girl, Amber Reeves. This affair was an important part of his breach with the Fabians, since the girl's father was a member of the society.[27]

The sexual values propounded in *Ann Veronica* are peculiarly Edwardian, and it released what has been called a 'counter-attack on Edwardian permissiveness' from the critics.[28] It is a flawed novel, certainly, over-assertive and negligently constructed, but Wells was writing in it the truth that he knew about the conflict between the conventions and sexual reality.

Finally, Wells believed that he knew, and could describe with authority, the *future*.

Beatrice Webb admired *The War in the Air* not for its prophecy but for its accurate presentation of low life.[29] Wells boasted about the accuracy with which he had predicted the nature of twentieth-century warfare (Wells, *Atlantic Edition*, vol.20, p.ix), and part of the interest of the book lies in the coexistence of these two things, prophecy and close observation of lower-class life. The two topics exist 'in solution' with only a most arbitrary plot holding them together.

Bert Smallways is seen escaping from the futile market-gardening life of his father. Bert 'hated diggin'' and was unable to run errands efficiently (like Mr. Polly) because of the 'strain of poetry in his nature' (*The War in the Air*, p.171).

His first break for freedom is from the garden to the bicycle shop. The bicycle figures constantly in Wells's novels from *The Wheels of Chance* onwards: a cheap, lower-class, democratic form of transport. This bicycle shop, run by one Grubb 'with blacksmeared face by day and a music-hall side by night' (p.171) operates at the lower end of the trade, hiring out broken-down bicycles to dockers and apprentices. Bert's father, a former coachman, is connected with the transport of the past. His former employers have been replaced by 'a new kind of gentleman altogether – a gentleman of most ungentlemanly energy, a gentleman in dusty oilskins and motor-goggles and a wonderful cap, a stink-making gentleman, a swift, high-class badger, who fled perpetually along high roads from the dust and the stink he perpetually made' (p.172).

Inevitably one thinks of Mr. Toad's passion for motorcars (a suggestion

---

[27] MacKenzies, p.226.
[28] Ibid., p.256.
[29] Quoted in Parrinder, p.150.

reinforced by Wells's reference to a badger) and of the motorcars in *Howards End* and *Man and Superman*. Bert buys a motorbike and sees airships and balloons rising above the Crystal Palace. Over Bun Hill where he lives a gyroscopic monorail train travels from London to Brighton: 'Old Smallways [his father] went to his grave under an intricate network of wires and cables' (p.175). The novel begins with a reliable insight – that the working-class adolescent mind is fascinated by the development of transport – and moves from there to take the implications of this into a future European conflict.

Perhaps Beatrice Webb is right about this book; its title-page seems to support her view. The sub-title, *And Particularly how Mr. Bert Smallways Fared*, suggests that the novelist has baulked at the prospect of inventing a completely understood aerial conflict among all the major powers – it would, indeed, be a monstrous undertaking – and has opted instead for an impressionist view given by a limited narrator.

The device by which Bert is manoeuvred into this central narrative position is farcical: he helps to steady the balloon in which Butteridge, inventor of the first stabilised flying-machine, has landed on Dymchurch beach, and is carried away when the balloon is released from Butteridge's weight. The balloon carries him to the centre of the 'German aeronautic park': he is mistaken for Butteridge and taken by Prince Karl Albert, the German Leader, 'big and blonde and virile and splendidly non-moral' (p.221) on the flagship of the German air-fleet to participate in the bombing of New York.

Among Bert's impressions there are some fine moments. Fires and slaughter always excite Wells, of course, and the attack on New York gives several opportunities:

'The little man on the pavement jumped comically – no doubt with terror – as the bomb fell beside him. Then blinding flames squirted out in all directions from the point of impact, and the little man who had jumped became, for an instant, a flash of fire and vanished' (p.278).

'As the airships sailed along they smashed up the city as a child will shatter its cities of brick and card. Below, they left ruins and blazing conflagrations and heaped and scattered dead' (p.279).

Wells concludes too easily that aerial warfare means the end of the world as we know it. He argues that since aerial warfare is a war without frontiers it must also be a war without end. A nation which has already effectively been destroyed can continue to drop bombs on its enemies as long as its airships are in operation. Wells's airships are cheap and easy to produce: the heavier-than-air machine in Wells's projection of the future has little part to play because only Butteridge (and a Japanese artist) have discovered the secret of stabilising them.

Wells looks down on his future world from a great height. He obviously enjoys writing sentences like: 'It was the collapse of the civilisation that had trusted to machinery, and the instruments of its destruction were machines' (p.301). He writes from an imaginary future after the events of the novel, in which there is a stable world government and from which: 'Nothing seems so precarious, so giddily dangerous, as the fabric of the social order with which the men of the opening of the twentieth century were content' (p.352).

The apocalyptic aspects of the book perhaps owe something to the fantasies of M.P. Shiel, *The Yellow Danger* (1898) and *The Purple Cloud* (1901), and to Richard Jefferies' impressive work in the genre, *After London* (1885). When the Chinese and Japanese attack Europe, Bert's German friend, Kurt, remarks blithely: 'The Yellow Peril was a peril after all!' (p.290). And the post-war population of the world in Wells's novel is decimated by a disease called the 'purple death'. In Shiel's novel the 'purple cloud' is a poison which destroys the population of the world except for one man and one woman. The post-apocalyptic ending of Wells's novel in which Bert and Edna settle down to breed eleven children and repopulate the earth is obviously close to this pattern.

The xenophobia in Shiel's books is part of the Edwardian popular mind, and Wells is reflecting this when he describes the popular neuroses of the period: 'Instead of the sturdy establishment in prejudice of Bert's grandfather, to whom the word 'Frenchified' was the ultimate term of contempt, there flowed through Bert's brain a squittering succession of thinly violent ideas about German competition, about the Yellow Danger, about the Black Peril, about the White Man's Burthen' (p.220).

Bert ceases to be the common man and becomes the narrator and survivor when he accidentally flies off in Butteridge's balloon. The balloon flight is like a scientific experiment, with Wells the novelist as the Godlike scientist: 'Bert Smallways was a vulgar little creature, the sort of pert, limited soul that the old civilisation of the early twentieth century produced by the million in every country of the world. He had lived all his life in narrow streets, and between mean houses he could not look over, and in a narrow circle of ideas from which there was no escape' (p.203).

The balloon flight gives him the escape he needs: 'It was as if Heaven was experimenting with him, had picked him out as a sample from the English millions to look at him more nearly and to see what was happening to the soul of man' (p.205).

Wells defies his son's criticism, then, because the 'truth that he knows' is too diverse to be confined to any one literary form; to have remained within the mode of *Love and Mr. Lewisham*, good though it is, would have been impossible for him.

The drive towards 'freedom', the disentangling of entangled man, is the dominant feature of his Edwardian books. The prophetic books, and the energy that Wells devoted to them, indicate a personal desire to sweep away, to undo, the infuriating obstructiveness of what he saw as the prejudice, stupidity and inertia of the people surrounding him. The *Faults of the Fabians* pamphlet and the whole struggle with the Fabians are symptomatic of this drive. And in his lighter books he could express the excitement of kicking away suburbia and replacing it with the delightful triumph of the will and the appetite. The Sea Lady complains, elegantly, that the English will not take off their clothes to enjoy their bodies, will not make love when they want to: 'You are so limited, so tied! The little time you have, you use so poorly. You begin and you end and all the time between it is as if you were enchanted, you are afraid to do this that would be delightful to do, you must do that though you know all the time it is stupid and disagreeable. Just think of the things ... you mustn't do ... sitting in stuffy ugly clothes ... hot tight boots, you know, when they have the most lovely pink feet, some of them' (*The Sea Lady*, 1902, p.98).

With this drive towards freedom goes the desire to Live, with a capital L: Capes could almost be echoing the Sea Lady when he advises Ann Veronica to 'find the thing you want to do most intensely, make sure that's it, and do it with all your might' (*Ann Veronica*, p.328) and declares 'We're going to live, Ann Veronica' (p.338). *The New Machiavelli* (1911) gives a vivid picture of defeated suburban man in 'Bromsted', Wells's childhood Bromley. Dick Remington is advised by his father never to become encumbered by property or responsibilities, but to 'Live' (p.31). Like Bert Smallways, Remington's father hates and resents gardening, the activity for the plodding, stupid man. When Remington Senior advises his son to 'Live' what he really seems to be saying is 'fly'. Drop the responsibilities like ballast, rise with the afflatus of your own genius: 'You and I are the brainy unstable kind, topside or nothing. And if ever those blithering houses [the rented property which his father finds an irksome responsibility] come to you – don't have 'em. Give them away! Dynamite 'em – and off! *Live*, Dick!' (p.31).

Flight, in both its aspects, seems to me the central feature of Wells's Edwardian temperament: flight upwards, giving one a perspective of authority and superiority on human affairs, and flight *away*, escape from any set of circumstances that might become a trap. Bert's flight in a balloon and Ponderevo's flight in his airship come to mind: the two novels were written very close together. All the four major novels deal in escape: Mr. Polly's flight from Fishbourne is the most obvious and exhilarating, but even Lewisham is escaping from an intolerable subjection, as a student, to a position of dominance as a householder and head of a family. The height of the giants in *The Food of the Gods* is flight in the other sense, the drive to a superior perspective. Trafford the super-intellect crashlanding his aeroplane in a vicarage garden in *Marriage* is a variation of the same pattern, the exalted mind opposing the constricted suburban world.

Undoubtedly in his own life Wells saw himself as 'the brainy unstable kind, topside or nothing'. He *will* dominate the Fabians, he *will* exercise the right to have mistresses as well as his wife, he *will* vindicate his sexual behaviour in *Ann Veronica*. The cool reception of *Love and Mr. Lewisham* at the beginning of the decade was a check to which he reacted by flight into prophecy and political activity. He returned to the novel with *Kipps* and *Tono-Bungay*, but it was the novel on a much bigger and more ambitious scale, as though having found that he could not impress the world with economical, well-shaped work, he had determined to compel respect with the sheer scale of his ambition in these later works. The hostile reaction to *Ann Veronica* is another check at the end of the decade; he reacts by writing more and more, becoming more and more gaseous and expanded (to extend the balloon image) and continues his vertical ascent leaving the art of the novel, the Edwardian period and his period of major achievement, behind.

Chapter Five: Arnold Bennett

1. 'The whole contention'

It is important to remember that in 1924, when Virginia Woolf read her famous attack on Bennett and the 'Edwardians' to the Heretics at Cambridge, she was speaking from anxiety. She feels that her own kind of writing is under attack from the other side for being 'insubstantial' and that Bennett is in a position of entrenched strength. For any young writer in the 1920s there was a feeling that Bennett was governing the literary market by his prestige and influence as a reviewer. A writer like Virginia Woolf who genuinely disliked Bennett's novels was bound to see him also as a major obstacle, a mediocrity who had made himself into an arbiter of taste by dint of application and sheer affrontery.

That said, there can be no doubt, as Samuel Hynes has pointed out, that Virginia Woolf is unfair to Bennett and that her case against him is substantially wrong.[1] She begins by speaking of 'The Edwardians' as Wells, Bennett and Galsworthy, arbitrarily excluding Forster on the grounds that he is 'Georgian' and Conrad because his Polishness 'sets him apart, and makes him, however admirable, not very helpful' (*Mr. Bennett and Mrs. Brown* (1924), p.10). She is angry with Bennett for describing in detail the houses in which people live (p.17) especially in *Hilda Lessways* (pp.14-15), and she sets up an amusing but misleading caricature of Bennett on a train describing the upholstery and advertisements in the carriage, and the clothes and gloves of 'Mrs. Brown' herself, and concerning himself with the question of whether Mrs. Brown's house is Freehold or Copyhold (p.16). She closes her case by saying that 'The Edwardians' (by which she now means Bennett alone, Wells and Galsworthy having been dropped from the essay after a brief flourish) 'have laid an enormous stress on the fabric of things. They have given us a house in the hope that we may be able to deduce the human beings who live there' (p.18).

---

[1] Samuel Hynes, 'The whole contention between Mr. Bennett and Mrs Woolf', in *Edwardian Occasions* (1972), pp.24-38.

Given the nature of her own art, Virginia Woolf's anxiety about Bennett is understandable. She feels that detailed and closely drawn setting and context are part of a dead Victorian convention and that she must make a strong case for overthrowing them. But it is not true to say that Bennett was 'never interested in character in itself' (p.12). And she betrays herself in a small way when she writes of Mrs. Brown: 'She came of gentlefolk who kept servants – but details could wait' (p.9). Bennett understands more clearly than she does that the 'details' matter to 'character', that social and economic status and geographical and historical situations bear crucially upon the personality.

The upper-middle-class of Virginia Woolf's novels are themselves personalities in given social and economic situations, and it is a mark of Virginia Woolf's fineness as a novelist that although the context is implied rather than stated one never loses the sense of it in her work. Her novels reveal what the essay would deny, that she and Bennett are actually rather alike, especially in their perception of women as socially conditioned beings: Bennett's Anna, Constance and Sophia, Virginia Woolf's Katharine Hilbery, Clarissa Dalloway, Mrs. Ramsay.

The differences, and they are of course very substantial, lie in the establishing of contexts rather than in the central matter of presentation of personality. To look at Virginia Woolf's essay again is to be struck by Bennett's paradoxical view of provincial life. Virginia Woolf's world is in a sense easy to present: the life of upper-middle-class people can be assumed as a norm existing in the reader's mind, the diction and styles will evoke recognition if not a sense of identification. Bennett has to present a way of life more or less unknown to a metropolitan readership.

In the best of his Five Towns writing, *The Old Wives' Tale*, 'The Death of Simon Fuge', *Anna of the Five Towns* and *Clayhanger*, he establishes a double perspective. Provincial working-class life is brutalised and stupid and at the same time strong, self-reliant and admirably energetic. Provincial middle-class life clumsily apes the manners of metropolis in some of its aspects but in others shows an appropriate and vigorous culture which exists in independence of, and indeed in successful competition with, the great artistic and intellectual centres. With this double perception of his Five Towns goes a further paradox which is constantly implied but never fully stated. It comes closest to full expression in *A Man from the North* and *Clayhanger*, presumably because Bennett is drawing on his own young manhood directly in those two books. In provincial life one is free and in chains. The closeness of the community and the strength of its traditions channel the energies and make for force, directness, a rooted sense of identity; but equally they make for conformity, the stifling of original thought, crippling constraint on creative innovation.

2. Clayhanger

In 1910 Arnold Bennett was regarded by many as *the* leading novelist of the day. A review in *The World* of Forster's *Howards End* complains that 'this novel has been one of the sensations of the autumn season, and, in that respect, it has been made – not widely – to overshadow Mr Arnold Bennett's *Clayhanger* which is a much greater book.'[2] The same critic objects to the *political* attitudes of the major Edwardian novelists (with the exception of Conrad): 'Mr Forster, in company with all the modern school of Wells, Galsworthy and Bennett, is one-sided in his sympathies. These writers cannot bring themselves to present fairly, as Henry James and George Meredith do, the side of English life supposed here to be represented by the Wilcoxes. Thousands of Wilcoxes did not die to make England, it was something far better. The modern intellectual will not see this, for his sympathies are radical. The type of Sir Philip Sidney is the real type, and it exists in plenty, but not obviously, like the Wilcoxes.'[3]

Bennett himself had handsome things to say about Forster's work when he reviewed it in *The New Age*, though he teases Forster for his sudden success with the '*élite*' and predicts that *Howards End* will not be his best book: 'No author's best book is ever the best received.'[4] He agrees, approvingly, that Forster is a 'radical' novelist.

It is a little startling that Bennett, Wells, Galsworthy and Forster could be seen as equally 'radical'. To a modern retrospect their political divergence seems clearly marked. Galsworthy never strayed far from the outlook of his class and Forster's liberalism is equally limited: though here the limitation is more a matter of temperament than of social affiliation. Wells's pungent aggressiveness is much closer to one's modern conception of 'radicalism' and Bennett, by contrast, is often thought of as conservative in outlook. He was certainly thought so by his enemies: Wyndham Lewis caricatured him as Samuel Shodbutt, the philistine autocrat of a modern Grub Street in *The Roaring Queen* (1936: not published, for fear of libel actions, until 1973), Ezra Pound makes him into the bloated, pampered Mr Nixon who advises the young poet to 'consider carefully the reviewer' in 'Hugh Selwyn Mauberley'. And even a close friend could misunderstand Bennett's political stance: Wells wrote to him in 1906 saying 'I want to make you a socialist'. Bennett replied temperately but with some slight irritation: he acknowledges that his life-style is not typically that of the radical writer ('I have been yachting with anti-socialists in Holland') but he goes on to say: 'You will find it impossible to make me a socialist, as I already am one. See?'[5]

[2] Philip Gardner (ed.), *E.M. Forster: The Critical Heritage* (1973), p.154.
[3] Ibid., p.155.
[4] Ibid., p.257.
[5] Harris Wilson (ed.), *Arnold Bennett and H.G. Wells* (1960), pp.136-7.

Clayhanger, Howards End and *The History of Mr. Polly* were all published in 1910 and are all concerned, from the different perspectives created by their writers' different temperaments, with freedom. The impediments in the way of Edwin Clayhanger's freedom are much more powerful than those obstructing the Schlegel sisters or Mr. Polly. A whole history of industrial conditioning has to be overcome, the Victorian inheritance embodied in Darius Clayhanger, Edwin's tyrannical father, has to be thrown off. And Edwin fails to throw it off; the personal ambition and sexual drive which he begins to show are signally defeated by the novel's pattern.

Wells insists that sexual freedom is an essential condition of the other freedoms. For Edwin Clayhanger the move towards sexual experience at the end of the novel seems tentative and colourless. Bennett notoriously found it difficult to write about sexuality and sexual attraction. Edwin Clayhanger comes across as a virgin in his late thirties who is quite contented with his celibacy, and motivated to marry Hilda Lessways partly by the feeling that a single person is a failure – he has the sad example of Janet Orgreaves, left at home looking after her extravagant and enfeebled parents – partly by the contrary pull of the examples of the male Orgreaves.

Clayhanger is a fresh departure among Bennett's various novels. After his major studies of women, *Anna of the Five Towns* and *The Old Wives' Tale*, Bennett in *Clayhanger* identifies and describes the repressiveness of provincial life as it effects a young male. The stance of the novel does not allow Edwin's overdetermined condition to seem an indictment of the society to which he belongs; he is sustained in the traditions of the Five Towns and imprinted with them until he has no other identity.

For Edwin the alternative to life in the Five Towns (in his father's printing works) is to become an architect, following the model of Osmond Orgreaves, his father-surrogate. In the later novels this ambition is fulfilled vicariously by his step-son George Cannon, Hilda's child. The pattern of *Clayhanger* declines to judge whether Edwin would have been better off if his ambition were fulfilled. His friend Charles Orgreaves escapes to become a doctor in London; the novel reveals that the apparent glamour of this escape is illusory, Charles finds it difficult to keep up appearances, his practice is in Ealing which is no less suburban than the Five Towns. Osmond Orgreaves has qualities that Edwin lacks, a developed sense of beauty, a capacity for hard bargaining, a flamboyant personality. He is a model that Edwin would find it impossible to follow, one may feel, and even in his father's printing business Edwin makes no more than a mediocre success.

As in the other Five Towns novels there is the sense that a Calvinist, predestining view of man in society is at work. Bennett himself had escaped from the uncongenial environment, had made the metropolitan success story against high odds. Edwin Clayhanger's story obviously embodies a flattering reflection on Bennett's own career: the man who does not have the energy and aggressiveness to escape when he is young will never 'make it' on his own, and is wise to accept whatever economic niche he may be lucky enough to inherit.

Part of Edwin's adverse conditioning is his ignorance. Bennett's experience made him acutely aware that knowledge is freedom, and for Edwin the knowledge, with the will and the sexual initiation, come too late: his insight into his own conditioning comes only when that conditioning has hardened round him. Edwin goes to Bursley Middle School, while Bennett went, like his Charles Orgreaves, to the superior Grammar School at Newcastle-under-Lyme (the 'Oldcastle' of the novel). Presumably, though, Bennett is drawing on his own experience when he describes Edwin's ignorance of his own history: 'That geographical considerations are the cause of all history had never been hinted to him, nor that history bears immediately upon modern life and bore on his own life. For him history hung unsupported and unsupporting in the air. In the course of his school career he had several times approached the nineteenth century, but it seemed to him that for administrative reasons he was always being dragged back again to the Middle Ages. Once his form had "got" as far as the infancy of his own father, and concerning this period he had learnt that "great dissatisfaction prevailed among the labouring classes, who were led to believe by mischievous demagogues", etc. But the next term he was recoiling round Henry the Eighth' (*Clayhanger*, p.12).

Edwin is taught nothing about the potteries, yet has an enquiring mind and would, if properly guided, come early to a mature knowledge of himself. He had also been taught 'absolutely nothing about political economy or logic, and was therefore at the mercy of the first agreeable sophistry that might take his fancy by storm' (p.13).

This ironic account of Edwin's education indicates, negatively, the kind of education that a young man in the Five Towns needed in order to escape. Bennett describes his own formal education as a kind of prison. His real education took place in his own time; his 'private enterprises' to which he stubbornly devoted himself out of school hours. His father would not allow him to go out in the evening or associate with the other youths of the district, and Bennett made good use of this enforced loneliness:

> 'I did acquire the habit of organising the hours of my day. I was compelled to acquire it, or I should have had no leisure at all for my own private enterprises.
>
> 'And my private enterprises alone interested. I cannot remember ever getting any pleasure out of the great official enterprise of learning. I never enjoyed school, and I assuredly never enjoyed home-lessons. Not until I was nearly forty did it suddenly occur to me that getting

knowledge was in itself rather fun' (Unpublished ms., Keele University Library).

Darius Clayhanger, Edwin's father, is based on Bennett's own father, and the close, stifling and strenuous relationship between father and son owes much to Bennett's recollection of this bruising and inhibiting relationship.

The most important fact in Edwin's history is one of which he remains ignorant until a late stage of the novel: the fact that his father as a child was sent to a workhouse. Like a Freudian trauma this wounding memory works at a deep level, determining his father's actions and thus the pattern of Edwin's early life. Darius's obstinacy, his refusal to give Edwin enough to live on, his intense possessiveness and competitiveness, are all expressions of neurosis springing from this source. Edwin cannot know the spring of his father's obsessions and is therefore helpless.

Perhaps the trauma is made too exclusively the root of Darius's behaviour, but one does not feel that the psychology of this figure is being handled with anything other than the most brilliant realism until the *dénouement* of his story is given. In his childhood Darius was rescued from a workhouse by Mr Shushions the Sunday School teacher; in maturity he learns that Shushions has become destitute, and has himself been taken to a workhouse and died there. It is at this moment, rather too mechanically and symmetrically, one may feel, that Darius begins to show symptoms of the 'softening of the brain' which will kill him in another two years and at last places power and initiative in Edwin's hands. The reader now has all the facts necessary for an understanding of Darius: facts still withheld from Edwin himself. '[Edwin was] unaware, with all his omniscience, that the being in front of him was not a successful steam-printer and tyrannical father, but a tiny ragged boy who could still taste the Bastille [workhouse] skilly and still see his mother weeping round the knees of a powerful god named Shushions' (p.334).

As well as Orgreaves and his father Edwin in adolescence is confronted with other models of masculinity, notably Big James, who works as a compositor in Darius's printing works. Big James is respected in a male-dominated working-class community for his height, his bass voice, and his beard; yet he is in fact a gentle bachelor with no ambition. The implication is that the virility of the industrial working-class can easily be deflected into display rather than directed towards achievement. Big James's chief pleasure is in his own singing, which communicates a powerful sense of masculine force and authority to the adolescent Edwin: 'It was majestic, terrific, and overwhelming. Many bars before the close Edwin was thrilled, as by an exquisite and vast revelation. He tingled from head to foot' (p.79).

A key to the paradox presented by Big James, the paradox of strength without effectiveness, is that he is an instinctive conservative accepting unquestioningly the industrial class system. Mr Shushions, very much more intelligent than Big James, ends his life a failure. In his senile old age Bennett remarks of him that he has 'lived too long'. But at no time has he been successful in worldly terms. His only achievement is to have made Darius Clayhanger what he is.

There are no developed studies of women in *Clayhanger*. Hilda Lessways, structurally the most prominent woman, is seen almost entirely in terms of externals. This is party because *Clayhanger* is designed as the first of a run of novels: Hilda, who is accepting Edwin as her lover in the last pages of the novel, is indicated and hinted at rather than developed, and in an explanatory note on his final page Bennett writes: 'In the autumn of 1911 the author will publish a novel dealing with the history of Hilda Lessways up to the day of her marriage with Edwin. This will be followed by a novel dealing with the marriage' (p.573).

This note makes the writing of the succeeding novels sound like a chore, and indeed the experience of reading *Hilda Lessways* and *These Twain* largely supports that suggestion, although in *Hilda Lessways* there is a particular technical satisfaction to be derived from reading scenes from *Clayhanger* repeated from the point of view of Hilda instead of Edwin. The explanatory note can be taken as freeing Bennett from the duty to present a full portrait of Hilda in the first novel, with the result that *Clayhanger* on its own is almost exclusively about a young man growing up in a man's world: a world which is materialist and realist, with success as its only recognised standard.

John Wain has remarked of Bennett: 'He presents people as simple organisms, moved ... by the predictable demands of their appetites and what they take to be their self-interest ... We miss the religious impulse ... an assent to the dark and mysterious, the intangible, the unbidden.'[6] He goes on to say that the interest in the religious revival in *Anna of the Five Towns* is external only, and that there is scarcely any 'religious' interest in any sense in *Clayhanger*. These points are true, and they are aspects of Bennett's attitudes to his own origins which Wain well characterises when he speaks of a 'slight but all-pervading irony which we find in his descriptions of Five Towns scenes and people.'[7] At the same time no one would ask Bennett to be Conrad, who does seem to me clearly to write with a 'religious' interest in Wain's sense of the term. To ask ultimate questions about the nature of life is to ask religious questions, and to be able to ask such questions one must be able to see man as free, isolated and alone, experiencing the epistemological crisis of the period. Bennett's Five Towns people are too firmly bedded in their history and their environment, even when reacting against those things, to experience or embody this crisis to the same degree.

6 John Wain, *Arnold Bennett* (1967), p.28.
7 Ibid., p.9.

The early part of the novel sees Edwin socially conditioned but with a 'blazing' desire for 'self-perfection'. The transcription from Bennett's own experience can be taken as direct. The young man from Hanley with no money, a speech impediment, a diffident social manner and a consciousness of considerable talent has an inner drive to 'self-perfection', which takes the place of religious intuitions and inquisitiveness.

The story of the young Edwin derives its energy from the tension between Edwin's ambitious, emergent identity and the inertia of the social situation surrounding him: 'Sundry experienced and fat old women were standing or sitting at their cottage doors, one or two smoking cutties. But even they, who in childbed and at gravesides had been at the very core of life for long years, they, who saw more than most, could only see a fresh lad passing along, with fair hair and a clear complexion, and gawky knees and elbows, a fierce, rapt expression on his straightforward, good-natured face. Some knew that it was "Clayhanger's lad", a nice-behaved young gentleman, and the spitten image of his poor mother. They all knew what a lad is – the feel of his young skin under his "duds", the capricious freedom of his movements, his sudden madnesses and shoutings and tendernesses, and the exceeding power of his unconscious wistful charm. They could divine all that in a glance. But they could not see the mysterious and holy flame for self-perfection blazing within that tousled head. And if Edwin had suspected that anybody could indeed perceive it, he would have whipped it out for shame, though the repudiation had meant everlasting death. Such is youth in the Five Towns, if not elsewhere' (pp.16-17).

This paragraph concludes the second chapter of the book, 'The Flame'. John Lucas has said of Bennett that one should not allow a critical discussion of his work to depend on quotation: 'The impact of his novel is gradual and cumulative. His best work is always much more impressive as a whole than as a sum of its parts.'[8] This is certainly true of *Clayhanger*. The above passage does not respond well to close reading – the old women could have been sharpened and made more specific, the 'mysterious and holy flame' is diluted by its epithets – yet as the last paragraph of an important chapter it establishes in the reader's mind a contrapuntal effect which is sustained throughout the novel; the contrast between Edwin's 'flame' of ambition and the Five Towns people glumly asserting a lifestyle which will extinguish that flame.

I have chosen to begin my discussion of Bennett with *Clayhanger* because it is his most autobiographical novel and the culmination of the best stage of his career. Bennett is Edwardian in all senses including that of strict chronology: all his best work, apart from *Riceyman Steps*, was done by the end of the decade.

Clayhanger's resemblance to Bennett's first novel, *A Man from the North* (by

[8] John Lucas, *Arnold Bennett: A Study of his Fiction* (1974), p.13.

'E.A. Bennett', 1898) has often been noted: each is the story of a young provincial who seeks freedom and personal success and fails to attain them. Richard Larch in *A Man from the North* escapes from the Five Towns and reaches London, but there allows himself to be trapped into suburban marriage and is baulked of his ambition to become a writer; the parallel with Wells's Mr Lewisham is close. In *Clayhanger* Edwin's childhood friend, Charlie Orgreaves, struggling to keep going as a doctor in Ealing, is just as much bound by the intractability of circumstance as Edwin himself. Indeed, in a sense Charlie is *less* 'free' than Edwin. Being bullied by his father and shut in by the closely controlled environment in Bursley finally enables Edwin to focus his aggressions. He is in no danger of the unmotivated drifting lethargy which overtakes Richard Larch in *A Man from the North*.

At the moment of his angry confrontation with his father Edwin's protracted adolescence can be seen at last giving way to maturity of a kind. The personality change is not forced, it is part of the closely observed, cumulative nature of Bennett's characterisation.

The following dialogue is well prepared for in the structure of the book: one knows that the pressure forming Edwin's personality has been steadily building so that he must react in this way at this point:

> '"What do you mean by calling me a thief?" Edwin and Darius were equally startled by this speech. Edwin knew not what had come over him, and Darius, never having been addressed in such a dangerous tone by his son, was at a loss.
>
> '"I never called ye a thief."
>
> '"Yes, you did! Yes, you did!" Edwin nearly shouted now. "You starve me for money, until I haven't got sixpence to bless myself with. You couldn't get a man to do what I do for twice what you pay me. And then you call me a thief. And then you jump down my throat because I spend a bit of money of my own."
>
> 'He snorted. He knew that he was quite mad, but there was a strange drunken pleasure in this madness' (p.268).

The passage has its disappointments: the snort, the madness, the 'knew not what' and the strange drunken pleasure should have been pruned away. Still, the particular localised world dominated by the moral outlook of Auntie Hamps, who 'leans hard' on Jesus, the narrowly channelled energy of the small businessman father fighting to become rich in a favourable economic climate, the provincial dandyism and prodigality of Orgreaves and the institutions created by these people – the glee-singing; the 'blood-tub', or travelling theatre; Florence Offlow's clog-dancing; the Young Men's Methodist Debating Society; the Mutual Burial Club (an anachronistic relic of earlier working-class poverty) – all these aspects of the Five Towns are brought to bear on Edwin in conflict with his own individuality at this point, making this paragraph a pivot of the action.

'The Flame', the title of the novel's second chapter, recalls the 1890s when Pater's hard gem-like flame was still beckoning young men towards an exacting intensity of aesthetic experience. *The Man from the North* is an 1890s novel, and Richard Larch has a good deal of the decadent/aesthetic temperament. 'On first arriving in London, he had projected a series of visits to churches famous either for architectural beauty or for picturesque ritual. A few weeks, however, had brought tedium. He was fundamentally irreligious, and his churchgoing proceeded from a craving, purely sensuous, which sought gratification in ceremonial pomps, twilight atmospheres heavy with incense and electric with devotion, and dim perspectives of arching stone' (*A Man from the North*, p.91).

Yet although *A Man from the North* and *Clayhanger* can both be seen as *Bildungsromane*, as novels of initiation and development, *A Man from the North* is very much a novel of the decadence while *Clayhanger* has the quite different characteristics of a 'condition of England' novel.[9]

In *Clayhanger* Bennett takes care to establish the factors in the history of the period which make Edwin a 'modern' man. *Clayhanger* spans almost the whole Victorian period, from 1835, when Darius was sent to the workhouse, to the 'flu epidemic of 1892. With his enthusiastic assent, as a social Darwinist, to the notion of 'progress', Bennett is able to take an Olympian view of the nineteenth century: in the chapter called 'Father and Son after Seven Years' he traces the differences between 1873 and 1880 in terms of the relationship between Edwin and Darius (Edwin ages from 16 to 23 in this period) and also in terms of the history of England.

> 'They both of them went on living on the assumption that the world had stood still in those seven years between 1873 and 1880. If they had been asked what had happened during those seven years, they would have answered: "Oh, nothing particular!"'
>
> 'But the world had been whizzing ceaselessly from one miracle into another. Board schools had been opened in Bursley, wondrous affairs, with ventilation; indeed ventilation had been discovered. A Jew had been made Master of the Rolls: spectacle at which England shivered, and then, perceiving no sign of disaster, shrugged its shoulders ... Herbert Spencer had published his "Study of Sociology"; Matthew Arnold his "Literature and Dogma"; and Frederick Farrer his Life of his Lord, but here the provinces had no difficulty in deciding, for they

---

[9] See my discussion of *Tono-Bungay*, above, pp.119-26.

had only heard of the last. Every effort had been made to explain by persuasion and force to the working man that trade unions were inimical to his true welfare, and none had succeeded, so stupid was he' (p.163).

There is a great deal more of this. I have selected sentences which illustrate Bennett's distance in time and place from his subject. He can write so well about the Five Towns because he has escaped from them; he can write about Victorian urban lower-middle-class English provincial life because he is an Edwardian man of letters living in Paris. He asserts both sides of Darwin's discovery equally: both the value of the continuity of human experience, and the importance of progress, of discovering a point in the continuum at which one breaks off to take one's own path.

All Bennett's major novels reflect a view of life which is ultimately despairing. There is a sense in which he is the most pessimistic of the Edwardians. The Orgreaves, who at the beginning of *Clayhanger* hold out to Edwin a hope of success and heroic endeavour, are decimated by the novel's action. At first the Orgreaves household with its conspicuous spending, its comfort, its unembarrassed belief in the value of pleasure, is a welcome antithesis to the harshness of the Clayhanger home. But the prosperity withers, the promising children leave, the attractive Janet becomes a passive spinster who is destined to nurse her fretful parents into their graves.

There are certain parallels with *Howards End*. The stagnant prosperity of the Wilcoxes is destroyed by Charles's imprisonment; the bored bachelor state of Edwin is radically disturbed by his discovery that Hilda's 'husband', now in prison, was never in fact married to her (his first conviction was for bigamy). Hilda's child, George, becomes the focus of hope for the future as does Helen Schlegel's baby in Forster's novel.

George's most effective function is to relate the novel's concern with education – the need for knowledge of oneself and one's environment – to the prosperous industrial setting. Prosaic, for Edwin, the process of pottery manufacture is a rich romantic experience for young George. Watching George's excitement as he visits a kiln, Edwin recalls his own childhood: as a boy he had wondered why clay had to be transported to the potteries from Cornwall (one of the many questions that his defective education has failed to answer). As a man he has acquired the answer by experience: the local clay is no longer good enough for fine ware, and is used only for the 'saggers' that hold the pottery during firing.

At the end of the novel Edwin is the product of a sustained struggle between his will and his environment. Neither has won. Although prevented from becoming an architect and leaving the Five Towns he has mastered his father (and sisters) and is about to rescue Hilda from bankruptcy in Brighton and fulfil his own ambitions vicariously through George. In chapter 3

Edwin's hatred of Brighton balances his earlier boredom with the Five Towns. The fashionable and the metropolitan would not suit him: 'For miles westwards and miles eastwards, against a formidable background of high, yellow and brown architecture, persons the luxuriousness of any one of whom would have drawn remark in Bursley, walked or drove or rode in thronging multitudes ... The air was full of the trot of glossy horses, and the rattle of bits, and the roll of swift wheels, and the fall of elegant soles on endless clean pavements; it was full of the consciousness of being correct and successful. Many of the faces were monstrously ugly, most were dissatisfied and querulous; but they were triumphant' (pp.476-7).

The young Edwin, wanting to escape from the tameness of the Young Men's Methodist Debating Society which believes in Moses as a 'serious historian' and in the 'doctrine of everlasting burning hell' (p.129), from 'the servitude and squalor of brutalised populations' (p.84) and from 'years of muddy inefficiency, of contentedness with the second-rate and the dishonest' (p.16), gives way to the self-reliant man who rescues Hilda from the cruel anonymity of fashionable Brighton and takes her back to a way of life which is now seen as warm, supporting and intimate. So firmly rooted in the Five Towns is Edwin's sense of his own identity that he could never have become one of Conrad's heroes, just as his creator could never have experienced Conrad's loneliness and alienation.

3. A Man from the North *and* Anna of the Five Towns

Bennett the realist, Bennett the materialist, Virginia Woolf's bogeyman Bennett who relentlessly chronicled the outsides of things and people: all these aspects of Bennett are there in *A Man from the North* (1898), but they coexist with what one may call 'Gothic' Bennett, a post-Swinburne, post-Pater, late- or last-Romantic who is more than a little in love with death. In *A Man from the North* Bennett allows himself to litter the stage with corpses. Richard Larch's parents, sister, brother-in-law all die before he reaches London: once there he presides over the death of his one literary friend, the failed laureate of the suburbs, Mr Aked. Richard sits at Mr Aked's bedside watching him die and reflecting on the stoicism of the hired nurse: '[Richard] marvelled that the nurse could be unmoved and cheerful in the midst of this piteous altercation with death. Was she blind to the terror in the man's eyes? ... [Aked begins to cough and is unable to stop:] Richard suddenly conceived a boundless respect for the nurse, who had watched whole nights by this tortured organism on the bed. Somehow existence began to assume for him a new and larger aspect; he felt that till that moment he had been going through the world with his eyes closed; life was sublimer, more terrible, than he had thought' (p.148).

Aked's role in the novel is completed by his death. He is an analogue of Richard himself, and Aked's ambition, to write a book about suburban London, is being fulfilled by Bennett the novelist in the act of writing his novel about Richard Larch's aspirations and failure.

Aked's death is a prolepsis of the death of Richard Larch's hopes. Like Wells's Lewisham and Hardy's Jude, Richard Larch has conflicting drives, one for fame and the other for sex, and the action turns on a competition between these drives in which sex wins. Literature is death. Richard Larch visits Mr. Aked in the British Museum Reading Room: 'In the centre of the reading-room at the British Museum sit four men fenced about by a quadruple ring of unwieldy volumes which are an index to all knowledge in the world ... All day long, from early morning, when the attendants, self-propelled on wheeled stools, run around the rings arranging and aligning the huge blue tomes, to late afternoon, when the immense dome is like a dark night and the arc lamps hiss and crackle in the silence, they answer questions, patiently, courteously ... Vague, reverberating noises roll heavily from time to time across the chamber, but no one looks up; the incessant cannibal feast of the living upon the dead goes speechlessly forward; the trucks of food are always moving to and fro, and the nonchalant waiters seem to take no rest' (pp.69-70).

The image of the Reading Room's scholars as cannibals feeding upon the dead substance of their kindred is decidedly good, consistent with and at the same time enhancing the recurrent theme of death in the book, and successfully challenging the cliché view of Bennett's realism. Angus Wilson, for example, is surely wrong when he writes that Bennett's case was 'the burial of Bennett's inspiration beneath the ruins of a collapsed tradition ... Bennett had nothing to replace the mammoth imaginative projections of his Victorian predecessors'.[10]

A Man from the North is an impressive first novel and a good novel of the English decadence. The deadening effect of suburban life, about which Forster was to write with such precision, is well-observed, the pervasive pessimism which might easily have become gratuitous (as it sometimes seems to in Gissing) is well prepared for by the story. The weak presentation of women is its major limitation.

John Lucas notes that Bennett's writing about women obeys no discernible rule of consistency. Some of his best characters are female, deeply registered and understood, yet elsewhere he allows himself a 'clubman's' stereotyped, stupid and condescending approach to women which taken out of context could, sadly, vindicate all the rude things Virginia Woolf says about him. *Anna of the Five Towns* (1902) fittingly follows *A Man from the North*. The first novel shows a young man's immature aspiration coming to terms

---

[10] Angus Wilson, 'Arnold Bennett's Novels', *The London Magazine* 1 (November 1954), pp.60-1.

with itself: *Anna of the Five Towns* is a moving and sensitive treatment of a girl caught in a similar predicament.

There are obvious differences: while the first novel marks the movement to London *Anna* is confined to the potteries, and while Richard has ambition (of a weak kind) Anna has none at all, indeed barely any egotism. The novel presents her from the outset as a crushed temperament, so intimidated by her father that she surrenders herself, without love, to the first masterful young man who offers to marry her – Mynors – and then learns too late that her sexual feelings are all for Willie Price, large, dependent, emotional, a 'baby'. Bennett solves this *impasse* by means of an awkward plot mechanism: Titus Price, Willie's father, kills himself, and Willie on learning that his father has embezzled the Sunday School funds is unable to bear the disgrace and throws himself down a mineshaft. The ending of the novel is weak and out of keeping with the rest. Bennett's final paragraphs become crudely melodramatic in tone, as though his preposterous makeshift conclusion is dragging the writing down to its own level.

That said, the book is remarkable for its tactful handling of a repressed girl's emergent identity. Two major repressive elements in Bennett's own childhood, a heavy father and evangelical Wesleyan Methodism, are brought to bear on a personality which, being young and female, is peculiarly vulnerable to such forces. The novel then confronts a question: what are the possibilities for a repressed young woman in the Five Towns? Anna's opportunities are far from typical because she is an heiress with a personal fortune of fifty thousand pounds, but the action shows convincingly that her father's tyranny has made this fortune meaningless to her. When first told of her inheritance 'Anna had sensations such as a child might have who has received a traction engine to play with in a back yard' (p.47).

Anna's money affects her destiny, though, obviously: in one sense it closes the trap on her by making her irresistibly attractive to the dominating Henry Mynors, in another sense it gives her a form of freedom by enabling her to win a climactic fight with her father over the destruction of a promissory bill forged by Willie Price.

Marriage to Mynors will be less than perfect, marriage to Willie Price would be impossible within the conventions of the Five Towns: the alternative to marriage is the dreadful genteel spinsterhood that will clearly overtake Beatrice Sutton, a gentle dutiful girl looking after aging parents as Janet Orgreaves does in *Clayhanger*. Beatrice Sutton's fate is prefigured by a minor character in the novel, Miss Dickinson: 'Miss Dickinson supported her mother, and was a pattern to her sex. She was lovable, but had never been loved. She would have made an admirable wife and mother, but fate had decided that this material was to be wasted. Miss Dickinson found compensation for the rigour of destiny in gossip, as innocent as indiscreet' (p.134).

Agnes, Anna's younger half-sister, is threatened with the same future. Part of Anna's motivation for marrying Mynors is to rescue her young sister (and herself, of course) from their father's tyranny.

Their father is exceptional in that he is a very wealthy miser but typical, as the novel stresses, in his exercise of domestic tyranny: 'The women of a household were the natural victims of their master: in his experience it had always been so ... He belonged to the great and powerful class of house-tyrants, backbone of the British nation, whose views on income-tax cause ministries to tremble' (pp.184-5).

Anna's struggle with this crude and forceful man is a subtle variation of a classic pattern. Landlord in her own right of the pottery works leased by Titus and Willie Price, she takes from her father's desk and destroys a bill forged by the Prices in order to save them. She is empowered to defy her father by her passion for Willie: in the pattern of Roman comedy, the young lover is spurred on by sexual feeling to seize the initiative and defy *senex iratus*.[11]

This simple opposition is buried under a layer of irony and denial. Anna is formally committed to Henry Mynors, she does not recognise her sexual interest in Willie, she does not understand herself at all. It is plain that she is 'frigid' (Bennett's word, p.323) in the modern sexual sense, and always will be, in her relationship with Mynors. Her sexual life will be lived against her instincts, a form of self-denial as difficult as the dedication to chastity hinted at as a possibility in the first description of her: she has the 'lenient curves of absolute maturity' but 'a face for the cloister' and 'that resigned and spiritual melancholy peculiar to women who through the error of destiny have been born into the wrong environment' (pp.7-8).

The religious element in this first description of Anna introduces the major context of the action, evangelical Wesleyan Methodism. Tellwright, her father, has in his day been an active Methodist because it gave him power, an 'unassailable position' in the local community (p.29), and Mynors' motivation is a slightly more disguised version of the same thing. The youngest son of a dispossessed family, Mynors' ambitions are social as well as economic: he loves Anna for her prospects and loves her the more when he learns just how rich she is. Anna tells him that she has fifty thousand pounds: 'The man of business was astonished and enraptured beyond measure. His countenance shone with delight ... He now saw himself the dominant figure in all the Five Towns' (pp.347-8).

This is not to say that his love for Anna is not 'real': but he is so conditioned by his environment, so firmly held in his economic and social

---

[11] For a discussion of this see Northrop Frye, 'The Mythos of Spring: Comedy', in *Anatomy of Criticism* (1957), pp.163-85.

context, that disinterested sexual passion of the kind that Anna wants is impossible for him.

For Anna, evangelical Methodism provides a temporary outlet for her romantic feelings and unfocused, sexually driven aspirations: 'She gazed at the stars and into the illimitable spaces beyond them, and thought of life and its inconceivable littleness, as millions had done before in the presence of that same firmament' (p.96). This questioning does not find an answer in Wesleyan Methodism. For all her passivity, Anna feels embarrassed among the naive converts and indignant with the commercially minded leader of the 'revival', whose 'cabinet photographs' are on sale outside the chapel door 'on application, at one shilling each' (p.94). This anger is an early feature of her quest for independence. Unable to focus clearly on the ugliness and falsehood of the religion in which she has, after all, been brought up, she turns her aggression inward upon herself and feels 'inexplicable dull anger – anger at her own penitence' (p.89).

Anna no more frees herself from Wesleyanism than from male domination. She admires and envies Mynors because men are 'not fettered like women' in religious matters, and are free to sin 'gloriously' (p.99). Mynors firmly intends to take control of her money: her marriage to him will exchange her father's tyranny for subjection to a man just as ruthless but more presentable.

For the novel, Anna's money provides a valuable ironic stance which enables Bennett to play off against each other the two levels of provincial society that he knew best: the doggedly self-reliant manufacturing class and the socially ambitious 'cultivated' class. Beatrice Sutton's pretentiousness is sharply contrasted with Anna's seriousness:

> '"Don't you adore chocolates?"
> '"I don't know," Anna lamely replied. "Yes, I like them."
> 'She only adored her sister, and perhaps God; and this was the first time she had tasted chocolate' (p.128).

Tellwright's miserliness here has had good effects: the puritan as against the fake metropolitan clearly has features to be admired. And indeed there is considerable admiration for the personal independence that Tellwright gains for himself by his life-style. When he becomes bored with Methodism in his fifties he immediately resigns from the preaching circuit: 'He at once yielded to the new instinct, caring naught for public opinion' (p.32). Anna's upbringing has made her in a sense more 'free' than Beatrice because less sensitive to the pressures of snobbery. The precise social gradations in this small community are subverted and made meaningless by the fact that Anna, the most inconspicuous woman in the place, is also the richest; this provides a good basic comic situation of which Bennett makes ample use. It provides the whole novel with an ironic perspective from which to perceive, for example, the 'carriage-owning' class of Bursley: 'The Clayton Vernons ventured only in wet weather to bring their carriage to chapel. Yet Mrs Sutton, who was a plain woman, might with impunity use her equipage on Sundays. This licence granted by Connexional opinion was due to the fact that she so obviously regarded her carriage, not as a carriage, but as a contrivance on four wheels for enabling an infirm creature to move rapidly from place to place' (p.6).

The consistently ironic treatment of all social aspiration in Bursley – the extreme ugliness of the park ('from its gilded gates to its smallest geranium slips it was brand-new, and most of it was red' (p.15)), the flimsy absurdity of Beatrice's drawing-room – makes way for an aesthetic of utility emerging from the book. The beautiful things are also practical: Anna's clean kitchen, much admired by Mynors, and Mynor's well-managed factory, equally admired by Anna. Sarah Vodrey is a pure example of this aesthetic in action, admired by the novel for working herself literally to death to clean the Prices' house, while the Prices themselves, by contrast, are very much to blame for the dirt and confusion of their 'bank': a 'pot-bank', a small factory in this case owned by Anna herself and rented and mismanaged by the Prices.

Judged by the standards indicated by this puritan aesthetic old Tellwright becomes a somewhat redeemed figure. He takes a practical view of money. His good investments are admired by Bursley, and there can be no doubt that Bennett shares that admiration and also shares Tellwright's belief in the rights of property. When John Lucas complains that Bennett does not focus in this novel on the real struggle of industrial life, the struggle between man and man (rather than that between man and nature, which is explored in the novel's opening chapter) he is asking too much. Bennett would not, and did not, regard class struggle as a subject for fiction, and if *Anna* were squeezed for a political stance it would be found to be on the side of the masters rather than the men.

When Anna is reproaching herself for Titus Price's suicide Bennett inserts an entirely detached authorial comment: 'She forgot that in pressing for rent many months overdue she and her father had acted within their just rights – acted as Price himself would have done in their place' (pp.278-9). With the death of Sarah Vodrey the novel's concern is to note and celebrate the stoicism and personality of the victim: 'After fifty years of ceaseless labour, she had gained the affection of one person, and enough money to pay for her own funeral' (p.341). The pathos of this ensures the reader's sympathy for Sarah as an individual, but it leaves undisturbed the novel's implicit acceptance of the system that has destroyed her.

4. 'The Death of Simon Fuge'

The short story 'The Death of Simon Fuge', published in *The Grim Smile of the Five Towns* (1907), has been as much over-praised as Conrad's 'The Secret Sharer', and for similar reasons. Academic literary critics have an understandable liking for short 'representative' texts, and 'Simon Fuge' seems to epitomise Bennett's mature appraisal of provincial life just as 'The Secret Sharer' can be held to be a limpid fable concisely setting out the archetypal Conradian personal crisis.[12]

The best aspects of 'The Death of Simon Fuge' have to do with the energy and cultural awareness of the industrial and professional middle-class of the Five Towns. This energy is bound up with the Five Towns' 'democracy'. Loring, a curator from the British Museum, is visiting the Five Towns to value some pottery and is entertained by Brindley, a local architect. Loring has noted in the London papers the death of Simon Fuge, a painter born in the Five Towns, once reputed to have spent a sensational night on a boat with two sisters, also from the district. Loring is intrigued to find that one of the sisters, Annie Brett, has now become a barmaid, and the other has married a wealthy man and moved into the middle class. Brindley reproaches Loring for his surprise: '"You must remember you're in a democratic district. You told me once you knew Exeter. Well, this isn't a cathedral town. It's about a century in front of any cathedral town in the world. Why, my good sir, there's practically no such thing as class distinction here"' (p.267).

The same kind of point is made in *The Card* (1911), where Denry Machin, the washerwoman's son, has cheated his way into a municipal ball given by the Countess of Chell: 'At first he had thought that four hundred eyes would be fastened on him, their glance saying, "This young man is wearing a dress-suit for the first time, and it is not paid for, either!" But it was not so. And the reason was that the entire population of the Town Hall was heartily engaged in pretending that never in its life had it been seen after seven o'clock of a night apart from a dress-suit' (p.13).

The class structure in *The Card* is used in a simple way: the provinces ape metropolitan distinctions but are temperamentally democratic, so that a man of enterprise and thick-skinned unscrupulousness like Denry can force his way through any social barrier. Social discrimination is used much more subtly than this in 'Simon Fuge'. Brindley, the architect who is a native of the place, asserts that the social habits and social gradations proper to the Five Towns are essentially different from those of London. Loring's experiences during his visit bear this out.

---

[12] Guerard (p.15) claims that with *Heart of Darkness* and *The Shadow Line*, *The Secret Sharer* is one of Conrad's symbolic masterpieces.

He is amazed to discover that Brindley and his friend Colclough, an industrialist who 'makes money and chooses to go to Paris and get the best motor-car he can' (p.26) are both good pianists, able to sight-read Richard Strauss's Domestic Symphony scored for two pianos. An unintentionally horrific notion, one may think, but also a fascinating reminder of the habits of amateur musicians in the days of the unreliable early gramophone. In the dirt of the potteries there is a live interest in books and music, and a great capacity for work – and, in particular, an admiration for the vigorous irreverence of the socially mobile. When Denry, in *The Card*, has succeeded in taking business from his employer and setting up on his own, the novel comments of him: 'He knew of a surety that he was that most admired type in the bustling industrial provinces – a card' (p.39).

It is interesting that there is no reference to religious life in 'Simon Fuge'. As an expression of humane aspirations in a hostile environment music seems to have taken the place occupied by religion in *Anna of the Five Towns* (it is relevant to note that Henry Mynors in that novel is a 'pleasing baritone' as well as a preacher).

One of Bennett's closest friends in Paris was Ravel, who could satisfy Bennett's avid amateur enthusiasm for music and who also shared with Bennett a voyeurist taste for sexual anecdote. It seems likely that the friendship springing up between the virginal and fastidious Loring and the vigorous men that he meets in the Five Towns is Bennett's friendship with Ravel transposed into a different context. As far as establishing the contrast between London and the provinces is concerned, the experiment is very successful: the Five Towns have not heard of Simon Fuge beyond the fact that they know his family. The middle-class of the place are intelligent and enlightened, certainly, but not to the extent of having to do with a minor 'Pre-Raphaelite' painter. The working-class of the district, whose interests, like their origins, the middle-class also share, are concerned with football, racing, and the rates. These facts lead steadily to the excellent joke at the end of the story where Loring points out the contrasting newspaper posters on Knype station:

'[The *Staffordshire Signal*:]

HANBRIDGE RATES
LIVELY MEETING
KNYPE F.C.
NEW CENTRE-FORWARD
ALL-WINNERS AND S.P.

'Now, close by this poster was the poster of the *Daily Telegraph*, and among the items offered by the *Daily Telegraph* was: "Death of Simon Fuge"' (p.291).

Part of the Simon Fuge myth has been his womanising: notably his adventure with two beautiful girls on Lake Ilam one summer night. Loring finds that this had no substance: Fuge lost an oar and went round in circles, then took the two sisters back to the station and they were home by eleven o'clock. The women themselves are uninteresting: one has married Colclough, Brindley's industrialist friend with the French motor-car, and has become domestic and virtuous. She is individualised only by the detail of her 'slight moustache', a reminder perhaps of her more sensuous past.

Her sister Annie Brett, the barmaid, is a fabricated figure, a composite of women that Bennett had used elsewhere. Like Bennett's Leonora (from the novel of the same name) Annie Brett 'had the mien of a handsome married woman of forty with a coquettish and superficially emotional past, but also with a daughter who is just going into long skirts', and like Beatrice Sutton from *Anna of the Five Towns* she is one of those women who 'are always frothing at the mouth with ecstasy. They adore everything, including God: ... They are stylish – and impenetrable' (p.257). There is a whole paragraph of such editorialising.

In short, Annie Brett is scarcely dramatised at all. The 'telling' has replaced the 'showing' almost completely. The narrator's bored attitude to women is balanced by the sniggering approach to sex among the men. Loring and Brindley swap dirty limericks, and Brindley then urges Loring to recite one to his friend Colclough. Colclough greets the two men who have just entered the house:

> '"Come along in, will you?"'
>
> '"Half-a-second, Ol," Mr. Brindley called in a conspiratorial tone, and, turning to me: "Tell him *the* Limerick. You know."'
>
> '"The one about the hayrick?"'
>
> 'Mr. Brindley nodded. There were three heads close together for a space of twenty second or so, and then a fearful explosion happened – the unique, tremendous laughter of Mr. Colclough' (p.272).

The men at their first meeting exchange smut in the hall before being introduced to the restraining presence of women. It is back to the world (or the implied world) of the Wilcox males in *Howards End*, with their separate room in the Ducie Street house where 'we fellows smoke'.

The story seems quite unembarrassed by this little scene, which is, it appears, presented as a laudable expression of the human solidarity, the freemasonry, that has sprung up among the three men. Otherwise male relationships are expressed in terms of competitiveness: smoking, drinking, even the interest in books and music, are entered into with the cold swagger of adolescents seeking to impress each other. Loring notes that Brindley is able to keep a match alight in the open air: 'The way in which that man kept the match alight in a fresh breeze made me envious. I could conceive myself rivalling his exploits in cigarette-making, the purchase of rare books, the interpretation of music, even (for a wager) the drinking of beer, but I knew that I should never be able to keep a match alight in a breeze' (p.266).

Is this to be taken ironically? And if not, what is Bennett doing with it? The answer has to be that the degree of seriousness in this story is slighter than its champions have claimed. Bennett is allowing himself to fall into the provincial success-story formula in which the whole of *The Card* is written, where philistine competitiveness is felt to have a self-justifying comic interest which needs no further significance.

5. The form of The Old Wives' Tale

Throughout his writing life Bennett had a great interest in music and architecture, and both these arts – music particularly – may be seen to have contributed to the methods and structure of *The Old Wives' Tale* (1908). It is often held that Bennett ought not to be considered with the masters of form, James and Conrad (and Ford) because he is just not that kind of writer; his virtues are said to lie in the direction of openness, humanity and other characteristics often loosely described as Dickensian in the popular sense (although Bennett himself found *Dombey and Son* 'appallingly vulgar' (*Journals*, p.320)). For John Lucas he was never a 'formalist': 'In spite of his early insistence on formal perfection, he is not really interested in the pattern and structure of his novels for their own intricate sakes.'[13]

I would not wish to suggest that the formal excellence of *The Old Wives' Tale* is there for its own intricate sake, but I do find in it a highly worked structure which gives a secure framework for Bennett's objectivity: the way the novel is organised facilitates the rhetoric with which Bennett presents 'life'. Indeed, in marked contrast with Wells, Bennett is a novelist whose social, religious and political attitudes are held in check in his fictions. He was a socialist and an atheist and a humanist, and at certain periods of his life he was a mystic (in *The Ghost* and *The Glimpse*) and a hedonist (in *The Grand Babylon Hotel* and *Lord Raingo*) but more than any of these things he was a novelist. In Bennett writing is autotelic. He has no vantage point from which to perceive his writing other than that provided by the work of art itself.

This could well account for the great fluctuations in the quality of the work: when he is good he is very very good, when he is bad he is appalling. Wells never writes as badly as Bennett can at his worst: however hasty and scrappy Wells's prose becomes his mind is usually kept at some degree of

---

[13] Lucas, p.12.

tension by the fight or argument in which he is engaged; since he usually has some extra-literary objective his intelligence continues to function after his art has been abandoned. In Bennett, if he allows his attention to the writing to slacken, the quality of thought, perception and sensitivity declines with it. Bennett has no external control: without his art he is lost.

Bennett tells us that Book One of the novel, 'Mrs. Baines', which is set in the Burslem of his childhood, was written in six weeks: 'It was fairly easy to me, because, in the seventies, in the first decade of my life, I had lived in the actual draper's shop of the Baines's, and knew it as only a child could know it' (Preface).

He then moved from Fontainebleu to London and found himself unable to get on with the book so wrote *Buried Alive* 'during January and February of 1908'. No one who has attempted to write a novel can fail to envy Bennett's facility. The implication here that the writing of *Buried Alive* was a form of holiday from the more serious task is not false modesty: he is simply stating what happened. It seems never to have occurred to Bennett that a 'holiday' might consist of the complete suspension of all work whatsoever. 'With regard to the French portion of the story,' he continues, 'it was not until I had written the first part that I saw from a study of my chronological basis that the Siege of Paris must be brought into the tale'.

The four books of the novel, 'Mrs. Baines', 'Constance', 'Sophia', and 'What Life Is', will bear a musical analogy. The three parts of Sonata form – exposition, development, recapitulation – loosely match the first three books of the novel. Exposition: the two sisters together and their struggle with their mother in 'Mrs Baines'. Development: the slow evolution of Constance into a mature woman in Bursley and her own struggle with the next generation represented by her son Cyril. Recapitulation: the movement back through time from the story of Constance as a middle-aged woman in Bursley to that of Sophia as a young woman in Paris in 'Sophia'. Book Four is a coda to the other three in which Sophia and Constance are reunited in their old age, and Sophia then dies leaving Constance to the harder fate of bleak survival into the unfamiliar and heedless world of the twentieth century. The title of Book Four, 'What Life Is', is very characteristically Edwardian, reflecting as it does the belief shared by the writers of the period that it was possible for art to know and express 'Life'.[14] The title here expresses a wish rather than an achieved fact, an impulse towards control, wholeness and order.

The four-part framework is underpinned by other elements for which the appropriate analogy is architecture rather than music. The analogy was in the air: in the 1907 preface to the New York edition of *The Portrait of a Lady* (pp.xi and xiv) Henry James had declared that fiction was a 'house' with

---

[14] 'The Edwardians were looking for ways to express their conviction that we can be religious about life itself' (Ellmann, 'Two Faces of Edward', p.196).

'windows' looking out on to the world, a building in which the central character is the 'corner-stone' and the growing novel, built on this figure, a 'structure'.

Bennett's preface to *The Old Wives' Tale* (the preface was first published in America in 1911) tells one nothing about the book's structural principles but defends the use of *two* central figures, or 'corner-stones' in James's term: 'I had the example and the challenge of Guy de Maupassant's "Une Vie".' Since Maupassant's novel was an exhaustive realist study of one woman's life, Bennett determined to 'go one better': 'Constance was the original; Sophia was created out of bravado.' The novel's more spectacular devices are balanced against each other with architectural symmetry and proportion. The hanging of Daniel Povey in Book Two is balanced by the guillotining of Rivain in Book Three. Chirac's escape by balloon from besieged Paris in defence of France in Book Three is balanced, and parodied, by Dick Povey's balloon-flight in defence of the independence of Bursley from the Federation of the Five Towns in Book Four.

Much of this duplication is attended by a comic or parodic *tone*, and the tone is perhaps part of the novel's total strategy by which the Five Towns of Bennett's childhood are kept at an objective distance. The irony of tone is supported by a reductive parallelism of events: chapters 4 and 5 of Book Two are called 'Crime' and 'Another Crime'. The first crime is Cyril Povey's theft of a florin: the second is Daniel Povey's murder of his wife. The point of the contrast is driven home by the behaviour of Samuel Povey, Cyril's father, who severely condemns the theft of the florin and passionately condones the murder. He martyrs himself in the effort to obtain a reprieve for his cousin Daniel, who is in due course hanged.

On one level this is a simple joke at the expense of a narrow provincial morality which is more disturbed by a crime against property than by a crime against life. But the situation is more complicated than that. After making Samuel Povey's limited outlook the subject of comic observation Bennett reverses the situation and draws attention to the man's latent dignity. Indeed, once Samuel Povey has worn himself out in his hopeless campaign for a reprieve for Daniel, Bennett as author intervenes in the first person. For most of the novel the narrative voice has been third-person free indirect speech, and this sudden intrusion of the first person is surprising but rapidly establishes itself as appropriate to the situation: '[Samuel Povey] died of toxaemia, caused by a heart that would not do its duty by the blood. A casual death, scarce noticed ... Samuel Povey never could impose himself on the burgesses [of Bursley]. He lacked individuality. He was little. I have often laughed at Samuel Povey. But I liked and respected him. He was a very honest man. I have always been glad to think that, at the end of his life, destiny took hold of him and displayed, to the observant, the vein of greatness which runs through every soul without exception. He embraced a cause, lost it, and died of it' (pp.238-9).[15]

Other events in Bursley contrast the epic with the comic in a similar way. The shooting of the mad elephant in Bursley Square is balanced against the 'killing' of old Baines by his daughter Sophia, when she spends a few fateful and fatal minutes flirting with Gerald Scales in the shop (Book One, chapter 4). Sophia as a young girl pulls out one of Samuel Povey's teeth: 'This was the crown of Sophia's career as a perpetrator of the unutterable' (p.21). This comic hyperbole takes on a fresh significance when Sophia elopes to Paris with Gerald Scales in Book Three. The extent of her capacity for perpetrating the unutterable as she grows to sexual maturity is still being explored.

Family quarrels expressed in terms of comic, or mock-epic, hyperbole recur often enough to be regarded as a subsidiary structural element. Constance takes Mr Povey's tooth from Sophia's workbox and throws it out of their bedroom window into St Luke's Square: 'She had accomplished this inconceivable transgression of the code of honour, beyond all undoing, before Sophia could recover from the stupefaction of seeing her sacred workbox impudently violated. In a single moment one of Sophia's chief ideals had been smashed utterly' (p.31).

Sophia defies her mother, shouting 'You are a horrid, cruel woman, and I hate you!': 'This was Mrs. Baines's first costly experience of the child thankless for having been brought into the world ... She had suddenly stumbled against an unsuspected personality at large in her house, a sort of hard marble affair that informed her by means of bumps that if she did not want to be hurt she must keep out of the way' (pp.56-7).

There is commonly a point of *peripeteia* or 'turn' in each of the novel's chapters, giving it basic binary elements of which the 'sonata form' that I have referred to is built up. Each chapter tends to fall into two parts, the first establishing the setting and context and the second, following the *peripeteia*, working out a dramatic conflict. In Book Three, chapter 2, for example, a chapter called 'supper', Gerald Scales gets into a quarrel with an English aristocrat in a French restaurant. The quarrel has no function beyond contributing to the steady, dismaying revelation of Gerald's unfitness to be Sophia's husband, and it could well be that the aristocrat is introduced largely to provide a point of *peripeteia* out of structural habit, as it were. Intrinsically it is not a strong scene. The English artistocrat is very lightly sketched and the whole of the quarrel is given in indirect speech: Bennett will not go to the trouble of dramatising it. It is 'the common, tedious, tippler's

---

[15] This is also, of course, a personal tribute to Bennett's father, on whom Samuel Povey is partially based.

quarrel. It rose higher and higher' (p.300), and the reader is left to fill in the particulars for himself.

The persistent use of this fundamental binary form, together with the sonata form and *coda* of the four books and the careful patterning of duplication and analogy among the characters and events impose order and unity on a novel which might well have threatened to disintegrate with a less disciplined framework. The subject is, after all, unwieldy: two lives separated in space and extended over a long period of time. To contain this subject one might well expect modernist narrative indirections, a controlled use of characterised narrators such as one finds in Conrad or Ford, or the impressionism of Forster where scenes separated in space and time are juxtaposed with the links left out. Bennett's method is more traditional and in a sense more honest than these. He has a great deal to communicate: the effect of historical perspective, environment, heredity, and *will* must all be taken into account when presenting the developing personalities.

In a way the Forsterian kind of impressionism *is* present. Bennett takes several dates in the lives of his characters and shows their lives at those moments, allowing the dramatic present to record the past and imply the future. But the connections between these islands of dramatised presentation are made in the omniscient, chronicle-writing manner common to Fielding, Trollope or John Cowper Powys: the tradition that still behaves, in Powys and other twentieth-century figures such as Henry Williamson and Paul Scott, as though Modernism had never happened. None of Bennett's chapters feels too long. One is impressed especially by the way in which i.is pacing is determined by his paragraphing: ample, generous blocks of prose, detailed in the way that James objected to as 'saturation'.

Because it covers so long a period, 1860 to 1906, and is placed in the drastically contrasted settings of Paris and Bursley, the sense of period and scene has to be re-established in each Book and often in each chapter. And as well as the problem of presenting a Victorian context in the dramatic present, in Book One, Bennett has set himself the special problem of presenting a provincial situation to a metropolitan audience.

By this time he had had a good deal of practice. *Anna of the Five Towns, Leonora* and the stories in *The Grim Smile of the Five Towns* all make this contrast (not to mention *Sacred and Profane Love*, which begins in the Five Towns and would have been a better novel if it had stayed there). The tone in which the Bursley setting of the 1860s is established in this novel is, then, a familiar one. Bursley is the place where the assumptions of upper-middle-class London are reflected in burlesque.

Constance's future husband, Samuel Povey, makes his first appearance in a borrowed phrase: he is a 'person universally esteemed, both within and without the shop' (p.14). This is presumably an echo of Jane Austen's 'truth universally to be acknowledged' and its comic point is the same as hers: the universe here is confined to St Luke's Square, Bursley, just as the universe of the opening sentence of *Pride and Prejudice* is confined to the blinkered consciousness of Mrs Bennet.

The comic method is exemplified in the chapter called 'Elephant' from Book One of the novel, in which the elephant that runs amok at the Bursley Wakes is shot dead, and Sophia 'kills' her father by flirting with Gerald Scales. 'On the previous night one of the three Wombwell elephants had suddenly knelt on a man in the tent; he had then walked out of the tent and picked up another man at haphazard from the crowd which was staring at the great pictures in front, and tried to put this second man into his mouth. Being stopped by his Indian attendant with a pitchfork, he placed the man on the ground and stuck his tusk through an artery of the victim's arm. He then, amid unexampled excitement, suffered himself to be led away' (p.67).

The elephant is shot and 'died instantly, rolling over with a soft thud'.

The detachment with which the elephant's violence is presented is matched by the objective description of John Baines's corpse: 'His face, neck and hands were dark and congested; his mouth was open, and the tongue protruded between the black, swollen, mucous lips; his eyes were prominent and coldly staring. The fact was that Mr Baines had wakened up, and, being restless, had slid out partially from his bed and died of asphyxia' (p.73).

Round these two dispassionately observed deaths is ranged a delicately established mock-genteel social order. Bennett is very good at this: 'It was the morning of the third day of Bursley Wakes: not the modern finicking and respectable, but an orgiastic carnival, gross in all its manifestations of joy. The whole centre of the town was given over to the furious pleasures of the people ... It was a glorious spectacle, but not a spectacle for the leading families. Miss Chetwynd's school was closed, so that the daughters of leading families might remain in seclusion till the worst was over. The Baineses ignored the Wakes in every possible way' (pp.66-7).

The notion that Bursley can have 'leading families', in a phrase suggesting grandeur on the scale of Trollope's political aristocracy, is both comic and true. Mrs. Baines's social ascendancy is just as real to herself and her neighbours as that of Trollope's Pallisers or Thackeray's Crawleys is to them, and is precisely felt in this dialogue with the school-mistress: '[Miss Chetwynd was] a pinched virgin, aged forty, and not "well off"; in her family the gift of success had been monopolised by her elder sister. For these characteristics Mrs. Baines, as a matron in easy circumstances, pitied Miss Chetwynd. On the other hand, Miss Chetwynd could choose ground from which to look down upon Mrs. Baines, who after all was in trade. Miss Chetwynd had no trace of the local accent; she spoke with a southern refinement which the Five Towns, while making fun of it, envied. All her O's had a genteel leaning towards 'ow', as ritualism leans towards Romanism' (p.59).

Jane Austen herself could scarcely have been funnier or more precise. The ironic method is the traditional one of comedy of manners: the class distinction of the Five Towns is presented in mock heroic form, invoking the differences felt in fashionable London and applying them to the inhabitants of Bursley. By including Miss Chetwynd Bennett ensures that these differences are felt to be significant as well as comic: 'It was an extremely nice question whether, upon the whole, Mrs. Baines secretly condescended to Miss Chetwynd or Miss Chetwynd to Mrs. Baines' (p.59).

Social distinction breeds mutual hostility which may occasionally break into open war, here as in Jane Austen, and the irony is never there purely for delight. Bennett is writing about the aggressions and anxieties felt by every provincial who has tried to rid himself of a regional accent when he refers to Miss Chetwynd's southern speech which the Midlanders simultaneously mocked and envied.

Mrs Baines's opening blow in the battle for ascendancy with Miss Chetwynd is her note of invitation to tea: 'lavender-coloured paper with scalloped edges, the selectest mode of the day' (p.60). This is painfully well-observed: Mrs Baines's limited nature is exposed to the reader and her vulgarity betrayed to Miss Chetwynd, on whom the 'selectest mode' will not, we may assume, make the impression intended. The effect, surprisingly, is to enlist the reader on Mrs Baines's side: there *is* something chill and false about the superiority that 'breeding' claims for itself, and something touching in Mrs Baines's social aspirations betraying her to Miss Chetwynd's judgment.

We know from his *Journals* that Bennett was happy with the writing of the first two books of *The Old Wives' Tale* and found that it came to him 'naturally'. And although the form is sophisticated and highly structured one's first response to these books is that they are true to life, that they convincingly present human growth. A fresh reader of Book One might miss its formal virtues but would certainly respond with pleasure to the major landmarks in Mrs Baines's battles with her daughters. Sophia expresses her wish to become a teacher, explodes with anger at her mother's repressiveness, and Mrs Baines loses the skirmish. This is reversed when Sophia 'kills' her father and withdraws her intention to become a teacher in remorse. Book One, chapter 7, 'A Defeat', records two major reversals for Mrs Baines, Constance and Samuel Povey becoming engaged and Sophia eloping with Gerald Scales. Mrs Baines has won some of the battles but has now clearly lost the war.

Book One, 'Mrs. Baines', is a short novel in itself, fifty thousand words long, and 'Constance', Book Two, is another self-contained narrative of the same length with parallel features. The birth and growth of Cyril, Constance and Samuel Povey's only child, illustrate the conscious 'realism', in the Zola and Maupassant sense, of the novel. Cyril is conceived because his father is sexually stimulated by conversation with his cousin Daniel Povey: 'For the ruling classes of Bursley, Daniel Povey was just a little too fanatical a worshipper of the god Pan. He was one of the remnant who had kept alive the great Pan tradition from the days of the Regency throughout the vast, arid Victorian expanse of years ... Daniel Povey had a way of assuming that every male was boiling over with interest in the sacred cult of Pan. The assumption, though sometimes causing inconvenience at first, usually conquered by virtue of its inherent truthfulness' (p.166).

Daniel Povey's behaviour is like Bennett's own, a matter of vicarious pleasure derived from sexual anecdote: a refreshing pastime, no doubt, in Victorian Burslem. Bennett is using the same kind of 'realism' when he describes the adolescent Cyril's mind at the age of thirteen: 'His parents, who despite their notion of themselves as wide-awake parents were a simple pair, never suspected that his heart, conceived to be still pure, had become a crawling, horrible mass of corruption' (p.200).

When Sophia falls in love with Gerald in Book Three the narrative works hard, and in some measure successfully, to show the enormous ignorance with which Gerald and Sophia must contend. At first Gerald perceives Sophia's sexuality entirely in terms of the new areas of skin revealed by the disarrangement of her clothes: 'She was his capture: he held her close, permittedly scanning the minutiae of her skin, permittedly crushing her flimsy silks' (p.278).

Sophia's own perception of the situation is less specifically sexual: '[She] thought of nothing but the intense throbbing joy of life, longing with painful ardour for more and more pleasure, then and for ever' (p.291).

Good though this is, Bennett's 'realism' is at its best in aspects of life which are at a remove from sexuality. He shows a fascinated sensitivity to human smells. At Cyril Povey's fourth birthday party: 'Although the window was slightly open, the air was heavy with the natural human odour which young children transpire. More than one mother, pressing her nose into a lacy mass, to whisper, inhaled that pleasant perfume with a voluptuous thrill' (p.181).

When Cyril becomes adolescent ('mysterious creature, this child, mysteriously growing and growing in the house!' (p.191)) the smells become more coarse. '[Constance] liked to feel him and to gaze at him, and to smell that faint, uncleanly odour of sweat that hung in his clothes' (p.199). When Cyril deserts his mother, now widowed, at the end of Book Two – at the end, then, of the short novel called 'Constance' – it is his turn to register his perception in terms of smell: 'Constance lifted her veil and kissed him; and kissed her life out. He smelt the odour of her crape. He was, for an instant, close to her, close; and he seemed to have an overwhelmingly intimate glimpse into her secrets; he seemed to be choked in the sudden strong emotion of that crape' (p.274).

6. 'The meaning of the word success'

For Conrad the writer-as-hero is a man of action, for Ford he is a gentleman-stoic, for Wells he is a social projectile in constant upward flight. For Bennett he is the provincial *arriviste*, refreshingly open about his pleasure in his own achievement. Success is the test, the middle-class economic success which comes only to the writer who can sell his wares: 'I am a writer, just as I might be a hotel-keeper, a solicitor, a doctor, a grocer, or an earthenware manufacturer' (*Mental Efficiency: And other Hints to Men and Women* (n.d.), p.102). The attitude is the reverse of Gissing's in *New Grub Street*. Gissing bemoans the fact that writing is an industry governed by economic laws: Bennett glories in it. For Bennett strength is *health* and health is morally self-validating. It replaces Christianity as the mark of the self-reliant, self-possessed man.

The title of Bennett's *Mental Efficiency* indicates sufficiently clearly an obsession with health as evidence of moral rectitude.[16] And his book reveals the way in which, for him, the moral universe has contracted until its dimensions are no greater than the dimensions of the self: 'There is only one single, unique, Force, Energy, Life. Science is making it increasingly difficult to conceive matter apart from spirit ... The same Force pervades my razor, my cow in my field, and the central *me* which dominates my mind: the same force in different stages of evolution. And that Force persists for ever. In such paths do I compel my mind to walk daily' (pp.147-8).

Success involves stress: 'Men destined for success flourish and find their ease in an atmosphere of collision and disturbance' (p.112).

In *How to Live on Twenty-Four Hours a Day* (1908) he applauds the successful man's confrontation with strain and declares his own taste for it: 'If you are not prepared for discouragements and disillusions; if you will not be content with a small result for a big effort, then do not begin. Lie down again and resume the uneasy doze which you call your existence. It is very sad, is it not, very depressing and sombre? And yet I think it is rather fine, too, this necessity for the tense bracing of the will before anything worth doing can be done. I rather like it myself. I feel it to be the chief thing that differentiates me from the cat by the fire' (pp.30-1).

The analogy is with the athlete: the 'strain' is the writer's equivalent of the 'wholesale attention given to physical recreation in all its forms', the 'gigantic debauch of the muscles' typical of Edwardian suburban Londoners. 'Poor withering mind!' thinks Bennett, priggishly (*Mental Efficiency*, p.23). Forster makes the same point about the Wilcoxes, who spoil the garden of Howards End by filling it with various kinds of athletic equipment.

[16] See my discussion of the general obsession with health in the period, above, pp.7-8.

Bennett's self-help books, *Mental Efficiency*, *How to Live on Twenty-Four Hours a Day* and *The Author's Craft* (1914) are bad for his image: they support the popular view of the aggressively philistine, money-grubbing, self-complacent figure pilloried by Virginia Woolf. Yet the emphasis on 'strain' and athletic self-discipline masks a deep insecurity. Bennett was constantly surprised by his own success and driven by an audacious need to 'keep up with' other writers. Reginald Pound has said 'the mainspring of [his] career was a desire to emulate, not an intention to excel'. He wanted to live like Balzac, Zola and Dumas: 'To write books and to conquer the social heights and command the homage of cities, to live in grand hotels and to own a yacht, to have a flat and a life of one's own in Paris!'[17]

Much that is virtuous, as well as all that is vulgar, in Bennett stems from this. *Anna of the Five Towns*, *The Old Wives' Tale* and *Clayhanger* owe their success partly to Bennett's modest estimation of himself as writer, his humble willingness to set out exhaustively the physical, economic and historical contexts in which his characters find themselves. The elaborate structure to which he committed himself in *The Old Wives' Tale* is another instance, in a way, of this humility. Bennett's commitment to its art is autotelic and ensures the consistently high standard of that work.

His commitment to work, success and self-reliance are not in the cause of any larger purpose. He has the temperament and behaviour of a sturdy mid-Victorian stripped of the moral values by which the Victorians lived. Hard work, success, pragmatism, ability to stand on one's own feet and an aggressive analysis of the existing social order: these things might seem to put him closer to Dickens and Thackeray than to, say, Oscar Wilde and John Gray. But Dickens and Thackeray are working securely *against* a society with resilient, unexamined assumptions about the nature of the hero. By the time Bennett writes no such assumptions are possible. The positives in his life and work are difficult to isolate, the negatives are easier: he believed in death, he believed in the cruelty of misfortune, the action of time, the built-in conditioning ironies of human history. Man has no moral existence beyond the frontiers of his human envelope and the five minutes through which his consciousness is moving. In the best of his 'self-help' books he describes the passengers on a motor-bus which has just run over a dog: 'All the persons in the motor-bus have come out of a past and are moving towards a future. But how often does our imagination put itself to the trouble of realising this?' (*The Author's Craft*, p.32).

The other part of Reginald Pound's observation animates many of Bennett's plots. Denry in *The Card* and Henry Shakespere Knight in *A Great Man* are mediocrities who make success for themselves by refusing to recognise any form of social, moral or (in Henry Knight's case) artistic

---

[17] Reginald Pound, *Arnold Bennett: A Biography* (1952), p.15.

superiority in others. Those who enjoy the fruits of success in *The Grand Babylon Hotel* and *Lord Raingo* have earned the right to do so by the same refusal. And this is perhaps where Bennett's identity and the drive of his heroes interlock most closely. The democratic outlook of the Five Towns that he refers to throughout his work and celebrates most seriously in 'The Death of Simon Fuge' gives scope to his own will-to-power, a stubborn, tactful, slow, systematic refusal to acknowledge any figure – other than the great French novelists of the past – as more than his equal.

If Bennett's novels can be seen falling into a broad pattern in which man struggles with his environment, the best novels are those in which the environment wins, in which the will of the hero is broken. Constance and Sophia are broken by the action of time in *The Old Wives' Tale*, Edwin Clayhanger by heredity and environment in the *Clayhanger* novels – though he is allowed, as Wells's Mr Lewisham is, the male consolations of marriage and headship of a household. In Bennett's serious novels women are on the whole stronger than men because better adapted to their circumstances, and this adaptation produces one of Bennett's funniest metaphors: Cyril and Constance crushed by the moral authority of Mrs Baines and Aunt Harriet when these two ladies convene (after Mrs Baines's widowhood) in St Luke's Square, Bursley: 'They referred to each other as oracular sources of wisdom and good taste. Respectability stalked abroad when they were afoot. The whole Square wriggled uneasily as though God's eye were peculiarly upon it … The younger generation was extinguished, pressed flat and lifeless under the ponderosity of the widows. Mr Povey was not the man to be easily flattened by ponderosity of any kind, and his suppression was a striking proof of the prowess of the widows; who, indeed, went over Mr Povey like traction-engines, with the sublime unconsciousness of traction-engines, leaving an inanimate object in the road behind them, and scarce aware even of the jolt' (*The Old Wives' Tale*, pp.120-1).

Sophia in *The Old Wives' Tale* ought to be a hero in the Wellsian sense. She has the courage to rebel against the authoritarian provincial life presented by the 'ponderosity of the widows' and to follow the direction of her sexual feeling for Gerald Scales ('Because she was mad for him she hated him furiously' (p.281)), which leads her in turn to France, 'a strange civilisation perfectly frank in its sensuality and its sensuousness, under the guidance of a young man to whom her half-formed intelligence was a most diverting toy' (p.296).

Her character prevents her from living out this promise – or, rather, for her Paris's freedom turns out to be illusory, a 'horrible, vile prison' (p.371) which her innate moral rectitude rejects. She has hereditary English virtues, 'this fragile slip of the Baines stock, unconsciously drawing upon the accumulated strength of generations of honest living' (p.287).

She returns to the bondage of the Five Towns, and the novel ends with its bleak and famous celebration of the triumph of death. Sophia visits the corpse of Gerald, who dragged her away from her provincial rectitude when she was a young girl, and recognises that 'it was the riddle of life that was puzzling and killing her': 'She was not sorry that Gerald had wasted his life, nor that he was a shame to his years and to her. The manner of his life was of no importance. What affected her was that he had once been young, and that he had grown old, and was now dead. That was all. Youth and vigour had come to that. Youth and vigour always came to that. Everything came to that' (p.540).

The Old Wives' Tale is a volcano, the Clayhanger trilogy is the crust forming as the lava cools. The Clayhanger books have the same basic configuration as *The Old Wives' Tale*. Edwin is a male Constance, battered and conditioned by struggles between the generations and against his environment. His father is the strongest of Bennett's portraits of his own father: Darius Clayhanger, rescued from sadistic beatings and homosexual rape in the workhouse by Mr Shushions, the Sunday-school teacher, has Victorian brutality, the aggressive thrust of the self-made man. Samuel Povey has the tenacity, unimaginativeness and anxious affection of Bennett's father and Earlforward (in *Riceyman Steps*) who is childless, has his fussy anal obsessiveness. Hilda is like Sophia: Sophia's escape to Paris is echoed in Hilda's marriage (bigamous, as it turns out) to a man who is half-French, Sophia fending for herself by exploiting her lodgers in the siege of Paris is echoed by Hilda keeping a boarding-house in Brighton.

When Hilda has accepted defeat, returned to the Five Towns and married Edwin (the pattern of Sophia returning to Constance repeating itself) Edwin turns into a Cyril Povey figure: 'He was now somebody's husband, and bearded, and perhaps occasionally pompous' (*These Twain* (1916), p.17).

His crusty domestic fussiness and his tender and embarrassed relationship with Hilda's son, George, complete the process: Edwin himself has now become another portrait of Bennett's father.

The contrast between metropolitan/southern and provincial lifestyles is restated and explored further in the Clayhanger books but still left unsolved. Restless – as well she might be – in her marriage to Edwin, Hilda becomes attracted to a badly sketched gentleman, Harry Hesketh, who 'had a beautiful moustache, nice eyes, hands excitingly dark with hair, and no affectations whatever' (p.265). In his house in Devon, 'Tavy Mansion', she experiences the disconcerting lack of identity which accompanies release from the constrictions of the industrial provinces:

'They were well-bred, and they were attended by servants who, professionally, were even better bred than themselves, and who were rendered happy by smooth words and good pay. They lived at peace with every one. Full of health, they ate well and slept well. They

suffered no strain. They had absolutely no problems, and they did not
seek problems. Nor had they any duties, save agreeable ones to each
other. Their world was ideal. If you had asked them how their world
could be improved for them, they would not have found an easy reply.
They could only demand less taxes and more fine days ... Whereas
Hilda and hers were forced to live among a brutal populace, amid the
most horrible surroundings of smoke, dirt and squalor. In Devonshire
the Five Towns was unthinkable; the whiteness of the window-curtains
at Tavy Mansion almost broke the heart of the housewife in Hilda ...

'Nobody in Bursley really knew the meaning of the word success'
(p.270).

'The meaning of the word success', which meant so much to Bennett the
writer-as-hero, is withheld from all his Five Towns characters. The most they
are allowed is an assertiveness against impossible odds. The gleesingers, for
the duration of the glee, enjoy complete success: 'The thing was performed
with absolute assurance and perfection' (*Clayhanger*, p.79). And the clog-
dancing in the same entertainment forces, so to speak, success out of the
conditions of failure: 'The clog, the very emblem of the servitude and the
squalor of brutalised populations, was changed, on the light feet of [Florence
Offlow] into the medium of grace. Few of these men but at some time of their
lives had worn the clog, had clattered in it through the winter's slush' (p.83).
The clog-dancer restores to the men a quality of reserve and subversive
aggressiveness, the qualities which made Darius Clayhanger prosperous:
'The men pulled themselves together, remembering that their proudest
quality was a stoic callousness which nothing could overthrow' (p.85).
Edwin's struggle with his father is a mark of his own necessary callousness,
the point at which he changes from the adolescent, 'inchoate, unformed,
undisciplined, and burning with capricious fires' (p.70) into the watchful
adult who looks on as Edwin talks to his selfish and stupid sister Clara: 'The
impartial and unmoved spectator that sat somewhere in Edwin, as in
everybody who possesses artistic sensibility, watching his secret life as from a
conning tower, thought how strange this was' (p.230).

As he locks his characters ever more securely in their chains Bennett
permits them this last freedom, a self-reflectiveness, a capacity to see that
they are playing roles determined for them by forces beyond their control.

Chapter Six: Galsworthy

1. John Galsworthy and Giles Legard

The linking together of Wells, Bennett and Galsworthy is well-established. Rebecca West united them as 'Edwardian Uncles' (see above, Chapter One, p.2). Virginia Woolf in *Mr. Bennett and Mrs. Brown* complained that the three of them left one with 'so strange a feeling of incompleteness and dissatisfaction'. Edwin Muir in his early study, *The Structure of the Novel* (1928), puts them together as writers of the 'Period Novel', which was 'less ambitious, less comprehensive; more immediate, more utilitarian' than the great Victorian novels. Unlike *War and Peace* or *Middlemarch*, 'this kind of novel is not audacious enough to attempt a picture of society valid for all time; its object is more modest and specific, to show us a section of contemporary society' (p.116). A modern critic has made the same point in a more sophisticated way: 'The post-1900 fiction of Wells, Bennett and Galsworthy is still perhaps responding too directly to sensed crisis to be "great art" or even "art" at all.'[1]

Others distinguish Galsworthy from Wells and Bennett, sometimes in a surprisingly deferential tone. He has been compared with Thomas Mann: 'In *Buddenbrooks* and *The Forsyte Saga* the bourgeoisie reached their highest degree of literary self-consciousness.'[2]

This traditional linking with Bennett and Wells is artificial. Bennett and Wells were better writers than Galsworthy, they were not 'gentlemen', and, as Edwin Muir noted, they dealt with upward social mobility with an excitement comparable to that with which the eighteenth century novelists deal with travel ('The counterpart of Smollett's travelling hero is Mr. Wells's climbing hero', Muir, p.32). Moral indignation, in Wells and Bennett, is seldom more than skin-deep and is always bound up with an aggressive, confident self-assertiveness. Galsworthy's temperament, by contrast, is characterised by a noble helplessness in the face of social cruelty. In his decency, liberalism, and narrowness of subject-matter he resembles Forster

---

[1] William Bellamy, *The Novels of Wells, Bennett and Galsworthy, 1890-1910* (1971), p.23.

[2] Gerhard Masur, *Prophets of Yesterday: Studies in European Culture, 1890-1914* (1963), p.249.

while his view of life is at time like Conrad's: 'a complex mixture of pessimistic scepticism and romantic faith'.[3]

Also, only when drawing on the personal conflict with his family caused by his affair with Ada does Galsworthy's writing reach distinction. Much of *The Man of Property* displays a degree of assurance and ironic control which is found nowhere else in Galsworthy, and is arrived at, presumably, because the family milieu is so 'known' that he does not become embarrassed by the problem of inventing it. In *The Man of Property* Galsworthy behaves with the confident omniscience of the Victorian novelist, an omniscience which is 'immanent', not 'transcendent'.[4] *The Man of Property* displays little sense of the epistemological crisis that one associates with Conrad and Ford. It kicks confidently at a secure social order. There is no suggestion that the kicking will cause the order to crumble, and when the direction of the novel demands that some alternative to the Forsyte family should be put forward the novel itself crumbles and the Forsytes remain intact. This is the point made by Lawrence in his attack on Galsworthy in 1928:[5] 'The man of Property has the elements of a very great novel, a very great satire' (p.58) but it 'fizzles out', because Galsworthy 'gave in to the Forsytes' (p.59). The only positive in the novel is Irene and Bosinney's 'doggish amorousness' (p.61).

Lawrence's objection here is not that sex is no good as a positive but rather the opposite, that Galsworthy can only imagine weak sex. What he needs is the strong sexuality of 'wolves and foxes' whose sex is 'wild and in act utterly private' (p.66). All he can offer is tame and public sex, 'like dogs copulating in the street, and looking round to see if the Forsytes are watching' (p.62). Galsworthy and Forster are alike in this: each attacks an existing social order using the devices of comedy, satire and extended commentary and each sets up illicit sex in its place. Giles in *Jocelyn*, Irene and Bosinney in *The Man of Property* compare with Lucy and George in *A Room with a View*, Maurice and Scudder in *Maurice*. Galsworthy is queasy and reluctant over illicit heterosexuality, just as Forster seems almost unable to write convincingly about the homosexual love affair in *Maurice*.

Galsworthy describes the objectives for his novels in his essay 'Vague Thoughts on Art'.[6] The novel is 'consolation' and 'fantasy' for the entrapped mind.[7] Human lives are 'grievous' to Galsworthy because 'we are shut up within ourselves'. 'To be stolen away from ourselves by Art is a momentary relaxation from that itching, a minute's profound, and as it were secret, enfranchisement' (p.258).

[3] Lord David Cecil, 'Joseph Conrad', *London Magazine*, 1 (September 1954).
[4] I take this contrast from J. Hillis Miller, *The Form of Victorian Fiction* (1968), pp.64-5.
[5] D.H. Lawrence, 'John Galsworthy', in Edgell Rickword (ed.), *Scrutinies* (1928), pp.52-72.
[6] *The Inn of Tranquillity: Studies and Essays* (1912), pp.254-78.
[7] I borrow these terms from Iris Murdoch's influential essay, 'Against Dryness', *Encounter* (January 1961), pp.16-20.

The period through which he is living presents a major challenge to the artist. Just as Conrad sees man caught in the epistemological flood in *Lord Jim* (I refer to Stein's famous image of the newly-born man fallen into the sea and working against the fluid medium for his survival) so Galsworthy sees the artist swimming in undammed water which is also, given his choice of phrase, the amniotic flow that accompanies the birth process: 'The waters are broken, and every nerve and sinew of the artist is strained to discover his own safety' (p.260). Here and elsewhere in the essay Galsworthy could well be quoting from the Stein chapter in *Lord Jim*: Stein spoke of the butterfly as the perfect product of evolution, 'the perfect equilibrium of colossal forces'. Galsworthy speaks of 'the Universe' as 'all of a piece, Equipoise supreme'. With his less subtle mind Galsworthy is less guarded than Conrad, and commits himself to a fairly simple expression of the need for an 'alternative' religious faith: 'Orthodoxy fertilised by Science is producing a fresh and fuller conception of life – a love of Perfection, not for hope of reward, not for fear of punishment, but for Perfection's sake ... The Western world awoke one day to find that it no longer believed corporately and for certain in future life for the individual consciousness ... Perfection, cosmically, was nothing but perfect Equanimity and Harmony; and in human relations, nothing but perfect Love and Justice. And Perfection began to flow before the eyes of the Western world like a new star' (pp.260-2).

The point of Galsworthy's essay is his perception that man has replaced God in the late Victorian consciousness: 'Perfection', meaning the perfection of the species, had become 'implicit everywhere, and the revelation of Him the business of our Art' (p.263). This substitution of man for God is widely recognised as a central event in late Victorian consciousness. For Beatrice Webb 'during the middle decades of the nineteenth century ... in England, the impulse of self-subordinating servitude was transferred, consciously and overtly, from God to man', and 'the good and evil of man's life became not divine, but social, values'.[8] In Galsworthy's essay man has replaced God and is now replacing art. The arts are merging with one another, 'the novel straining to become the play, the play the novel, both trying to paint' ('Vague Thoughts on Art', p.265), and the boundary between art and life has also become indistinct: 'The power of Art is the disengagement from Life of its real spirit and significance' (p.271). God, having been expelled, reappears as the 'Creative Purpose' with man as his work of art in a closing rhetorical question: 'What are we – ripples on the tides of a birthless, deathless, equipoised Creative Purpose – but little works of Art?' (p.278).

Obviously one function of this essay is to vindicate Galsworthy's own literary habits: his didacticism, his overt moral and social objectives. His altruism is artistically disabling, the more socially engaged Edwardian

---

[8] Quoted by Bellamy, p.12.

novels are well-constructed but dead: *The Island Pharisees, Fraternity, The Country House, The Patrician*. *The Man of Property* is so much better than the other fictions, so much more responsibly a work of art, that it could be the work of a different writer. The only other novel that compares with it is the very first novel *Jocelyn* (1898).

What *Jocelyn* and *The Man of Property* have in common is that they are the products of anger and personal frustration rather than benign social observation. *Jocelyn* was first published under Galsworthy's pseudonym, 'John Sinjohn', was disowned by him and never reprinted in his lifetime, and has recently had a second edition. In the introduction to this edition Catherine Dupré, who has also written a biography of Galsworthy, points out that much of the interest of the novel is in the knowledge that its heroine is based on Galsworthy's wife, Ada, who was married to his cousin. Ada and Galsworthy were unable to live together openly, and force a divorce, until after the death of Galsworthy's father.

In *Jocelyn* the formal obstruction to happiness is the fact that Giles Legard is married to an invalid wife, but the real obstruction is Jocelyn's temperament and her dislike of sex. Ostensibly an irresistibly feminine and passive victim, the dramatised Jocelyn comes over as frigid and sexually cruel. As Catherine Dupré points out, it is reasonable to conclude that Galsworthy has accurately observed Ada's behaviour without allowing his infatuation with her to be disturbed. Ostensibly the conventions and the fact that he is a married man cause Giles Legard's sexual torment, but the dramatisation makes it quite clear where the real responsibility lies.

Galsworthy notoriously uses animals to counterpoint the behaviour of his human characters and he liked to set scenes of sexual rejection in stables. In *The Patrician* (1911) Lady Barbara Caradoc feeds a carrot to a horse which has been nuzzling in her pockets, and then rejects the advances of Lord Harbinger. Her face has an expression which 'was not a cruel look, had not a trace of mischief, or sex malice, and yet it frightened him by its serene inscrutability'. And Lord Harbinger pleads, pathetically: 'You know what I feel: don't be cruel to me!' (p.148).

The prototype of this scene appears in *Jocelyn* where Giles Legard at a clandestine meeting in a stable begs Jocelyn to become his mistress and she refuses him: 'At last he said, rather because his feelings fought for expression than that the words were those he wished to speak, "What's the matter, Jocelyn? Why do you treat–?" She stamped her foot upon the straw of the stall, and without saying a word, went out of the stable. He stood there, biting his moustache, dumb with pain and dismay, and the pony thrust its wet nose against the pocket of his coat' (pp.41-2).

A woman refuses sex, an animal offers affection. In the case of *Jocelyn* the act of writing is itself a sexual act performed vicariously. Just as Forster wrote homosexual stories for sexual relief, so Galsworthy, one may legitimately surmise, both focuses and eases the tensions caused by his relationship with Ada in this throwing-off of the proprieties: 'His will made no further remonstrance. All that he thought of, day and night, was to be near her. Conventional morality ceased to be anything to him but a dim, murky shadow, falling at times across the path of his longing. He was face to face with two very grim realities ... his great unslaked thirst, and his dread of bringing her harm. He was unable to see issues clearly outlined under the pressure of the throbbing passion which possessed him' (p.42).

'The pressure of the throbbing passion' in the passage quoted above is an Elinor Glyn *cliché* as far as its expression goes, but interesting here because it is a release of personal frustration, a verbal orgasm on the page.

The dramatisation makes it clear that Jocelyn is both frigid and more than half aware of the pain that she is inflicting: 'He clasped his hands on her knees, and she bent her head ... A great trembling passed through his frame.' With a refinement of cruelty she says: 'I *want* to be good to you, dearest. What does anything matter while you are wretched? What can I do? What can I do?' (pp.74-5). There is a hatred which is, presumably, still unconscious, in the way Giles perceives her appearance as she rejects him: 'A delicate oval face, cold as the moonlight itself; averted with unseizable eyes, profound and dark, with the lids drooping over them and circles of black beneath; lips drawn together, cruelly set; cheeks colourless; between the brows a slight furrow; and over all the waving dark hair gathered back from the low forehead' (p.80).

Irene in *The Man of Property* (1906), also based on Ada, is similar in behaviour: constantly 'averse', consistently passive with an 'alluring strangeness' (p.48). (Though unlike Jocelyn, Irene is blonde: she has 'dark brown eyes and golden hair, that strange combination, provocative of men's glances, which is said to be the mark of a weak character' (p.48).)

Like Elinor Glyn's and Henry Harland's heroes, Giles Legard is vaguely upper-class, aimlessly noble and sexually passive.[9] Lawrence objected that the Forsytes were all 'social beings' and therefore inhuman.[10] Giles Legard and Jocelyn Ley are inhuman for the opposite reason; they are deracinated, almost devoid of social or familial context. Giles's parents have died in his childhood, Jocelyn's have died entrusting her to her aunt, Mrs Travis, the only 'social' being in Lawrence's sense that this novel presents.

Both appear to be only children. Giles has never had a profession, has married a Polish invalid (the novel doesn't explain why) and spent all his adult life abroad. Gambling at Monte Carlo is his only pursuit. When he fell in love with Ada the young Galsworthy was an equally aimless figure. Harrow and New College, dabbling in the law, some agreeable travel, and

---

[9] See the discussion of 'Dandyism', above, pp.17-20.
[10] Lawrence, op. cit., p.54.

the publication of some feeble Kiplingesque short stories at his own expense (*From the Four Winds* by 'John Sinjohn', 1897): his biography up to this point had been uneventful. Giles's life is 'indifferent, gentle egotism', 'resigned humdrum, bored and gentle pleasure-seeking' (pp.15 and 18). One sees the point of another of Lawrence's remarks: 'The Galsworthy heroes are all weirdly in love with themselves.'[11]

Nevertheless, Giles's undirected laziness has its artistic point. When sexual arousal comes to him he is defenceless: as a man devoid of other interests he is condemned to be stirred and changed or broken by his sexuality. This scheme is set out on the first page and steadily followed through. The plotting of *Jocelyn* is flimsy, the characterisation conventional and the *dénouement* trite. But the novel remains permanently interesting for the exposed, vulnerable subjectivity with which its anti-hero's feeling is presented.

2. The Man of Property

Giles Legard fondles his dog because Jocelyn has shown it the affection that she won't show him, Horace Pendyce in *The Country House* steps on his dog and makes it squeal as he breaks his wife's heart over their errant son, Lady Casterley in *The Patrician* crushes a hornet as she persuades her granddaughter, Barbara Caradoc, to give up her unsuitable lover. Galsworthy's use of animals can be much more subtle than this, though, and occasionally in *Jocelyn* animals are used in a way that anticipates the central body of animal imagery in *The Man of Property* (1906): 'If you scratch a Russian you come to a Tartar, if you scratch a human being you come to an animal; only in some cases you scratch more, in others less. In Mrs. Travis' case you scratched less. She suggested nothing so much as a large Persian cat' (*Jocelyn*, p.26).

The detachment and control of *The Man of Property* are far removed from the subjective passion of *Jocelyn* and the didacticism and idealism of the other Edwardian novels. One cannot claim that it is an unflawed masterpiece: the Irene-Bosinney relationship is a relative failure; the reader has no access to the nature of the sexual attraction between them and finds it difficult to imagine. And some of the relationships in Old Jolyon's family strain one's credulity: Old Jolyon has not seen his son, it seems, for fourteen years (although he buys his pictures and they live within a mile or so of each other), and Young Jolyon has not seen his daughter June for the same period of time. Divorce and remarriage were certainly sources of disgrace in the

[11] Ibid., p.64.

period but Galsworthy has surely over-simplified the situation to gain his effect here.

The Man of Property is central to the Edwardian period, defining what the period thought literary success, liberal high-mindedness and alert economical honest craftmanship consisted of. It also exemplifies more clearly than any other work, including *Howards End*, the dilemma of the liberal imagination in the period. Galsworthy holds his own opinions at a distance. The Forsytes 'collected pictures ... and were supporters of such charitable institutions as might be beneficial to their sick domestics' (p.20).

The objectivity of the novelist's eye is shared by Young Jolyon, who is the narrative centre of much of the novel. As an artist himself he is able to stand outside the present and comment on his father as a representative of the Victorian order which is about to be swept away: 'In his great chair with the book-rest sat old Jolyon, the figure-head of his family and class and creed, with his white head and dome-like forehead, the representative of moderation, and order, and love of property. As lonely an old man as there was in London. There he sat in the gloomy comfort of the room, a puppet in the power of great forces that care nothing for family or class or creed, but moved, machine-like, with dread processes to inscrutable ends. This was how it struck young Jolyon, who had the impersonal eye' (p.41).

But Old Jolyon too is introspective and thoughtful. This is a fine touch, as he is Galsworthy's own father and the barrier to Galsworthy's happiness. It is difficult for any writer to portray his father objectively. Butler's *The Way of All Flesh* and Gosse's *Father and Son* present Victorian fathers who are seen with insight, certainly, but with umistakable hatred. Galsworthy in his novel has detached himself from his hatred as well as from everything else.

Soames, too, is part of the Victorian order to be swept away, although he is also in a sense an evolutionary survival and success. Soames's rape of Irene is an act of marital imperialism, and in this he is like his uncle Nicholas, an imperialist in the literal sense who 'had succeeded during the day in bringing to fruition a scheme for the employment of a tribe from upper India in the gold-mines of Ceylon ... As he had often forcibly argued, all experience tended to show that a man must die; and whether he died of a miserable old age in his own country, or prematurely of damp in the bottom of a foreign mine, was surely of little consequence, provided that by a change in his mode of life he benefited the British empire' (pp.47-8).

Soames setting out to build a country house at Robin Hill shares his uncle's disposition and is presented ironically as the explorer, charting the dark continent of his own country: 'Soames the pioneer-leader of the great Forsyte army advancing to the civilisation of this wilderness, felt his spirit daunted by the loneliness, by the invisible singing [larks], and the hot, sweet air' (pp.70-1).

Soames's wish to build himself a country house is a *parvenu* aspiration, which is of course the point of the novel's title: the novel is about vulgarity. The Forsytes have come from humble, innocently rustic origins in Dorset. James Forsyte, Soames's father, has visited the ancestral village and returned unimpressed by what he found: with the necessary tendency in the Forsytes to glorify their antecedents, who were tenant farmers and small builders, Aunt Hester refers to her father as 'an owner of houses' and to her grandfather as one who 'had to do with land' (p.19).

Only Old Jolyon has the 'desperate honesty' to see his ancestors as: '"Yeomen – I suppose very small beer." Yet he would repeat the word "yeomen" as if it afford him consolation' (p.20). Compare Forster's romantic use of the word 'yeomen' to describe the ancestors of Ruth Wilcox in *Howards End*. In sensing that the word 'yeomen' asks to be used ironically Galsworthy displays more literary tact, on this topic, than does Forster.

As in *Howards End, Tono-Bungay, Heartbreak House* and Galsworthy's *The Country House*, houses, the physical buildings, are of central importance. Like James Forsyte, Galsworthy's father, a solicitor, had made money from speculation in property in London, and in the novel 'from their father, the builder, [the Forsytes] inherited a talent for bricks and mortar'. The sites, sizes, styles of their houses represent their aspirations: 'Their residences, placed at stated intervals round the park, watched like sentinels, lest the fair heart of this London, where their desires were fixed, should slip from their clutches, and leave them lower in their own estimations' (p.20).

Each of the houses is then itemised – 'Old Jolyon in Stanhope Place; the Jameses in Park Lane; ... The Soameses in their nest off Knightsbridge' (pp.19-20). Each Forsyte is carefully given a setting, or perhaps the word should be 'habitat', the word used by Young Jolyon in chapter 10 where the Forsytes are explicitly compared with animals. Jolyon's mansion in chapter 2 has the 'rich brown atmosphere peculiar to back rooms in the mansion of a Forsyte' (p.25). Soames's house is small and fussy: 'The inner decoration favoured the First Empire and William Morris. For its size, the house was commodious; there were countless nooks resembling birds' nests, and little things made of silver were deposited like eggs' (p.73).

Irene is a childless bird; a 'captive owl, bunched in its soft feathers against the wires of a cage' (p.373). The eggs are artificial, the nest is a death-trap.

The homes of the two artists, Young Jolyon and Bosinney, contrast sharply with these opulent interiors. Jolyon, having quarrelled with his father over his divorce and remarriage, is forced to live modestly in St John's Wood, a 'pokey' place with 'an air of shabbiness', steps that need painting, and a scruffy pear-tree as the principal ornament of its small garden (pp.93-4). Bosinney lives in absolute squalor with a roughly made bed, dust everywhere, 'a few shirts and collars, a pair of muddy boots' (p.350). Yet Bosinney is a 'gentleman', something Soames ardently desires to be.

Bosinney is a member of the Hotch Potch Club, which has refused to elect Old Jolyon and took Young Jolyon only because his father's money has bought him a gentleman's education.

The Forsytes have made the movement that Wells, Bennett and Forster, as well as Galsworthy, see as crucially representative of Edwardian and late Victorian economic life, the movement from the country, or the provincial town, into London. To attain the status that Bosinney enjoys by birth Soames must complete this obliteration of the 'Yeoman', 'Superior Dosset' Forsyte, by moving back from London into the country on a new social level; no longer tenant farmer but quasi-country gentleman. Bosinney the gentleman-architect knows exactly how to catch the fancy of Soames the *arriviste* solicitor. He describes the designs of the new house, Robin Hill: 'The principle of this house ... was that you should have room to breathe – like a gentleman!' (p.107). He sneeringly advises Soames to go to a rival who builds for manufacturers if he finds Bosinney's house too expensive. Soames's vanity, as Bosinney intended it should be, is hooked: 'He had been identified with a gentleman; not for a good deal of money now would he be classed with manufacturers' (p.109).

Soames is Galsworthy's central anti-hero, the representative Forsyte who inhabits a well-observed social paradox. Property both qualifies and disqualifies him for gentility. The drive to set himself up at Robin Hill is inseparable from the drive to dominate Irene. The rape of Irene is an expression of the property impulse which could never be the act of a gentleman within the novel's – that is to say, within Bosinney's – understanding of the term: 'Soames had exercised his rights over an estranged and unwilling wife in the greatest – the supreme act of property' (p.322). The two acts of possession, of the house and of the woman, are elegantly matched: by raping Irene, Soames loses any hope of living in Robin Hill with her, and the novel closes with Old Jolyon intending to buy the house for his newly reconciled son, Young Jolyon, the disinherited and disgraced outsider whom the novel's reversals will now make the 'Man of Property' of the title. While Soames's sexual initiative disqualifies him for gentility it at the same time confers on him the badge of evolutionary success. With the other Forsytes he has the necessary qualities for survival, and he ends the novel by closing the door of his lair with Irene trapped inside.

The novel's *dénouement* has Bosinney run down and killed in the fog. His death may be a suicide brought on because his gentlemanly susceptibilities are unable to withstand the horror of Soames's rape of Irene. George Forsyte has followed Bosinney through the fog and overheard (improbably) a soliloquy which would indicate a suicidal state of mind: 'His [George Forsyte's] fancy wandered in the fields of this situation; it impressed him; he guessed something of the anguish, the sexual confusion and horror in Bosinney's heart. And he thought: "Yes, it's a bit thick! I don't wonder the poor fellow is half-cracked!"'' (p.322).

Bosinney's death is not seen from within. Galsworthy originally intended to make it explicitly suicide but was dissuaded by Edward Garnett, and leaves the story of Bosinney with the ambiguous ending that it has now.[12] Bosinney is observed by George but also by Young Jolyon, who has less evidence than George but more insight. Jolyon is voicing Edward Garnett's objection to the novel's original ending when he argues with himself that Bosinney would not have killed himself 'in the full sweep of passion' for Irene (p.369). George Forsyte knows, as Jolyon does not, that Soames has raped Irene and that Irene has reported this to Bosinney in her distress.

When he gives Bosinney suicidal feelings on learning that his mistress has been forced by her husband Galsworthy may well be drawing on his own experience with Ada and her husband. Soames is more successful in sexual competition; Bosinney, discouraged and neutered by the knowledge that he has been worsted by Soames, has perhaps destroyed himself. Galsworthy does not attempt to explore Bosinney's mind beyond George's speculation about his 'sexual confusion and horror' where Conrad, writing about Heyst, for example, could have made such a psychological process full and detailed. Soames survives, Bosinney is extinguished and his death completes the pattern of evolutionary images in the novel. Soames has a capacity for primitive sexual violence which belies his physical appearance: 'Skin-like immaculateness has grown over Soames, as over many Londoners' (p.74). But he shares with the other Forsytes the animal quality which equips them to survive in a world in which Bosinney is extinguished. Young Jolyon gives to Bosinney his 'Diagnosis of a Forsyte' (chapter 10) in the form of a biological essay: '"This little animal, disturbed by the ridicule of his own sort, is unaffected in his motions by the laughter of strange creatures (you [Bosinney] or I). Hereditarily disposed to myopia, he recognises only the persons and habitats of his own species, amongst which he passes an existence of competitive tranquillity"'' (p.221).

In the wholly successful opening chapter the Forsytes behave like a herd of cows when Bosinney enters: 'Like cattle when a dog comes into the field, they stood head to head and shoulder to shoulder, prepared to run upon and trample the invader to death' (p.9). Compare the English travellers on the train in *The Island Pharisees* (1904) who react as 'animals at the first scent of danger' to the presence of two young foreigners in their carriage (p.6).

The Forsytes are 'an upper-middle class family in full plumage', and the favoured observer is 'admitted to a vision of the dim roads of social progress, has understood something of patriarchal life, of the swarmings of savage hordes, of the rise and fall of nations' (p.3). Swithin is a 'pouter-pigeon' and a 'turkey-cock' (pp.14-15), Soames is a 'mouse' and a 'bull-dog' (pp.125 and

---

[12] Catherine Dupré, *John Galsworthy*, p.103.

132), both sneaking and obstinate. Collectively the Forsytes are a 'tree' as well as a 'herd': Darwin's tree illustrating the descent of man. Their show of solidarity at Aunt Ann's funeral illustrates the 'law of property underlying the growth of their tree' (p.119). Bosinney, the strange dog, the cat, the lion, is in the anomalous position of being both an outsider and also a member of the family (to the extent that he is engaged to June Forsyte): hence Young Jolyon's feeling that his death affects the whole family, cuts into the 'wood of their tree' and delivers the Forsytes a blow from which they will never recover (p.368). The solidarity displayed at Aunt Ann's funeral has been broken. In their imperial aspect the Forsytes control the energies of their subject peoples as though they were zoo-keepers containing lesser animals. Young Jolyon feels sympathy for a caged tiger at the zoo (Bosinney's animal) while his father complacently finds it 'humanising and educational to confine baboons and panthers' (p.190).

The notion of inheritance is inextricably bound up with these images of evolution. The first chapter of the novel gives a tableau in which the Forsytes are immortal. They 'did not die: death being contrary to their principles, they took precautions against it, the instinctive precautions of highly vitalised persons who resent encroachments on their property' (p.4).

This contains the seeds of its own ironic destruction, these rich old people are certain to be defeated by the action of time. The death of Aunt Ann is an elaborately prepared symbolic event. The tough Victorian world shifts and gives way, time unsticks, and the elder Forsytes, a dying species, are translated into mythology as the dinosaurs were turned into dragons. At Robin Hill, while Bosinney and Irene enjoy their first sexual encounter in the woods below, Swithin dozes off in the sun and becomes an ancient, discredited god, 'like some image blocked out by the special artist of primeval Forsytes in Pagan days' (p.150).

This pattern of evolutionary success and failure is accompanied by the Art-Property conflict. Bosinney makes art, Soames buys it. Obviously Soames's purchasing of pictures is primarily an act of property, but it answers another need as well. His purchases are 'nearly all landscapes with figures in the foreground, a sign of some mysterious revolt against London' (p.63). They are Soames's pastoral world, a retreat for the mind from life's urgent urban contingencies. (As too is St Paul's cathedral, visits to which 'enabled him to concentrate his thoughts' (p.66).)

The Forsytes *need* art. Old Jolyon goes to the opera and finds himself dismayed by the changes that have overtaken it: 'There was no opera now! That fellow Wagner had ruined everything; no melody left, nor any voices to sing it' (p.34). Swithin's dreadful modern sculpture and the 'love of ormulu' reflected in his over-decorated bachelor apartments are the products of an inability to distinguish between beauty and luxury (p.43). In his case, bad taste in art is a symptom of dissatisfaction with himself: he surrounds himself with luxury to combat 'a sense that a man of his distinction should never have been allowed to soil his mind with work' (p.44). For Soames, Robin Hill is a work of art (a pastoral retreat in the literary sense) as well as a guarantee of gentility. Therefore although Bosinney is an evolutionary failure he retains an ultimate power. Bosinney's revolt against Soames's niggling over the price of Robin Hill is the 'eternal position of Art towards Property' (p.173). Soames hates Bosinney because he needs him, Bosinney is destroyed because he is too good an artist to leave the Forsytes untouched.

Soames and Bosinney are locked in sexual and economic conflict. The sexual conflict stirs up undercurrents which are never fully in the novelist's control. The source of this difficulty is the characterisation of Irene. Galsworthy himself was uncomfortable with the character: 'The figure of Irene, never, as the reader may possibly have noticed, present, except through the senses of other characters, is a concretion of disturbing Beauty impinging on a possessive world' (*The Man of Property*, p.vi).

Although directed by the novel to admire and love Irene, the reader is also free to make his own objective judgment of her as she sulks or cowers, upstages her 'friend' June Forsyte, ensnares and finally destroys Bosinney. Bosinney has much in common with Giles Legard and may resemble the young Galsworthy when he met and fell in love with his bored, sultry, married cousin Ada: an immature ex-public schoolboy, idealistic and sexually ignorant, easily trapped, unbalanced by the sexual 'horror' of the rape.

Bosinney also is 'present' largely 'through the senses of other characters'. The novel works against its own current of feeling: Bosinney and Soames are drawn towards each other by the house and the woman, and their mutual attraction-repulsion is explored in this scene:

> '[Soames] "Let women into your plans ... and you never know where it'll end."
> '"Ah!" said Bosinney, "women are the devil!"
> 'This feeling had long been at the bottom of Soames's heart; he had never, however, put it into words.
> '"Oh!" he muttered, "so you're beginning to –"
> 'He stopped, but added, with an uncontrollable burst of spite:
> '"June's got a temper of her own – always had."
> '"A temper's not a bad thing in an angel."
> 'Soames had never called Irene an angel. He could not so have violated his best instincts, letting other people into the secret of her value, and giving himself away. He made no reply' (p.68).

Solidarity between the men and a mutual agreement that women are the cause of all the trouble in the world: it begins for a moment to resemble the groundplan of all Forster's novels. In addition to the equivocal, detached treatment of Irene there is evidence that the novel is the work of someone who is fundamentally misogynist. Aunt Hester's interminably boring gossip, Winifred's vulgar desire to see 'the common people making love' (p.228), 'the little McAnder' who is a 'New Woman' (p.286), 'Little Francie's' fatuous but successful music (her 'Kensington Coil' has a 'sweet dip in it') (p.200): none of these are the inventions of a writer who has much respect for women.

The Forsyte men, like Forster's Wilcoxes, have at least the justification of a significant role in English life. For young Jolyon they are 'half England, and the better half, too, the safe half, the three per cent. half, the half that counts' (p.238). It is part of the novel's detachment, and therefore part of its success, that it denies its own instincts. The friendship between Soames and Bosinney must not be allowed to develop, the failure of Soames's marriage must be blamed on Soames, not on Irene. 'She was ever silent, passive, gracefully averse; as though terrified lest by word, motion, or sign she might lead him to believe that she was fond of him; and he asked himself: must I always go on like this?' (p.76).

Soames is a novel reader and is interested in plays about conjugal problems: he takes Irene to the theatre often. He believes that the improvement of his marriage will be 'only a question of time' (p.76) as it is in the novels and plays which are to his taste. Real heroism in Soames would require the strength to scrap his marriage and start again; real heroism in Bosinney would require the strength to be honest with Soames and himself and then escape from the Forsytes altogether.

3. The Country House

Galsworthy found *The Country House* (1907) easy to write, expected it to have as much success as *The Man of Property* and was disappointed by its cooler reception.[13] The novel's principal difficulty is that it 'was to do for the country what *The Man of Property* did for the town' (p.138). For his Forsytes Galsworthy was able to draw on his own relations while for the squirearchical Pendyces of *The Country House* he had to draw on people he knew less well, the rather grand people in whose houses he had been a guest.

Horace Pendyce, owner of Worsted Skeynes, the country house of the title, is brutal and stupid and his companion the Rector, the Reverend Hussell Barter, is a sexually insatiable Puritan who has forced his wife to have eleven children while condemning any relaxation of sexual restraint in others. The dramatic situation is like that of *The Man of Property* at an earlier stage. Horace Pendyce is quarrelling with his son George because of George's

[13] Dupré, p.138.

involvement with a married woman, Helen Bellew. Helen Bellew's husband cites George as co-respondent but drops the case after the intervention of George's mother, Mrs Pendyce; Helen Bellew rejects George who can then be reconciled to his father.

The simplicity of the targets in *The Country House* suggests that Galsworthy is becoming fatally bored by the business of characterisation. Horace Pendyce's obduracy, oppressiveness and obtuseness are sketched in thick, broad outlines in the opening pages: 'His wife was a Totteridge, and his coverts admirable. He had been, needless to say, an eldest son. It was his individual conviction that individualism had ruined England, and he had set himself deliberately to eradicate this vice from the character of his tenants. By substituting for their individualism his own tastes, plans, and sentiments, one might almost say his own individualism, and losing money thereby, he had gone far to demonstrate his pet theory that the higher the individualism the more sterile the life of the community. If, however, the matter was thus put to him he grew both garrulous and angry, for he considered himself not an individualist, but what he called a "Tory Communist" ... Mr. Pendyce had other peculiarities, in which he was not too individual. He was averse to any change in the existing order of things, made lists of everything, and was never really so happy as when talking of himself or his estate' (p.6).

The Reverend Hussell Barter is characterised in equally generalised and frankly dull terms, and the only fully sympathetic figure in the novel, Pendyce's wife, causes Galsworthy's critical faculties to collapse altogether. The novel is ostensibly an attack on the hereditary powers of the county families and the country houses that are the physical symbol of that power. One would have expected that the first items to be dropped from the vocabulary of the novel, given its theme, would be 'lady' and 'gentleman' as terms of commendation. Yet on her first appearance it is announced that Mrs Pendyce's bosom 'hid the heart of a lady' (p.14). At the moment at which she decides to leave her bullying husband Galsworthy produces a paragraph of extraordinarily muddled prose. Margery Pendyce is representative of England, she has in her spirit 'something' which unknown to her is 'her country's civilisation, its very soul, the meaning of it all – gentleness, balance'. Her virtues are hereditary. She comes from an older family than the Pendyces and has a 'gentle soul' whose 'strength was the gift of the ages'. This strength would, it seems, be fatally impaired if she had had any proletarian ancestors. Fortunately she had not: 'In Margery Pendyce ... there was no irascible and acrid "people's blood", no fierce misgivings, no ill-digested beer and cider – it was pure claret in her veins – she had nothing thick and angry in her soul ... That which she had resolved she must carry out, by virtue of a thin, fine flame, breathing far down in her – so far that nothing could extinguish it ... It was not "I will not be over-ridden" that her spirit felt, but "I must not be over-ridden, for if I am over-ridden, I, and in

me something beyond me, more important than myself, is all undone"'
(p.214).

The muddle into which the upper-class liberal can get himself is felt here
in an acute form. Like the embarrassing bits of atavism and snobbery which
crop up in Forster, Galsworthy's praise of Mrs Pendyce's ancestors threatens
to wreck his theme.

The contrast between Margery Pendyce and her husband's family is like
that between Ruth Wilcox and the family into which she has married in
Howards End. The difference is that Forster is on the whole conscious of the
contradictions that threaten his novel. That is one of the reasons why Forster
uses *two* country houses, Howards End and Oniton Grange, to illustrate his
points. Galsworthy blunders straight in. The question one would like to ask
is why all these people are presented as exemplary types? The breakdown of
the Pendyce marriage is just plausible as a difference between two
individuals, but as a representative conflict between old English virtues and
modern English brutalism it simply will not work.

The real difficulty with the book is, perhaps, that Galsworthy is forced by
his chosen topic to write disapprovingly about things that he actually loved.
He enjoyed house-parties, shooting and fishing (though not hunting), the
elaborate ceremony of Edwardian upper-class life, and one can suspect that
he enjoyed the sheer dullness of the squirearchy as compared with the
irritable company of other writers or the expatriate colonies among whom his
wife insisted on moving on her endless excursions abroad. He shares with
Horace Pendyce his love of dogs, a motif which is very much overworked in this
novel. As Pendyce in his disappointment with his son makes plans to
disinherit him, he treads three times in the course of one chapter on his
favourite dog; he is hurting himself, as the symbol makes all too plain, by
hurting what he loves (Part 2, chapter 4). The feature which partially
salvages the novel and prevents it from falling apart altogether is the
landscape itself.

The mythologising of the English landscape in the Edwardian period is an
important feature of its quest for alternative religious and social values. *The
Country House* is dedicated to W.H. Hudson (with particular reference to *The
Purple Land*). Hudson's *Nature in Downland* had defined the nature of, and the
appeal of, the English landscape for the whole decade. (It was greatly
admired by Ford Madox Ford.) Love of the landscape is an overwhelmingly
'legitimate' emotion which can coexist respectably with Galsworthy's kind of
liberalism. The Pendyces are of the land and the landscape, and to that
extent admirable, but their stupidity disqualifies them for this stewardship.
The institutions governing the land are too few and too hereditary: 'Just as
round the hereditary principle are grouped the State, the Church, Law, and
Philanthropy, so round the dining-table at Worsted Skeynes sat the Squire,
the Rector, Mr. Paramor, and Gregory Vigil' (p.168). The land itself exerts a

dumb attraction over Vigil. He leaves Worsted Skeynes and on the way back
to London in the train looks out at the landscape: 'Throughout the whole of
his journey up to town he looked out of the window, and expressions half
humorous and half puzzled played on his face. Like a panorama slowly
unrolled, country house after country house, church after church, appeared
before his eyes in the autumn sunlight, among the hedgerows and the coverts
that were all brown and gold; and far away on the rising uplands the slow
ploughman drove, outlined against the sky' (pp.71-2).

This is the point at which all Edwardian liberals confront an insoluble
paradox. The hereditary leaders must go without changing this hereditary
beauty. But how can that be guaranteed? If the Pendyces, Wilcoxes or
owners of Up Park are done away with, what will take their place?

4. Fraternity

In *The Country House* Galsworthy attempts the squirearchy, and in *Fraternity*
(1909) he seems to be exploring Bloomsbury. *Fraternity* presents surprising
parallels with the life and work of Virginia Woolf. The people involved are
London intellectuals who dabble in the arts and politics and have Social
Consciences. Its opening feels like a mix of *Mrs. Dalloway* and Virginia
Woolf's biography: a Mrs Cecilia Dallison is shopping for a dress with which
to charm her husband. Her sister, Bianca, is a painter and a practical,
independent-minded woman, on bad terms with her husband. This
incestuousness – two brothers marrying two sisters – and the way their little
London houses express their personalities all have a smell of Bloomsbury.
Cecilia Dallison looks at her brother-in-law Hilary's house: 'The queer
conceit came to Cecilia that it resembled Hilary. Its look was kindly and
uncertain; its colour a palish tan; the eyebrows of its windows rather straight
than arched, and those deep-set eyes, the windows, twinkled hospitably; it
had, as it were, a sparse moustache and beard of creepers, and dark marks
here and there, like the lines and shadows on the faces of those who think too
much. Beside it, and apart, though connected by a passage, a studio stood,
and about that studio – of white rough-cast, with a black oak door, and
peacock-blue paint – was something a little hard and fugitive, well suited to
Bianca, who used it, indeed, to paint in' (p.6).

Her husband is a 'Barrister in an official position', an establishment figure
like Virginia Woolf's Richard Dalloway, but she wants to keep in touch with
her sister's friends: 'Since Hilary wrote books and was a poet, and Bianca
painted, their friends would naturally be either interesting or queer', and she
views them with 'pleasurable dread' (p.9). Old Mr Stone, the philosopher,
and father of Cecilia and Bianca, could well be based on Leslie Stephen's
nervous and quasi-senile physical appearance: 'very thin and rather bent,

with silvery hair, and a thin silvery beard grasped in his transparent fingers' (p.7). (One can almost hear Sir Leslie pulling at his moustache and saying aloud: 'Oh, *why* won't my whiskers grow?') Cecilia has a daughter, Thyme, about whom she feels the kind of anxiety that Clarissa Dalloway feels about her Elizabeth. There the resemblances end: Thyme involves herself in social work with her doctor cousin, Martin Stone, and is forced by the experience to acknowledge that she is not suited to it. She has wanted to help the poor for aesthetic rather than philanthropic reasons: 'I only care because they're ugly for me to see!' (p.301). Thyme's name is a pun, of course: she is of the time, caught up in the social changes of the day and registering them for the upper classes. In the same way Mr Stone is a thinker seeking the philosopher's stone, or the 'Key to All the Mythologies', as George Eliot had it. He also resembles Shaw's Captain Shotover in *Heartbreak House* and Barrie's Grandpa Reilly in *Little Mary* (1903), who is writing a 'book about the English Aristocracy' showing that all the evils of Edwardian England are the result of overeating.

Another type-figure is Mr Purcey ('Purse-y'), the wealthy parvenu whose favourite activity is driving around London in his motor-car, an A.1 Damyer (an adaptation of Daimler, presumably; but a pun on 'Damn-Yer' – the attitude of the motorist – is probably also intended). Old Mr Stone is writing a book on 'Universal Brotherhood' which is, of course, the subject of the novel's title, *Fraternity*. The novel presents itself as a discussion novel like Shaw's or Granville-Barker's or Galsworthy's own discussion plays. Its title and its type characters place it with *Justice, Strife, Waste* and *Getting Married* (or Wells's *Marriage*, equally a discussion novel). It is all too neatly constructed, setting up a high life group whose pattern is reflected by low-life figures. Mrs Hughs and her husband quarrel over a model, Miss Barton, who has been boarded with them by the Dallisons. The model causes the Hughs marriage to break up. Hughs, who has been shell-shocked in the Boer War (suggesting a slight parallel with Virginia Woolf's Septimus Smith, again in *Mrs. Dalloway*), fancies her, and attacks his wife with a bayonet when she tries to keep him from the model. He is sent to prison; this is no help to Mrs Hughs whose baby dies of starvation because her milk dries up under stress. Upper-class justice can be seen to have destroyed the helpless, confused working-class people just as it destroys the Joneses in *The Silver Box*. The model is the sexual centre of the novel, and a necessity for old Mr Stone. (One would like to draw a comparison with the relationship between Ellie Dunn and Captain Shotover in *Heartbreak House*.)

Mr Stone himself is a fine comic invention, though the quotations given from his book are over-long. Perhaps Galsworthy wants the reader to attend to them seriously; they all begin with the phrase 'in those days', and then list a series of social evils of the present. Mr Stone acknowledges, when it is pointed out to him, that the model's presence in his room gives him pleasure:

'It must be due to the sex instinct not yet quite extinct. It is stated that the blackcock will dance before his females to a great age, though I have never seen it' (p.207). His habit of swimming in the Serpentine every morning almost drowns him: 'Mr. Stone, seated at the bottom, was doing all he could to rise' (pp.235-6). He is rescued by Hilary, his son-in-law and in a sense his rival for the model's attentions.

If the temperately comic characterisation of Mr Stone is the novel's success, Hilary's relationship with the model is its worst failure. The model begins and ends the novel. It opens with discussion of a painting of her by Bianca Dallison, Hilary's wife. The painting stimulates a spiteful attack from a rancorous art-critic – a fine vignette of a man whose 'natural male distaste for the works of women painters' and 'acid temperament' leads him to 'revel in an orgy of personal retaliation' (p.41): '"We learn that 'The Shadow', painted by Bianca Stone, who is not generally known to be the wife of the writer, Mr. Hilary Dallison, will soon be exhibited ... This very *fin-de-siècle* creation, with its unpleasant subject ... is a somewhat anaemic piece of painting. If Mr. Dallison, who finds the type an interesting one, embodies her in one of his very charming poems, we trust the result will be less bloodless"' (p.42).

Yet Hilary's relationship with the model *is* bloodless. He leaves his wife but is unable to commit himself to the model. Galsworthy refers, as Wells did in *The Sea Lady*, to Burne-Jones's painting *The Depths of the Sea* (1887). The painting could almost be a dream-painting of male sexual fear. A mermaid has her arms round a naked sailor, and drags him down into the water. It is possible that she does not know that he is drowning, but the Giaconda smile on her face suggests that she does know and is deriving sexual pleasure from his death. One of her arms covers his genitals as though castrating him. Bianca, the painter who has made the model a street-walker, now makes her into the mermaid: '"He'll never abandon you; his conscience is too tender. But you'll be round his neck – like this!"' Bianca raised her arms, looped, and dragged them slowly down, as a mermaid's arms drag at a drowning sailor' (p.332).

With her Hilary feels trapped by the 'mystery of sex' (p.357), but when he kisses her she disgusts him: 'The touch of her lips was moist and hot. The scent of stale violet powder came from her, warmed by her humanity. It penetrated to Hilary's heart. He started back in sheer physical revolt' (p.337). The illicit sex that seems to be breaking through the class barriers and making 'fraternity' into a reality is blocked by what are presumably class, or aesthetic, objections from Hilary: the model is over-willing and not clean. It is surprising that Lawrence did not single out this relationship for scorn rather than the Irene-Bosinney relationship.

I began by saying that Wells, Bennett and Galsworthy should not be seen as a group. Extraordinary attempts have been made to give intellectual seriousness to the traditional grouping. William Bellamy sees the Edwardian literature of the three as 'art characterised by its overt interest in therapy – not simply therapy in the shape of social reform, but a transference from teleologies to direct remedial action undertaken on behalf of the self. The later fiction might be called a literature of exhortation.'[14] I take this to mean that in their Edwardian novels the three writers tended to 'tell' rather than 'show', that they sacrificed dramatic presentation to the easier business of presenting their opinions. Bellamy goes to great lengths to make Galsworthy look as interesting as the other two writers. *Fraternity*, in his view, is 'post-Chekhovian music in the counterpointing of its atomised consciousness'.[15] He discusses the tramps in the park who appear at the end of chapter 9: Hilary is walking in search of the little model, and the tramps prick his social conscience: 'In the centre of the lane a row of elm-trees displayed their gnarled, knotted roots. Human beings were seated there, whose matted hair clung round their tired faces. Their gaunt limbs were clothed in rags; each had a stick, and some sort of dirty bundle tied to it. They were asleep. On a bench beyond, two toothless old women sat, moving their eyes from side to side, and a crimson-faced woman was snoring ... A little farther on two young men in working-clothes were looking straight before them, with desperately tired faces. They, too, were silent' (*Fraternity*, p.90).

Bellamy sees in this scene 'the scenery of Beckett and early Picasso': 'One requires some training in *fin-de-siècle* fantasy, perhaps, to see this as a kind of space-warp, with the pastoral world and the urban existing in explosive simultaneity.'[16] Galsworthy's unexciting prose is itself part of the artistic endeavour, it seems: 'The manifest inability of Galsworthy to imagine is here being exploited in a quite modern way', and Galsworthy should be compared with Ford Madox Ford, 'his art depending for its effectiveness ... upon certain epistemological inadequacies in the imagining consciousness.'[17]

These observations seem to me sheer nonsense. The writing of the tramps passage is dull, as is so much of Galsworthy's writing, because Galsworthy's compassion has outrun his powers of imaginative observation. *Fraternity* cannot possibly be elevated into a 'modernist' work of art, and to compare it with Beckett is crazy. It is a neatly constructed, kind book by a genial philanthropist who doesn't know his characters well enough to make them interesting.

Most novelists write best about what they know best. It takes a very unusual talent, like Conrad's or Graham Greene's, to rise to the challenge of inventing convincingly a human situation in a setting of which one has only a visitor's knowledge. Wells and Bennett could write well over comparatively

[14] Bellamy, p.22.
[15] Ibid., p.188.
[16] Ibid., p.200.
[17] Ibid., p.199.

large areas. Bennett's strength lay in the Five Towns of his childhood but he can invent the siege of Paris (*The Old Wives' Tale*) or the back streets of London (*Riceyman Steps*) with impressive conviction. Wells writes best, one could argue, when revisiting his childhood and frustrated young manhood in *Love and Mr. Lewisham, Kipps* and *Tono-Bungay*, but all Wells's scientific romances are energised and interesting, even at their most slight. Science and the will-to-power that fantasy represents were themselves part of his life, part of his 'known' and felt experience. Galsworthy's range is much narrower. *The Man of Property* demonstrates an innate capacity for social comedy when he knows his subject confidently, and the plays, *The Silver Box, Strife* and *Justice* especially, demonstrate a capacity for organising an argument into actable and entertaining dramatic form so that its points are clear without resorting to Shavian 'arias'. This is by no means a despicable talent. The failure of the other Edwardian novels suggests that Galsworthy did not know his own talent and was determined to be, like Wells and Shaw, a polymath and prophet, a critic of the age.

5. 'Danaë', The Patrician *and the ascetic ideal*

Galsworthy's fragment 'Danaë', issued by his wife after his death in *Forsytes, Pendyces and Others* (1935), is the first part of what later became *The Country House*. The seventy-eight pages of 'Danaë' have what *The Country House* lacks: wit, assurance, and a close knowledge of the social milieu presented. The fragment opens with a board meeting at which Anthony Thornworthy, Chairman of 'Bhang and Sciatic' and an elderly ruffian of the London business world, is resisting demands for higher wages from a trades union leader. The situation is a mix, one may say, of Galsworthy's *Strife* and Granville-Barker's *The Voysey Inheritance*. Old Thornworthy is on the verge of the 'abyss' (that classically Edwardian word) of bankruptcy (p.10) and kept going largely by his own and his son's directors' fees from Bhang and Sciatic. His personality is modelled on that of his antecedent, 'Squire Baldwin Thornworthy'.

Thornworthy then is the opposite of the Forsytes: he is decayed gentry forced to move into the city and work for his living, but retaining the sturdy individualism of a Regency country gentleman. He has inherited 'Squire Baldwin's' furniture and with it 'something of the atmosphere which belonged to the hard-riding, port-drinking, free-loving days of the Squire, when the country was orthodox and Christian to a man, in the loyal belief that the British temperament was the ideal, original soil for Christian seed, and good hard hitting in Commerce, camp, and Church, the first teaching of Christ' (p.56).

Anthony Thornworthy is the strongest male figure in 'Danaë', just as Old Jolyon is the strongest male figure in *The Man of Property*. Galsworthy celebrates the doughtiness of these Victorian patriarchs in similar terms except that in 'Danaë' there is a conspicuously new element, 'Christian seed' and 'the first teaching of Christ'.

Thornworthy is failing physically: he has to be helped onto the underground train by two porters: 'It was as good as a play to see the old fellow try to get into the train by himself! So – the porters to each other; but down in their hearts was a deep, unvoiced admiration for that vain, heroic effort renewed each day. And it was the most gentle, the most delicate of pushes that heaved the feeble, bulky form into place' (p.17).

Like the Forsytes he is tenacious of health as his most valued property, and this tenacity is expressed in a finely written passage about his interest in food: 'When Anthony ate, he employed great methods. One knew him at once for a man of courage, of stubborn tenacity, of a shrewd if not cynical judgment. As he was very feeble, he protected his chest with his napkin ... In entertainment he gave of the best, with Roman splendour causing creatures to be brought from long distances, and vegetable substances to be cooked in peculiar ways. To recoil before difficulty was foreign to his temperament; and strawberries grew for him in January. The longest and happiest hours of his old age were passed with a fork in his hand' (pp.63-4).

His greed reminds one of the passage about the traditional Forsyte saddle of mutton ('succulent, and – tasty') in *The Man of Property*. For old Thornworthy Christianity and aggressive individualism support each other. His Victorian economic individualism is obsolete and there is nothing to replace it: the moral fragmentation of Edwardian life is represented by the divergent philosophies of the younger male figures. George Forsyte, son of Roger (the same George who witnesses Bosinney's stricken wanderings through the London fog in *The Man of Property*) is in love with Danaë Thornworthy who is now unhappily married to the drunken Jasper Bellew. (This element of 'Danaë' is the starting-point for *The Country House*, Danaë's interesting symbolic name having been changed to the prosaic and insignificant 'Helen'.) George is an unthinking hedonist, his values are those of the turf but he has inherited Victorian qualities which unfit him to be the lover of Danaë: 'To George, born and bred to commercialism, this passion for a married woman, coming not in his first youth, was charged with the countless doubts and fears that hover around passion in a fundamentally commercial mind' (p.34).

George, James and Young and Old Jolyon Forsyte, all of whom appear in 'Danaë' are of course dropped from *The Country House*. The character who remains, though much altered, is the most extraordinary of Galsworthy's Edwardian creations, Gregory Vigil. In *The Country House* he is 'the radical'

but in 'Danaë' he is a Christian. He trained for the priesthood but renounced
the church after talking to a young clergyman who denied the resurrection of
the body (p.38).

By the time it breaks off 'Danaë' is settling down to become a discussion
novel, closely resembling a Shavian discussion play with Young Jolyon as
(say) John Tanner and Gregory Vigil as a more fanatical male Major
Barbara. The Danaë/Bellew plot, in which George and Gregory compete for
the favour of Danaë who (on the last page of the fragment) still allows her
drunken husband into her bed, might have gone in any direction.

Danaë herself has an amoral sexuality which is exuberantly celebrated (in
marked contrast with the air of noble martyrdom that surrounds Helen
Bellew): Danaë is 'like a ripe cornfield in the afternoon sun when a breeze
blows over it', and is amply built with 'the swelling billowy look' (p.26). As a
discussion novel 'Danaë' displays and demonstrates the crippling lack of
moral imperatives in the Edwardian period. Young Jolyon believes that
economic individualism is still the country's only moral imperative, that
Socialism is the same individualism taken up by the working class and given
a new name: 'Each workman looks to his own future; his individualism,
hopefulness, selfishness, obstinacy, idealism, call it what you like' (p.74).
Vigil's Christianity, 'near and personal', is so vague (though 'certain and
arranged' in his own mind) that it cannot stand up for a moment to young
Jolyon's sceptical conviction that selfishness is the rule.

The food scene leads Jolyon to reflect: 'It's the strangest thing in life – that
we should have to cut off little bits of pigs and sheep, and absorb them, in
order to enable us to contemplate God and the differential calculus' (p.65).
One can see why the fragment ends where it does. As a discussion novel it
would be a walk-over for Jolyon's scepticism, as a novel of sexual intrigue it
would get hopelessly bogged down in the intricacies of Vigil's Christian
celibacy and George's caution. (Presumably Jaspar Bellew would have to die
of drink before this plot could get anywhere at all.) Yet it is a pity that
Galsworthy abandoned the city milieu of 'Danaë' for the upper-class county
set in *The Country House*. Pruned and reorganised 'Danaë' might have been a
much sharper and more challenging work than *The Country House* in which, as
I have suggested, Galsworthy seems infected by a spreading malaise, a
feeling that characterisation is no longer worth the bother.

What, for Galsworthy, is heroism? It seems to be located in sexual self-
denial. *Jocelyn*, 'Danaë' and *The Man of Property* cause some confusion because
there sexual restraint is wrong: the basis of Gregory Vigil's somewhat
bullying religious convictions, the source of Bosinney's unhappiness, or Giles
Legard's sufferings. But in the later novels Helen Bellew gives up George
Pendyce, Hilary Dallison resolves to live alone, Mrs Lees Noel is persuaded
to give up Eustace Miltoun. The Christian celibacy mocked in the Gregory
Vigil of 'Danaë' has become an unequivocal virtue in *The Patrician*. Miltoun is

a Christian martyr, his face 'the face of one who would burn in his own fire sooner than depart from his standards' (p.80). He has a hereditary resemblance in face and personality to Cardinal Caradoc 'who suffered for his faith in the sixteenth century. Ascetic, crucified, with a little smile clinging to the lips and deep-set eyes, he presided, above the blueish flames of a log fire' (p.31). Asceticism is the key to Miltoun's life. The name of his home, Monkland Court, underlines this theme, and his childhood and young manhood has been characterised, entirely convincingly, by loneliness. At what is obviously New College he keeps to himself: 'Remaining, so long as custom permitted, in lodgings, outside his College, and clinging thereafter to remote, panelled rooms high up, overlooking the gardens and a portion of the city wall. It was at Oxford that he first developed that passion for self-discipline which afterwards distinguished him. He took up rowing; and, though thoroughly unsuited by nature to this pastime, secured himself a place in his College "torpid"' (p.30).

Like his predecessors in Galsworthy's fictions, Gregory Vigil and Hilary Dallison, he is subject to passionate impulses: 'Now and then he was visited by those gusts which come to the ascetic, when all life seemed suddenly caught up and devoured by a flame burning night and day, and going out mercifully, he knew not why, like a blown candle' (p.30).

But he is sexually inexperienced, 'leading a life of almost savage purity, with one solitary breakdown' (p.33). All Galsworthy's Edwardian male protagonists can be seen as engaged in struggles with their own sexual natures. There is a chronologically ascending scale of self-control. Giles Legard and Bosinney have a humanist duty to submit to passion. George Pendyce is freed from Helen Bellew by his mother's intervention: Hilary Dallison escapes from the model (as well as from his wife) because of the physical revulsion that he feels when the model kisses him. Shelton (of *The Island Pharisees*) rejects Antonia Dennant because she is 'tyrannous'. The pattern of *The Patrician* closely resembles that of *The Country House*: Audrey Noel, trapped by her marriage to a clergyman, renounces her claims on Miltoun as a result of Lady Casterley's intervention so that Miltoun's political career will not be blighted.

Miltoun is consciously living by archaic standards. In the Edwardian world the only disgrace, sexually, is bad publicity. Miltoun tells his father that he must resign his seat in the House of Commons because of his relationship with Audrey Noel and Lord Valleys replies: 'How many men are there into whose lives there has not entered some such relation at one time or another? This idea would disqualify half the nation' (p.258).

Solomon and his sister Danaë in 'Danaë' are both easily and unreflectively promiscuous. What seems to have happened is that having thrown down the Victorian edifice in *Jocelyn* and *The Man of Property* Galsworthy found himself stuck for subjects to write about. The Candide-like young Frenchman and the spectator Shelton in *The Island Pharisees* are weak characters in a thinly observed, over-symmetrical book. By giving Miltoun a Christian conscience, by making him a 'Monk' and a 'Milton' – a hereditary Puritan, in short – Galsworthy creates an artificial conflict within the relaxed atmosphere of Edwardian England.

The struggle with one's sexuality is a tiny theme. The novelist insists that Miltoun's story is a 'tragedy ... the human spirit driven to the wall' (p.277) but the reader refuses to believe it. Miltoun's sufferings, like Dallison's and Shelton's, are self-induced. The most energising feature of these sexual struggles is the unconscious hatred of women that the novels betray at their climactic moments.

> 'In that letter there was something tyrannous, a denial of his right to have a separate point of view. It was like a finger pointed at him as unsound person. In marrying her he would be marrying not only her, but her class – her class' (of Antonia Dennant, *The Island Pharisees*, p.283).

> 'Suddenly she sprang at him, wreathed her arms round his neck, and fastened her mouth to his. The touch of her lips was moist and hot. The scent of stale violet powder came from her, warmed by her humanity. It penetrated to Hilary's heart. He started back in sheer physical revolt' (*Fraternity*, p.337).

> 'Silent, but quivering all over, she clung to him in the hall; and this passion of emotion, without sound to give it substance, affected him profoundly. How terribly sensitive and tender she was! She seemed to have no armour. But though so stirred by her emotion, he was none the less exasperated. She incarnated at that moment the life to which he must now resign himself – a life of unending tenderness, consideration, and passivity' (*The Patrician*, p.252).

Passivity: this, finally, is the dominant characteristic of the Galsworthy erotic hero. The Victorians, Thornworthy, Old Jolyon, Mr Stone in *Fraternity*, have their manhood but belong to the past. The men of the present have surrendered their manhood.

Fraternity is a highly schematic novel about the failure of the classes to relate to each other. Hilary and Thyme Dallison are repulsed by the dirt and smells of the lower class. Thyme's revulsion from the poor is aesthetic, 'they're ugly for me to see', and so is Hilary's sexual revulsion from the little model. Only Old Mr Stone is able to bridge the gap between the classes. Like the working-class people, Mr Stone *smells*: his old tweed suit has an aroma of peat and potatoes which makes people avoid him. In the novel's last pages he approaches death, acknowledges that his book on Universal Brotherhood will never be completed, and achieves an impersonality which is itself an expression of the 'Brotherhood' that he has been working for: 'Bianca saw her father's fragile arms stretch out into the night through the sleeves of his white garment, as though expecting to be received at once into the Universal Brotherhood of the thin air' (p.346).

Mr Stone's final detachment from himself reminds me of Heyst's detachment, his impersonal courtesy, his native asceticism. And it is possibly more than a coincidence that an image similar to the disembodiment of Mr Stone occurs in Galsworthy's 1890s story, 'The Doldrums', in which Conrad himself is the principal character. The story is based on an actual event on board the *Torrens* where the young Galsworthy first met Conrad. The opium-addicted doctor, who like Conrad's *Lord Jim*[18] has (in Conrad's accent): 'An eyged father, you know, a parson in Yorkshire' ('The Doldrums', *Forsytes, Pendyces and Others*, p.200) is dying. Only 'Armand' (Conrad) knows that he is an opium addict, but another young officer, 'Raymond', sees the figure of the doctor on deck at the moment of his death: 'His head was bent back, and his hands thrown up; he was like a shot bird that's towering for air, you know, but there was no sound, no choke or gasp – I listened for it, but there was none, not even a sigh!' (p.204).

'Armand' offers this explanation: 'It is perhaps the twilight of the body, you know, and the dawning of the soul – it is that breathless space which these old crafts of our bodies have to go through, you know, where there is no life, and not yet death – the Doldrums of our individualities hanging in the wind' (pp.205-6).

An impersonality verging on the supernatural, a state of withdrawal which confers peace, a passivity which becomes a sanctuary: Conrad's Heyst, Galsworthy's Miltoun, Hilary Dallison and Gregory Vigil, have in common this form of heroism which is an ultimate, if unattainable, ideal.

---

[18] Jim's father is an 'old parson' in Essex who 'fancied his sailor son'. The father of Leggatt in Conrad's 'The Secret Sharer' is 'a parson in Norfolk'.

Chapter Seven: E.M. Forster

1. Maurice *and Edwardian Forster*

Forster's Edwardian novels misrepresent him. They are comedies, and with the exception of *Howards End* they are comedies of a restricted kind. I take *A Passage to India* to be a novel of major importance, the one work on which Forster's reputation stands or falls, and I take the Edwardian novels, including *Howards End*, to be not more than good minor novels. An excellent recent study of Forster, the first to give full weight to the posthumous homosexual writings, argues that the comedies are 'as critical of the deadness of the middle class' as those of Galsworthy but seem lighter – and are more attractive to read – because they employ 'deft social shorthand' instead of the 'laboured documentation of the Edwardian realists, Galsworthy, Bennett and Wells'.[1] This critic ought not to restate the heresy which has Wells, Bennett and Galsworthy as an indistinguishable trio: otherwise I would not wish to dispute what he says. Forster's range, his ability to write about 'what he knows', is even more restricted than Galsworthy's. The fact that he was homosexual is crucially relevant here. Samuel Hynes was one of the first to describe this aspect of Forster accurately. His homosexuality 'made his literary and social existence possible': 'Forster may have disliked and resented his condition – it seems clear that he did – but it was as central to his art as to his sexual being; to say that he was homosexual is to define not only his private nature, but the nature of his imagination.'[2]

As far as his personality goes, the benign father-figure toddling about King's who became a legend in his own lifetime has been replaced by the more sharply focused, less flattering portrait given in Furbank's biography:[3] a personality which was spinsterly, gossiping, manipulative and physically cowardly, though also affectionate, generous and loyal to his friends.

One obvious point of resemblance between Galsworthy and Forster is that they had independent incomes. They did not need to make their way socially and economically, as Wells and Bennett and Shaw had to. Their impulse to

[1] John Colmer, *E.M. Forster: The Personal Voice* (1975), pp.15-16.
[2] Samuel Hynes, 'Forster's Cramp', *Edwardian Occasions*, p.115.
[3] P.N. Furbank, *E.M. Forster*, 2 vols (1977-8).

write is part of their sense of separation from the class to which they belonged. Forster understands sexual frustration and writes about it intelligently. Caroline Abbott in *Where Angels Fear to Tread* and Charlotte Bartlett in *A Room with a View* are well observed minor figures driven by sexual deprivation. Adela Quested in *A Passage to India* is unbalanced by sexual repression and imagines herself attacked by Dr Aziz in the Marabar Caves. Margaret Schlegel in *Howards End* (1910) fears that the 'pressure of virginity' may make her as cranky as a pathetic spinster of her acquaintance who imagines that the postman is in love with her (p.157).

The posthumous homosexual writings, especially *Maurice* (1971), reflect the personal difficulties from which these portraits of frustration were drawn. The manuscripts of *Maurice* illustrate most revealingly Forster's perception of his own sexuality. The manuscript *Maurice* is a naive sexual utopia: Scudder, the gamekeeper who becomes Maurice's lover, is not a person but a list of physical specifications of sexual fantasy of the simplest kind. Maurice lies in bed at Penge, the home of his unsatisfactory undergraduate friend Clive Durham, and hears a ladder scrape against the window-sill of his room. Racked by sexual frustration Maurice has called 'Come!' from his bedroom window: an involuntary act by which he surprised himself but also gained some psychological relief (p.163). The vibration of the ladder is caused by Scudder, the gamekeeper, who has heard Maurice's cry and is climbing, absurdly enough, up to his room: 'Who was climbing up to him, who? From whom did the maddening vibration ascend: From an athlete, beautiful and young, who desired him and whom he desired' (unpublished typescript, King's College Library, Cambridge). In this early draft the writing lurches on until it reaches this inimitable consummation: 'His body had overleapt class, and that night it yearned to feel corduroys, despite him. He called it lustful ... but his body would not be convinced of this. Chance had mated it too perfectly, and it recalled the myriad details that made up a physical joy, and the joy it had given to a body as passionate as itself, and as beautiful, and as young' (Ibid.). As verbal masturbation this may have its point, but as novel-writing it is hopeless. The Scudder of the manuscript is the merest phantasmal expression of Maurice's sexual loneliness: the Scudder of the published text is a surprisingly good portrait of a well-observed working-class boy.

Chapter 44, one of the novel's best, was written later than 1914, possibly as late as the 1950s.[4] It gives an entirely convincing post-coital dialogue between Maurice and Scudder against the background of Scudder's impending emigration. Scudder is cheeky and resentful, full of class hatred: '"Don't talk to me about Penge ... Oo! Mah! Penge where I was always a servant and Scudder do this and Scudder do that and the old lady, what do you think she once said? She said 'Oh would you most kindly of your

[4] See Furbank, vol. 2, p.304 and passim.

goodness post this letter for me, what's your name?' What's yer name! Every day for six months I come up to Clive's bloody front porch door for orders, and his mother don't know my name. She's a bitch. I said to 'er, 'What's yer name? Fuck yer name.' I nearly did too"' (p.214). But the revised and improved Scudder could never be more than what is known in homosexual circles as a one-night stand. The cancelled final chapter gives an impossible pastoral situation in which Maurice has become a woodman and lives with Scudder in a hut. Lytton Strachey told Forster that the Maurice/Scudder relationship would not last more than six weeks (*Maurice*, Forster's terminal note, p.238) and all critics since the novel's publication have agreed with that. What would Maurice and Scudder have found to talk about all those years in their hut? In his terminal note Forster says that: 'A happy ending was imperative. I shouldn't have bothered to write otherwise' (p.236). At first the happy ending was rather vaguely conceived: having found that Scudder had missed his ship for South America, Maurice was to turn happily back to England to look for his lover. But the question of 'how ... was he actually going to find Alec?' was raised by a friend in the 1950s, and Forster added the chapters 'in which Maurice is brought safely to Alec's arms'.[5]

Forster wanted Maurice both to have the excitement of illicit sex with a working-class boy and to have the stability and companionship of a homosexual marriage. He did not have experience on which to draw: in his own case his relationship with Bob Buckingham was very much interrupted by Buckingham's marriage and by the presence of Forster's mother, who survived until Forster himself was sixty-six. Furbank's biography makes it clear that there was not much sex in the relationship with Buckingham, indeed Buckingham in 1964 said he had never even known that Forster was homosexual.[6] Whatever the truth of that, it is clear that Forster's mother was his constant companion so that his freedom to choose sexual partners was severely restricted. It seems from Furbank's biography that he got on well with his mother, that their gossipy relationship fed his novels rather in the way that Jane Austen's relationship with Cassandra can be presumed to have fed hers. But there is no doubt that Forster never lived as most adult homosexuals live and therefore in an important way he was simply not equipped to write about Maurice's predicament realistically.

Maurice's sexual centre has to be regarded as a failure: otherwise *Maurice* seems an almost distinguished novel written against hopeless odds. It is 'Edwardian' in the sense that it belongs to the pre-1914 world, but also in the far more important sense that Maurice is a central Edwardian figure, the suburban business man who is also a domestic tyrant, a Forsyte or Wilcox whose sex-drive forces him into articulacy. As an undergraduate Maurice

---

[5] Ibid., p.304.
[6] Ibid., pp.168 and 319.

falls in love with Clive Durham, heir to a decayed country estate. The relationship, based on Forster's friendship with H.O. Meredith[7] is unconsummated. Maurice belongs to the 'suburban classes' (*Maurice*, p.74) and has a grandfather in Birmingham, the ultimate suburban city. Clive with his hereditary country house belongs to the class which still presided over Edwardian England but was now, as Wells saw in his account of Bladesover in *Tono-Bungay*, in its last decline. Clive's Penge is a nest feathered in the eighteenth century: 'The feathers were inclined to blow about now. A hundred years had nibbled into the fortune, which no wealthy bride had replenished, and both house and estate were marked, not indeed with decay, but with the immobility that precedes it' (p.77).

One may compare this with the passage about Bladesover which is probably the best single paragraph in Wells's *Tono-Bungay*: 'The great houses stand in the parks still, the cottages cluster respectfully on their borders, touching their eaves with their creepers, the English countryside – you range through Kent from Bladesover northward and see – persists obstinately in looking what it was. It is like an early day in a fine October. The hand of change rests on it all, unfelt, unseen; resting for a while, as it were half reluctantly, before it grips and ends the thing for ever. One frost and the whole face of things will be bare, links snap, patience end, our fine foliage of pretences lie glowing in the mire' (*Tono-Bungay*, p.16).

In *Maurice* the neat social order – upper-class Clive, middle-class Maurice, working-class Scudder – depends for its neatness on the Edwardian situation. So does the absence of physical sex between Maurice and Clive: one can just believe that these undergraduates in the 1890s saw themselves as lovers without going to bed together. When Forster was a member of the Cambridge Apostles homosexuality was much discussed but it was not yet the 'done thing' for members of the society to have affairs.[8] Indeed the dramatic dating of the novel – from Maurice's schooldays in the 1880s to the 'present' in 1913 – permits one to see the difference between the platonic relationship with Clive and the sexual relationship with Scudder in terms of the difference between Victorian decorum and Edwardian libertinism.

The novel seeks to show the novelty of its subject-matter as a strength: 'Their love scene [a dialogue between Maurice and Clive] drew out, having the inestimable gain of a new language. No tradition over-awed the boys. No convention settled what was poetic, what absurd. They were concerned with a passion that few English minds have admitted, and so created untrammelled. Something of exquisite beauty arose in the mind of each at last, something unforgettable and eternal, but built of the humblest scraps of speech and from the simplest emotions' (p.83).

---

[7] Furbank, op. cit., vol.1, pp.60ff.
[8] Ibid., p.78.

The experience of reading the novel suggests that the opposite of this is true. If *Maurice* had a tradition of homosexual literature on which to draw it would be subtler and better-written as well as simply more convincing than it is.

Socially, the homosexual in Edwardian society is a spectator, an anthropologist observing the busy egotistical lives of alien tribes, a man whose relationships with women, if they are achieved at all, are built up by analogy and ingenuity. The homosexual becomes, then, the weak onlooker, the detached cerebral analyst and moralist, the fastidious dilettante, the Edwardian Forsterian persona.

The homosexuality provides a key to the emotional situations in the earlier novels: the curiously void sexual relationship between Agnes and Gerald in *The Longest Journey*, the intense relationships between pairs of male figures, Philip Herriton and Gino in *Where Angels Fear to Tread*, Rickie Elliot and Stephen Wonham in *The Longest Journey*. In this last novel the relationship of 'half-brother' is an awkward substitution for the sexual attraction that certainly exists between Stephen and Rickie: there is no reason, after all, why half-brothers should like each other. Sexual feeling and cultural difference make for the strong, vivid relationship between Fielding and Aziz and (in Part Three, the 'Temple' section of the novel) between Ralph Moore and Aziz in *A Passage to India*.

Forster is a novelist of only one kind of emotional *impasse* and of only one period. Furbank writes about this most perceptively: 'Forster was one of those who have only one novel to write ... He received his whole inspiration – a vision, a kind of plot, a message – all at once, in early manhood ... For this reason he was content to use and re-use many of the same plot-materials: for instance the jaded traveller unable (for what reasons he cannot tell) to respond to the scenes he or she has come to visit; or the picnic or party of pleasure invaded by panic forces ... For the same reason, the social types and manners which ruled his imagination were those of his Edwardian youth. This was no small difficulty for a realistic novelist, though it would not have arisen for a poet. He already found it so with *A Passage to India*, and evidently it was bound to grow with every year or decade.'[9]

Sexual unorthodoxy as a theme is not 'enough' in Forster, any more than it is enough in Galsworthy. Maurice buys a wedding present for Clive: 'While paying three guineas he caught sight of himself in the glass behind the counter. What a solid young citizen he looked – quiet, honourable, prosperous without vulgarity. On such does England rely. Was it conceivable that on Sunday last he had nearly assaulted a boy?' (p.141).

He despises the clients of his stockbroking firm, and his clerks and partners all of whom are timid, joyless suburban people like himself: 'They

---

[9] Furbank, op. cit., vol.2, pp.132-3.

had never struggled, and only a struggle twists sentimentality and lust together into love. Maurice would have been a good lover. He could have given and taken serious pleasure. But in these men the strands were untwisted; they were either fatuous or obscene, and in his present mood he despised the latter least' (pp.202-3).

This editorial passage both expresses the theme of the novel with honourable clarity and exemplifies the novel's weaknesses. Maurice as a good lover, giving and taking serious pleasure, is something Forster cannot dramatise. Maurice's homosexuality qualifies him precisely for his present unhappiness and his role as a sharp but impotent observer of Edwardian suburban complacency and timidity: he saw 'from the faces of his clerks and his partners, that they had never known real joy. Society had catered for them too completely' (p.202). And Maurice is part of this society. Like Galsworthy, Forster is unable to set up a convincing alternative to the society that he wishes to attack.

2. Where Angels Fear to Tread

Far too much has been written about Forster. During his long life the five published novels attracted at least double that number of full-scale books of literary criticism: since his death and the release of *Maurice* and the rest of the posthumous material there has been a further spate. Yet it is impossible to omit him from a study of the Edwardian novel. The Forsterian non-player, the nervous tourist looking on and reluctantly becoming embroiled in, and damaged or rehabilitated by 'life', is a crucial figure for one's understanding of the period. The defining feature of his identity, a feature more important even than the sexual disfunction and its concomitant emotional detachment, is the fact that he is a product of the suburb, a product of the convenient, debased compromise between country and town which is itself a physical feature of the period.[10]

The four Edwardian comedies have a single theme: the Forsterian onlooker is forced by redemptive love to surrender his detachment and become involved in human relationships. *Where Angels Fear to Tread* (1905) was the first published of the novels (though *A Room with a View* was the first planned). It is a precociously assured work, exhaling throughout the savour of beginner's luck: it is short, fifty thousand words or so divided into ten chapters, and depends heavily on dialogue, carefully wrought visual effects and sharply ironic observation. Its principal device is to take the English class system and compare its acquired values – the suburban outlook of the Herritons in Sawston – with its inherited values: those of Caroline Abbott

[10] See Chapter One above, pp.8-10.

and Lilia Theobald, both of whom are of higher social standing than the suburban Herritons. When the Herritons receive a letter from Mrs Theobald announcing Lilia's engagement to an unsuitable Italian Mrs Herriton betrays her social insecurity: '"Read me the letter. My hands are dirty. How intolerable the crested paper is"' (p.10).

Thus from the beginning of the first novel Forster alights on what was to be one of his most effective topics: the small horizons, limited aspirations, social anxieties and petty cruelties of suburbia. The first chapter suggests an important contrast between Sawston, the suburb 'within easy reach of London', and Yorkshire, where the Theobald family and Mr Kingcroft, Lilia's disappointed lover, come from. But these characters fade from the action, and the central contrast in the book is that developed between Sawston and Monteriano.

Philip Herriton is obviously a self-portrait of the young Forster, but he is also an anti-hero, nerveless and incompetent. The British upper-class ideal of action has become a weak middle-class desire to be an 'honourable failure' (p.121). Forster is having his social perceptions both ways, so to speak: the suburbs are despised from both the top and the bottom ends of the social spectrum, and Philip Herriton is both 'of' the suburban limitations and able to rise above them. Indeed, the novel is organised round the story of his conversion from priggishness to spontaneity.

While spontaneity, delight and fullness of life are vested in Gino and his Italian men friends, the women in the novel are the custodians of principle and moral conviction. Forster is at pains to show that Harriet is consistent, although detestable, and to balance her he creates the figure of Caroline Abbott: noble, chaste, and dramatically the least interesting figure in the novel. Lilia marries an Italian, Gino, who is unsuitable by Sawston standards, and has a child by him. She dies leaving the child alone with its father, and Philip and Harriet Herriton are sent by their domineering mother to 'rescue' the baby from Gino. Caroline Abbott accompanies them and rebukes Philip for his indecisiveness over the baby's future: '"I expect you to settle what is right and to follow that. Do you want the child to stop with his father, who loves him and will bring him up badly, or do you want him to go to Sawston, where no one loves him, but where he will be brought up well?"' (p.120). Philip's response is a formal declaration of the paralysing effect that his suburban upbringing has had on him: '"Some people are born not to do things. I'm one of them; I never did anything at school or at the Bar. I came out [on a previous interfering visit to Italy] to stop Lilia's marriage, and it was too late. I came out intending to get the baby and I shall return an 'honourable failure'. I never expect anything to happen now, and so I am never disappointed"' (p.121).

This nervelessness is socially determined, and works perfectly convincingly on that level: but knowledge of Forster's homosexuality enables one to see that Philip's disfunction is sexual as well as social, and that his aesthetic pleasure in Monteriano, in Italians in general and Gino in particular is an expression of an otherwise blocked sexuality. Much of his pleasure in Monteriano is associated with physical contact with Gino: at the opera house he is 'enchanted by the kind, cheerful voices, the laughter that was never vapid, and the light caress of the arm across his back' (p.97). Gino is affectionate and outgoing, it is natural to him to express friendship physically: he lays 'a sympathetic hand on Philip's knee' as they sit at the Café Garibaldi in Monteriano's tiny Square (p.123) and discuss objectively Philip's predicament (he is under pressure from his mother and Harriet to take the baby back to England, but his friendship with Gino makes him reluctant to do so).

Harriet kidnaps the baby on her own initiative and it is accidentally killed when the hired carriage overturns: Philip's arm is broken in the same accident. This is followed by the extraordinary scene in which Gino punishes Philip for the baby's death by twisting his broken arm: in his grief Gino becomes like a stock figure in homosexual art, a tortured St Sebastian who abruptly turns the tables to become the torturer and is then comforted by Caroline Abbott (who in her turn has become an image from the fine arts, a Renaissance Madonna): 'Her eyes were open, full of infinite pity and full of majesty, as if they discerned the boundaries of sorrow, and saw unimaginable tracts beyond. Such eyes he [Philip] had seen in great pictures but never in a mortal. Her hands were folded round the sufferer [Gino], stroking him lightly, for even a goddess can do no more than that' (p.139).

If homosexuality is the novel's secret spring its ostensible concerns are public and social. One paragraph will seem to speak a language which is still current, the next will appear to work from attitudes and assumptions that have vanished. So slow is English social change that most of the points made about the English class system in the Edwardian period will seem current to a modern reader: Mrs Theobald and Mr Kingcroft as decayed gentry are natural enemies of the emergent London-based business class to which the Herritons belong. But the relationship between the English visitors and the inhabitants of Monteriano is based on assumptions which now seem wholly obsolete and are best described as imperial: the Italians are *racial* inferiors of the English.

Any middle-class Edwardian Englishman was wealthy by Italian standards: hence the community of English expatriates making private incomes stretch in the Florence of *A Room with a View*. The sense of the Italians as 'primitive' man is one that Forster can exploit when he celebrates Gino's spontaneity and energy: it is not unlike the contrast that Conrad makes between the energy of the negroes and the hollowness of the whites in *Heart of Darkness*. In the first three novels, *Where Angels Fear to Tread*, *The Longest Journey* and *A Room with a View* this pattern repeats itself: the spontaneous primitives, Gino, Stephen Wonham and George Emerson (the last two are 'primitive' in the sense that they are English lower-class) are set up in contrast with the inhibited, suburban figures, Philip, Rickie Elliot, Cecil Vyse. Gino is the most successful of Forster's primitives because he is the least loaded with significance.[11] He is a Darwinian hero compared at the crises of his life to an animal: he lies with his head against the door like a dog waiting for his child to be born, he growls when pursuing Philip to torture him. As narrative centre Philip Herriton determines the novel's method: he begins as tourist and observer and ends as participant. The whole of Monteriano is transformed from a decorative frieze to a community which has a living relationship with Philip as Gino moves into his life.

The tourist Philip is Forster's self-portrait: 'A tall, weakly built young man, whose clothes had to be judiciously padded on the shoulder in order to make him pass muster. His face was plain rather than not, and there was a curious mixture in it of good and bad. He had a fine forehead and a good large nose, and both observation and sympathy were in his eyes. But below the nose and eyes all was confusion, and those people who believe that destiny resides in the mouth and chin shook their heads when they looked at him' (p.54).

In the first part of the novel the omniscient narrative voice is associated with Philip's consciousness. Take the beginning of chapter 2: 'When the bewildered tourist alights at the station of Monteriano, he finds himself in the middle of the country. There are a few houses round the railway, and many more dotted over the plain and the slopes of the hills, but of a town, medieval or otherwise, there is not the slightest sign' (p.15). As tourist, 'emissary of civilisation and ... student of character' (p.117) he has to be broken and changed by the epic encounter with Gino, the point in the novel at which its religious, moral and sexual themes come together. But the transformation does not take him very far. The suburban temperament has been enlarged, not replaced by something else. There is no *fundamental* opposition between Monteriano and Sawston as there would be if Monteriano were a rural setting instead of a medieval city (or as there is between Sawston and Wiltshire in the next novel, *The Longest Journey*). Monteriano represents an escape into a satisfactory *urban* world, with its cafés and its florid opera-house; urban amenity without the narrowness and ugliness of Sawston. It also represents a successful conspiracy against women.

The omniscient narrator speaks with unmistakable pleasure of the subordinate role allotted to women in Monteriano: 'Italy is such a delightful place to live in if you happen to be a man. There one may enjoy that exquisite luxury of Socialism – that true Socialism which is based not on equality of

---

[11] As contrasted with the over-weighted figure of Stephen Wonham: see below, p.220.

income or character, but on the equality of manners. In the democracy of the *caffè* or the street the great question of our life has been solved, and the brotherhood of man is a reality. But it is accomplished at the expense of the sisterhood of women. Why should you not make friends with your neighbour at the theatre or in the train, when you know and he knows that feminine criticism and feminine insight and feminine prejudice will never come between you! Though you become as David and Jonathan, you need never enter his home, nor he yours. All your lives you will meet under the open air, the only roof-tree of the South, under which he will spit and swear, and you will drop your h's, and nobody will think the worse of either' (pp.35-6). Above all, the escape from Sawston to Monteriano is an escape from female domination into a *masculine* world.

3. The Longest Journey

Monteriano is a male arcadia and *Where Angels Fear to Tread* is in its feline way a *macho* novel. Philip's pull towards Caroline Abbott is a matter of religious devotion rather than sex: 'He had reached love by the spiritual path' (p.141) – and in any case comes to nothing. (Since Caroline is in her turn infatuated with Gino, Philip's feeling for her can reasonably be seen as a displaced expression of his own erotic attraction to Gino.) In *The Longest Journey* (1907) Forster as novelist faces up to the fact that in the social world which is the novelist's material women are, irreversibly, *there* and something has to be done about them. In the first novel the women were killed off (Lilia) ridiculed (Harriet and Mrs Herriton) or etherealised out of existence (Caroline). In *The Longest Journey* the women are deadly enemies of the men's happiness: Agnes Pembroke will separate Rickie from his friends if she can, Mrs Failing takes an abominable pleasure in humiliating Stephen Wonham and bringing him up badly.

In his personal life Forster on the whole disliked women, and in *The Longest Journey* Agnes and Mrs Failing are characterised with full, sustained, venomous clarity. Thereafter Forster relents or perhaps feels a need to redress the balance. *A Room with a View* is the first novel to have a woman, Lucy Honeychurch, as its central figure: though this benign portrait is balanced somewhat by other female figures, the emotionally crippled Miss Bartlett and the coarse-minded literary hack Miss Lavish. *Howards End* goes further, and can be seen as an extended act of propitiation towards the sex that he disliked: Margaret and Helen have Bloomsbury right-mindedness and romantic idealism respectively, and Mrs Wilcox is all but deified.

None of the men in *Howards End* can stand up to these powerful females: Mr Wilcox is bullied and broken, Leonard Bast patronised and unsettled. Indeed it is the high-handed busy-bodying of the Schlegel sisters that kills

Leonard Bast and gets Charles Wilcox sent to prison. None of this resentment is allowed to make itself felt in the novel, of course: Forster's determination to be fair to women forces him to write against the grain from beginning to end.

The passage in *The Longest Journey* where Gerald Dawes kisses Agnes is seen by most Forster critics as a mark of Forster's incapacity with heterosexual relationships: but my view is that Forster is enacting the progress of Rickie Elliott's perceptions. Rickie is an unseen observer of Gerald and Agnes and a moment before he has been hating Gerald who had bullied him at school: Gerald was the kind of boy who 'twisted up the arms of little boys, and ran pins into them at chapel, and struck them in the stomach when they were swinging on the horizontal bar' (p.49). When Gerald kisses Agnes her face, to Rickie's perception, from being a thing, an inanimate object, becomes a 'star': 'Her face had no expression. It stared at the intruder and never saw him. Then her lover kissed it, and immediately it shone with mysterious beauty like some star' (p.49).

Rickie's response to this is a gust of adolescent lyricism which one critic has called 'Wagnerian':[12] 'He seemed to be looking down coloured valleys. Brighter they glowed, till gods of pure flame were born in them ... The riot of fair images increased. They invaded his being and lit lamps at unsuspected shrines' (pp.49-50).

There is a sharp and intriguing contrast between Rickie's lyrical awareness of Agnes here and her spiteful perception of him. When Rickie, in obedience to his impulse to idolise Agnes, offers part of his income to Gerald Dawes so that Gerald and Agnes can marry he is angrily rebuffed. Gerald reacts particularly against Rickie's 'abnormality', his crippled foot, and Agnes is pleased to learn that Gerald has bullied Rickie at school: she 'had a thrill of joy when she thought of the weak boy in the clutches of the strong one' (p.63). This is followed immediately by Forster's most startling piece of artistic retribution. The next sentence runs: 'Gerald died that afternoon. He was broken up in the football match' (p.64).

Agnes is permitted a moment of pathos at Gerald's death, although this scene is spoilt by Gerald's closing line. 'I shan't do as a spirit,' he remarks, with a lightness of phrase which is quite unsuited to him and is in any case highly unlikely if Gerald is supposed to be dying of his injuries (p.65). Thereafter Agnes is a pure, vigorously drawn bitch. She is particularly well observed in the Sawston scenes, where she is anxious to prevent Rickie (now her husband) from talking to people who might interest him, and can only tolerate Ansell when she can regard him as a social failure. Ansell in his turn, probably quoting Shaw's *Man and Superman*, sees Agnes as 'the emissary of Nature, and Nature's bidding has been fulfilled. But man does not care a damn for Nature – or at least only a very little damn. He cares for a hundred things besides, and the more civilised he is the more he will care for these other hundred things, and demand not only a wife and children, but also friends, and work, and spiritual freedom' (p.103).

The other female villain, Mrs Failing, is drawn with greater complexity and less success. She is a somewhat confused portrait partly because the novel works to temper its loathing and give her some redeeming elements. The simplest way to see her is as another Forsterian tourist like the expatriates in the Italian novels: in this case a woman who passes through life seeing it as an amusing spectacle. Her youth was different: she married Mr Failing because he was a serious socialist and philosopher, she adopted Stephen Wonham out of a form of altruistic commitment. In middle age she has become incapable of 'seriousness' – a major crime in this novel where Ansell dismisses Agnes by saying that 'she is not serious. She is not truthful' (p.104) – and Stephen Wonham has become her toy, kept by her because his own seriousness, and roughness, make a flattering foil to her capriciousness. She regrets the past: 'The world was not so humorous then, but it had been more important' (p.116), and she is capable of some 'good' actions. If it is true that she is based on Marianne Thornton, Forster's great-aunt who left him enough money when he was eight to make him independent for life, the reasons for the mixed and tempered treatment of her are clear.

Surprisingly, Mrs Failing has something in common with Ansell, Rickie's undergraduate friend: they are both 'against Nature', they are both intrigued by Stephen's qualities. This unlikely conjunction is an outcome of the radical confusion into which the novel gets itself over the differences among Cambridge, Sawston and Wiltshire. For Ansell Nature is ranged with Agnes, the life-force and everything that is destructive of civilisation and friendship: for Rickie Nature is a pastoral dream evolved at Cambridge (his magical dell on the road to Madingley is part of this dream) which finds its 'realistic' equivalent in Wiltshire and centres on the figure of Stephen. Nature, then, is good in Wiltshire, bad in Sawston, and to be 'against' Nature is tonic in Cambridge but destructive in Wiltshire.

The source of the tangle is to be found in the displacement of the novel's real emotional drive. The authentic emotional focus is Cambridge, and the elaborate treatment of Wiltshire conveys an enthusiasm for the rural which is theoretical rather than felt. Rickie's real passion is not for his dead mother, nor for his half-brother Stephen, nor for Ansell (though Ansell does show a strong attachment to Rickie) but for his rooms at King's: 'Just then he loved his rooms better than any person. They were all he really possessed in the world, the only place he could call his own. Over the door was his name, and through the paint, like a grey ghost, he could still read the name of his predecessor. With a sigh of joy he entered the perishable home that was his for a couple of years' (pp.73-4).

Rickie is the weakest of Forster's heroes, a cripple who is killed at the end of the novel in the act of saving his half-brother's life: a resounding *cliché* which the novel presents with unabashed ingenuousness. 'Wearily he did a man's duty' (p.351): the one strong action of his life finishes him off. The novel's pattern resembles that of *Where Angels Fear to Tread*: a timid and reluctant male figure encounters redemptive love. But *The Longest Journey* is a mixed and irritating book: part of its trouble is that the theme of redemptive love exists in at least two forms. For much of the novel one supposes that the redemptive figure is Ansell, the homosexual philosopher who is 'not a gentleman', but it emerges that the emotional centre of the novel is supposed to be Stephen Wonham, Rickie's half-brother, the spontaneous Wiltshire rustic.

F.C. Crews says of *The Longest Journey* that it takes up the idea of the 'hero' 'as it is ironically developed in *The Ordeal of Richard Feverel*.'[13] But I think Crews is attributing more subtlety to *The Longest Journey* than is actually present. When *The Longest Journey* calls Stephen a 'hero' it uses the word in a traditional, straightforward sense. Stephen is a Nietzschean hero, amoral and direct, a man of large appetites and uncomplicated passions.

Mrs Failing's view of heroes is, indeed, ironic, but her view is not the novel's. Agnes says: 'To me ... a hero has always been a strong wonderful being.' Mrs Failing reacts: 'Ah, wait till you are the dragon. I have been a dragon most of my life, I think. A dragon that wants nothing but a peaceful cave. Then in comes the strong, wonderful being, and gains a princess by piercing my side. No, seriously, my dear Agnes, the chief characteristics of a hero are infinite disregard for the feelings of others, plus general inability to understand them' (p.131).

The basis of the love between Stephen and Rickie is fraternal. But the novel wants to have this relationship both ways – to make Stephen the lover, and leader, of Rickie as well as his brother: 'Stephen was man first, brother afterwards. Herein lay his brutality, and also his virtue' (p.332).

It seems to me that the novel is not ironic here: that Rickie's attitude to Stephen is identical with the novel's: 'Stephen was a hero. He was a law unto himself, and rightly. He was great enough to despise our small moralities. He was attaining love. This evening Rickie ... felt it worth while to sacrifice everything for such a man' (p.347).

This is heavily proleptic, of course, since Rickie finds Stephen, drunk, trying to cross the railway-line and is run over by a train in the act of saving Stephen's life. The epilogue makes it clear that Stephen still drinks but has learnt to temper the habit, that he is grateful to Rickie in a dumb way but able to express his gratitude only by living well as a husband and father and by naming his daughter after his and Rickie's mother, and that he is benefiting

[13] F.C. Crews, *E.M. Forster: The Perils of Humanism* (1962), p.103.

from the posthumous sale of Rickie's stories.

Crews has it that this ending is anti-heroic: 'The consummately normal Stephen, who shows himself to be an affectionate husband and father, has escaped from the categories of both hero and mock-hero' (Crews, p.103).

This seems to me a mis-reading. When Rickie discovers that Stephen has broken his promise and is drinking again, he reacts as follows: 'Stephen was a law to himself. He had chosen to break his word, and would break it again. Nothing else bound him. To yield to temptation is not fatal for most of us. But it was the end of everything for a hero' (p.349).

Crews reads this as meaning that Stephen is no longer a hero. But surely it means the opposite: that Stephen's romantic force, untrammelled by any conventions, will in the end destroy him. The pattern is somewhat confused, but it seems clear that the effect of Rickie's sacrifice of his own life is to deflect Stephen's romantic force from drink into family life. Crews is surely wrong, also, to describe Stephen's family life as 'consummately normal'. The epilogue is at pains to stress the strangeness of Stephen's behaviour as husband and father. He is seen taking his baby daughter out in the open on the downs (where he has often slept alone before his marriage and where he spent his wedding night). His wife loves him but cannot control him: he will 'talk nonsense' to the little girl, and his wife accepts that she is being 'kept in line'. In short, romantic force makes him a tyrant and prophet, father of a master-race.

The novel concludes as a dialogue between Mrs Failing's assertion of the power of the conventions and Stephen's romantic heroism. Mrs Failing urges Rickie to go back to his wife Agnes, the conventional thing to do: '"We are conventional people, and conventions – if you will but see it – are majestic in their way, and will claim us in the end. We do not live for great passion or for great memories, or for anything great." [Rickie] threw up his head. "We do"' (p.341).

In Rickie's case the conventions win, of course: Rickie dies at Cadover, Mrs Failing's house, telling her that she was right. But in the whole novel it is the romantic concept of heroism, in the person of Stephen, that wins. Forster knew that *The Longest Journey* was an outdated novel and that his concept of a hero was obsolete: hence, I suspect, his obstinate preference for it over his other works.

4. A Room with a View

The Longest Journey, the worst of Forster's Edwardian novels, was its author's own favourite: *A Room with a View*, which seems to me by far the best of the four (including *Howards End*), was not rated very highly by Forster. He called it 'toshy, but one trusts inoffensive' (Letter to E.J. Dent, 30 June 1907), and 'slight, unambitious and uninteresting, but – in rather an external way – the characters seem more alive to me than any others that I have put together' (Letter to Nathaniel Wedd, 25 June 1908).[14]

I think Forster called it 'toshy' because it is a *formal* comedy: Lucy Honeychurch, a lawyer's daughter from Surrey, falls in love with a lower-middle-class man, George Emerson, the son of a homespun philosopher. They fall in love in Florence: the relationship is helped by a murder witnessed by Lucy which drives her in panic into George's company, and by a visit to Fiesole where Lucy loses her chaperone, the virginal Miss Bartlett, and is kissed by George.

I agree with Oliver Stallybrass that Forster probably felt that he had betrayed his own findings about art in *A Room with a View*. In a paper on 'pessimism in literature', delivered December 1906, Forster wrote 'The woman of today ... may marry, but her marriage is certainly not an *end*, either for herself or for her husband.'[15] Since this novel *does* end with marriage one can see that Forster may have felt detached and cynical about it.

A look at the early versions of *A Room with a View*, now published as *The Lucy Novels: Early Sketches for A Room with a View*, gives one another explanation for Forster's sense of detachment from the novel in its final version. The change from the Lucy manuscripts to the published novel is achieved by modifying and to some extent reversing the impulses of the manuscript.

The manuscript is characterised by an irritable dislike of women's company in foreign pensions. Indeed, the writing seems to have begun as a personal act of aggression, the expression of a need to defend himself from the suffocating presence of the English ladies in the pensions at which he and his mother stayed in Italy in 1901-2. Lucy, shut in her pension in Florence with other English ladies, chafes at the boredom of her situation: 'This was Florence, but her life would be where she ate and slept. Even if she escaped between meals, she would be obliged to give an account twice daily of her doings and hear them criticised' (*The Lucy Novels*, p.18).

The first 'Lucy' novel had a hero called Arthur, or Tancred, who was based on H.O. Meredith: the fellow-undergraduate with whom Forster was in love for a time and on whom Clive in *Maurice* is based. The theme of the first 'Lucy' strongly resembled that of *Where Angels Fear to Tread*: a contest between English suburban and Italian spontaneous values.

English suburbia is represented by the ambition of the English community in Florence to build an Anglican church. The plot was to centre on a concert to raise money for this church, a concert at which a Mrs Flint-Carew – a

14 Both letters quoted by Oliver Stallybrass in his introduction to E.M. Forster, *A Room with a View* (1908) (Abinger Edition, 1977), p.xiii.
15 Quoted by Stallybrass, p.xvi.

heavily satirised sample of female vanity – was to display her singing. The murder in which Lucy meets George Emerson survives from the original 'Lucy', but here it is 'Arthur' who witnesses the murder on his own. The murder itself is characterised by a strong homoerotic element which is edited out of the final version completely: 'Arthur hurried to the Fountain of Neptune, and as he was strong enough to push men aside and not too chivalrous to push women, he soon clambered over the bronze groups of Tritons and Satyrs and reached the central basin. On the rim lay a young man of twenty, stripped almost naked ... Blood was dripping quickly off him ... He was one of those handsome Italians of the lower classes who may be seen by the dozen in any Tuscan town. He was magnificently made and his splendid chest swelled and contracted with every spurt of the blood' (p.36).

From its unpromising beginnings in *The Lucy Novels* Forster develops *A Room with a View* into a very successful small formal comedy. The love between Lucy Honeychurch and George Emerson is prohibited by class distinction as understood by Charlotte Bartlett, Lucy's thwarted spinster cousin. Lucy is in danger of marrying the aesthete Cecil Vyse, but the comic action in Florence (Italy is again the source of spontaneous, as against socially determined, behaviour) rescues her, loosens the conventions, and permits her to marry George.

As compared with its predecessor the objectivity of this comedy is a marked technical gain: the unlovable characters are treated with detachment rather than loathing (Cecil Vyse, Miss Lavish, Mr Eager) and the characters to be admired are handled with delicate equivocation. Mrs Honeychurch and Freddie, Lucy's mother and brother, are permitted to be suburban and stupid as well as fundamentally good-hearted, Mr Emerson is prosy and sententious even when he is right, his son George may be a steady lover but he is also an awkward and taciturn one. By firmly holding the balance of the comedy Forster is able to keep in reserve some elegantly turned surprises: the moment at which George kisses Lucy on Fiesole, the discovery that Miss Lavish has observed this kiss and used it in her slushy novel, the startling and well-timed revelation that Charlotte Bartlett's repressed romanticism has driven her to act against her nature and give aid to the lovers at the turning point of the action.

It is important for the novel's pattern that Lucy and Charlotte are *alike* – that Lucy may well turn into Charlotte if she allows her life to be governed by the same conventions – and in the first scene they are unanimously dismayed by the fact that Signora Bertolini is a cockney and that old Mr Emerson offers them his room:

'They were tired, and under the guise of unselfishness they wrangled. Some of their neighbours interchanged glances, and one of them – one of the ill-bred people whom one does meet abroad – leant forward over the table and actually intruded into their argument. He said:

'"I have a view, I have a view."

'Miss Bartlett was startled. Generally at a pension people looked them over for a day or two before speaking, and often did not find out that they would "do" till they had gone. She knew that the intruder was ill-bred, even before she glanced at him' (p.3).

Miss Bartlett looks round to see whether all the residents of the pension are as vulgar as the Emersons: 'Two little old ladies, who were sitting farther up the table, with shawls hanging over the backs of the chairs, looked back, clearly indicating "We are not; we are genteel"' (p.4).

The encounter with Mr Beebe, the clergyman from Tunbridge Wells, begins to pull together the erotic and social themes: '"I *am* so glad to see you," said the girl, who was in a state of spiritual starvation, and would have been glad to see the waiter if her cousin had permitted it' (p.5).

For 'spiritual' read 'sexual', and one has a good example of Forster's comic method throughout the book. Beneath the stifling decorum of the narrative voice raw sexuality and violence are present: the 'well-bred' ironic omniscient narrator translates these pressures into social, aesthetic or 'spiritual' terms. When Lucy falls in love with George it is ostensibly for 'aesthetic' reasons: he has behind him the magnificent 'view' of the book's title.

Like Wilde and other writers of comedy (Noël Coward and Joe Orton are twentieth-century examples) Forster had discovered that a writer who expresses himself with decorum can say anything he likes. Take Mr Beebe's attitude to Lucy: 'Girls like Lucy were charming to look at, but Mr Beebe was, from rather profound reasons, somewhat chilly in his attitude towards the other sex, and preferred to be interested rather than enthralled' (p.32). In short, he is homosexual. So is Cecil Vyse, whom Lucy has unwisely agreed to marry: '"He's only for acquaintance,"' says George. '"He is for society and cultivated talk. He should know no one intimately, least of all a woman"' (p.165).

English class perception is a strength as well as a weakness. It is unable to cope with the raw violence of Italian experience, but for the emotionally insufficient – Mr Beebe, Charlotte Bartlett, Cecil Vyse – it provides a form of protection and control. Mr Beebe perceives the Honeychurch house, Windy Corner, as a place which will 'do': the same phrase is used by Charlotte in the Pension Bertolini to describe those fellow-English who are socially acceptable. By a subtle manipulation of this Mr Beebe convinces himself, and by extension the reader, that the Honeychurch house passes the appropriate tests: 'The situation was so glorious, the house so commonplace ... The late Mr Honeychurch had affected the cube, because it gave him the most accommodation for his money ... So impertinent – and yet the house "did"; for it was the home of people who loved their surroundings honestly' (p.175).

Summer Street is 'half suburban' but felt to be acceptable because it is redeemed by right feeling: the ugly villas 'Albert' and 'Cissie', are admissible because the Emersons have rented one of them. The conflict between the rural and the pastoral expressed in *The Longest Journey* and the loathing of suburbs expressed in *Where Angels Fear to Tread* are resolved by this double perspective on 'half-suburban' Summer Street. It is a tame landscape compared with Italy, the 'lake' beneath its pinewoods is no more than a pond, but approached with the right feelings it can be an adequate and consoling landscape.

The unnamed 'Twelfth Chapter' in which Freddie, George Emerson and Mr Beebe bathe in the pool is rightly celebrated. It is, of course, a discreet subversive homosexual orgy in the middle of the respectable world: 'a call to the blood and to the released will' (p.133). This is why Mr Beebe responds to its appeal: it is a place which cannot be touched by 'motor-cars and Rural Deans', his rich parishioners and his seniors in the Church (p.130).

Forster has revalued his earlier hatreds: women and suburbs are admitted into the comedy's resolution. The emergent middle-class Honeychurches are better able to accept George in Surrey than could Miss Bartlett in the prickly and socially vulnerable English community in Florence. And George, although so shadowy a characterisation, has a sexual force registered again by Mr Beebe, who responds to George's *smell*: George 'bowed his head, dusty and sombre, exhaling the peculiar smell of one who has handled furniture' (p.127).

5. Howards End

A Room with a View is a wholly successful comedy partly because it is unambitious. The social comedy is a moral comedy, Lucy and George at the close are securely united in a secure middle-class world. Yet the novel at times refers to the radical disconnection of private sensibility from our outer experience which was to characterise *Howards End*: 'It so happened that Lucy, who found daily life rather chaotic, entered a more solid world when she opened the piano. She was then no longer either deferential or patronising; no longer either a rebel or a slave. The kingdom of music is not the kingdom of this world; it will accept those whom breeding and intellect and culture have alike rejected' (*A Room with a View*, p.29).

Nothing further is made of this in *A Room with a View*, but it clearly anticipates the scene in which Helen Schlegel meets Leonard Bast while listening to Beethoven in the Queen's Hall. Music represents freedom from the tyranny of the class system and privacy for the beleaguered ego.

Howards End is Forster's Bloomsbury novel. The breakdown of 'connection' between sensibility and action is also the distinction that

Bloomsbury felt between its own high-mindedness and the philistinism of Edwardian London. If it were only a novel about Bloomsbury *Howards End* would probably be a success, but as it stands it seems to me an honourable failure, a noble attempt to do far too much and to be too many kinds of writer. To his own natural gift for comedy Forster adds Galsworthy's generous moral indignation, Wells's sweeping historical generalisations, Shaw's subversive 'discussions'. The mixture can't work. To turn the pages and note how often Forster's ambition has betrayed him into being pompous or sentimental or just plain dull is to be reminded of the brilliance of *A Room with a View* and of how difficult it is to follow success of that kind.

Howards End is a consciously political book. It looks back to Gladstonian liberalism and to rural England and laments the replacement of these things by the new business class of suburban England. Mrs Wilcox's family, the Howards, were decayed farming gentry while the Wilcoxes, the family into which she has married, are the new class. Her friend Margaret Schlegel, being half German, belongs to neither group but 'spiritually' she belongs to the Howards. The novel sees hope in this situation. Because there are still people like Margaret (like Bloomsbury, in other words), intelligent cultivated liberals with altruistic instincts, the good qualities of traditional England may survive.

Settings have been important in all Forster's novels: Sawston and Italy, Wiltshire and Cambridge, Summer Street and Florence. In *Howards End*, as the title indicates, the settings are to carry major significance. The Wilcoxes are masters of most of England, especially London (as are Galsworthy's Forsytes) but also Shropshire, and they even control the flow of the Thames, the national river. They have become the nominal owners of Howards End also, but this bit of England, at least, remains spiritually independent of them: because of its name (Ruth Wilcox's maiden name is perpetuated, after she has surrendered it in marriage, in her house), its mystical qualities which speak only to initiates (the pigs' teeth in the wych elm have never been noticed by the Wilcoxes) and its *hostility* to the Wilcoxes, all of whom suffer from hay fever when they go there. (They don't seem to suffer from hay fever in Shropshire, which is presumably far more rural than Howards End: the novel doesn't explain why not.)

Parts of *Howards End* can be seen as the illustration of a literary theory: 'To speak against London is no longer fashionable. The Earth as an artistic cult has had its day, and the literature of the near future will probably ignore the country and seek inspiration from the town. One can understand the reaction. Of Pan and the elemental forces, the public has heard a little too much – they seem Victorian, while London is Georgian – and those who are for the earth with sincerity may wait long ere the pendulum swings back to her again' (p.102).

Forster is noting the tendency of the period towards urban literature,

Bennett's Five Towns, Gissing's London, Joyce's Dublin. His lament for the death of a rural literary tradition is revived in Margaret's thoughts as she walks towards Howards End. This passage is blatantly editorial, a discursive essay addressed to the reader over Margaret's shoulder: 'Why has not England a great mythology? Our folklore has never advanced beyond daintiness, and the greater melodies about our country-side have all issued through the pipes of Greece. Deep and true as the native imagination can be, it seems to have failed here. It has stopped with the witches and the fairies ... England still waits for the supreme moment of her literature – for the great poet who shall voice her, or better still, for the thousand little poets whose voices shall pass into our common talk' (p.249).

The literature of the countryside is to be centred on farmhouses, the home of the 'yeoman' who is a persistent point of reference in the novel, and who can be trusted to hold humane and right-thinking opinions: ' "Left to itself," was Margaret's opinion, "this country would vote Liberal." The comradeship, not passionate, that is our highest gift as a nation, was promised by it, as by the low brick farm where she called for the key' (p.249).

The novel is clear that both Schlegels and Wilcoxes are intruders in this yeoman farmers' setting. Both are middle-class not landowning, and belong to the civilisation of luggage. Forster seems regretfully to note that although the country house is no longer available to him, a liberal, as a point of reference, it had certain positive qualities, it was a custodian of civilisation: 'The feudal ownership of land did bring dignity, whereas the modern ownership of movables is reducing us again to a nomadic horde ... Historians of the future will note how the middle classes accreted possessions without taking root in the earth, and may find in this the secret of their imaginative poverty' (p.141).

The novel is trapped in the Edwardian liberal dilemma: it dislikes what it sees of the future, but does not want to be backward-looking. The conventional taste for 'the country' is Victorian, in a pejorative sense, and is exemplified by Leonard Bast's dreary reading matter: Stevenson's *Prince Otto*, E.V. Lucas's *The Open Road*, the novels of Richard Jefferies (misjudged by Forster, in my view: Jefferies is rather good) and George Borrow. But against this conventional taste it sets up its hope for 'a thousand little poets' or its faith in personal relations, which as Helen asserts 'are the real life, for ever and ever' (p.27).

Bloomsbury and the rural are not easy bedfellows but the novel is determined to work them both in. 'Personal relations' is of course the Bloomsbury *credo*: it also belongs to the Cambridge Apostles, and this aspect of *Howards End* looks back to *The Longest Journey*. Forster never fully came to terms with Vanessa and Virginia Stephen, and was happiest with Bloomsbury before it became Bloomsbury: that is to say, when the 'group' was exclusively male and lived at Cambridge. There is a very significant small reference to Cambridge in *Howards End* which is strongly reminiscent of Rickie's passion for the place in the earlier novel. Tibby, the Schlegel's effeminate but clever brother, is to go to Oxford where he will develop further the chill self-centredness which is already his leading characteristic. His egocentricity, the novel asserts, would have been cured at Cambridge: 'The august and mellow University [Oxford], soaked with the richness of the western countries that it has served for a thousand years, appealed at once to the boy's taste: it was the kind of thing he could understand, and he understood it all the better because it was empty. Oxford is – Oxford: not a mere receptacle for youth, like Cambridge. Perhaps it wants its inmates to love it rather than to love one another: such at all events was to be its effect on Tibby' (p.100).

There is another reference to Cambridge, that sacred place in the Forsterian mythology, in connection with Leonard Bast. Leonard's life is divided into compartments: the clerk who tries to retain a degree of cockney self-possession, the struggling husband trapped by an aging prostitute, the autodidact who hopes that the Schlegel sisters will improve his mind. This portrait is almost certainly based on one of Forster's contacts with working-class boys here translated into heterosexual terms and seen from the boy's point of view. Leonard meets an undergraduate on a train to Cambridge and is invited back to 'coffee after hall': but he becomes shy and takes care not to leave the hotel where he is staying. The fact that the undergraduate tries to establish 'personal relations' with this unknown young man is applauded by the novel as Cambridge/Bloomsbury liberalism at its best.

Oliver Stallybrass suggests that the Schlegel girls are drawn from the heart of Bloomsbury, being based on Vanessa and Virginia Stephen: Helen's 'tense wounding excitement' (p.209), her obsessiveness, her hatred of religion, her tendency to become 'over-interested in the subsconscious self' (p.181) could all be aspects of Virginia Stephen. When Helen is secretly pregnant she conceals herself from her family: Henry Wilcox concludes that she has gone mad and prepares a trap for her. After collaborating in the trap Margaret recoils from her husband when she sees that he (and the doctor accompanying him) are classifying Helen: 'Margaret's anger and terror increased every moment. How dare these men label her sister! What horrors lay ahead! What impertinences that shelter under the name of science!' (pp.268-9).

Virginia Stephen herself, as Virginia Woolf, was to express hatred of the impertinence of science in very similar terms in *Mrs. Dalloway*, where Holmes and Bradshaw precipitate the suicide of Septimus Smith.

Margaret sees the situation as the defence of abnormality against normality and the defence of women against men. This can be related to other patterns in the novel: the defence of learning against philistinism, enlightenment against prejudice, the universities against the public schools. During the train-journey to Evie's wedding at Oniton the Wilcox men display stifling solicitude. Margaret feels divided about their sexist treatment of her. She 'bowed to a charm of which she did not wholly approve', but retains her intellectual superiority: she 'said nothing when the Oxford colleges were identified wrongly' (p.196). The train is a 'forcinghouse for the idea of sex' (p.196), but Margaret and Helen are opposed to conventional sexual differentiation: 'Male and female created he them' is a 'questionable statement' (p.196).

The end of the novel is heavily weighted towards Bloomsbury values. Charles is sent to prison for the death of Leonard Bast, Henry Wilcox is forced to recognise that he has no right to judge Helen for her sexual submission to Leonard. Margaret and Helen and Helen's baby (by Leonard) preserve the fragile integrity of liberal humanism: Bloomsbury has taken over the 'yeoman's' farmhouse to keep its moral superiority intact while the 'red rust' of the outer suburbs of London encroaches on the fields surrounding it.

Lawrence was mistaken in thinking that *Howards End* seeks to rehabilitate the business people *as* business people.[16] Margaret attempts to see good in the aggressions that make the Wilcoxes successful, but the perspective of the novel's omniscient narrator on this is rather different. When Margaret tries to convert Henry to her way of thinking over his sexual misconduct by exhortation she fails: it requires the whole machinery of the plot to change his attitudes by force.

The business mind is more entrenched and less flexible than Margaret allows for, and in one of his teasing discursive paragraphs which seems to promise more than it actually says Forster reflects on the characteristics of this mind: 'If necessary he would deny that he had ever known Mrs Bast [Leonard's wife and Henry's former mistress] ... Perhaps he never had known her ... All was so solid and spruce, that the past flew up out of sight like a spring-blind, leaving only the last five minutes unrolled. As is Man to the Universe, so was the mind of Mr Wilcox to the minds of some men – a concentrated light upon a tiny spot, a little Ten Minutes moving self-contained through its appointed years' (p.232).

Like the scene in which the Wilcoxes are described as lacking the part in the middle of the head which says 'I', this paragraph stops short of becoming a theory and is left as a suggestion. It conveys clearly enough, though, the notion that the Wilcox mind is immature: its narrow practicality is worse than the selfish inconsequentiality of Tibby, who has at least the

[16] Lawrence to Forster, 20 September 1922, Harry T. Moore (ed.), *Collected Letters*, vol.2, (1965), p.716.

excuse of being only eighteen: 'At Oxford he had learned to say that the importance of human beings has been vastly over-rated by specialists' (p.237).

Tibby's flippancy, Helen's mysticism, Paul's sexual incontinence, Henry's self-deception, Leonard's false literariness, all fall short of maturity. Margaret, unlike these figures, does not attempt to arrive at a formed philosophy of life: her openness and willingness to encounter experience are what set her apart and fit her to be Ruth Wilcox's heir.

6. The defeat of comedy

I have been discussing *Howards End* as though it were a failure, which on the whole I think it is, but quite a lot of it works and it is important to do the novel justice.

The first eleven chapters are very good. Helen is kissed by Paul Wilcox, Mrs Munt blunders off to Howards End to interfere, the Wilcoxes take a flat opposite the Schlegels' house in Wickham Place, Margaret is rude to Ruth Wilcox, apologises, and goes Christmas shopping with her; she is rude a second time and tries to make up for it by accompanying Ruth Wilcox on an impulsive visit to Howards End but this is cut short by an unexpected meeting with Mr Wilcox and Evie. Ruth Wilcox dies, her family receive a letter saying that she wished Howards End to go to Margaret. They discuss the letter and decide they can suppress it.

The virtues of these chapters are comedy, economy, lucky selection, accurate observation, hilarious mimicry. Mrs Munt is a useful comic character through whose limited vision the Schlegel household and its relationship with the Wilcoxes is mediated. Her brother-in-law had been 'peculiar and a German' (p.11). She quarrels with Charles Wilcox but is silenced by the presence of a 'member of the lower orders', a shop-assistant loading shopping into Charles's car: '"Esprit de classe" – if one may coin the phrase – was strong in Mrs. Munt. She sat quivering while a member of the lower orders deposited a metal funnel, a saucepan and a garden squirt beside the roll of oilcloth' (p.18).

Mrs Munt is bullied by Tibby for missing the transitional passage on the tympany in Beethoven's Fifth: '"I do in a *way* remember the passage, Tibby, but when every instrument is so beautiful it is difficult to pick out one thing rather than another"' (p.35).

The German cousin Frieda Mosebach is an equally successful comic figure, heavily interfering in Helen's love-life in an English which brilliantly just misses the rhythm of the language's idioms. When reproached by her sister for her relationship with Paul Wilcox Helen chants, clowning in a cockney accent: 'Meg, Meg, I don't love the young genterman', and Frieda

Mosebach feels obliged to force the point home: '"Most certainly her love has died," asserted Fräulein Mosebach' (p.62). Frieda and Mrs Munt are Forster's representative German and Briton, stupid, well-meaning, patriotic and obtuse. They are seen by Margaret as the 'gutter press of the private emotions' (p.60), commonplace people who unintentionally make trouble between individuals just as cheap journalism makes trouble between the two nations: 'The remark "England and Germany are bound to fight" renders war a little more likely each time that it is made, and is therefore made the more readily by the gutter press of either nation' (p.60).

After chapter 11 the writing of *Howards End* is often dismayingly soggy, nervously assertive, uncertainly proselytising. But as the novel loses its way the comic virtues of Frieda and Mrs Munt remain intact, and one only wishes that the novel gave them more space than it does.

In chapter 19 they engage in a duel over the respective virtues of England and Pomerania. Frieda, now a married woman, is taken up on to the Purbeck Hills (with Helen Schlegel) by Mrs Munt 'to be impressed'. Frieda 'said that the hills were more swelling here than in Pomerania' and then compares the mud of Poole harbour unfavourably with the 'tideless Baltic' of her native land:

> 'Rather unhealthy Mrs. Munt thought this would be, water being safer when it is moved about. "And your English lakes – Vindermere, Grasmere – are they, then, unhealthy?"
>
> '"No, Frau Liesecke; but that is because they are fresh water, and different. Salt water ought to have tides, and go up and down a great deal, or else it smells. Look, for instance, at an aquarium."
>
> '"An aquarium! Oh, *Meesis* Munt, you mean to tell me that fresh aquariums stink less than salt? Why, when Victor, my brother-in-law, collected many tadpoles –"
>
> '"You are not to say 'stink'," interrupted Helen; "at least, you may say it, but you must pretend you are being funny while you say it."
>
> '"Then 'smell'. And the mud of your Poole down there – does it not smell, or may I say 'stink, ha, ha'?"
>
> '"There always has been mud in Poole harbour," said Mrs Munt, with a slight frown. "The rivers bring it down, and a most valuable oyster fishery depends upon it."
>
> '"Yes, that is so," conceded Frieda; and another international incident was closed' (p.165).

I would cheerfully ditch all the solemn parts of *Howards End* – the pompous paragraphs about England's lack of a 'great mythology' and the world as a 'melting-pot' – for the sake of more of such scenes. And indeed, if Forster could write comic dialogue so well, with such economy, such elegant bitchiness, such tact, why did he not give us more in *Howards End*?

One answer to this question is to be found in the manuscripts, now published by Edward Arnold, 1973.[17] Here Forster gave more space to Mrs Munt and her eccentricities, and it seems likely that his first intuition was better than his revisions. Whenever Mrs Munt is present in the published text as a limited narrator the novel recovers its forward impetus and its comic balance. The novel first sees the Wilcox household through Mrs Munt's eyes, in chapter 3, and the effect is finely satirical. When Mrs Wilcox appears, though, the novel drops Mrs Munt in favour of an omniscient voice and immediately the prose becomes weak and windy: 'One knew that she worshipped the past, and that the instinctive wisdom the past can alone bestow had descended upon her' (p.19).

After the first eleven chapters Mrs Munt is largely edited out, and the prophetic, omniscient, turgid voice takes over.

Howards End is so very nearly a good novel that its self-defeating pomposity is infuriating. Presumably it is pompous because it is ambitious: Forster knows that he is a master of comedy, he has displayed a perfect technical control of the form in *A Room with a View*. Here he forces himself to go further. Perhaps the most successfully dramatised part of the novel, apart from Mrs Munt and Frieda, is the relationship between Margaret and Helen. They are well-observed, fully created individuals and it is difficult for the Wilcoxes to stand up to them as foils. Despite all his skill Forster cannot make Margaret's marriage to Henry seem as plausible as he would wish. Margaret's motivation remains obscure because of its purity. She acknowledges to Helen that she does not love Henry, and if she does not have much in common with him intellectually and morally – and the fact that she does not is the whole basis of the Wilcox/Schlegel dialogue – then her decision to marry him is left looking whimsical and improbable. If Forster had made her slightly less high-principled, or slightly more desperate – older, plainer, poorer – her need for a husband could have been passed off without an essential loss of integrity or plausibility, as is Charlotte Lucas's marriage to Mr Collins in *Pride and Prejudice*. As it is, the Margaret/Henry relationship is never reciprocal. Henry bullies and dominates and is then morally 'broken' by Charles's imprisonment and is dominated in his turn. Whether he is also bullied is not shown, but his destiny at the end of *Howards End* seems distinctly unenviable. It is impossible to imagine this married couple sharing a joke or getting into bed together. Helen and Margaret perpetuate Bloomsbury in Arcadia, the baby grows into a youthful Forster (one may assume), and their victim works out a life-long penance, nursing his hay-fever in the shuttered dining-room of Howards End.

[17] E.M. Forster, *The Manuscripts of Howards End* (1973).

Afterword

Conrad is obviously a giant and I have given him a proportionately large share of my discussion. Forster, for me, is a self-defeating master of comedy whose *Howards End* collapses under the weight of its own seriousness and whose *A Room with a View* is his most successful Edwardian work (I exclude *A Passage to India* from my consideration). Bennett, Wells and Ford Madox Ford I would regard as major novelists in their respective ways and Galsworthy as a decent, muddled liberal whose personal predicament enabled him to write one good novel. I have not tried to force these writers to resemble one another, since it is clear that they don't, but I have sought instead to show that the Edwardian period presented specific challenges to which these writers were forced to respond, each in the way that suited him best.

The conventions of the novel require that the protagonist – the 'hero' in the sense in which traditional storytelling uses that word – shall have certain objectives, certain clear drives, desires and imperatives. The writers of this period are working within a received convention from which this central force – the machine which drives Fielding's novels, or Smollett's, vigorously forward – is missing. The male protagonist is beset by doubts and anxieties: yet he must still act as a 'hero', he must behave as though the old world of established certainties still exists, since that world has determined the dramatic shape with which these writers are working. *Victory*, as I have tried to show, demonstrates this difficulty at its most acute: Heyst's complex asceticism exists within the frame of a puppet show full of 'flat' good and bad characters with which, to the novel's detriment, he is obliged to interact. At his best Conrad makes the problem itself into the novel's subject: *Lord Jim* is a self-referential fiction in which the reader must collaborate with Marlow as he lovingly (but finally in vain) seeks to apprehend and present the fine grain of Jim's personality and ideals. Jim is never fully known but he is *loved* – by Marlow and therefore by the reader – which enables this novel to evade, with its own peculiar and supreme artistry, the difficulty of presenting an anti-hero within a dramatic action which requires a hero.

Ford Madox Ford's evasions are different: Edward Ashburnham and Tietjens are left high and dry, obstinately loyal to loyalty when the objects of their loyalties, mistress, wife or country, have been exposed as fraudulent or malign. In Wells the subversive lower-class male's drive towards power again effectively displaces the emphasis from the uncomfortable vacuum at the centre of the Edwardian novel: *The War in the Air* may end in a pointless and suicidal strife between nations who have nothing left to fight for, but Bert Smallways, as his name indicates, has his own small objectives to which he can still confidently aspire after the disappearance of the civilisation from which he sprang. For Bennett the 'hero' is history itself, the stupid life-support system of contingencies operating in time and presented in discrete detail: a system without which his people have no identity, but in which they are deprived of freedom. And in Galsworthy and Forster muddled liberalism takes the form of sexual rebellion which mildly shakes but cannot disturb the social order within their respective imaginative worlds. These writers are all forced to come to terms with the inherent contradiction that must exist between the devalued and directionless state in which the early twentieth-century hero found himself and the received literary conventions in which he still had to be dramatised and presented.

Bibliography

This list is in three parts: 1. The six major novelists discussed; 2. Other primary works; 3. All secondary works. London is the place of publication unless specified.

Primary Sources 1
Conrad, Ford, Wells, Bennett, Galsworthy and Forster

JOSEPH CONRAD. All novels, tales, essays and collaborations (but see also under Ford) referred to are cited from *The Collected Edition of the Works of Joseph Conrad* (Dent, 1946-55). Other works referred to are:

> *Congo Diary: And Other Uncollected Pieces* (ed. Zdzislaw Najder). New York: Doubleday, 1978.
>
> *Heart of Darkness* (Norton Critical Edition, ed. Robert Kimbrough). New York: Norton, 1971.
>
> *Letters to William Blackwood and David S. Meldrum* (ed. William Blackburn). Durham, N. Carolina: Duke University Press, 1958.
>
> *Letters to R.B. Cunninghame Graham* (ed. C.T. Watts). Cambridge: Cambridge University Press, 1969.
>
> *Conrad's Polish Background: Letters to and from Polish Friends* (ed. Zdzislaw Najder). Oxford University Press, 1964.
>
> *Letters from Conrad* (ed. E. Garnett). Nonesuch Press, 1928.
>
> *Letters of Joseph Conrad to Marguerite Poradowska, 1890-1920* (ed. J.A. Gee and P.J. Sturm). New Haven: Yale University Press, 1940.

FORD MADOX FORD [also Ford Madox Hueffer]. All major works referred to (*The Good Soldier, The Fifth Queen*, the Tietjens tetralogy) are cited from *The Bodley Head Ford Madox Ford* (Bodley Head, 1962-72). Other works referred to are:

Ancient Lights: And Certain New Reflections. Chapman and Hall, 1911.

Mr. Apollo. Methuen, 1908.

The Benefactor. Brown, Langham and Co., 1905.

A Call: The Tale of Two Passions. Chatto and Windus, 1910.

Collected Poems. Max Goschen, 1914.

The Critical Attitude. Duckworth, 1911

An English Girl. Methuen, 1907.

Mr. Fleight. Howard Latimer, 1913.

The Half Moon. Eveleigh Nash, 1909.

Hans Holbein the Younger. The Popular Library of Art, Duckworth, 1905.

Henry James: A Critical Study. Martin Secker, 1913.

Joseph Conrad: A Personal Remembrance. Duckworth, 1924.

[with Conrad] *The Nature of a Crime*. Duckworth, 1924.

[as 'Daniel Chaucer'] *The New Humpty-Dumpty*. Bodley Head, 1912.

The Portrait. Methuen, 1910.

Return to Yesterday: Reminiscences, 1894-1914. Gollancz, 1931.

[with Conrad] *Romance*. Methuen, 1903.

[as 'Daniel Chaucer'] *The Simple Life, Ltd*. Bodley Head, 1911.

The Soul of London. Alston Rivers, 1905.

The Spirit of the People: An Analysis of the English Mind. Alston Rivers, 1907.

Thus to Revisit. Chapman and Hall, 1921.

The Young Lovell: A Romance. Chatto and Windus, 1913.

Letters of Ford Madox Ford (ed. R.M. Ludwig). Princeton N.J.: Princeton University Press, 1965.

H.G. WELLS. Most novels discussed (e.g. *Love and Mr. Lewisham, The War in the Air, Kipps, Tono-Bungay, The History of Mr. Polly, The New Machiavelli*) are cited from the Odhams Press library edition. Wells's prefaces are cited from *The Works of H.G. Wells: Atlantic Edition* (Unwin, 1924-27). There is a very helpful bibliography, *H.G. Wells: A Comprehensive Bibliography* (H.G. Wells Society, 1968). Other works referred to are:

The Anatomy of Frustration: A Synthesis. Cresset, 1936.

Ann Veronica: A Modern Love Story. Fisher, Unwin, 1909.

Anticipations: of the Reaction of Mechanical and Scientific

Progress upon Human Life and Thought. Chapman and Hall, 1902.

Boon. Fisher, Unwin, 1915.

'The Chronic Argonauts', in Bergonzi, *The Early H.G. Wells* (see Secondary Works).

The Country of the Blind. Nelson, 1911.

The Discovery of the Future. Fisher, Unwin, 1902.

Early Writings in Science and Science Fiction (ed. Robert M. Philmus and David Y. Hughes). Berkeley and Los Angeles: University of California Press, 1975.

Experiment in Autobiography: Discoveries and Conclusions of a Very Ordinary Brain (since 1866) (two volumes). Gollancz, 1934.

The First Men in the Moon. Newnes, 1901.

The Food of the Gods and How it Came to Earth. Macmillan, 1904.

The Island of Dr. Moreau. Heinemann, 1896.

In the Days of the Comet. Macmillan, 1906.

Mankind in the Making. Chapman and Hall, 1903.

Marriage. Macmillan, 1912.

Mind at the End of Its Tether. Heinemann, 1945.

A Modern Utopia. Chapman and Hall, 1905.

New Worlds for Old. Constable, 1908.

The Plattner Story and Others (including 'In the Abyss'). Methuen, 1897.

The Sea Lady: A Tissue of Moonshine. Methuen, 1902.

Socialism and The Family. Fifield, 1906.

Tales of Space and Time. Harper, 1900.

The Time Machine. Heinemann, 1895.

Twelve Stories and a Dream. Macmillan, 1903.

The War of the Worlds. Heinemann, 1898.

The Wealth of Mr. Waddy: A Novel (ed. Harry T. Moore and Harris Wilson). Carbondale: Southern Illinois University Press, 1969.

H.G. Wells: Journalism and Prophecy (ed. W. Warren Wagar). Bodley Head, 1964.

The Wheels of Chance: A Holiday Adventure. Dent, 1896.

When the Sleeper Wakes: A Story of the Years to Come. Harper, 1899.

The Wife of Sir Isaac Harmon. Macmillan, 1914.

Arnold Bennett and H.G. Wells (ed. Harris Wilson). Hart-Davis, 1960.

George Gissing and H.G. Wells (ed. Royal A. Gettmann). Hart-Davis, 1961.

Henry James and H.G. Wells (letters and essays, ed. Leon Edel and Gordon N. Ray). Hart-Davis, 1958.

ARNOLD BENNETT. Works referred to are:

Anna of the Five Towns. Chatto and Windus, 1902.

The Author's Craft. Hodder and Stoughton, 1914.

Books and Persons: Being Comments on a Past Epoch, 1908-11. Chatto and Windus, 1917.

The Card. Methuen, 1910.

Clayhanger. Methuen, 1910.

The Grim Smile of the Five Towns. Chapman and Hall, 1907.

The Ghost. Chatto and Windus, 1907.

The Glimpse. Chapman and Hall, 1909.

Hilda Lessways. Methuen, 1911.

How to Live on 24 Hours a Day. Hodder and Stoughton, 1908.

The Journals: Four Volumes (ed. Newman Flower). Cassell, 1932-3.

The Journals (with additional material, selected and ed. Frank Swinnerton). Penguin 1971.

Leonora, Chatto and Windus, 1903.

A Man from the North. Bodley Head, 1898 (as 'E.A. Bennett').

Mental Efficiency. Hodder and Stoughton, 1911.

The Old Wives' Tale. Chapman and Hall, 1908.

The Old Wives' Tale (with preface added). Hodder and Stoughton, 1912.

Sacred and Profane Love. Chatto and Windus, 1905.

Teresa of Watling Street. Chatto and Windus, 1904.

These Twain. Methuen, 1916.

(*Letters*: see under Wells)

JOHN GALSWORTHY. Works referred to are:

A Commentary. Grant Richards, 1908.

The Country House. Heinemann, 1907.

Forsytes, Pendyces and Others (includes 'Danäe' and 'The Doldrums'). Heinemann, 1935.

Fraternity. Heinemann, 1909.

From the Four Winds. Fisher, Unwin, 1897 (as 'John Sinjohn').

The Inn of Tranquillity: Studies and Essays. Heinemann, 1912.

The Island Pharisees. Heinemann, 1904 (revised 1908).

Jocelyn (1898, as 'John Sinjohn'). Duckworth/ Sidgwick and Jackson, 1976.

The Man of Property. Heinemann, 1906.

The Patrician. Heinemann, 1911.

The Plays of John Galsworthy. Duckworth, 1929.

E.M. FORSTER. All novels with the exception of *The Longest Journey* are referred to in *The Abinger Edition of E.M. Forster*, Arnold, 1971-, as are *The Life to Come, The Lucy Novels, The Manuscripts of Howards End, Goldsworthy Lowes Dickinson* and *Two Cheers for Democracy*. Other works referred to are:

Aspects of the Novel. Arnold, 1927.
The Celestial Omnibus. Sidgwick and Jackson, 1911.
Collected Short Stories. Sidgwick and Jackson, 1948.
The Longest Journey. Blackwood, 1907.

Primary Sources 2

Barker, H. Granville	*Three Plays: The Marrying of Anne Leete, The Voysey Inheritance, Waste*. Sidgwick and Jackson, 1909.
Barrie, J.M.	*The Plays of J.M. Barrie* (ed. A.E. Wilson). Hodder and Stoughton, 1942.
Beerbohm, Max.	*The Happy Hypocrite*. John Lane, 1897.
	Zuleika Dobson. Heinemann, 1911.
Benson, A.C.	*From a College Window*. Smith, Elder, 1906.
Benson, E.F.	*As We Were*. Longmans, 1930.
	The Babe, B.A., 1897.
Benson, R.H.	*The Light Invisible*. Isbister, 1903.
	Lord of the World. Pitman, 1907.
	None Other Gods. Hutchinson, 1910.
	The Sentimentalists. Pitman, 1906.
Bergson, Henri	*Creative Evolution*. Macmillan, 1928.
Buchan, John	*Prester John*. Nelson, 1910.
Chesterton, G.K.	*The Ball and the Cross*. John Lane, 1909.
	The Flying Inn. John Lane, 1914.
	Manalive. Nelson, 1912.
	The Man Who Was Thursday. Arrowsmith, 1908.
	The Napoleon of Notting Hill. Bodley Head, 1904.
Childers, Erskine	*The Riddle of the Sands*. Smith, Elder, 1903.
'Corvo, Frederick Baron' [also Fr. Rolfe]	*The Desire and Pursuit of the Whole*. Cassell, 1934.
	Hadrian the Seventh: A Romance. Chatto and Windus, 1904.
	The Venice Letters (ed. Cecil Woolf). Cecil and Amelia Woolf, 1974.
The English Review	(ed. Ford, 1908-9).
Gissing, George	*The Private Papers of Henry Ryecroft*. Constable, 1903.
Glyn, Elinor	*Three Weeks*. Duckworth, 1907.
Graham, R.B. Cunninghame	*Thirteen Stories*. Heinemann, 1900.
	A Vanished Arcadia. Heinemann, 1901.
Grahame, Kenneth	*The Golden Age*. John Lane, 1900.
	The Wind in the Willows. Methuen, 1908.
Harland, Henry	*The Cardinal's Snuff-Box*. John Lane, 1900.
	The Lady Paramount. John Lane, 1902.
	My Friend Prospero. John Lane, 1904.
	The Royal End. Hutchinson, 1909.

Hichens, Robert	*The Garden of Allah*. Methuen, 1904.
Hudson, W.H.	*Green Mansions*. Duckworth, 1904.
The Independent Review	(1903-1907).
James, William	*The Varieties of Religious Experience*. Longmans, Green, 1902.
	After London: Wild England. Cassell, 1885.
	Dubliners (1914). Jonathan Cape, 1956.
Jefferies, Richard	*A Portrait of the Artist as a Young Man* (1916).
Joyce, James	Jonathan Cape, 1952.
Kipling, Rudyard	*Actions and Reactions*. Macmillan, 1909.
	The Day's Work. Macmillan, 1898.
	Kim. Macmillan, 1901.
	Puck of Pook's Hill. Macmillan, 1906.
	Rewards and Fairies. Macmillan, 1910.
	Stalky and Co. Macmillan, 1899.
	Traffics and Discoveries. Macmillan, 1904.
Le Queux, William	*The Great War in England in 1897*. Tower, 1894.
	The Invasion of 1910. Eveleigh Nash, 1906.
London, Jack	*The People of the Abyss*. Isbister, 1903.
Machen, Arthur	*The Great God Pan*. John Lane, 1894.
	The Hill of Dreams. Grant Richards, 1907.
Mason, A.E.W.	*The Broken Road*. Smith, Elder, 1908.
Masterman, G.F.	*Seven Eventful Years in Paraguay*. Sampson, Low, 1869.
Masterman, C.F.G.	*The Condition of England*. Methuen, 1909.
	From the Abyss. R.B. Johnson, 1902.
	'The Social Abyss' *Preachers from the Pew* (ed. W.H. Hunt). W.H. Lord, n.d.
Maugham, W. Somerset	*Liza of Lambeth*. Unwin, 1897.
	Mrs. Craddock. Heinemann, 1902.
Maupassant, G. de	*A Woman's Life* (*Une Vie*, 1882; trans. Antonia White). Hamish Hamilton, 1949.
Moore, George	*Esther Waters*. Walter Scott, 1894.
	The Untilled Field. Unwin, 1903.
Moore, G.E.	*Principia Ethica*. Cambridge: Cambridge University Press, 1903.
Morrison, Arthur	*A Child of the Jago*. Methuen, 1896.
	The Hole in the Wall. Methuen, 1902.
The New Age	(ed. Alfred Orage).
Nordau, Max.	*Degeneration*. Heinemann, 1895.
	The Malady of the Century. Heinemann, 1896.
Pater, Walter	*The Renaissance* (1873). Macmillan, 1910.
Reid, Forrest	*The Garden God*. Long Acre, 1905.
Russell, Bertrand	*Autobiography: 1872-1914*. Allen and Unwin, 1967.
	'The Free Man's Worship', *The Independent Review*, I, No.3 (December, 1903), pp.415-24.
Sackville-West, Victoria	*The Edwardians*. Hogarth, 1930.
Saki [H.H. Munro]	*The Chronicles of Clovis*. John Lane, 1912.
	The Unbearable Bassington. John Lane, 1912.
	When William Came. John Lane, 1914.
Shaw. G. Bernard	*Cashel Byron's Profession* (1886, revised 1901). Constable, 1930.

All references to Shaw's plays are to:
The Bodley Head Shaw, Bodley Head, 1971-1974.

Shiel, M.P.	*The Purple Cloud*. Chatto and Windus, 1901.
	The Yellow Danger. Grant Richards, 1898.
Stacpoole, H. de Vere	*The Blue Lagoon*. Fisher, Unwin, 1908.
Stephens, James	*The Crock of Gold*. Macmillan, 1912.
Symons, Arthur	*Studies in Prose and Verse*. Dent, 1904.
	The Symbolist Movement in Literature. Heinemann, 1899.
Thomas, Edward	*The Heart of England*. Dent, 1906.
	The South Country. Dent, 1909.
Tressell, Robert	*The Ragged Trousered Philanthropists* (1914). Panther, 1975.
Wodehouse, P.G.	*The Gold Bat*. Black, 1904.
	Mike: A Public School Story. Black, 1909.
	The Pothunters. Black, 1902.
	Psmith in the City. Black, 1910.
	The Swoop! Or How Clarence Saved England. Alston Rivers, 1909.
	The White Feather. Black, 1907.
Yeats, W.B.	*Ideas of Good and Evil*. Bullen, 1903.
	Introduction, *Oxford Book of Modern Verse*. Oxford University Press, 1936.

Secondary Sources

Amis, Kingsley	*Rudyard Kipling and his World*. Thames and Hudson, 1975.
Andreach, Robert J.	*The Slain and Resurrected God: Conrad, Ford and the Christian Myth*. University of London Press, 1970.
Baines, Jocelyn	*Joseph Conrad: A Critical Biography*. Weidenfeld and Nicolson, 1960.
Barker, Dudley	*The Man of Principle: A View of John Galsworthy*. Heinemann, 1963.
Beckson, Karl	*Henry Harland: His Life and Work*. The Eighteen-Nineties Society, 1978.
Beer, J.B.	*The Achievement of E.M. Forster*. Chatto and Windus, 1962.
Bellamy, William	*The Novels of Wells, Bennett and Galsworthy: 1890-1910*. Routledge and Kegan Paul, 1971.
Benkovitz, Miriam J.	*Frederick Rolfe: Baron Corvo*. Hamish Hamilton, 1977.
Bergonzi, Bernard	*The Early H.G. Wells: A Study of the Scientific Romances*. Manchester: Manchester University Press, 1961.
	H.G. Wells: A Collection of Critical Essays. Englewood Cliffs, N.J.: Prentice-Hall, 1976.
	Heroes' Twilight: A Study of the Literature of the Great War. Constable, 1968.

The Turn of a Century: Essays on Victorian and Modern English Literature. Macmillan, 1973.

Berthoud, Jacques — *Joseph Conrad: The Major Phase.* Cambridge: Cambridge University Press, 1978.

Bocock, Robert — *Freud and Modern Society.* Nelson, 1976.

Bradbury, Malcolm — *Possibilities: Essays on the State of the Novel.* Oxford University Press, 1973.

Brent, Peter — *The Edwardians.* B.B.C., 1972.

Buckley, J.H. — *Season of Youth: The Bildungsroman from Dickens to Golding.* Cambridge, Mass.: Harvard University Press, 1974.

Burrow, J.W. — *Evolution and Society.* Cambridge: Cambridge University Press, 1966.

Carrington, Charles — *Rudyard Kipling.* Macmillan, 1955.

Cavaliero, Glen — *A Reading of E.M. Forster.* Macmillan, 1979.

The Rural Tradition in the English Novel. Macmillan, 1977.

Cecil, Lord David — 'Joseph Conrad', *The London Magazine*, I, (September, 1954), pp.54-71.

Chapple, J.A.V. — *Documentary and Imaginative Literature, 1880-1920.* Blandford, 1970.

Cockburn, Claud — *Best-Sellers: The Books that Everyone Read, 1900-1939.* Sidgwick and Jackson, 1972.

Colmer, John — *E.M. Forster: The Personal Voice.* Routledge, 1975.

Connolly, Cyril — *Enemies of Promise.* Routledge, 1938.

Cooper, Christopher — *Conrad and the Human Dilemma.* Chatto and Windus, 1970.

Cox, C.B. — *Joseph Conrad: The Modern Imagination.* Dent, 1974.

Crankshaw, Edward — *Joseph Conrad: Some Aspects of the Art of the Novel* [1936]. Macmillan, 1976.

Crews, F.C. — *E.M. Forster: The Perils of Humanism.* Oxford University Press, 1962.

Crompton, Louis — *Shaw the Dramatist.* Allen and Unwin, 1971.

Cruse, Amy — *After the Victorians.* Allen and Unwin, 1938.

Daiches, David — *Some late Victorian Attitudes.* Andre Deutsch, 1969.

Daleski, H.M. — *Joseph Conrad: The Way of Dispossession.* Faber, 1977.

Dangerfield, George — *The Strange Death of Liberal England.* Constable, 1936.

Dickson, Lovat — *H.G. Wells.* Macmillan, 1969.

Drabble, Margaret — *Arnold Bennett: A Biography.* Weidenfeld and Nicolson, 1974.

Duncan-Jones, E.E. — 'Some Sources of *Chance*', *The Review of English Studies, XX*, (November, 1969), pp.468-71.

Dupré, Catherine — *John Galsworthy: A Biography.* Collins, 1976.

Dyson, A.E. — *Between Two Worlds: Aspects of Literary Form.* Macmillan, 1972.

The Crazy Fabric. Macmillan, 1965.

Eagleton, Terence — *Exiles and Emigrés.* Chatto and Windus, 1970.

Ellmann, Richard (ed.) — *Edwardians and Late Victorians.* New York: Columbia University Press, 1959.

Ellmann, Richard — *Golden Codgers: Biographical Speculations.* Oxford University Press, 1973.

Ensor, R.C.K. — *England, 1870-1914.* Oxford University Press, 1946.

Fleishman, Avrom, — *The English Historical Novel.* Baltimore: Johns Hopkins Press, 1971.

Conrad's Politics. Baltimore: Johns Hopkins Press, 1967.

Friedman, Alan, — *The Turn of the Novel.* Oxford University Press, 1966.

Furbank, P.N. — 'Chesterton the Edwardian', *G.K. Chesterton: A Centenary Appraisal* (ed. J. Sullivan). Elek, 1974.

E.M. Forster: A Life, I and II. Secker and Warburg, 1977 and 1978.

Fussell, Paul — *The Great War and Modern Memory.* Oxford University Press, 1975.

Galsworthy, John — 'Joseph Conrad: A Disquisition', *Fortnightly Review, LXXXIII,* (1908), pp.627-33.

Gardner, Philip (ed.) — *E.M. Forster: The Critical Heritage.* Routledge, 1973.

Gibbons, Tom — *Rooms in the Darwin Hotel: Studies in English Literary Criticism and Ideas, 1880-1920.* Nedlands: University of Western Australia Press, 1973.

Gilbert, Elliot L. — *The Good Kipling.* Manchester: Manchester University Press, 1972.

Gill, Richard — *Happy Rural Seat: The English Country House and the Literary Imagination.* Yale: Yale University Press, 1972.

Goldring, Douglas — *The Last Pre-Raphaelite: Ford Madox Ford.* MacDonald, 1948.

South Lodge: Reminiscences of Violet Hunt, Ford Madox Ford and the English Review Circle. Constable and Co., 1943.

Graham, Kenneth — *English Criticism of the Novel: 1865-1900.* Oxford University Press, 1965.

Green, Peter — *Kenneth Grahame: A Study of his Life, Work and Times.* John Murray, 1959.

Greene, Graham — *The Lost Childhood.* Eyre and Spottiswoode, 1951.

Gross, John — *The Rise and Fall of the Man of Letters.* Weidenfeld and Nicolson, 1969.

Green-Armitage, Adrian — 'The Religion of Joseph Conrad', *The Tablet* (December 7th, 1957), pp.501-2.

Guerard, A.J. — *Conrad the Novelist.* Oxford University Press, 1958.

Guetti, James — *The Limits of Metaphor.* Ithaca: Cornell University Press, 1967.

Hawthorn, Jeremy — *Joseph Conrad: Language and Fictional Self-Consciousness.* Arnold, 1979.

Hay, Eloise Knapp — *The Political Novels of Joseph Conrad.* Chicago: University of Chicago Press, 1963.

Hearnshaw, F.J.C. (ed.) — *Edwardian England: 1901-1910.* Ernest Benn, 1933.

Henkin, Leo J. — *Darwinism in the English Novel: 1860-1910.* New York: Russell and Russell, 1963.

Henn, T.R. — *Kipling.* Edinburgh: Oliver and Boyd, 1967.

Hepburn, James G.   *The Art of Arnold Bennett.* Bloomington: Indiana University Press, 1963.

Hewitt, Douglas   *Conrad: A Reassessment.* Bowes and Bowes, 1952.

Hillegas, Mark R.   *The Future as Nightmare: H.G. Wells and the Anti-Utopians.* New York: Oxford University Press, 1967.

Hodges, Robert R.   *The Dual Heritage of Joseph Conrad.* Paris: Menton, 1967.

Hough, Graham   *Image and Experience: Studies in a Literary Revolution.* Duckworth, 1960.
            The Last Romantics. Duckworth, 1948.

Howe, Irving   *Politics and the Novel.* New York: Horizon Press, 1960.

Hynes, Samuel   *Edwardian Occasions: Essays on English Writing in the Early Twentieth Century.* Routledge, 1972.
            The Edwardian Turn of Mind. Princeton: Princeton University Press, 1968.

Jackson, Holbrook   *Romance and Reality.* Grant Richards, 1911.

James, Henry   *The Art of Fiction: And Other Essays.* New York: Oxford University Press, 1948.

Jean-Aubry, G.   *Joseph Conrad: Life and Letters, I and II.* Heinemann, 1927.
            The Sea Dreamer: A Definitive Biography of Joseph Conrad. Allen and Unwin, 1957.

Jepson, Edgar   *Memories of an Edwardian and neo-Georgian.* Richards, 1937.

Johnson, Bruce   *Conrad's Models of Mind.* Minneapolis: University of Minnesota Press, 1971.

Johnstone, J.K.   *The Bloomsbury Group.* Secker and Warburg, 1954.

Jones, Alun R.   *The Life and Opinions of T.E. Hulme.* Gollancz, 1960.

Jones, Michael P.   'A Paradise Lost: Conrad and the Romantic Sensibility', *Critical Quarterly, XVIII,* No. 4 (Winter, 1976), pp.37-49.

Kagarlitski, J.   *The Life and Thought of H.G. Wells.* Sidgwick and Jackson, 1966.

Karl, F.J.   *Joseph Conrad: The Three Lives.* Faber, 1979.

Keating, Peter (ed.)   *Into Unknown England 1866-1913.* Manchester: Manchester University Press, 1976.

Kennedy, J.M.   *English Literature: 1880-1905.* Sampson, Low, Marston, 1913.

Kermode, Frank   *The Sense of an Ending.* New York: Oxford University Press, 1967.

Kirschner, Paul   *Conrad: The Psychologist as Artist.* Edinburgh: Oliver and Boyd, 1968.

Lawrence, D.H.   *Collected Letters* (2 vols: ed. Harry T. Moore). Heinemann, 1965.

Lee, Robert, F.   *Conrad's Colonialism.* The Hague: Mouton, 1969.

Lester, John A.   *Journey Through Despair, 1880-1914: Transformations in British Literary Culture.* Princeton: Princeton University Press, 1968.

Lewis, C.S.   *They Asked for a Paper.* Geoffrey Bles, 1962.

Lewis, Wyndham — *The Roaring Queen*. Secker and Warburg, 1973.

Lodge, David — *Language of Fiction*. Routledge, 1966.

Lucas, F.L. — *The Decline and Fall of the Romantic Ideal*. Cambridge: Cambridge University Press, 1936.

Lucas, John — *Arnold Bennett: A Study of his Fiction*. Methuen, 1974.

MacKenzie, Norman and Jeanne — *The Time Traveller: The Life of H.G. Wells*. Weidenfeld and Nicolson, 1973.

MacShane, Frank (ed.) — *Ford Madox Ford: The Critical Heritage*. Routledge, 1972.

MacShane, Frank — *The Life and Work of Ford Madox Ford*. Routledge, 1965.

Malbone, R.G. — '"How to be": Marlow's Quest in *Lord Jim*', *Twentieth Century Literature X*, No. 4, (January, 1965), pp.172-80.

Marrot, H.V. — *The Life and Letters of John Galsworthy*. Heinemann, 1935.

Masur, Gerhard — *Prophets of Yesterday: Studies in European Culture, 1840-1914*. Weidenfeld and Nicolson, 1963.

Megroz, R.L. — *Joseph Conrad's Mind and Method*. Faber, 1931.

Meisel, Martin — *Shaw and the Nineteenth Century Theatre*. Princeton: Princeton University Press, 1963.

Meixner, John A. — *Ford Madox Ford's Novels*. Oxford University Press, 1962.

Meyer, Bernard C. — *Joseph Conrad: A Psychoanalytic Biography*. Princeton: Princeton University Press, 1967.

Meyers, Jeffrey — *Fiction and the Colonial Experience*. Ipswich: Boydell Press, 1973.

Homosexuality and Literature: 1890-1930. Athlone, 1977.

Miller, J. Hillis — *The Disappearance of God*. Cambridge, Mass.: Harvard University Press, 1963.

The Form of Victorian Fiction. Notre Dame: University of Notre Dame Press, 1968.

Poets of Reality: Six Twentieth Century Writers. Cambridge, Mass.: Harvard University Press, 1966.

Minney, R.J. — *The Edwardian Age*. Cassell, 1964.

Mizener, Arthur — *The Saddest Story: A Biography of Ford Madox Ford*. Bodley Head, 1971.

Moers, Ellen — *The Dandy*. Secker and Warburg, 1960.

Morf, Gustav — *The Polish Heritage of Joseph Conrad*. Sampson, Low, Marston, 1930.

The Polish Shades and Ghosts of Joseph Conrad. New York: Astra Books, 1976.

Moser, Thomas — *Joseph Conrad: Achievement and Decline*. Cambridge, Mass.: Harvard University Press, 1957.

Muddiman, Bernard — *The Men of the Nineties*. Henry Danielson, 1920.

Muir, Edwin — *The Structure of the Novel*. Hogarth, 1928.

Murdoch, Iris — 'Against Dryness', *Encounter*, (January, 1961), pp.16-20.

Nettels, Elsa — *James and Conrad*. Athens, Ga.: University of Georgia Press, 1977.

Newell, Kenneth B.   *Structure in Four Novels by H.G. Wells.* The Hague: Mouton, 1968.

Nowell-Smith, S. (ed.)   *Edwardian England: 1901-1914.* Oxford University Press, 1964.

Orwell, George   *Collected Essays, Journalism and Letters* (4 vols). Secker and Warburg, 1968.

Parrinder, Patrick   *H.G. Wells.* Edinburgh: Oliver and Boyd, 1970.

Parrinder, Patrick (ed.)   *H.G. Wells: The Critical Heritage.* Routledge, 1972.

Pearson, Hesketh   *Bernard Shaw.* Collins, 1942.

Pound, Reginald   *Arnold Bennett.* Heinemann, 1952.

Praz, Mario   *The Hero in Eclipse in Victorian Fiction,* (trans. Angus Davidson). Oxford University Press, 1956.

Pritchett, V.S.   *The Living Novel.* Chatto and Windus, 1946.

Rank, Otto   'The Myth of the Birth of the Hero' [1914], *The Myth of the Birth of the Hero and Other Writings.* New York: Random House, 1964.

Ray, Gordon N.   *H.G. Wells and Rebecca West.* Macmillan, 1974.

Read, Donald   *Edwardian England: 1901-1915.* Harrap, 1972.

Rickword, Edgell (ed.)   *Scrutinies: By Various Writers.* Wishart, 1928.

Rosenfield, Claire   *Paradise of Snakes.* Chicago: University of Chicago Press, 1967.

Ross, R.H.   *The Georgian Revolt.* Faber, 1967.

Routh, H.V.   *Towards the Twentieth Century.* Cambridge: Cambridge University Press, 1937.

Ruthven, K.K.   'The Savage God: Conrad and Lawrence', *Critical Quarterly X,* (Spring and Summer, 1968), pp.39-54.

Said, Edward W.   *Joseph Conrad and the Fiction of Autobiography.* Cambridge, Mass.: Harvard University Press, 1966.

Sandison, Alan   *The Wheel of Empire: A Study of the Imperial Idea in Some Late Nineteenth and Early Twentieth Century Fiction.* St Martin's Press, 1967.

Sherry, Norman (ed.)   *Conrad: The Critical Heritage.* Routledge, 1973.

Sherry, Norman   *Conrad's Eastern World.* Cambridge: Cambridge University Press, 1966.

                             Conrad's Western World. Cambridge: Cambridge University Press, 1971.

                             Conrad and His World. Thames and Hudson, 1972.

Sherry, Norman (ed.)   *Joseph Conrad: A Commemoration.* Macmillan, 1976.

Sinclair, Andrew   *Jack: A Biography of Jack London.* Weidenfeld and Nicolson, 1978.

Spender, Stephen   *The Struggle of the Modern.* Hamish Hamilton, 1963.

Stead, C.K.   *The New Poetic.* Hutchinson University Library, 1964.

Stern, J.P.   *On Realism.* Routledge, 1973.

Stevenson, Lionel   *Darwin Among the Poets.* Chicago: University of Chicago Press, 1932.

Storr, Anthony   *The Dynamics of Creation.* Secker and Warburg, 1972.

Street, Brian V. — *The Savage in Literature: Representations of 'Primitive' Society in English Fiction 1858-1920*. Routledge, 1975.

Swinnerton, Frank — *The Georgian Literary Scene, 1910-1935*. Hutchinson, 1935.

Swinnerton: An Autobiography. Hutchinson, 1937.

Symonds, Arthur — *Notes on Joseph Conrad*. Myers and Co., 1925.

Symons, A.J.A. — *The Quest for Corvo*. Cassell, 1934.

Tanner, Tony — 'Nightmare and Complacency: Razumov and the Western Eye', *Critical Quarterly IV*, No. 3, (Autumn, 1962), pp.197-214.

Thomson, David — *England in the Nineteenth Century*. Penguin, 1955.

Thompson, Paul — *The Edwardians*. Weidenfeld and Nicolson, 1975.

Thorburn, David — *Conrad's Romanticism*. New Haven: Yale University Press, 1974.

Tomkins, J.M.S. — *The Art of Rudyard Kipling*. Methuen, 1959.

Trewin, J.C. — *The Edwardian Theatre*. Basil Blackwell, 1976.

Van Ghent, Dorothea — *The English Novel: Form and Function*. New York: Rinehart, 1953.

Wagar, W.W. — *H.G. Wells and the World State*. New Haven: Yale University Press, 1961.

Wagner, Geoffrey — 'Ford Madox Ford: The Honest Edwardian', *Essays in Criticism XVII*, (1967), pp.75-88.

'The Novel of Empire', *Essays in Criticism XX*, (1970), 224-42.

Watt, Ian — 'Joseph Conrad: Alienation and Commitment', *The English Mind* (ed. Watson and Davies). Cambridge: Cambridge University Press, 1964.

Watts, Cedric and Davies, Laurence — *Cunninghame Graham: A Critical Biography*. Cambridge: Cambridge University Press, 1979.

Weeks, Donald — *Corvo*. Michael Joseph, 1971.

West, Geoffrey — *H.G. Wells: A Sketch for a Portrait*. Howe, 1930.

West, Rebecca — *The Strange Necessity: Essays and Reviews*. Jonathan Cape, 1928.

Wilding, Michael — 'The Politics of *Nostromo*', *Essays in Criticism XVI*, (1966), pp.441-56.

Wiley, Paul L. — *Conrad's Measure of Man*. Madison: University of Wisconsin Press, 1954.

Novelist of Three Worlds: Ford Madox Ford. Syracuse: Syracuse University Press, 1962.

Williams, Raymond — *The English Novel from Dickens to Lawrence*. Paladin, 1974.

Wilson, Angus — 'Arnold Bennett's Novels', *The London Magazine I*, (November, 1954), pp.60-1.

The Strange Ride of Rudyard Kipling. Secker and Warburg, 1977.

Wilson, Edmund — *The Wound and the Bow*. Cambridge, Mass.: Houghton, Mifflin, 1941.

Woolf, Virginia — *Mr. Bennett and Mrs. Brown*. Hogarth, 1924.

A Writer's Diary. Hogarth, 1964.

Index

Amis, Kingsley, 16
Andreach, R.J., 97
Arnold, Matthew, 102
Austen, Jane, 176, 210, 232

Baines, Jocelyn, 61, 81
Bayley, John, 44n
Bellamy, William, 183n, 185n, 201
Bennett, Arnold, vii, 8, 81, 93, 105, 125, 127, 139, 144, 150-82, 183, 191, 200, 201, 202, 208, 227, 233
Benson, A.C., 5n
Benson, E.F., 5n, 19
Benson, R.H., 5
Bergonzi, Bernard, 1, 6, 8n, 199n, 138, 143
Blackwood, Algernon, 10
Bradbury, Malcolm, 84n
Brontë, Emily, 37
Brown, Ford Madox, 92, 94-5, 103
Browning, Robert, 109
Buchan, John, 20-1, 46n, 99
Buckley, J.H., 28n
Burnaby, Fred, 35
Burne-Jones, Edward, 92, 200
Butler, Samuel, 189
Barrie, J.M., 199

Campbell, Roy, 2
Carlyle, Thomas, 35
Cecil, Lord David, 184n
Chesterton, G.K., 4, 5, 8
Childers, Erskine, 8
Colmer, John, 208n
Connolly, Cyril, 1
Conrad, Joseph, vii, 7n, 22, 23-4, 25, 27-91, 95-6, 97-101, 102, 111-12, 115-18, 124, 126, 143, 150, 161, 170, 174, 178, 184, 185, 201, 207

'Corvo, Baron', 5, 17, 18-19
Cox, C.B., 39, 50-1
Crews, F.C., 220-1
Cunninghame Graham, R.B., 35, 58n, 90

Daiches, David, 3n, 4n, 62n, 63n
Daleski, H.M., 51n
Dangerfield, George, 22
Dickens, Charles, 2, 37, 68-9, 70, 74, 83, 125, 132n, 133, 170, 179
Dickinson, G. Lowes, 5n, 22
Dostoievsky, Fyodor, 74
Duncan-Jones, E.E., 82-3
Dupré, Catherine, 23n, 186, 195n

Edel, Leon, 143n
Eliot, George, 3, 199
Ellmann, Richard, 1, 3, 171n

Ford, Ford Madox, vii, 7n, 22, 67, 89, 92-118, 126, 170, 174, 178, 184, 197, 201, 233
Forster, E.M., vii, 1, 2, 4, 5, 7, 9, 10, 22, 69, 139, 150, 152, 153, 160, 174, 178, 184, 186, 191, 195, 197, 198, 208-32, 233
Fielding, Henry, 174, 232
Frye, Northrop, 164n
Furbank, P.N., 208, 209, 210, 211n, 212
Fussell, Paul, 10n

Galsworthy, John, vii, 2, 7, 20n, 22, 23, 69, 150, 152, 183-207, 208, 211, 212, 226
Gardner, Philip, 152n
Garnett, Edward, 41, 72n, 90, 192
Gibbons, Tom, 3n, 39n

Gissing, George, 21, 22, 162, 178, 227
Glyn, Elinor, 19, 20, 81, 187
Gosse, Edmund, 189
Grahame, Kenneth, 9, 11-12, 137
Granville-Barker, H., vii, 23, 202
Gray, John, 179
Green, Peter, 11n
Greene, Graham, 105, 201
Guerard, A.J., 45, 47, 87, 167n

Hardy, Thomas, vii, 81
Harland, Henry, 17, 19-20, 187
Hay, E.K., 39n, 40
Hawthorn, Jeremy, 37n
Henkin, Leo J., 3n, 73n
Hichens, Robert, 5
Hodges, R.R., 28n
Hough, Graham, 4n, 32, 60, 81
Hudson, W.H., 9, 81, 197
Hunt, Violet, 97, 111
Hunt, William Holman, 92, 93
Hynes, Samuel, 1, 150, 208

Jackson, Holbrook, 17, 22
James, Henry, vii, 22, 59, 69n, 74, 83, 90, 97, 98, 102, 103, 104, 111, 115, 126, 132, 136, 143, 170, 171-2
James, William, 5n, 7
Jean-Aubry, G., 74n, 89n
Jefferies, Richard, 147, 227
Johnstone, J.K., 4n
Joyce, James, vii, 17, 227

Karl, Frederick, 61, 97, 116n
Keating, Peter, 7n
Kermode, Frank, 3
Kimbrough, Robert, 44
Kipling, Rudyard, 9, 12-17, 19, 22, 37, 93, 101

Lawrence, D.H., vii, 93, 103, 184, 187, 188, 200, 229
Le Queux, William, 8
Lewis, Wyndham, 2, 93, 152
Lodge, David, 126, 143
London, Jack, 7, 9, 27
Lucas, John, 157, 162, 166, 170
Ludwig, R.M., 92n

Machen, Arthur, 10, 17-18

MacKenzie, Norman and Jeanne, 126n, 127n, 130, 145n
Mann, Thomas, 183
Marsh, Richard, 10
Mason, A.E.W., 13, 20, 46n
Masterman, C.F.G., 7, 9, 22, 23, 25
Masterman, G.F., 58
Masur, Gerhard, 183n
Maugham, W. Somerset, 1, 7n, 81
Meixner, John, A., 104, 108
Meredith, George, 2
Meyer, Bernard, 39, 40
Meyers, Jeffrey, 27
Miller, J. Hillis, 3n, 184n
Minney, R.J., 3n
Mizener, Arthur, 97, 109-10, 111, 116n, 117
Moore, George, 81, 101, 102, 143
Moore, G.E., 4
Morris, William, 92, 96, 117, 119
Morrison, Arthur, 7
Muir, Edwin, 183
Murdoch, Iris, 184n

Najder, Zdislaw, 61
Nettels, Elsa, 69n
Newell, Kenneth, 126, 127n, 144
Nordau, Max, 7

Orage, Alfred, 22
Orwell, George, 27

Parrinder, Patrick, 132n, 143, 145n
Pater, Walter, 4, 159, 161
Patmore, Coventry, 82
Pinker, J.B., 22, 94, 117
Pound, Ezra, 2, 93, 152
Pound, Reginald, 179
Powys, John Cowper, 174

Ray, G.N., 143n
Reid, Forrest, 10
Rickword, Edgell, 184n
Rossetti, D.G., 92
Rossetti, W.M., 92, 95
Russell, Bertrand, 5, 6, 25
Ruthven, K.K., 41n, 42

Sackville-West, Victoria, 6
'Saki', 8, 9, 10, 19
Scott, Paul, 174

Scott, Walter, 99
Shaw, G.B., vii, 24-5, 81, 93, 94, 199, 202, 204, 208, 226
Sherry, Norman, 48n, 67n, 72n
Shiel, M.P., 8, 10, 147
Sinclair, Andrew, 27
Smollett, Tobias, 233
Stallybrass, Oliver, 222, 228
Stephens, James, 10
Stevenson, R.L., 99, 227
Storr, Anthony, 40n
Swinburne, A.C., 92, 161
Swinnerton, Frank, 1
Symons, Arthur, 4

Tanner, Tony, 75, 77
Thackeray, William, 175, 179
Thomas, Edward, 9, 10
Tressell, Robert, 7n
Trollope, Anthony, 174, 175

Wagar, W.W., 142n
Wagner, Geoffrey, 28, 117
Wain, John, 156n
Watt, Ian, 6
Watts, C.T., 58n
Waugh, Evelyn, 5
Webb, Beatrice, 145
Weeks, Robert P., 144n
Wells, H.G., vii, 2, 6, 7, 8, 22, 23, 67-8, 69, 74, 81, 93, 94, 101, 104, 119-49, 150, 152, 153, 178, 180, 183, 191, 198, 200, 201, 202, 208, 211, 226, 233
West, Anthony, 144
West, Rebecca, 2, 183
Wilde, Oscar, 17, 95, 119, 179
Williams, Raymond, 39n
Williamson, Henry, 174
Wilson, Angus, 14, 15, 162
Wodehouse, P.G., 8, 19
Woolf, Virginia, 1, 2, 150-1, 161, 162, 179, 183, 198-9, 227, 228

LIBRARY
OKALOOSA-WALTON JUNIOR COLLEGE

·00011184·